Transforming Encounters and Critical Reflection: African Thought, Critical Theory, and Liberation Theology in Dialogue

Transforming Encounters and Critical Reflection: African Thought, Critical Theory, and Liberation Theology in Dialogue

Selected Articles Published by MDPI

MDPI • Basel • Beijing • Wuhan • Barcelona • Belgrade

MDPI

Selected by

Justin Sands
North-West University Potchefstroom
South Africa

Anné Hendrik Verhoef
North-West University Potchefstroom
South Africa

Editorial Office
MDPI
St. Alban-Anlage 66
Basel, Switzerland

This is a selected of articles published online by the open access publisher MDPI from 2017 to 2018 (available at: http://www.mdpi.com/journal/religions/special_issues/transforming).

For citation purposes, cite each article independently as indicated on the article page online and as indicated below:

LastName, A.A.; LastName, B.B.; LastName, C.C. Article Title. *Journal Name* **Year**, *Article Number*, Page Range.

ISBN 978-3-03897-151-1 (Pbk)
ISBN 978-3-03897-152-8 (PDF)

Contents

About

Justin Sands is a postdoctoral fellow at the North-West University, Potchefstroom, South Africa. He received his PhD in theology at KU Leuven, Belgium, and is currently pursuing a PhD in philosophy at the University of Fort Hare, South Africa. His research ranges from fundamental and systematic theology to hermeneutic phenomenology, the critique of metaphysics, and African and decolonial thought. This is the second time he has guest edited a project for Religions and MDPI. His monograph, *Reasoning From Faith: Fundamental Theology in Merold Westphal's Philosophy of Religion*, was recently published by Indiana University Press.

Anné Hendrik Verhoef is an associate professor in philosophy at the Faculty of Humanities at the North-West University, Potchefstroom, South Africa. He studied at the University of Stellenbosch and at the Catholic University of Leuven in Belgium. In 2008, he received his doctorate with a thesis on the relation between time and the Trinity. His interests are in the philosophy of religion, metaphysics, the philosophy of Paul Ricoeur, ethics, and the philosophy of happiness. His research focuses mainly on transcendence and the transcendent in contemporary culture, and its relation to ethics, politics, meaning of life and happiness. He is the associate editor of the journal *Transformation in Higher Education*.

religions

MDPI

Editorial

Introduction to "Transforming Encounters and Critical Reflection: African Thought, Critical Theory, and Liberation Theology in Dialogue"

Anné H. Verhoef

School of Philosophy, North-West University, Potchefstroom 2520, South Africa; anne.verhoef@nwu.ac.za;
Tel.: +27-18-299-1569

Received: 8 May 2018; Accepted: 19 June 2018; Published: 20 June 2018

Abstract: This special issue of *Religions*, entitled "Transforming Encounters and Critical Reflection: African Thought, Critical Theory, and Liberation Theology in Dialogue", brought together diverse international scholars and experts to think together on the intersection of African Thought, Critical Theory, and Liberation Theology. One of the aims of this special issue, and of the preceding conference (as stated in the call for papers), was to explore the complex relationship between the West's pervasive (capitalistic) culture and epistemologies, and the current post-colonial context of (southern) Africa. As such, it provided a platform to engage questions regarding the relationship between colonialism, capitalism, and culture through both a philosophical and theological lens. The final publication of all articles in the special issue not only achieved the above set aims, but accomplished even more by opening up new creative pathways of thinking about the three traditions that were brought into conversation (and not only within their intersection).

Keywords: transforming encounters; Critical Theory; Liberation Theology; African Philosophy

---

This special issue of *Religions*, entitled "Transforming Encounters and Critical Reflection: African Thought, Critical Theory, and Liberation Theology in Dialogue", brought together diverse international scholars and experts to think together on the intersection of African Thought, Critical Theory, and Liberation Theology. One of the aims of this special issue, and of the preceding conference (as stated in the call for papers), was to explore the complex relationship between the West's pervasive (capitalistic) culture and epistemologies, and the current post-colonial context of (southern) Africa. As such, it provided a platform to engage questions regarding the relationship between colonialism, capitalism, and culture through both a philosophical and theological lens.

The final publication of all articles in the special issue not only achieved the above set aims, but accomplished even more by opening up new creative pathways of thinking about the three traditions that were brought into conversation (and not only within their intersection).

In total, eleven articles were published, and they were well representative of all three traditions. They can be loosely grouped together as described below, although some articles pertinently explore the intersection of the traditions (e.g., Lamola, Resane, Sands, and Verhoef) while others focus on the dialogue between some of these traditions (e.g., Resane and Gerber). The grouping here is, thus, mainly pragmatic in nature in order to assist with further discussion of the themes.

Part 1: African Thought. This part includes themes like decolonization, Traditional African Religion, African Philosophy, African rationality, and questions about African epistemologies. There is an overlap and dialogue within this group on various points with Liberation Theology and Critical Theory, as will become clear in all the authors' work.

Kelebogile T. Resane, "Transparent Theological Dialogue—"*Moseka Phofu Ya Gaabo Ga a Tshabe Go Swa Lentswe*" (A Setswana Proverb). Resane's article focuses on "transparent theological dialogue" and his starting point is the Setswana proverb, "one must fight impatiently for what rightly belongs to him or her" (Resane 2018). He argues from a traditional African proverb and notion of dialogue back to its applicability to theological discourse, but with the aim of explicitly critiquing corruption in the socio-political context. All three themes—African Thought, Critical Theory, and Liberation Theology—thus come together in this elucidating article on transparent dialogue. The African proverb is helpful here because it asks for an impatient "fighting" for the marginalized and poor, and Resane links this to the church's calling to liberate the oppressed masses. Such a transparent dialogue between the traditions can, as he argues, help communities to experience liberation on different levels.

Joel Mokhoathi, "From Contextual Theology to African Christianity: The Consideration of Adiaphora from a South African Perspective". In the same spirit of Resane's "transparent dialogue" between African traditions and theology, Mokhoathi argues that proponents of contextual Christianity might have overlooked some critical aspects of African cultural and religious heritage. There is much more to learn from Traditional African Religion than what is often acknowledged by Christian theologians. Mokhoathi lists two examples, namely the pragmatic nature of the African cultural and religious heritage, and the African traditional methods of healing. These things must not "fall in between" (adiaphora) (Mokhoathi 2017) within a dialogue, but rather be brought to the fore to explore and value its richness for the community as a whole.

Lawrence O. Ugwuanyi, "Towards a Rational Kingdom in Africa: Knowledge, Critical Rationality and Development in a Twenty-First Century African Cultural Context". Ugwuanyi's article broadens the discussion of African Thought by explicitly engaging with the colonial and post-colonial challenges it faces. He critiques the assumptions on which modern states were built in post-colonial Africa as "an outcome of a wrong knowledge design" (Ugwuanyi 2018). He proposes in its place a more African "knowledge design" in which the term "rational kingdom" functions as a pointer to the "community of reason marked by critical conceptual self-awareness driven by innovation and constructivism". Ugwuanyi's aim here is to find more authentic African sources to address African problems in a decolonized context.

Schalk H. Gerber, "From Dis-Enclosure to Decolonisation: In Dialogue with Nancy and Mbembe on Self-Determination and the Other". The theme of African Thought and decolonization is taken further in Gerber's article. He specifically asks what comes after the logic of the colonizer. This question is pertinent in a world dominated by the "all-enclosing Western worldview" (Gerber 2018), which leads to various political, economic, social, and intellectual oppression. Gerber argues that both the Continental philosophy of religion and African philosophy address this question, and he then proceeds to look at Jean-Luc Nancy and Achille Mbembe's thoughts in this regard. In dialogue with these two thinkers, he sees decolonization as the "dis-enclosure of the world", which opens up a space for an alternative ontology that acknowledges our existence as always being-in-the-word with others. Dis-enclosure, as an alternative ontology of decolonization, implies for Gerber the responsibility for the "reparation of the dignity of the whole of humanity within our shared world".

Part 2: Critical Theory. Gerber's incorporation of Jean-Luc Nancy's alternative ontology in his concept of decolonization serves in a way as a bridge to the themes addressed by the papers in the Critical Theory tradition. Specific themes that are prominent in this section are freedom, determinism, embodiment, facticity, existentialism, authenticity, and transcendence. Authors such as Sartre, Agamben, Merleau-Ponty, Adam Smith, and Žižek are discussed.

Abraham Olivier, "The Freedom of Facticity". Olivier's article about the "freedom of facticity" asks in a very definite way: "How free are we from the facticity of situations, particularly ones in which we are subject to collective identification?" This links immediately to the above themes discussed under African Thought, such as decolonization, African rationality, racism, and freedom. Olivier elaborates on his initial question by adding more questions: "How free are we to change the situations—places, environments, histories, others—to which we inevitably belong and which subject us to collective identities? How free are we from identification in terms of others? How free are we to transform such identification?" (Olivier 2018). The relevance of these questions lies for Olivier in the harmful effects of collective ascriptions, and in the pressing demands to change it. Olivier argues that it is not through freedom that one has a situation with limited options (Sartre), but that it is "on the basis of a situation and the limits of its options that we are set free to have choices". Our situations enable us to have options of choice (a heteronomous freedom), and therefore, individuals cannot be sufficiently free if "oppressive situations that legitimize collective labeling, such as racism, are still allowed to exist". It is on this point where Olivier's work has the potential to productively engage with African Thought and Liberation Theology, but also with other traditions like existentialism.

Marcos A. Norris, "Existential Choice as Repressed Theism: Jean-Paul Sartre and Giorgio Agamben in Conversation". The discussion of Sartre and freedom continues in the next article, written by Norris. He brings Sartre's notion of existential authenticity (sovereign decisionism) into conversation with the work of Giorgio Agamben. Norris indicates in his article how Sartre's sovereign decisionism parallels "how modern democratic governments conduct themselves during a state of emergency" (Norris 2018), and secondly, how Sartre's existential authenticity models secularized theism. The implication of this is for Norris that "an existential belief in sovereign decision represses, rather than profanes, the divine origins of authoritarian law". A link between existentialism and theism is hereby emphasized by Norris, which accentuates the importance of the dialogue between (amongst others) Critical Theory and Liberation Theology.

Mark Rathbone, "Adam Smith, the Impartial Spectator and Embodiment: Towards an Economics of Accountability and Dialogue". Rathbone's article brings the economic reality of our lives and freedom into play. Rathbone argues that Adam Smith's economics are far more complex than mere self-interest as a driver of commerce. There is not a clear causality to be found here, and the relationship is much less deterministic than often perceived. To move away from the deterministic jargon often used to describe an individual's behavior, Rathbone explores the embodied phenomenology of Merleau-Ponty, which can offer "a theory of behavior that goes beyond a particular society's perceptions of acceptable behavior" (Rathbone 2018). Rathbone concludes that it is in the "hyper-dialectic of the flesh" where one can found accountability and dialogue in moral assessment. This is needed to create a more "responsible" economy from which not only the rich will benefit.

Anné H. Verhoef, "Encountering Transcendence: Žižek, Liberation Theology and African Thought in Dialogue". In a vein of dialogue between the three traditions discussed in this special issue, Verhoef explores the notion of transcendence as an entry point to this dialogue. His specific focus is on how transcendence is encountered by the philosopher Slavoj Žižek as a post-metaphysical thinker. Verhoef argues that Žižek's notion of the "gap in immanence" has some crucial implications for a notion of freedom. Verhoef then asks if African thought—specifically Traditional African Religion—and Liberation Theology allow for such a "gap in immanence" or for a kind of transcendence (Verhoef 2017). He argues that a lack of such a notion might be detrimental for freedom (ironically in "Liberation" Theology, and in African Thought as "decolonization") and a return to a deterministic understanding of being, life, and ethics.

Part 3: Liberation Theology. Verhoef's article ends with a discussion of freedom and Liberation Theology. This is only one of the themes that connect Critical Theory to Liberation Theology and African Thought. In this section on Liberation Theology, themes such as incarnation, Kairos, religious epistemology, praxis, political theology, and interdisciplinary methodology receive prominence. Authors that are centrally referred to in this section include Karl Marx, Joseph Cardinal Cardijn, Leonardo Boff, Clodovis Bof, Mikhail Bakhtin, Albert Nolan, Paul Tillich, and Louis Althusser.

Malesela J. Lamola, "Marx, the Praxis of Liberation Theology, and the Bane of Religious Epistemology". Lamola asks in his article whether religious epistemology can aid in the transformation of the world to the same effect as Marxist Theory. In answering this question, he problematizes the transcendentalism that Liberation Theology places on social practice. He argues that the theology of revolution is a type of Hegelian theosophy which, in effect, loses its socio-materialist basis (of Marx), and eventually, praxis. He concludes that Liberation Theology has limited efficacy for socio-political transformation because of its inherent transcendentalist and rationalistic orientation (Lamola 2018).

Sands's article, however, gives an interesting alternative view on the praxis aspect of Liberation Theology (and the other traditions).

Ian Bekker, "Kairos and Carnival: Mikhail Bakhtin's Rhetorical and Ethical Christian Vision". A more positive outlook on the praxis of Liberation Theology is found in the article by Bekker. He focuses on the term "Kairos", which for modern liberation theologians at least, refers to the breakthrough of the divine into human history. Kairos is important because it implies a consciousness of the present, as well as the need for responsive action. Bekker explores the potential of this concept by linking it to Bakhtin's work and his emphasis on carnival, or the flesh (Bekker 2018). The importance of the corporal and praxis of Liberation Theology (in contrast to Lamola's view) is highlighted by Bekker when he makes the connections explicit between Bakthin's carnivalesque vision and a Christian reading of the ethical importance of Kairos (with its links to incarnation).

Justin Sands, "Introducing Cardinal Cardijn's See–Judge–Act as an Interdisciplinary Method to Move Theory into Practice". Sands continues this emphasis on the praxis of Liberation Theology, but his discussion also attempts to incorporate African Thought and Critical Theory at the same time (Sands 2018a). His question is how one can translate theories (created by dialogue on colonialism and capitalism, for example) into practice. The following question is how to enact on these theories as one collective group. Sands finds recourse in the method of Joseph Cardinal Cardijn's See–Judge–Act. He proposes this interdisciplinary method as a framework to move from theory to praxis, which will not cede away the core principles of each discipline. Sands first discusses Cardijn's articulation of the method, and then, explores how two liberation theologians (Leonardo Boff and Clodovis Boff) employed this method in their theological framework. Sands concludes with an exploration of how this method might be beneficial for other traditions such as African Thought and Critical Theory. The ethical praxis—which is often questioned in this special issue—is thereby creatively addressed by Sands.

In Summary

To bring such diverse traditions like African Thought, Critical Theory, and Liberation Theology in dialogue initially seemed like an unlikely (or even impossible) task. With this special issue, and the preceding conference, it became clear, however, that such a dialogue is indeed possible and also very fertile. It is fertile especially in terms of the reconceptualization of key concepts which link these traditions—like freedom, justice, dialogue, praxis, ideology critique—but also in terms of the reconceptualization of these terms within each tradition. In that sense, the first part of the title of the special issue, namely "Transforming Encounters and Critical Reflection", indeed became the intellectual experience of dealing with these three traditions in dialogue.

The eleven authors of this special issue all contributed in their own right to this valuable discussion, and in the future, more deliberations on the same themes will hopefully take place. This introductory discussion of their work is my own interpretation; and where I brought them in conversation with each other, it was done through my own creative linking of their themes. The conference and the special issue were not structured in a way that they responded to each other. Of course they (and others) are welcome, now that all the articles are published, to respond to each other, and to continue the dialogue in that way. In the conclusion of this special issue, Justin Sands identify some points for further reflection. He argues that all authors "partially (or perhaps provisionally) agree that liberation entails embodied communal responsibility as being-with others, the importance of transparent dialogue, the need for new rationalities to enter the discussion of African self-determination, while also highlighting the dangers of appropriating these new rationalities when bringing them into an African context or when moving theory into praxis" (Sands 2018b).

A special word of thanks to the editorial staff of *Religions* who were of great assistance in every step of the process. Thank you to Justin Sands, who initiated most of this conference, and who co-edited the special issue with me. Thank you also to the Transforming Encounters Research Group (North-West University) who helped organize the initial conference, the National Research Foundation of South Africa who gave us a grant to host it, and especially to Danelle Fourie who worked extremely hard to made it such a success.

Conflicts of Interest: The author declares no conflict of interest.

References

Bekker, Ian. 2018. Kairos and Carnival: Mikhail Bakhtin's Rhetorical and Ethical Christian Vision. *Religions* 9: 79. [CrossRef]

Gerber, Schalk Hendrik. 2018. From Dis-Enclosure to Decolonisation: In Dialogue with Nancy and Mbembe on Self-Determination and the Other. *Religions* 9: 128. [CrossRef]

Lamola, Malesela John. 2018. Marx, the Praxis of Liberation Theology, and the Bane of Religious Epistemology. *Religions* 9: 74. [CrossRef]

Mokhoathi, Joel. 2017. From Contextual Theology to African Christianity: The Consideration of Adiaphora from a South African Perspective. *Religions* 8: 266. [CrossRef]

Norris, Marcos Antonio. 2018. Existential Choice as Repressed Theism: Jean-Paul Sartre and Giorgio Agamben in Conversation. *Religions* 9: 106. [CrossRef]

Olivier, Abraham. 2018. The Freedom of Facticity. *Religions* 9: 110. [CrossRef]

Rathbone, Mark. 2018. Adam Smith, the Impartial Spectator and Embodiment: Towards an Economics of Accountability and Dialogue. *Religions* 9: 118. [CrossRef]

Resane, Kelebogile Thomas. 2018. Transparent Theological Dialogue—"*Moseka Phofu Ya Gaabo Ga a Tshabe Go Swa Lentswe*" (A Setswana Proverb). *Religions* 9: 54. [CrossRef]

Sands, Justin. 2018a. Introducing Cardinal Cardijn's See-Judge-Act as an Interdisciplinary Method to Move Theory into Practice. *Religions* 9: 129. [CrossRef]

Sands, Justin. 2018b. Transforming the Conversation: What Is Liberation and from What Is It Liberating Us? A Critical Response to "Transforming Encounters and Critical Reflection: African Thought, Critical Theory, and Liberation Theology in Dialogue". *Religions* 9: 194. [CrossRef]

Ugwuanyi, Lawrence Ogbo. 2018. Towards a Rational Kingdom in Africa: Knowledge, Critical Rationality and Development in a Twenty-First Century African Cultural Context. *Religions* 9: 96. [CrossRef]

Verhoef, Anné Hendrik. 2017. Encountering Transcendence: Žižek, Liberation Theology and African Thought in Dialogue. *Religions* 8: 271. [CrossRef]

religions

MDPI

Article

Transparent Theological Dialogue—"*Moseka Phofu Ya Gaabo Ga a Tshabe Go Swa Lentswe*" (A Setswana Proverb)

Kelebogile Thomas Resane

Department of Historical & Constructive Theology, University of the Free State, Bloemfontein 9301, Free State, South Africa; ResaneKT@ufs.ac.za

Received: 29 November 2017; Accepted: 9 February 2018; Published: 9 February 2018

Abstract: This paper looks into the definition of Setswana[1] proverb: *Moseka phofu ya gaabo ga a tshabe go swa lentswe* (One must fight impatiently for what rightly belongs to him or her). The proverb is used to express the African thought of transparent dialogue that can be applied in theological deliberations; leading to sound theological conclusions adequate to address the corruption in the socio-political landscape. Transparency is explained from the African concept of addressing socio-political struggles. Theology calls for robust dialogue for the alternative society. This calls for understanding of African thought of fighting impatiently for the marginalized and the poor—a mandate that is similar to the church's calling for liberating the oppressed masses through dialogue with others and communities in context. A special exploration is made through the symbiosis of *dogma* and *kerygma* for the incessant intervention of theology on behalf of the silent masses. An appeal is made for liberation theology and mainstream theology to dialogue in order for communities to experience salvation authentically.

Keywords: theology; dialogue; *kerygma*; transparency; liberation

1. Introduction

A socio-cultural approach is applied in this paper to reinforce the importance of theological dialogue as a way of addressing injustice in social structures. The central theme of transparency in dialogue is promoted as a preferred alternative, since it is supported by *dogma* and *kerygma* that speaks on behalf of the victims of social injustice. To strengthen this socio-cultural approach a biblical example of Paul's relationship with the Corinthians is cited, together with Romans 10's injunction of *homologia* and *credo*. The historical silence of mainstream theology is challenged to synergize with the liberation theology in order to bring a balance between a belief system (*dogma*) and the confession of faith.

This Setswana proverb serves as a guideline, an appeal, or encouragement during the times of crises when intervention seems far-fetched. It carries a connotation of waiting patiently, of patriotism, standing for what rightly belongs to one, and perseverance during and after a dialogue. It is an African expression of remaining resilient and waiting for positive outcomes. The proverb is used in sociological context of human interactions aiming to find a solution, and in theological dialogue for the same intended solution. The roots and the meaning of the proverb orbits around the justice system in a Setswana culture. The patriot or the arbitrator (who unlike in the normal justice system is not a private mediator, but a participant in legal processes) pleads incessantly for justice to take its course. Theologians are beset with struggles for political reactions, economic crisis, and human dignity degradation perpetuated by the neo-colonialist regimes in the highest echelons of political

---

[1] Setswana is one of the Southern African language groups, mostly spoken in Botswana, South Africa and Namibia. It is estimated that more than seven million people speak it.

occupations. The silent and suffering masses find themselves in this sphere and try to philosophize in order to interpret their demise and misery. There is the need for theological voice from African understanding of dialogue deliberated in and through transparency.

Moseka phofu ya gaabo ga a tshabe go swa lentswe is used in this paper as a special appeal to theology to speak vigorously, vivaciously, and vividly. The speaking into the situation is precipitated by *dogma*, which is a theological conviction, "the mysteries of faith" that must be complemented with *kerygma*, which is "the truth that is openly proclaimed in the church" (Sauter 2003, pp. 24–25). Since this proverb carries the meaning of patriotism, it can be ascribed theologically as promoting Christian *apologia*. Just as much as patriotism is an attachment to one's homeland, so is theologians' attachment to *dogma* and *kerygma*. Just as this attachment is emotional and relates to one's ethnic, cultural, political or socio-historical aspects, so should theologians be attached to common history, faith confessions, and liturgical traditions. Theologians are not called to be the secret agents of God's kingdom, but the heralds who are "to make a dramatic declaration in an atmosphere of importance and wonder" (Resane 2010, p. 87). Their voice should be the proclamation and the declaration of the new order, which is God's kingdom (Resane 2010, p. 86). Their acts of *kerygma* are expected to be vocal and audible enough in the chaotic world—and this should be incessant. This is a *moseka phofu* (a herald) who is not afraid to lose voice to defend what rightly belongs to her. In the African worldview, a *moseka phofu's* voice is loud and clear. His voice warns the community of the ensuing danger. He alerts the society of the authorities' intentions, like the king's coming, new directions to be taken or even calling the assembly. This tells us that in this context, engagement in dialogue should be an incessant theological deliberation undertaken in a transparent procedures and processes. Theology is a rhetoric which is concerned with the power to speak or speaking truth to power. This is done through passion, as ((Smit 2014, p. 33), in Dibeela, Lenka-Bula & Vellem) in reference to Boesak defines it as theological convictions that undergird passion for political and rhetorical power.

2. Transparent Theological Dialogue

2.1. Transparency in Theological Dialogue—One Biblical Example

In the recent past, transparency is associated with winning back the disillusioned followers, subordinates, or partners (consumers, stakeholders, students etc.). Historically, in Setswana culture, the voice of *moseka phofu* was an alarm that broke the silence or disillusionment in the community. In certain instances, it was the voice signaling an ensuing or emerging hope. In politics, transparency is a buzzword used to obtain public office. In general, transparency means clear, unhindered honesty in the way duties are undertaken. One business diary gives a transparency definition that is closer, if not wholly theological, as a

> lack of hidden agendas or conditions, accompanied by the availability of full information required for collaboration, cooperation, and collective decision making . . . an essential condition for a free and open exchange whereby the rules and reasons behind regularity measures are fair and clear to all participants (Transparency n.d.).

It is, therefore, linguistically correct to conclude that transparency is the full, accurate, and timely disclosure of information. Theologians are the transparent interlocutors of the mind of God in socio-economic structures of society. *Moseka phofu* (in this case, a theologian) is a transparent communicator of *dogma* into the human situation to enable humanity to assess and regain the meaning of life. Kusmierz (2016, p. 161) also captures this that:

> Theology that takes up the challenge of contributing to the shaping of common life can only be meaningful and relevant if it takes into account its social, political, and economic context.

This theologian is like a believer who exists for others not just for himself. He cannot operate as an island. Moseka phofu is a full member of the community that he is willing to die for, rescue from hardships, or alerting them of the new order. His mandate is the patriotic service to the community. This paper promotes the *moseka phofu* whose endeavor is the recovery of the notion of theological dialogue in contemporary post-liberation South African context. This dialogue calls for accountability to the community where he/she belongs:

> Obviously, being part of the faith community the believer is no island and has no exclusive claim to wisdom or to the guidance of the Spirit. He is *accountable to his community of faith* for ethical decisions (Loubser 2005, p. 327).

Political liberation had come, yet not liberation in totality. West (2017, p. 186) resonates this reality that

> While political and legal liberation have been secured in South Africa, we have been forced to recognize that we have less liberation than we had imagined.

The new focus of struggle is for socio-economic justice, where theology must be vocal in South Africa. Unfortunately, it occupies the back seat, what Tshaka (2015, p. 7) alludes to that

> The perception was, we assume, that once political power is gained, the economy would simply conform to the dictates of politics.

In theology, the bottom line transparency is walking together in the light; letting the left hand know what the right hand does. Theologians as the depositories of empirical knowledge of *dogma* walk together for mutual support to form the united voice, especially in the corrupt socio-political landscape. Theological silence in times of crises is not justified. Ecumenical cooperation becomes effective when transparency is constituent to *kerygmatic* efforts and attempts in redressing the imbalances in the society. Transparency puts a damper on ecclesiastical fragmentations.

> Fragmentary denominational existence put at risk the testimonial and *kerygmatic* integrity of the one whole Christian church. Different and conflicting brands of Christianity present ironical testimonies and proclamations amidst a spiritually hungry world that has overwhelmingly grown by billions (Delotavo 2012, p. 163).

There are many biblical examples of transparency, but one selected here is to drive the point home. The biblical example of transparency selected is that of Paul's dealing with the Corinthian Church in his second letter to them. In the introductory part of the letter (2 Cor 1:1–24), he addresses the complaint that he had not been open and honest with them. He takes a great delight that his conduct among the Corinthians has always been transparent. He did not display machinations of worldly wisdom, as his abeyance of his visit to them was intended for positive outcomes. The historical interactions with them was permeated by integrity and transparency that would hopefully breed trust (2 Cor 1:12). His continuous and direct involvement with them authenticates his word to them (1:17–20); and this will enhance their understanding, after listening to him. Transparency enhances mutual trust.

In theological dialogue, transparency does not mean freedom of revelation of all information one may possess. There are confidentialities that cannot be divulged, though confidentiality cannot be an excuse to prevaricate, manipulate others, portraying or masquerading in a falsely positive light. When questions surface about motives, a solid record of accomplishment of openness and reliability will be the best antidote for misplaced doubts.

Transparency is so important to Paul's relationship and ministry with the Corinthians that he returns to the theme throughout the letter. *We refuse to practice cunning or to falsify God's word; but by the open statement of the truth, we commend ourselves* (2 Cor. 4:2). *We have spoken frankly to you Corinthians; our heart is wide open to you* (2 Cor. 6:11).

2.2. Theological Dialogue

Dialogues often take the form of theological consultations, which highlight differences and seek ways of coming closer together through new understandings, reinterpretation or correction of misunderstandings, and healing of divisions. The process of discussion itself brings people closer together and helps to break down barriers in social spaces, necessitating the need for social scientists' interventions. Theologians are also the social scientists. Auerbach (2017) of the African Leadership University in the daily Conversation captures this correctly:

> Social scientists often assign themselves the role of deconstructor: unpacking power, race, capitalism and consumption with glorious self-righteous abandon. My colleagues and I recognise that we cannot work alone, and require our students to play a central role in contributing to the university's outputs.

Moseka phofu dialogues with the surroundings and people in immediate precincts. To *seka*, which is the root or verb of *moseka*, (legal or communal debate) cannot take place on the mountaintop or at the periphery of the community. *Tsheko* (court case) takes place at the *kgotla* (court) which is always at the centre of the village. The case is stated and debated with and within the community. *Moseka phofu* is part of the community. These people are not apart from him/her. *Tsheko* is a communal dialogue, not like in the normal court of justice where there is the accused and the accuser with the magistrate presiding. In this context, *moseka phofu* is an advocate, arbitrator or reconciler who patiently plead for what rightly needs action for the plaintiff and the accused. The participants carry different personalities and dialoguing with them may bear some dissenting ideas. It is true that

> Dialogue makes participants more sympathetic to one another, even when they disagree, and assists enormously in preparing the ground for negotiation or decision-making on emotion-laden issues (Resane 2017a, p. 204).

In dialogue, consensus is reached. Dialogue brings the warring parties to the table to foster the unified action plan in order to address the situation; or clarify any misunderstanding. In theological dialogue, fragmentations, misunderstandings, and misinformation are all addressed because:

> Dialogue is a special kind of discourse that enables people with different perspectives and worldviews to work together to dispel mistrust and create a climate of good faith (Resane 2016, p. 62).

Dialogue kicks theologians out of their *parochial silos*. When the voice of *moseka phofu* reverberates, citizens stand attention to listen or to leave or enter a *laager* for safety. Theological safety is not inside the *laager* or a *silo*, but is in jumping out and crossing the dividing walls of self-righteous or self-imposing enclaves such as race, power, economy, traditions, gender, institutions etc. Disagreements in open dialogues are inevitable, but the mutual understanding of the differing opinion or ideology calms down the potential of conflicts and mistrust. Ratzinger (1987, pp. 73–74) referring to Catholic-Anglican dialogues asserts:

> Affirmation and criticism are not mutually exclusive: each demands the other. Only when both are joined together do we get an authentic vehicle for true dialogue.

The similar truth is affirmed by Ford (2013, p. 166) that

> a theology, which tries to avoid such differences by claiming some unquestionable certainty, or an overview of everyone else, is implausible and unwise.

In dialogue, all voices are heard and respected. It is unacceptable for authentic voices to keep silence during the dialogue. This is especially to African theologians who tend to keep their peace during the dialogues. Their rich insights are muzzled, consequently omitted in crucial policymaking processes. It is a fact that "For us to assess the impact of the voice in its variations, we really need to know what it is" ((Gaie and Tabalaka 2015, p. 379), in Chimhanda, Molobi & Mothoagae). The silent voice during theological dialogues disserves the think tank.

Moseka phofu is therefore like a person who speaks from the faith position. He enters the public debate and translate any claims or concerns deriving from their faiths into a language that is comprehensible—deemable as reasonable—to individuals outside that particular (or outside any) belief system (Fokas 2009, p. 128).

Jesus Christ can be cited as a real *moseka phofu*, for he walked and lived among the people. He was the Word that lived (tabernacled, tented) among us (John 1:14) as an ordinary man. Indeed, "the cost of ordinariness is involvement in the affairs of people" (Fernando 1995, p. 42). For Jesus, the presence and the proclamation were inseparable. When John the Baptist opted for solitary ministry by moving to the desert, Jesus opted for going to the towns and villages where people were populated. "So, the teaching of Jesus was relevant because He moved among people and knew what was in them" (Fernando 1995, p. 43).

3. Dogma and Kerygma

Dogma as well as creeds are the response of believers to the Word of God. Theology is a response to *dogma* as *regula fidei* (Rules of faith) and *articulus fidei* (Articles of faith); and in many ways as *veritas* (truth). *Dogma* is a decision to live out (theologise) truth in the social context, because the context is where theology is practiced. That is where liberation theology in its varied aspects, becomes *id quod ubique, quod semper, quod ob omnibus creditum est* (A valid Christian conviction believed and confessed). Liberation theology plunges into evil social structures; and becomes a genuine mode or expression of the Christian faith.

3.1. Dogma as Homologia and Credo—Theology in Action

The manner of speaking of the way *dogma* is communicated is known as *homology*, which is the speech of consent. Sauter (2003, p. 28) points out that homology

is language that gives a simple and unrestricted Yes to God's action and therefore must be unconditionally and under all circumstances affirmed.

The Greek *homologein*, in theological context, means

to declare things that all can hear, to declare what is binding, and at the same time to declare one's own acceptance of what is said, to agree to it, to consent, to confess (Sauter 2003, p. 29).

The key text is Romans 10:9—"If you confess (*homologia*) with your mouth 'Jesus is Lord', and believe (*credo*) in your heart that God raised him from the dead, you will be saved". Wethmar alludes to the fact that "The term *homologia* is indicative not of the content of faith as a deed or an act". Confession is an act rather than just a content. The Christian faith is not merely theoretical talk without any obligation. Faith requires a commitment and a decision. Confession is an enactment of Christian faith, a decision and commitment. Confession (*homologia*) and belief (*credo*) are a symbiotic relationship. *Credo* is a description of the saving work of Christ as content of the Christian faith and as the basis of a commitment to Christ. Commitment and content are inseparable. Commitment to *dogma* is a confession and belief in incarnation of the love of God by bringing *soteriological* realities to the context where faith is lived and practiced. *Dogma, homologia* and *credo* operate in a balance overflowing out of passion. External practices are the results of intrinsic motivations. This balance is captured by De Gruchy (2011, p. 10) that

Studying theology is a necessary and important academic activity, whereas doing theology is more—it is as a faith-praxis, a committed engagement, a way of being, a passion.

In the same spirit, liberation theology takes biblical text further by expressing the *lex esedenti –lex orandi* (What I know is what I say) further. In this context,

The biblical text becomes a catalyst in the exploration of pressing contemporary issues relevant to the community; it offers a language so that the voice of the voiceless may be heard ((Modise 2015, p. 4), in Chimhanda, Molobi & Mothoagae).

Soteriological experiences are not only spiritual, but also total human liberation. This includes the effects of social justice in the evil society. The incarnation of the love of Christ is the ultimate *soteriological* experience for humanity. This becomes feasible when *dogma* is articulated to address human miseries in diverse form. It should always be by *bona fides* that "*dogma* aims to articulate the universal implications of the Christian faith" ((Gunton 1998, p. 5), in Pfitzner and Regan). *Dogma* is not a dead *quaere* (inquiry), but a *viva voce* (living voice) in the community "regarding beliefs and practices that are considered essential to the identity or welfare of the group in question" (Lindbeck 1984, p. 74). It is the voice of the people, therefore *a vox populi, vox Dei* (the voice of the people is the voice of God). That is why it is crucial that the church is perceived, rightly so, as belonging or some form of embodiment. From this embodiment, the voice becomes united and vocal, and in and through the body, theology becomes vocal and practical. Vosloo (2017, p. 224) captures Smit's idea that

> Being Christian and being church has to do with "belonging". It also has significant implication for the way one thinks about theology. Theology is done in community.

3.2. Kerygma as a Liberative Dunamis

This Greek word, *kerygma*, is translated proclamation and it refers to various forms of the ministry of the word in mission such as preaching, witnessing, providing literature, theological education etc. It is a joyful invitation to communion with Jesus and His followers. However, it is not a means of scaring people to God with the fear of hell. Proclamation brings the preacher and the audience closer. Some of the famous missiologists in South Africa correctly admonish us that:

> We do not proclaim from the distance, from the security of some haven of self-righteousness, but that we come very close to the people we are inviting, in relate to them in solidarity because we are as much in need of the good news as they are (Kritzinger et al. 1994, p. 143).

The British theologian, Macquarrie (1997, p. 10) drives the point home:

> Gospel is preaching or proclamation; it is a first order language, which is unselfconscious, a language in which faith speaks in order to awaken faith through the transmission of the good news on which faith has been founded. Christology on the other hand has taken a step back, so to speak, and has become self-conscious and self-critical.

The salvific experiences do not emanate prophetically from the political status quo. The Old Testament narratives are not shaped by the royal stories but by the prophets. "The real actors of history are the prophets. History is written from the perspective of the prophets" (Wittenberg 2012, p. 97). The knowledge of *dogma* encourages the liberation theologians to be *kerygmatic* as prophets to confront the imbalances in the society. As *moseka phofu,* they are not afraid to *swa lentswe* (lose voice), fighting for the righteousness of faith and civic righteousness. This theology is the involved theology.

> We do not have the luxury of the distant view of earth from space, where the airless void refuses to carry the world's cries of despair. We hear the cries all around us and wonder what we are being called to do about it all (Thiemann 1991, p. 98).

Liberation theology as the theology that addresses the current socio-cultural scenes, conscientizes *dogmatists* to contribute towards "the shaping of industries, nations, institutions, professions, cultures, and practices of all sorts" (Ford 2013, p. 173). It challenges the mainstream theology to stand up from the upper room laurels and move to the public square to become prophetic. The current scenario of corruption in socio-political landscape can be refuted through prophetic theology. Nolan (2012, p. 118) points out that

> Prophetic Theology would then mean the outright condemnation of the worship of money in all its forms and a call to action, a call to participate in the struggle against economic injustice.

This happens when theology advocates a clear option for the poor in the South Africa of today. It is when theology speaks prophetically for the redemption of humanity from the snares of socio-political injustice, oppression, and all forms of marginalization and capture. Koopman (2010, p. 54) reminds us that:

> This option for the poor indicates how God works in the world, namely from the particular to the universal. The option for the poor, therefore, also does not imply that even the poor are ends in themselves. In the redemption and liberation of the poor and wronged God is working towards the liberation of all, also of oppressors.

This cannot be achieved in silence. Koopman (2009, pp. 122–23) elsewhere alludes to the fact that prophets are critics. They denounce the realities that are in conflict with the ideals of the new society. It is therefore; accurately conclusive that theology is the vehicle by which the arguments are voiced. Just as a moseka phofu is a vital member of a society, so is theologians as the community members; and as communal people, speak prophetically and in humility. Thiemann (1991, p. 135) highlights this that:

> Theologians carry on the conversation, not from a privileged position above tradition, but from within the polyphony of voices that constitute the Christian community.

This brings the liberative *dunamis* that the voices are within the societal structures where theology is practically appropriated for the benefit of the community in need. Fernando (1995, p. 42) also attests this that:

> Ministering to people provides the context out of which we preach and teach. Without this we may produce a lot of excellent material, but the material will lack the penetrating insight that is needed to effect change for good in the lives and thinking of people.

3.3. Rationale for the Return of Liberation Theology

Theology in South Africa is silent in socio-political landscape. It fails to fight impatiently in matters of morality, human rights abuse, poverty escalation, gender-based abuse, the excessive *realpolitik* as it contends with *vox populi* on the grassroots. Theology, though in the social strata of society, is not on the cutting edges of the marginalized poor. It is failing its legitimate mandate as a moseka phofu.

> South Africa is at the crossroads as its moral compass is being eroded by unscrupulous people. Since the arrival of freedom and democracy, the voice of the Church is not audible enough to usher and lead people to God. Corruption in the form of oppression of the poor is at an alarming level. The beneficiaries are social elites and political demagogues. Ethics in political governance had become opaque. The populace finds it incomprehensible regarding politics and Church's role in public policies. The opacity in moral values had magnified beyond explanation (Resane 2017b, p. 1).

The emergence of liberation theology over fifty years ago was due to a genuine concern for biblical social justice. It took theology out of *silos* when almost all major academic theologians were white, middle class and male.

> It has attempted to take theology out of the academic ivory tower of the West into the streets . . . it has shifted the focus of theological engagement from the intellectual discourse of the Western philosophy to the life and death struggles of poor and oppressed communities ((Modise 2015, p. 3), in Chimhanda, Molobi & Mothoagae).

Due to its stress on the importance of the wisdom and insight of the poor as the focal point, liberation theology is a *moseka phofu* to return to the community and conscientise it of its responsibility in the hurting and the marginalized poor. Theologians on the mainstream are invited to opt for openness in dialogue. There should never be a space for neutrality in advocating economic justice. Mind shift is inevitable. This is a theological tug-of-war, but needs to be overcome. It is a struggle that demands the taking of sides, leaving no room for neutrality. Resisting neutrality and making ethical decisions draws attention to the importance of *prophetic virtue* (Le Bruyns 2012, p. 84).

Doing theology includes the critical or prophetic capacity to challenge the politics of abstractions that deny people social justice and economic freedom. The inescapable conclusion is that "God has a concern with the quality of political and economic structures" (Brown 1978, p. 89).

Liberation theology contributes immensely to the interpretation of the Bible and the *praxis* of the Christian faith. De Gruchy (1991, pp. 131–32) is correct that liberation theology helps contemporary Reformed theologians to return to their inherent liberating dimensions of their *dogma* and traditions especially the doctrines of grace, justification, sanctification, ecclesiology, the law and the covenant. Liberation theology has a track record of being a starting point of theological relevance; it is a

> theology focused on the interpretation of scripture in conjunction with God's intention
> for mankind, within a given context—an exercise also known as contextualization
> (Nyiawung 2010, p. 1).

4. Conclusions

If theology in South Africa believes in transparent, relevant, and bold dialogue, then it has to come to terms with the fact that liberation theology should be engaged, as it opens "the horizons of those who suffer vicious oppression and domination in their land of birth" (Vellem 2010, p. 3). Conviction espoused in this paper is consonant with Peters (2000, p. 347) that "theology can enhance the quality of social life in the world at large by offering a vision of ecumenic wholeness and a proleptic ethic". Theology is legitimized by its prophetic role in social strata of the society. Its voice is a *moseka phofu* who is not afraid to *go swa lentswe* for the sake of societal transformation. The body of what we believe and what we confess should incarnately be vocal and visible in the cultural context where humanity is at stake. As pointed out in this paper, a theologian is a *moseka phofu* who is not a private arbitrator, but a public champion of justice—whose voice echoes through the social structures pleading for justice to take its course. Theologian speaks within the socio-cultural context. Outside this context, *dogma* and theology in general, "seems barren and lifeless" (McGrath 1997, p. 12). A liberating theology, therefore, should emphasize the humanization that includes working for the humanity of all racial groups in order to gain a status as a deeply pastoral theology. This means that mainstream theology should be both pastoral and prophetic. It should be a passionate theology geared to care giving for the marginalized poor masses in distress. Steyn and Masango (2011, p. 2) stress this:

> This pastoral care should find its motivation from within the caregiver's theological
> convictions, in order to find sufficient energy to sustain the care that is offered.

The mainstream theology must come out of the *silos*, and cease being *parochial*. Silence is not the best theology in praxis. *Kerygma* is *dogma* verbalized. Theology has to dialogue in public spaces for assertion of its own legitimacy. This can be achieved through dialogue with the liberation theologies of the time. Theological dialogues must be transparent with a goal of achieving maximum results for ecclesiastical and societal transformation. Theology must fight patiently for its convictions that are consonant with Christian *dogma* and *credo*. In agreement with Van der Kooi and van den Brink (2017, p. 27):

> It is crucial for theology to think from a perspective of the future of the kingdom that God
> has promised, and to act accordingly. This orientation will result in a critical theology that
> is at right angles with the status quo of injustice and inequality.

Theological consonance with *dogma* and *credo* situates theology in the right place where *praxis* is most needed. The church in South Africa, and Africa at large, faces the challenges in socio-cultural contexts. Tesfai (1996, p. 95) highlights the reality:

People are dying of hunger; they are victims of malnutrition, diseases, and economic exploitation. National life is collapsing or on the verge of doing so.

This is the context where the *moseka phofu's* voice must echo and resonate the sound with patriotic insistence and patience through transparent dialogues. Theology as a *moseka phofu* must come out into the public space; ascend from parochial throne and presence itself in the grassroots centers, from periphery to the center. For in the postmodern era:

> Theologising should be grass roots, communitarian, doxological, provisional, applied and contextual, rather than addressing questions that interest a theological guild (Murray 2004, p. 302).

This truth has been the focus of this paper. Theology should be vocal and unapologetically assert itself at the center stage of world and human affairs. As Naudé (2015, p. 133) remarks: "theology in a new key needs to be complemented by theology with a new voice". Theology must be chiefly concerned with reasoning about relation between God and God's creation (including humans), together with their ethical behaviors (Pietersen 2015, p. 120). Furthermore, theology as a *moseka phofu* must become patriotic in such a way that its prophetic utterances can be heeded by humanity in all spheres of life. There is no doubt that the bottom line remains:

> A recognition of theology as a critical inquiry emerging out of deeply held religious convictions can greatly enrich the cultural, intellectual, and spiritual life of our society (Thiemann 1991, p. 167).

Theological declarations, as epistemological as they may be, should transcend all structural delimitations in order to shape the *cosmos* eschatologically. The exuberance of the 1980s and the 1990s of prophetic appeals to the then South African government to dismantle apartheid should be revived. As in those days, the appeals should take the form of "strongly worded synodical resolutions and press statements, often issued by churches jointly" ((Kritzinger 2013, p. 108), in Plaatjies-Van Huffel and Vosloo). This contribution cannot be silent or through some docile behavior, for it is appropriate for theologians "to reflect on the proper nature of Christian contributions to deliberation about ethical issues in secular public platforms" (Biggar 2011, p. 48). Theological voice is critical in and as endeavors to restore justice in South Africa. Its voice like a moseka phofu should resonate in the halls of civil and social justice, as well as on the ecclesiastical platforms to address injustices in societal structures. The mainstream theology is invited to collaborate with liberation theologies in order to expedite balanced justice in a currently corrupt South Africa where human dignity and degradation is becoming a norm.

Acknowledgments: This research project is financially sponsored by the Transforming Encounters and Critical Reflection: African Thought, Critical Theory, and Liberation Theology in Dialogue.

Conflicts of Interest: The author declares no conflict of interest.

References

Auerbach, Jess. 2017. What a new university in Africa is doing to decolonise social sciences. *The Conversation*, May 13.

Biggar, Nigel. 2011. *Behaving in Public: How to do Christian Ethics*. Grand Rapids: W.M. Eerdmans Publishing Company.

Brown, Robert McAfee. 1978. *Theology in a New Key: Responding to Liberation Themes*. Philadelphia: Westminster Press.

De Gruchy, John. 1991. *Liberating Reformed Theology: A South African Contribution to an Ecumenical Debate*. Grand Rapids: Eerdmans Publishers.

De Gruchy, John. 2011. Transforming Traditions: Doing Theology in South Africa Today. *Journal of Theology for Southern Africa* 139: 7–17.

Delotavo, Alan J. 2012. *Contemporary Evangelicalism and the Restoration of the Prototypal Church*. London: FreshIdeasBooks.

Fernando, Ajith. 1995. *The Supremacy of Christ*. Wheaton: Crossway Books.

Fokas, Effie. 2009. Welfare at the Intersection between Theology and Politics: A Global Perspective. *Journal of Theology for Southern Africa* 133: 126–44.

Ford, David F. 2013. *Theology: A Very Short Introduction*. Oxford: Oxford University Press.

Gaie, Joseph. B. R., and Abel Tabalaka. 2015. The Ontology and Intricacy of a Voice: Toward a Philosophy of a Voice. In *African Theological Reflections: Critical Voices on Liberation, Leadership, Gender and Eco-Justice*. Edited by Chimhanda, Fransica H., Victor M. S. Molobi and Itumeleng Daniel Mothoagae. Unisa: Pretoria.

Gunton, Colin Ewart. 1998. *Dogma*, the Church and the Task of Theology. In *The Task of Theology Today*. Edited by Pfitzner, Victor C. and Hilary D. Regan. Grand Rapids: Eerdmans Publishers, pp. 1–54.

Koopman, Nico. 2009. Public Theology as Prophetic Theology: More than Utopianism and Criticism. *Journal of Theology for Southern Africa* 134: 117–30. [CrossRef]

Koopman, Nico. 2010. Churches and Public Policy Discourses in South Africa. *Journal of Theology for Southern Africa* 136: 41–56.

Kritzinger, Klippies. 2013. The Struggle for Justice in South Africa (1986–1990): The Participation of the Dutch Reformed Mission Church and the Dutch Reformed Church in Africa. In *Reformed Churches in South Africa and the Struggle for Justice: Remembering 1960–1990*. Edited by Plaatjies-Van Huffel, Marry-Anne and Robert Vosloo. Stellenbosch: Sun Press, pp. 92–117.

Kritzinger, Johannes J., Piet Meiring, and Willem A. Saayman. 1994. *On Being Witnesses*. Halfway House: Perskor, Orion Publishers.

Kusmierz, Katrin. 2016. *Theology in Transition: Public Theologies in Post-Apartheid South Africa*. Zurich: LIT Verlag GmbH & Co., KG Wien.

Le Bruyns, Clint. 2012. Religion and the Economy? On Public Responsibility through Prophetic Intelligence, Theology and Solidarity. *Journal of Theology for Southern Africa* 142: 80–97.

Lindbeck, George A. 1984. *The Nature of Doctrine: Religion and Theology in a Postliberal Age*. Louisville: Westminster, Kentucky: John Knox Press.

Loubser, Gys M. H. 2005. Paul's Ethic of Freedom: No Flash in the Galatian Pan. *Neotestamentica: Journal of the New Testament Society of South Africa* 39: 313–37.

Macquarrie, John. 1997. *Jesus Christ in Modern Thought*. London: SCM Press.

McGrath, Alister E. 1997. *The Genesis of Doctrine: A Study in the Foundation of Doctrinal Criticism*. Grand Rapids: W.M. Eerdmans Publishing Company.

Modise, Leepo J. 2015. Liberation Theology as doing theology in post-apartheid South Africa: Theoretical and practical perspectives. In *African Theological Reflections: Critical Voices on Liberation, Leadership, Gender and Eco-Justice*. Edited by Chimhanda, Fransica H., Victor M. S. Molobi and Itumeleng Daniel Mothoagae. Pretoria: UNISA, pp. 2–17.

Murray, Stuart. 2004. *Post-Christendom: Church and Mission in a Strange New World*. Milton Keynes: Paternoster Press.

Naudé, Piet. 2015. *Pathways in Theology: Ecumenical, African and Reformed*. Stellenbosch: SunMedia.

Nolan, Albert. 2012. A Luta Continua: The Struggle and Theology: Yesterday, Today and Tomorrow. *Journal of Theology for Southern Africa* 143: 116–18.

Nyiawung, Mbengu D. 2010. The prophetic witness of the church as an appropriate mode of public discourse in African societies. *HTS Teologiese Studies/Theological Studies* 66: 1. [CrossRef]

Peters, Ted. 2000. *God—The World's Future: Systematic Theology for a New Era*, 2nd ed. Minneapolis: Augsburg Fortress.

Pietersen, Herman Johan. 2015. *The Four Types of Christian Theology*. Johannesburg: Knowledge Resources Publishing.

Ratzinger, Joseph. 1987. *Church, Ecumenism, and Politics: New Endeavors in Ecclesiology*. San Francisco: Ignatius Press.

Resane, Thomas. 2010. Proclamational Evangelism must be Balanced with Incarnational Evangelism to Validate Postmodern Evangelism. *The South African Baptist Journal of Theology* 19: 86–103.

Resane, Thomas. 2016. Africanising a theological discipline: Paradigm shifts for the new trends. In *Theology and the (Post) Apartheid Condition: Genealogies and Future Directions*. Edited by Venter, Rian. Bloemfontein: Sun Press.

Resane, Thomas. 2017a. *Communion Ecclesiology in a Racially Polarised South Africa*. Bloemfontein: Sun Media.

Resane, Thomas. 2017b. The Church's prophetic role in the face of corruption in the South African socio-political landscape. *Pharos Journal of Theology* 98: 1–13. Available online: http://:www.pharosjot.com (accessed on 11 September 2017).

Sauter, Gerhard. 2003. *Gateways to Dogmatics: Reasoning Theologically for the Life of the Church*. Grand Rapids: W.M. Eerdmans Publishing Company.

Smit, Dirkie. 2014. Resisting 'Lordless Powers': Boesak on Power. In *Prophet from the South: Essays in Honour of Allan Aubrey Boesak*. Edited by Prince, Dibeela, Puleng Lenka-Bula and Vuyani Vellem. Stellenbosch: Sun Press.

Steyn, Tobias H., and Maake J. Masango. 2011. The theology and praxis of practical theology in the context of the Faculty of Theology. *HTS Teologiese Studies/Theological Studies* 67: 2. [CrossRef]

Tesfai, Yacob. 1996. *Liberation and Orthodoxy: The Promise and Failures of Interconfessional Dialogue*. Maryknoll and New York: Orbis Books.

Thiemann, Ronald F. 1991. *Constructing a Public Theology: The Church in a Pluralistic Culture*. Louisville: Westminster, Kentucky: John Knox Press.

Transparency. n.d. BusinessDictionary.com. WebFinance, Inc. Available online: http://www.businessdictionary.com/definition/transparency.html (accessed on 20 July 2017).

Tshaka, Rothney S. 2015. The black church as the womb of black liberation theology? Why the Uniting Reformed Church in Southern Africa (URCSA) is not a genuine black church? *HTS Teologiese Studies/Theological Studies* 71: 3. [CrossRef]

Van der Kooi, Cornelis, and Gijsbert van den Brink. 2017. *Christian Dogmatics: An Introduction*. Grand Rapids: W.B. Eerdmans Publishing.

Vellem, Vuyani S. 2010. Prophetic Theology in Black Theology, with special reference to the *Kairos document*. *HTS Teologiese Studies/Theological Studies* 66: 1. [CrossRef]

Vosloo, Robert. 2017. *Reforming Memory: Essays on South African Church and Theological History*. Stellenbosch: SunMedia.

West, Gerald O. 2017. The Co-optation of the Bible by 'Church Theology' in Post-liberation South Africa: Returning to the Bible as a 'Site of Struggle'. *Journal of Theology for Southern Africa* 157: 185–98.

Wittenberg, Gunther. 2012. *Resistance Theology in the Old Testament: Collected Essays*. Pietermaritzburg: Cluster Publications.

     MDPI

Article

From Contextual Theology to African Christianity: The Consideration of Adiaphora from a South African Perspective

Joel Mokhoathi

Faculty of Theology and Religion, Department of Religion Studies, University of the Free State, Bloemfontein 9301, South Africa; MokhoathiJ@ufs.ac.za

Received: 7 November 2017; Accepted: 6 December 2017; Published: 8 December 2017

Abstract: The move towards contextual Christianity in Africa is an essential venture if Christianity is to communicate with the African cultural heritage. As a universal religion, Christianity has to find an expression within the cultural context. However, the contextualization of Christianity in Africa appears to have permitted the practice of syncretism. It has resulted in the emergence of African Christianity, which is the amalgamation of Christianity and African Traditional Religion. The amalgamation of Christianity and African Traditional Religion appears to overlook the essence of both religions as there is currently no clarity on how Christianity can best be expressed within the African cultural and religious heritage. This paper employs the document review method to explore the things that fall in between—"adiaphora", which the proponents of contextual Christianity may have overlooked with regard to the African cultural and religious heritage. These include the pragmatic nature of the African cultural and religious heritage, and the African traditional methods of healing.

Keywords: contextualization; African Christianity; African Traditional Religion; African cultural and religious heritage

---

There is an eminent move towards contextual Christianity in African scholarship. A great number of African scholars contend for the contextualization of Christianity, which aims at providing a link between the African cultural and Christian underpinnings. But what seems to be lacking in this debate is the critical evaluation of how Christianity can fully be expressed or practiced within the cultural context. Even though it is apparent that Africans yawn to experience Christianity within their cultural setting, it still remains to be established how Christianity can best be communicated within an African cultural context. So far, the contextualization of Christianity seems to have permitted syncretism. It has resulted in the emergence of "African Christianity", which is the amalgamation of Christianity and African Traditional Religion (ATR). The amalgamation of Christianity and African Traditional Religion appears to overlook the essence of both religions, as the elements of one religion are expressed through the other. In this paper, I argue that there are "things in between"—*Adiaphora*, which the proponents of contextual Christianity seem to have overlooked with regard to the African cultural and religious heritage. These include the pragmatic nature of the African cultural and religious heritage; and African traditional methods of healing.

Within the modern missiological debate, there are scholars who contend that the attitude of early missionaries towards the African cultural and religious heritage was often misguided (Fiedler 1996; Mugambi 2002; Sanou 2013). Early missionaries are accused of being too much involved with their own culture (colonialism included), did not understand much of the African culture, and worked hard to destroy what they did not understand (Fiedler 1996, p. xi; Mokhoathi 2017, p. 2f; Sanou 2013, p. 7). This error, according to Mugambi (2002, p. 520), resulted in the perception of the Christian identity as equivalent to the western cultural and religious heritage. Following western precedence, conversion was determined by behavioural norms, in which African converts had to abandon their traditional African customs and adopt the western ones (Oduro et al. 2008, p. 37).

In that context, African converts were forced to live double lives (Mugambi 2002; Oduro et al. 2008). Mugambi depicts this dichotomy in the following manner:

> On the one hand, they accepted the norms introduced by the missionaries who saw nothing valuable in African culture. On the other hand, the converts could not deny their own cultural identity. They could not substitute their denominational belonging for their cultural and religious heritage. Yet they could not become Europeans or Americans merely by adopting some aspects of the missionaries' outward norms of conduct. (Mugambi 2002, pp. 519–20)

The strain of having to live by double standards for African converts brought about some difficulties in the appreciation of the Christian identity. The principal concern was: "What should be the proper relationship between Christian identity and a Christian's cultural identity?" (Mugambi 2002, p. 520). As expected, there were no simple answers to this enquiry. But suggestions towards the consideration of inculturation (Magesa 2004; Mbiti 1975; Bujo 2003)[1]; the reformation or reconstruction of Christianity in Africa (Mugambi 1995; Shorter 1975); and the Africanisation of Christianity, seemed to be more favourable (Oden 2007; Van der Merwe 2016; Akao 2002).

All these approaches sought to make Christianity more communicative with the African cultural and religious heritage (Bediako 1994, p. 15; Fasholé-Luke 1975, p. 267). In this regard, Oden (2007, p. 93) argues that "[m]any African Christians today have a deep conviction that they must think in terms that are indigenously African because this is what has been most neglected". This deep seated conviction, which tends to lean back to African forms of thought and expression, has become the premise and a solid foundation of African theology (Nwibo 2010, p. 36; Mbiti 1977, p. 83). African theology is the embodiment of the contextualization of Christianity. Muzorewa attests that African theology is an "attempt to respond to a mandate to construct a biblically-based and relevant theology that speaks to the spiritual needs of the African people" (Muzorewa 1985, p. 96). Thus, the goal of African theology[2] is to construct a biblically-based and relevant theology that can meet the spiritual needs of African people.

The implications therefore, of African theology, are that imported theologies do not sufficiently touch the hearts of African believers because they are couched in a language that is foreign to them (Muzorewa 1985, pp. 96–97). And, that the building of communication between Christianity and the African cultural and religious heritage is best left for African theologians because they know how best to contextualize Christianity in a manner that can fully communicate with their African cultural and religious heritage (Muzorewa 1985). Thus, in this argument, Christianity needs to assume a local and Africanised temperament, where it can be communicated in a language that Africans can understand and appreciate; and be articulated in a manner that can touch the hearts of Africans. In its reproduction, it is exclusively the task of African theologians to contextualize Christianity so that it may fully communicate with the African cultural context. As to how this can be done, it is not clear. But what is apparent is that the contextualization of Christianity has resulted in the emergence of African Christianity.

---

[1] Tinyiko Maluleke (Maluleke 2005, p. 477) alludes to the urgency at which Africans sought to make Christianity communicate with their African cultural context. He notes that "from various fronts, African Christians insisted that the church of Africa and its theology must bear an African stamp". In his view, this insistence moved beyond theological and ecclesiastical matters as other African thinkers also attempted to construct "African philosophy", "African literature", "African art", and "African architecture".

[2] It is worth noting that some African scholars draw distinctions between "African theology" and "Black theology", while others see the two concepts as interconnected. Manas Buthelezi (Buthelezi 1986, p. 220), for instance, seems to favour the notion of "Black theology" more than that of "African theology"; while Desmond Tutu (Tutu 1986, p. 262) regards both "African theology" and "Black theology" as soulmates (cf. Motlhabi 1994, pp. 113–41).

The term "Christian", in this paper, is used to refer to "a person who has accepted the Christian faith and made a firm decision to become a follower of Jesus Christ." (Mugambi 2002, pp. 516–17). In consequent, "Christianity" is regarded as an institute which affirms the Lordship of Jesus Christ, as the Son of God, who brings about the process of reconciliation between humanity and God (Barker 2005, p. 2). Against this background, Christianity is taken to be a "non-cultural entity", which only finds a sense of expression within a cultural medium (Mugambi 2002, p. 516). On this ideal, Mugambi (2002, p. 517) employs an analogy to epitomise how Christianity floats with different cultures: "One missionary scholar liked the Christian faith to a jockey who rides a racing horse as long as the horse is a faster runner. When the horse loses its racing ability, the jockey chooses another horse, and by so doing he remains on the racecourse".

Giving his own interpretation to this analogy, Mugambi (2002, pp. 517–18) further asserts that:

> Christianity began within the Jewish culture. That culture became incapable of sustaining the Christian faith because the leaders of Judaism believed that the new faith was a threat to the Jewish culture [. . .]. Then it was greatly influenced by Greek philosophy, without being swallowed by it. In the fourth century Christianity became the popular religion of the Roman Empire, after the conversion of Emperor Constantine [. . .]. During the modern missionary enterprise Christianity was riding on western culture.

This analogy, therefore, seems to qualify the scholastic language of speaking of Christianity as having arrived in Africa as part of the Western campaign of civilization, which was meant to redeem the 'Dark Continent' from the claws of ignorance and devilish superstitions (Bediako 1992, p. 225; Bosch 1991, pp. 227, 312–13). In this narrative, Christianity was equated to western culture, hence the need for African Christianity arose.

African Christianity is the amalgamation of Christianity and African Traditional Religion (Maluleke 2010, p. 370; Mndende 2013, p. 79). It is a form of Christianity that draws from both the Christian faith and African Traditional Religion for some ethico-spiritual principles. It is evidenced by the reverting of Christians back to African traditional practices and the consultation of traditional healers[3]. In this narrative, it becomes difficult for Africans to plainly choose between Christianity and their African traditional practices. Christianity connects them to God while African traditional practices provide a lasting bond with their ancestors. In such a situation, they tend to lack the aspiration to part ways with Christianity and to totally abandon the ATR. According to Mbiti (1969, p. 223), the other reason why Africans cannot simply choose between Christianity and ATR is that Christianity has been in existence for a very long time in Africa. It has influenced the lives of Africans for so long that "it can rightly be described as an indigenous, traditional and African religion" (Mbiti 1969, p. 223).

The term "African Traditional Religion (ATR)", in this paper, assumes a singular connotation. This stands against the popular perception that, as an umbrella term for various African religions, the term should be used in plural (Mndende 2013, pp. 76–77). African scholars like Mbiti (1990, pp. 1–5) initially followed this direction, as he referred to "ATR" in plural (as African religions). He used the term in this manner to account for the different beliefs and traditions that are found in African ethnic groups (Adamo 2011, p. 5). However, Mbiti (1990, p. 13) later revised his position on the second edition: "in the first edition I spoke about "African religions" in the plural to keep alive the diversity of African religiosity [. . .]. I now use the singular, "African religion," more than the plural expression".

The word "traditional" is included "to indicate that these religions emerged among traditional communities in specific regions before they came into contact with other world religions and cultures" (Crafford 2015, p. 2). Thus, the use of "ATR" in the singular is perceived to be more approving because it accounts for the common racial origin of Africans and the similarities of their culture and religious

---

[3] Traditional healers do not perform the same functions, nor do they fall into the same category but each traditional healer has a field of expertise, with their own methods of diagnosis and a particular set of knowledge in traditional medicines (cf. Ilse Truter 2007, pp. 57–58).

beliefs (Idowu 1973, pp. 103–4). Shorter (1975, p. 1) further asserts that the "ATR" should be spoken of in the singular because of the basic unity of African religious systems:

> Although they (African religious systems) were separate and self contained systems, they interact with one another and influenced one another to different degrees. This justifies our using the term African Traditional Religion in the singular to refer to the whole African religious phenomena, even if we are, in fact, dealing with multiplicity of theologies.

Thus, the common racial origin of Africans and the similarities in their culture and beliefs, deems it appropriate to conceive of the ATR in the singular rather than in plural.

Due to the amalgamation of Christianity and ATR, a different form of Christianity has emerged in Africa. It is African Christianity. Since its emergence, scholars like Maluleke (2010, p. 370) noted that "[t]he very notion of "African Christianity" appeared to depict something to be handled with caution and suspicion, if it was not to be rejected altogether". This is because the very concept of "African Christianity" lacked the requisite history, culture and theological traditions for Christianity to take on a distinguishable African identity, and the suggestion that Christianity was universal and therefore did not need to be qualified as "African" (Maluleke 2010, p. 370). This implies that the concept of "African Christianity" was, to begin with, uncalled for.

African Christianity does not have the necessary history, the cultural backing or theological traditions that may distinctively give it an "African" identity. Furthermore, as a universal religion, Christianity cannot simply be reduced to an "African" concept. This may lower the "universal standards" of Christianity and fit it with the local "African standards" (Maluleke 2010, p. 372). Thus, the concept of "African Christianity" remains a point of contention in African scholarship. Maluleke (2010, p. 372) further notes that the notion of "African Christianity" is too wide and covers a great scope to be meaningfully examined. But in an effort to signify the nature and temperament of Christianity when amalgamated with ATR, which in turn produces a new form of Christianity—"African Christianity", Mndende (2013, p. 79) used the following diagram (Figure 1):

The above diagram (Figure 1) shows that "African Christianity" is a result of the amalgamation of Christianity and ATR. It is the product of syncretism, from which the ethico-spiritual principles of Christianity are practiced in conjunction with those of the ATR. From an outsider's view, the amalgamation of Christianity and ATR appears to dilute the purity of Christianity or that of the ATR, as both religions seem to lose their uniqueness when expressed with the other (Bediako 1994, p. 14; Hastings 1989, pp. 30–35). This form of expression therefore, may easily be interpreted as the distortion of the originality of both systems, since there is presently no definite clarity on how both systems come or work together (Hastings 1989). Adamo (2011, p. 16) further notes that many Christian theologians consider the dialogue between Christianity and ATR to be a step towards syncretism.

He expresses this idea in the following manner: "In fact, the question of inculturation or Africanisation of Christianity is seen as a corruption of Christianity, because Christianity must be Christocentric. As a result, (the) Christian religion is absolutised" (Adamo 2011, p. 16). McGuire (2008, p. 189) traces the hesitation of blending Christianity with other religions from the era of the Reformation. She asserts that "[t]oward the end of the Long Reformation, theologians gave the term "syncretism" a pejorative connotation: It came to mean the blending of foreign, non-Christian elements with (putatively "pure", "authentic") Christian beliefs and practices" (McGuire 2008, p. 189). In that sense, syncretism was regarded as the corruption of the Christian faith.

Contrary to this, anthropologists such as Stewart (1994, p. 274) argue for the move beyond "syncretism" to "hybridity". Shaw and Stewart (1994, p. 26) further states that syncretism is "the process by which cultures constitute themselves at any given point", and McGuire (2008, p. 190) notes that "[a]ll cultural traditions—including religious traditions—are based on this kind of inter-penetration and interaction with external influences". This seems to suggest that "all religions are necessarily syncretic and continually changing, as people try to make sense of their changing social worlds, including other cultures with which they come in contact" (McGuire 2008, p. 192).

This, probably, warrants the review of the referral of African Christianity, which is, indeed, the amalgamation of Christianity and ATR, as "syncretism". As Oden (2007, p. 93) argued, "Christianity meets the criterion of indigenous or traditional African religion, since it has twenty centuries of sustained presence in Africa".

However, due to the lack of clarity on how Christianity can best be practiced within the African cultural and religious heritage, there is a developed sense of realisation that Christianity in Africa is syncretised with traditional practices (Jebadu 2007, p. 246; Onuzulike 2008, p. 6; Mndende 2009, p. 1). Some research studies conducted in this field indicates that the nature of Christianity that is commonly practiced by Africans is dichotomous—it is the combination of Christianity and ATR (Ntombana 2015, p. 106; Amanze 2003, p. 43; Matobo et al. 2009, p. 105). The amalgamation of these two traditions therefore, has raised some concerns for some Christian institutions. The Pastoral statement of the Southern African Catholic Bishops (2006, p. 1), for instance, states that there are Catholic Christians who search for healing from *Sangomas*[4]. The Pastoral statement further notes that some priests go so far as to "act as *Sangomas*" by calling upon the ancestors for healing (Southern African Catholic Bishops 2006, p. 1).

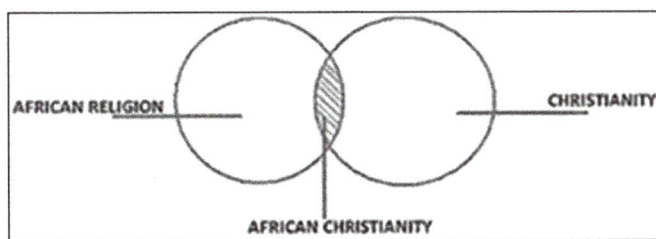

Figure 1. The nature of African Christianity. Source: Mndende (2013). Law and Religion in South Africa: An African Traditional Perspective.

Scholars such as Ntombana (2015, p. 105) also notes that there are professed Christians within the Mainline or Mission Churches, who tend to revert to African traditional practices or consult traditional healers for healing. The falling back of Christians to African traditional practices appears to be a developed phenomenon in Africa. What makes this phenomenon even more disquieting is that there are priests or pastors who go over-board to becoming traditional healers, while professing to be *'bona fide'* Christians. To this, scholars such as Mlisa (2009, p. 8) argue that "it is no longer a shame to see a well-educated person or Christian in *igqirha*'s (diviner) regalia or wearing white beads both at church and at work". The acceptance of syncretism, by African Christians, has become a practical realism in South Africa.

This is largely a result of the contextualization of Christianity in Africa, it opened doors for syncretism. The main concern with the contextualization of Christianity in Africa is that African scholars did not attend to the consideration of *adiaphora*. They have mainly focused on the positive and negative aspects of the African cultural heritage. They tend to elevate the positive and reject the negative (Lado 2006, p. 11). The positive aspects include practices such as hospitality, humaneness (*Ubuntu*), respect—of God, of life, of ancestors, of elders or of nature, etc. These are highly encouraged (Mbiti 1969; Bujo 2003; Futhwa 2011). The negative aspects include practices such as witchcraft, stealing, killing, human sacrifices, disregarding ancestors, interfering with community life, etc. These

---

[4] A *Sangoma* or diviner is the most senior of the traditional healers. She or he is a person who defines an illness (diagnostician) and also divines the circumstances of the illness in the cultural context. Diviners are known by different names. For example, they are known as *Igqirha* in Xhosa, *Ngaka* in Northern Sotho, *Selaoli* in Southern Sotho, and *Mungome* in Venda and Tsonga. But most South Africans generally refer to them as *Sangomas*—from the Zulu word *Izangoma* (cf. Ilse Truter 2007, p. 57).

are firmly discouraged (Magesa 1998; Awolalu 1976; Awolalu and Dopomu 1979). In this sense, the contextualization of Christianity in Africa appears to have been mainly concerned with the integration of positive aspects of the African cultural heritage into the Christian faith (Lado 2006, p. 11). This is at the exclusion of those things that fall "in between". I refer to these as "*adiaphora*".

Since the contextualization of Christianity in Africa has mainly focused on the integration of positive aspects of the African cultural heritage into the Christian faith, it appears to have overlooked the two influential components of the African cultural and religious heritage. These are, namely: the pragmatic nature of the African cultural and religious heritage; and the traditional methods of healing. These are what calls for the consideration of "things in between (*adiaphora*)". By this, I suggest that the contextualization of Christianity in Africa should not only consider the positive or negative aspects of the African cultural and religious heritage, but should also take into account the nature of such a cultural and religious heritage. This is because the cultural and religious heritage of many Africans serves as their worldview—that is, the way they see the world, understand wellness and get to maintain balance in their lives.

This worldview is complete, not dichotomous. It encompasses both the positive and negative, and those things that fall "in-between". Its wholeness therefore, calls for the consideration of *adiaphora*, especially when it comes to the contextualisation of Christianity. The term "*adiaphora*", in biblical terms, refers to "disputable matters" (1 Corinthians 8 vs. 4–7). St. Paul, for example, employs this concept to address the liberty of conscience. He notes that one can eat food sacrificed to idols, but it should not be in the presence of a believer with a weaker conscience[5]. In this sense, the notion of "*adiaphora*" is evoked. St. Paul appears to be suggesting that eating food sacrificed for idols is "debatable"—if there is no one who may be harmed by it, it is permissible; but if the conscience of a weaker believer may be harmed, it is discouraged. This applies both ways—there is no apparent sense of right and wrong.

But in this paper, "*adiaphora*" denotes "indifferent things" (Evans 2009, p. 23). This suggests that the term clearly encapsulates the nature of the African cultural and religious heritage. It is something that cannot be sensibly differentiated. This is because the elements of culture are closely aligned to those of the religious heritage. In that sense, it is difficult to separate the cultural from the religious heritage. They are both intertwined. This entails that when an African convert becomes a Christian, they carry both their cultural and religious heritage with them, and these are often incorporated to their new Christian way of life. But as research has shown, this process tends to produce the assimilation of dual identities (Mugambi 2002, pp. 519–20). This is mainly because African converts do not know how to express their Christian faith within their cultural context. They ultimately resolve to blend Christianity with African traditional practices.

In this impression, Christianity finds it difficult to absorb the entire richness of the African cultural and religious heritage, and to transform the intricate aspects of that cultural and religious heritage which do not match with its ideals. In this sense, some African traditional practices, which are neither seen as positive nor negative, such as the ritual reincorporation of the living-dead (*ukubuyisa*), the ritual inclusion of babies into the clan (*pitiki*), the rite of passage into manhood (*lebollo*), or the consultation of traditional healers, are allowed to form part of this Christian identity.[6] These traditional practices form part of the African cultural and religious heritage, and are neither seen as positive nor negative. Instead, they assume a neutral position.

For the reason that these traditional practices are perceived as neutral, one cannot tell whether they are part of the cultural or religious heritage. They fall on both sides. In this sense, they cannot

---

[5] For further discussions on this matter (cf. Carson 2015, pp. 385–56).

[6] African Independent or Initiated Churches (AICs), for instance, have taken a firm and decisive position on the inclusion of African traditional rituals into their Christian system. In most AICs, there is no apparent contradictions in the practice of African traditional rituals, which include the veneration of ancestors, with one being a committed Christian (cf. Ntombana 2015, pp. 106–7).

simply be disregarded as negative[7]. Their status is neutral. What appears to disquiet many institutions, however, about this situation, is that many professed Christians tend to substitute Christianity and its principles with African traditional practices. They often search for answers or immediate interventions outside the bounds of the Church (Ntombana 2015, p. 108), and tend to pretend as if the church is sufficiently meeting or catering for their needs. In such a predicament, many African believers claim to be "*bona fide*" Christians while supporters of ATR in private (Mndende 2009, p. 8).

As a pragmatic system, the ATR contains a set of beliefs and ritual practices that promise immediate returns, whereas mainstream Christianity largely insists on faith and hope (Lado 2006, p. 18; Hammond-Tooke 1974, p. 318). Therefore, when moments of crises occur within the Christian setting, believers are often encouraged to pray (or are prayed for) and advised to patiently wait for God's intervention. Scriptural readings like James 1 (verses 2 and 3) seems to suggest that the occurrence of "trials" and "suffering" in a believer's life equals the test of character, which in turn develops one's faith and the level of perseverance[8]. In this setting, faith and hope are prominent features. An alternative to mainstream Christianity and its methods of healing, is the use of conventional medicines.

These are commonly known as western medicines. Truter, for instance, notes that conventional medicines are usually associated with curing diseases of the physical body, and are based on the principles of science, technology, knowledge and clinical analysis which are developed in Northern America and Western Europe (Truter 2007, p. 57). These mainly focus on the physical, emotional, psychological, and social aspects of individuals, families and communities but tend to ignore the spiritual. Traditional medicines[9], on the other hand, are said to be "intertwined with cultural and religious beliefs", and are "holistic in nature". In this sense, they do not only focus on the physical, emotional, psychological, and social aspects of the individuals, families and communities, but also cater for spiritual conditions (Truter 2007, p. 57). Traditional medicines therefore, seem to be mostly favoured by Africans.

The pragmatic nature of traditional beliefs and ritual practices therefore, seem to underpin the manner in which African people attend to pressing matters. Because they obtain immediate returns from them, many professed Christians tend to revert back to African traditional practices for worrying socio-spiritual issues. This is because Mainstream Christianity lacks this attitude. An exception can be found with Pentecostal and Charismatic Churches. Commenting on the foundations of Christian villages, by missionaries around the nineteenth century, Isichei (1995, p. 199) notes that it was "no coincidence that a number of Christian prophetic movements were founded during the 1918 flu pandemic, which made the limitations of both western and traditional medicines painfully apparent".

Thus, Pentecostal and Charismatic Churches possess a form of pragmatism which appears to compete with mainstream Christianity[10] and ATR. To this, Anderson (2000, p. 66) notes that African Pentecostal Churches proclaim a message of deliverance from sickness and from oppression of evil spirits, and the message of receiving the power of the Holy Spirit, which enables people to survive in a predominantly hostile traditional spirit world. In this sense, African Pentecostal and Charismatic Churches become an attractive religion that offers solutions to all problems of life, and not just the spiritual ones (Anderson 2000, p. 66). This is what is lacking in mainstream Christianity, hence many professed Christians tend to revert back to African traditional practices.

---

[7] Wallace Mills (Mills 1995, pp. 153–72), however, notes that missionaries rejected the practice of traditional rites and customs. Among the Xhosas, for instance, traditional rites and customs such as circumcision (initiation rites), *lobola* (dowry, or bride-price), the drinking of traditional beer, etc. were opposed by missionaries.

[8] James 1 vs. 2–3 reads as follows: "Consider it pure joy, my brothers, whenever you face trials of many kinds, because you know that the testing of your faith develops perseverance" (NIV translation).

[9] According to Richter (2003), the WHO Centre for Health Development defines African traditional medicines as "the sum total of all knowledge and practices, whether explicable or not, used in diagnosis, prevention and elimination of physical, mental, or societal imbalance, and relying exclusively on practical experience and observation handed down from generation to generation, whether verbally or in writing".

[10] Mainstream Christianity, in this paper, refers to those Christian churches that follow the Nicene Creed and include the Roman Catholic Church, Eastern Orthodox, Anglican and major Protestant churches (cf. The New Encyclopaedia Britannica 2007).

Within the African traditional setting, when people are overwhelmed by crises, they are encouraged to consult traditional healers, prophets or seers (Mogoba 2011, p. 176; Hammond-Tooke 1974, p. 318). These promise immediate returns. In that manner, the Christian principles of faith and hope are often abandoned for traditional interventions. This is a process which seems to suggest that "pressing matters need immediate interventions", since African converts look for quick answers from traditional healers. Furthermore, this appears to create disparity in the church as a system that requires the exercise of patience is constantly compared against or substituted by a fast-paced system, which promises immediate returns. By leaning back to African traditional practices, believers substitute Christian principles for traditional interventions.

Due to the lack of clarity on how Christianity can best be expressed within the African cultural and religious context, scholars are divided in their understanding of this matter. There are currently three guiding perspectives regarding the amalgamation of Christianity and African Traditional Religion. The first is that of conservative Christians. In this perspective, Christian scholars like Jarvis (2009, p. 43) argue that Christianity does not permit the inclusion of African cultural and religious beliefs that conflict with the revelation of God as found in the Bible. Therefore, African Christians must renounce and break away from these cultural and religious beliefs. In this sense, African Christians are encouraged to renounce their traditional cultures and religious beliefs that pertain to the "fear of evil spirits, evil spells, curses, or the anger or favour of spirits of ancestors" (Jarvis 2009, p. 44)[11].

The second is the African rigorist perspective. This is the perspective that seeks to preserve the African cultural and religious heritage of indigenous people, which was handed down by the forebears of the present generation (Mbiti 1975, p. 12). Within this perspective, scholars like Mndende argue that Africans must not mix their African Traditional Religion with other religions such as Christianity or Islam. The amalgamation of African Traditional Religion with other faiths like Christianity or Islam is interpreted, by Mndende (2009, p. 1), to be the constraint of 'true' African spirituality. In this sense, the perspective maintains that indigenous people should preserve their African Traditional Religion and not mix their African traditional cultures and religious practices with Christian or Islamic elements. Those who amalgamate the African Traditional Religion with Christianity or Islam, are said to be "sitting on the fence" (Mndende 2009, p. 1).

The third and last perspective is that of moderate African religionists. This perspective assumes a middle ground. It argues that both Christianity and African Traditional Religion can be amalgamated or made to work together (Mlisa 2009, p. 9; Hirst 2005, p. 4). This is because Christianity has strongly influenced the Africans to an extent that they have to integrate Christian values into their cultural value systems (Mbiti 1975, p. 14). Within this perspective, Christianity is the means by which African Christians get to relate with God, while African traditional practices provide some form of socio-spiritual context which connects them to their ancestors (Mbiti 1992, p. 264). In this sense, Christianity and ATR are understood to be related systems of thought and practice.

The rationale for the positions taken by both conservative Christians, and African rigorist religionists appears to be reasonable. Both Christianity and African Traditional Religion seek to preserve some form of purity by waning off any signs of religious infiltration into their distinctive beliefs. In this context, both the conservative Christian and African rigorist perspectives, seem to assume a protective position. They both seeks to keep syncretism away from their distinctive faiths. However, the manner in which both Christianity and African Traditional Religion approaches this issue appears to be problematic.

---

11 Simon Maimela (Maimela 1985, p. 71) seems to have addressed this issue when he noted that for many Africans "the church is not interested in their daily misfortunes, illness, encounter with evil and witchcraft, bad luck, poverty, barrenness—in short, all their concrete social problems [...]. Most Africans often do not know what to do with their new, attractive Christian religion and yet one which dismally fails to meet their emotional and spiritual needs". He also framed this as the strength of AICs—they give Africans "an open invitation to bring concrete social problems to the church leadership".

As suggested by Jarvis (2009, p. 43), the only possible way in which Africans may fully become Christians is when they renounce their cultural and religious beliefs, which conflict with the revelation of God as found in the Bible. In this regard, one cannot be a devout Christian while holding to their traditional culture and religious beliefs. This argument seems to speak directly to the concern of this paper. How are Africans to measure and extract those cultural and religious beliefs that stands against the word of God, when their cultural and religious elements are intertwined? Does not this, ultimately, lead towards the abandonment of the entire African heritage? For that matter, how can Africans attain a sense of ignorance (or lack of fear) for the reality of evil spirits, evil spells, curses, or the anger or favour of spirits of ancestors, when that is an integral part of their lived experiences?[12]

However, scholars like Mbiti (1975, p. 130), and Leonard (1906, p. 429) have shown that the total break away of Africans from their cultural roots and religious beliefs is almost an impossible mission. This is because the traditional culture and religious beliefs of Africans form part of their identity. Leonard (1906) expressed this sentiment in the following manner: "The religion of these natives (Africans) is their existence and their existence is their religion [...]. The entire organisation of their common life is so interwoven with it that they cannot get away from it [...]" (Leonard 1906, p. 429).

Some sixty-nine years later, Mbiti (1975) observed a similar attitude regarding the total break away of Africans from their traditional culture and religious beliefs:

> [W]hen Africans migrate in large numbers from one part of the continent to another, or from Africa to other continents, they take religion with them. They can only know how to live within their religious context. Even if they are converted to another religion like Christianity or Islam, they do not completely abandon their traditional religion immediately: it remains with them for several generations and sometimes centuries. (Mbiti 1975, p. 13)

It therefore appears to be difficult for Africans to entirely abandon their traditional culture and religious beliefs. Even if they do eventually abandon these, it is a process that takes several generations, and sometimes centuries. Their new Christian identity is often adopted in conjunction with the old African traditional and religious identity. As Mbiti (1975, p. 13) contended, this is because their African religion is their way of life and "within that religious way of life, they know who they are, how to act in different situations, and how to solve their problems". The act of asking Africans to renounce their cultural and religious beliefs in order to be Christians therefore, seems to be a huge ask on the part of conservative Christianity.

The African rigorist perspective, as well, appears to pose some problems. It seems to suggest that one cannot freely experience their 'true' African spirituality when they amalgamate the ATR with other faiths like Christianity (Mndende 2009, p. 1). The expression of 'true' African spirituality appears to come only when indigenous people continue to preserve their African cultural and religious heritage which was handed down to them by the forebears of the present generation. In this manner, one cannot embrace the ATR together with other religions because this denotes that they are "sitting on the fence" (Mndende 2009, p. 1).

The supposed contradiction of embracing the ATR together with Christianity is remarked upon by Mndende (2009) as follows:

> One wonders how one can officiate in a ritual professing ancestors as intermediaries between humanity and God, and at the same time go to church and preach that Jesus is the way, the truth and the life? Surely these two practices are based on mutually exclusive, irreconcilable tenets of faith; a contradiction in terms. (Mndende 2009, p. 8)

Thus, the African rigorist perspective argues that one cannot be an African religionist while a Christian at the same time. This perspective however, seems to overlook the reality of people who

---

12 For further discussions on this matter (cf. Anderson 2000, pp. 30–31).

amalgamate the two systems—Christianity and ATR, and hold that they are related systems of thought and practice. It is a known fact that there are Africans who regard themselves as Christians while they are also traditional healers, or continue to practice their traditional customs (Mlisa 2009, p. 8; Hirst 2005, p. 4). This African rigorist view seems to undermine the existence of such a reality. This view further seems to suggest that converting to Christianity, as Mbiti (1975, p. 13) and Leonard (1906, p. 429) argued, is almost impossible because Africans find it difficult to renounce their traditional cultures and religious beliefs.

Leonard (1906, p. 429) seem to have endorsed this sentiment when he pointed out that Africans can only freely express themselves within their religious context: "[T]hey eat religiously, drink religiously, and sing religiously". In this regard, the religion of Africans is said to be an overarching factor that is intimately interwoven to their cultural expressions, from which no other religion can replace. In this form of expression, Africans are said to "eat religiously, drink religiously and (even) sing religiously" (Leonard 1906, p. 429). Even though this may possess some truth, it is not always the case. Jarvis (2009, p. 34) notes that there are Africans who converted to Christianity, that have completely broken away from the influence of their cultures and religious beliefs—particularly from the influence of venerating ancestors.

The last perspective, which assumes the middle ground, seems to address the realism of Africans who live with the awareness of the influence of Christianity on the ATR, and also acknowledge the impact exerted by the ATR on Christianity. On the one hand, there are African religionists who argue that Christianity has strongly influenced Africans so much that they had to incorporate Christian values into their cultural systems (Mlisa 2009, p. 9). On the other hand, there are Christians who argue that Christianity cannot be expressed or communicated outside a cultural medium and therefore the African cultural heritage must give context to the expression of Christianity (Mugambi 2002, p. 519).

The separation of Christianity from the African culture, in this perspective, is said to have resulted in a life of double standards among African converts (Pityana 1999, p. 137; Mtuze 2003, p. 8). This view, therefore, maintains that Christianity must find an expression within the cultural context. In this backdrop, where the terms of one religion are expressed through the other, Mugambi (2002, p. 518) notes that "[s]cholars are now predicting that in the twenty-first century Christianity will be riding on the cultures of Africa and Asia". Therefore, this seems to suggest that the expression of Christianity within the African cultural context is the only realistic premise for African Christianity.

This perspective however, seems to raise a number of concerns. The first is that the practices of both Christianity and ATR appear to be contradictory. Mndende (2009, p. 8), for instance, argues that one cannot simply officiate in a ritual that profess ancestors as mediators between humanity and God, and then turn to preach that Jesus is the way, the truth and the life. Therefore, the practices of these two systems are "based on mutually exclusive, irreconcilable tenets of faith; a contradiction in terms" (Mndende 2009, p. 8).

The second concern is that there are no definite boundaries between the plain elements of the African cultural and religious heritage (Mndende 2009, p. 117). Both the elements of the African cultural heritage and religious heritage are seen as overlapping, and thus are often thought of as an item. In this overlap, there is no distinction between traditional customs and religious beliefs. One can therefore not identify the cultural heritage from the religious life of Africans. Due to this limitation, the calling of traditional healers is often perceived as part of the African cultural heritage, instead of being looked at, only, as the aspect of the African religious life[13].

As the integral part of the African cultural heritage, divination is principally accepted on the bases, and explained in terms of one's cultural lineage—in terms of Xhosa divination, Zulu divination, or any other African agnatic groups' system of divination (Hirst 2007, pp. 218–19). In this context,

---

[13] Nokuzola Mndende (Mndende 2013, p. 78) exemplifies this intersection when she states that "rituals are special gatherings of the clans aimed at communal religious practices". This means that some agnatic group rituals carry a religious significance, even though they are taken as communal.

the connection of one with their clan is imperative; as the call to divination is transmitted, or may be responded to wholly within one's agnatic group (Hirst 2005, p. 3). This call is said to come from the ancestors (Mlisa 2009, p. xii). The ancestors are deceased senior males of the agnatic group or clan, who are the descendants of the common great-grandfather (Hammond-Tooke 1974, pp. 17–19)[14]. But in the *Mpondo* tradition, the concept of ancestors also includes all the deceased old people, and not just the deceased senior males (Hunter 1936, p. 123).

Because ancestors play a significant role in African cosmology, their status has often been overly elevated (Muzorewa 1985, p. 12). Some Christians go so far as to equate Jesus Christ with ancestors (Nxumalo 1981, p. 67)[15]. According to Nyamiti (1984, p. 9), this is a paradigm which begins with "African ancestral beliefs and practices and tries to confront these with the Christian teaching on the saviour". African theologians such as Charles Wanamaker (Wanamaker 1997, p. 296) Kwame Bediako (Bediako 1994, p. 99), and Francois Kabasele (Kabasele 1991, p. 46) seem to advocate for this Christology. However, scholars such as Jarvis (2009, pp. 25–27) have been very critical of the elevation of ancestors. He maintains that "it is God who should be held in awe, not the spirits of the ancestors, or any other spirit" (Jarvis 2009, p. 43). Because ancestors form part of the African cultural and religious heritage, their role and position within the African cultural setting, and Christian church (AICs) will always be an open-ended discussion—They seem to connect Africans to their cultural and religious heritage.

Therefore, due to the prevalence of these variant perspectives, the status of Christians who amalgamate Christianity with ATR remains a heated debate in South Africa. As a result, many Africans have resolved to live by double standards, professing to be Christians in public, while reverting to the practice of ATR in private (Ntombana 2015, p. 105). This is a phenomenon which scholars like Mbiti (1992, p. 264) describe as "religious concubinage". It is a phenomenon whereby believers acknowledge one religion in public while they practice another in private. Mathema (2007, p. 5) contends that these are professed Christians who derive some form of satisfaction from African traditional practices.

The contextualization of Christianity in Africa therefore, is undoubtedly a necessary venture. Christianity needs to communicate with the African cultural and religious heritage. This means that it needs to be couched in a language that Africans can understand and appreciate, and further be presented in a manner that does not require the alienation of Africans from their cultural heritage. But in that endeavour, all aspects of the African cultural and religious heritage must be considered, not only the positive and negatives. These include the pragmatic nature of the African cultural and religious heritage, as well as the methods that Africans use to respond to moments of crises. Perhaps, the consideration of these may pave a way towards the exploration of methods in which Africans may be assisted in becoming genuine Christians without falling back to African traditional practices, or having to rely on traditional interventions for pressing issues.

Again, this consideration may require the exploration of the viability of traditional methods of healing—that is, which traditional remedies are to be acceptable or non-acceptable; which should be considered harmless or harmful against the Christian faith; and which traditional remedies, to some extent, can be tolerated or incorporated into the Christian system. Of course, this discussion may have to consider and critically evaluate the role of traditional healers, herbalists or seers as collaborators in the administration of traditional remedies, which I suppose may not be an easy task to undertake. But the role of traditional healers, herbalists or seers cannot be taken for granted. They are the primary givers of traditional remedies, which promise immediate returns. Perhaps the consideration of these

---

14 For further discussions (cf. Mayer and Mayer 1974, p. 151; Wilson 1982, p. 27).
15 Jabulani Nxumalo (Nxumalo 1981, p. 67) asserts the following: "In my view, there is a relationship between Christ and the ancestors, for the simple reason that Christ died too. He is therefore an *idlozi* (the living-dead) to us, since those who are dead are *amadlozi* (plural of *idlozi*) for us. Therefore Christ and those who have died are united together. We call them together in Christ".

"things in between" may provide the necessary clarity on how Christianity can best be expressed and practiced within the African cultural and religious heritage.

Conflicts of Interest: The author declares no conflict of interest.

References

Adamo, David T. 2011. Christianity and the African Traditional Religion(s): The Postcolonial Round of Engagement. *Verbum et Ecclesia* 32: 1–10. [CrossRef]

Akao, John O. 2002. The Task of African Theology: Problems and Suggestions. *Scriptura* 81: 341–43. [CrossRef]

Amanze, James N. 2003. Christianity and Ancestor Veneration in Botswana. *Studies in World Christianity* 8: 43–49. [CrossRef]

Anderson, Allan. 2000. *Zion and Pentecost: The Spirituality and Experience of Pentecostal and Zionist/Apostolic Churches in South Africa*. Pretoria: Unisa Press.

Awolalu, Omosade J., and Adelumo P. Dopomu. 1979. *West African Traditional Religion*. Ibadan: Onibonoje Press & Book Industries.

Awolalu, Omosade J. 1976. Sin and its Removal in African Traditional Religion. *Journal of the American Academy of Religion* 44: 275–87. [CrossRef]

Barker, Gregory A. 2005. *Christianity: A Guide to Christianity*. Oxford: The Subject Centre for Philosophical and Religious Studies.

Bediako, Kwame. 1992. *Theology and Identity: The Impact of Culture upon Christian Thought in the Second Century and Modern Africa*. Oxford: Regnum Books International.

Bediako, Kwame. 1994. Understanding African Theology in the 20th Century. *Themelios* 20: 14–20.

Bosch, David J. 1991. *Transforming Mission: Paradigm Shifts in Mission Theology*. Maryknoll: Orbis Books.

Bujo, Bénézet. 2003. *Foundations of an African Ethic: Beyond the Universal Claims of Western Morality*. Nairobi: Paulines Publications Africa.

Buthelezi, Manas. 1986. Toward Indigenous Theology in South Africa. In *Third World Liberation Theologies: A Reader*. Edited by Dean W. Ferm. Maryknoll: Orbis Books, pp. 205–21.

Carson, Donald A. 2015. On Disputable Matters. *Themelios* 40: 383–88.

Crafford, Dionne. 2015. African Traditional Religions. In *South Africa, Land of Many Religions*. Edited by Arno Meiring and Piet Meiring. Wellington: Christian Literature Fund.

Evans, Richard G. 2009. Sancta Indifferentia and Adiaphora: "Holy Indifference" and "Things Indifferent". *Common Knowledge* 15: 23–38. [CrossRef]

Fasholé-Luke, Edward W. 1975. The Quest for an African Christian Theology. *The Ecumenical Review* 27: 267. [CrossRef]

Fiedler, Klaus. 1996. *Christianity and African Culture: Conservative German Protestant Missionaries in Tanzania, 1900–1940*. Leiden and Boston: E. J. Brill.

Futhwa, Fezekile. 2011. *Sesotho Afrikan Thought and Belief Systems*. Alberton: Nalane Publication.

Hammond-Tooke, David W. 1974. *The Bantu-Speaking Peoples of Southern Africa*. London: Routledge & Kegan Paul Publication.

Hastings, Adrian. 1989. *African Catholicism—An Essay in Discovery*. London: SCM Press.

Hirst, Manton M. 2005. Dreams and Medicines: The Perspective of Xhosa Diviners and Novices in the Eastern Cape, South Africa. *Indo-Pacific Journal of Phenomenology* 5: 1–22. [CrossRef]

Hirst, Manton M. 2007. A River of Metaphors: Interpreting the Xhosa diviner's myth. *Journal of African Studies* 56: 217–50. [CrossRef]

Hunter, Monica. 1936. *Reaction to Conquest: Effects of Contact with Europeans on the Pondo of South Africa*. Oxford: Oxford University Press.

Idowu, Bolaji E. 1973. *African Traditional Religion: A Definition*. London: SCM Press.

Isichei, Elizabeth. 1995. *A History of Christianity in Africa: From Antiquity to the Present*. Grand Rapids: William B. Eerdmans Publishing Company.

Jarvis, Michael. 2009. *Ubuntu Christianity*. Wellington: Fact and Faith Publications.

Jebadu, Alexander. 2007. Ancestral Veneration and the Possibility of its Incorporation into the Christian Faith. *Exchange* 36: 246–80. [CrossRef]

Kabasele, Francois L. 1991. Christ as Ancestor and Elder Brother. In *Faces of Jesus in Africa*. Edited by Robert J. Schreiter. New York City: Orbis Books, pp. 116–27.

Lado, Ludovic. 2006. The Roman Catholic Church and African Religions: A problematic encounter. *The Way* 45: 7–21.

Leonard, Arthur G. 1906. *The Lower Niger and It's Tribes*. London: Macmillan and Company, Ltd.

Magesa, Laurenti. 1998. *African Religion: The Moral Traditions of Abundant Life*. Nairobi: Paulines Publications Africa.

Magesa, Laurenti. 2004. *Anatomy of Inculturation: Transforming the Church in Africa*. Maryknoll: Orbis Books.

Maimela, Simon S. 1985. Salvation in African Traditional Religion. *Missionalia* 13: 63–77.

Maluleke, Tinyiko S. 2005. Half a Century of African Christian Theologies: Elements of the Emerging Agenda for the Twenty-First Century. In *African Christianity: An African Story*. Edited by Ogbu. U. Kalu. Pretoria: University of Pretoria, pp. 469–93.

Maluleke, Tinyiko S. 2010. Africanised Bees and Africanised Churches: Ten Theses on African Christianity. *Missionalia: Southern African Journal of Mission Studies* 38: 369–79.

Mathema, Zacchaeus A. 2007. The African Worldview: A Serious Challenge to Christian discipleship. *Ministry, International Journal for Pastors* 79: 5–7.

Matobo, Thope A., M. Makatsa, and Emeka E. Obioha. 2009. Continuity in the Traditional Initiation Practice of Boys and Girls in Contemporary Southern African Society. *Studies of Tribes and Tribals* 7: 105–13. [CrossRef]

Mayer, Philip, and Iona Mayer. 1974. *Townsmen or Tribesmen: Conservation and the Process of Urbanization in a South African City*. Cape Town: Oxford University Press.

Mbiti, John S. 1969. *African Religions and Philosophy*. London: Heinemann Educational Publishers.

Mbiti, John S. 1975. *Introduction to African Religion*. London: Heinemann Educational Books.

Mbiti, John S. 1977. The Biblical Basis for Present Trends in African Theology. In *African Theology en Route: Papers from the Pan-African Conference of Third World Theologians, Accra, December 17–23 1977*. Edited by Kofi Appiah-Kubi and Sergio Torres. Maryknoll: Orbis Books, pp. 83–94.

Mbiti, John S. 1990. *African Religions and Philosophy*. Oxford: Heinemann International.

Mbiti, John S. 1992. *African Religions and Philosophy*, 2nd ed. revised; London: Heinemann Educational Books.

McGuire, Meredith B. 2008. *Lived Religion: Faith and Practice in Everyday Life*. Oxford: Oxford University Press.

Mills, Wallace G. 1995. Missionaries, Xhosa Clergy and the Suppression of Traditional Customs. In *Missions and Christianity in South African History*. Edited by Henry C. Bredenkamp and Robert J. Ross. Johannesburg: Witwatersrand University Press, pp. 153–72.

Mlisa, Nomfundo L. 2009. Ukuthwasa, the Training of Xhosa Women as Traditional Healers. Ph.D. Thesis, University of the Free State, Bloemfontein, South Africa.

Mndende, Nokuzola. 2009. *Tears of Distress: Voices of a Denied Spirituality in a Democratic South Africa*. Dutywa: Icamagu Institute.

Mndende, Nokuzola. 2013. Law and Religion in South Africa: An African Traditional Perspective. *Nederduitse Gereformeerde Teologiese Tydskrif* 54: 74–82. [CrossRef]

Mogoba, Mmutlanyane S. 2011. The Religious Background to African Christianity: African Traditional Religion. In *The Journey of Hope: Essays in Honour of Dr Mmutlanyane Stanley Mogoba*. Edited by Itumeleng Mekoa. Cape Town: The Incwadi Press, pp. 170–85.

Mokhoathi, Joel. 2017. Imperialism and its effects on the African Traditional Religion: Towards the liberty of African Spirituality. *Pharos Journal of Theology* 98: 1–15.

Motlhabi, Mokgethi G. 1994. Black or African Theology? Towards an Integral African Theology. *Journal of Black Theology in South Africa* 8: 113–41.

Mtuze, Peter T. 2003. *The Essene of Xhosa Spirituality: And the Nuisance of Cultural Imperialism: Hidden Presences in the Spirituality of the annaXhosa of the Eastern Cape and the Impact of Christianity on Them*. Florida Hills: Vivlia Publishers and Booksellers.

Mugambi, Jesse N. K. 1995. *From Liberation to Reconstruction: African Christian Theology after the Cold War*. Nairobi: East African Educational Publishers.

Mugambi, Jesse N. K. 2002. Christianity and the African Cultural Heritage. In *Christianity and African Culture*. Edited by Jesse. N. K. Mugambi. Nairobi: Acton Publications, pp. 516–42.

Muzorewa, Gwinyai. H. 1985. *The Origins and Development of African Theology*. Maryknoll: Orbis Books.

Ntombana, Luvuyo. 2015. The Trajectories of Christianity and African Ritual Practices: The Public Silence and the Dilemma of Mainline or Mission Churches. *Acta Theologica* 35: 104–19. [CrossRef]

Nwibo, Joseph. 2010. A Brief Note on the Need for African Christian Theology. Paper presented at the Cursus Godsdient Onderwijs (CGO-HBO), Lienden, The Netherlands, September 22.

Nxumalo, Jabulani A. 1981. Zulu Christians and Ancestor Cult: A Pastoral Consideration. In *Ancestor Religion in Southern Africa*. Edited by Heinz Kuckertz. Transkei: Lumko Missiological Institute, pp. 65–78.

Nyamiti, Charles. 1984. *Christ as Our Ancestor: Christology from an African Perspective*. Gweru: Mambo Press.

Oden, Thomas C. 2007. *How Africa Shaped the Christian Mind: Rediscovering the African Seedbed of Western Christianity*. Westmont: InterVarsity Press Books.

Oduro, Thomas, Hennie Pretorius, Stan Nussbaum, and Bryan Born. 2008. *Mission in an African Way: A Practical Introduction to African Instituted Churches and Their Sense of Mission*. Wellington: Christian Literature Fund and Bible Media Publication.

Onuzulike, Uchenna. 2008. African Crossroads: Conflicts between African Traditional Religion and Christianity. *The International Journal of the Humanities* 6: 163–69. [CrossRef]

Pityana, Nyameko B. 1999. The Renewal of African Moral Values. In *African Renaissance: The New Struggle*. Edited by William M. Makgoba. Sandton: Mafube Publishing, pp. 137–48.

Richter, Marlise. 2003. Traditional Medicines and Traditional Healers in South Africa. Discussion Paper Prepared for the Treatment Action Campaign and AIDS Law Project. Available online: http://www.tac.org.za/Documents/ResearchPapers/Traditional_Medicine_briefing.pdf (accessed on 29 November 2017).

Sanou, Boubakar. 2013. Missiological Perspectives on the Communal Significance of Rites of Passages in African Traditional Religions. *Journal of Adventist Mission Studies* 9: 39–52.

Shaw, Rosalind, and Charles Stewart. 1994. Introduction: Problematizing syncretism. In *Syncretism/Anti-Syncretism: The Politics of Religious Synthesis*. Edited by Charles Stewart and Rosalind Shaw. London: Routledge Press, pp. 1–26.

Shorter, Aylward. 1975. *African Christian Theology: Adaptation or incarnation?* Michigan: Geoffrey Chapman.

Southern African Catholic Bishops. 2006. Ancestor Religion and the Christian Faith. Paper presented at Resolution 2.5.2 of the Plenary Session of the Southern African Catholic Bishops' Conference, Mariannhill, KwaZulu Natal, South Africa, August 11.

Stewart, Charles. 1994. Syncretism as a Dimension of National Discourse in Modern Greece. In *Syncretism/Anti-Syncretism: The Politics of Religious Synthesis*. Edited by Charles Stewart and Rosalind Shaw. London: Routledge Press, pp. 127–44.

The New Encyclopaedia Britannica. 2007. *Mainstream Christianity: Definition*. Chicago: Encyclopaedia Britannica, Inc.

Truter, Ilse. 2007. African Traditional Healers: Cultural and Religious Beliefs Intertwined in a Holistic Way. *SA Pharmaceutical Journal* 74: 56–60.

Tutu, Desmond. 1986. Black Theology and African Theology: Soulmates or Antagonists? In *Third World Liberation Theologies: A Reader*. Edited by Dean W. Ferm. Maryknoll: Orbis Books, pp. 256–64.

Van der Merwe, Dirk. 2016. From Christianising Africa to Africanising Christianity: Some hermeneutical principles. *Stellenbosch Theological Journal* 2: 559–87.

Wanamaker, Charles A. 1997. Jesus the Ancestor: Reading the Story of Jesus from an African Christian Perspective. *Scriptura* 62: 281–98. [CrossRef]

Wilson, Monica. 1982. The Nguni People. In *A History of South Africa to 1870*. Edited by Monica Wilson and Leonard Thompson. Cape Town: David Philip Publication, pp. 75–130.

religions

MDPI

Article

Towards a Rational Kingdom in Africa: Knowledge, Critical Rationality and Development in a Twenty-First Century African Cultural Context

Lawrence Ogbo Ugwuanyi

Department of Philosophy, University of Abuja, P.M.B 117, Abuja, Nigeria;
lawrence.ugwuanyi@uniabuja.edu.ng or lawrenceogbougwuanyi@gmail.com

Received: 31 January 2018; Accepted: 7 March 2018; Published: 26 March 2018

Abstract: This paper seeks to locate the kind of knowledge that is relevant for African development in the twenty-first century African cultural context and to propose the paradigm for achieving such knowledge. To do this, it advances the view that the concept of twenty-first century in an African context must be located with the colonial and post-colonial challenges of the African world and applied to serve the African demand. Anchored on this position, the paper outlines and critiques the wrong assumption on which modern state project was anchored in post-colonial Africa and its development dividend to suggest that this is an outcome of a wrong knowledge design that is foundational to the state project and which the project did not address. It proposes a shift in the knowledge paradigm in Africa and suggests critical self-consciousness as a more desirable knowledge design for Africa. It applies the term 'rational kingdom' (defined as a community of reason marked by critical conceptual self-awareness driven by innovation and constructivism) to suggest this paradigm. 'Innovation' is meant as the application of reason with an enlarged capacity to anticipate and address problems with fresh options and 'constructivism' is meant as the disposition to sustain innovation by advancing an alternative but more reliable worldview that can meet the exigencies of modernity in an African cultural context. The paper then proceeds to outline the nature of the rational kingdom and its anticipated gains and outcomes. It applies the method of inductive reasoning to advance its position. To do this it invokes selected but crucial areas of African life to locate how the developmental demands of these aspects of life suggest a critical turn in African rationality.

Keywords: critical rationality; development; Africa; kingdom

1. Introduction

At the beginning of the African quest for independence, Kwame Nkrumah, the Ghanaian president widely known as the father of modern African political freedom project, is credited with having made a popular assertion: "seek ye first the political kingdom and all other things will be added unto you."[1] This position is a strong expression of faith in the future of the African state. However, more than half a century after Nkrumah made this significant statement there is doubt on the merit of what has been added to Africa in terms of development, which to a large extent questions the validity of the assumption. This position is strongly justified especially given that another Ghanaian scholar and intellectual Kwesi Prah recently said, "little has been achieved in the 50 years of Africa's independence which can be seriously described as developmental" (Prah 2011, p. 156). This paper applies this position to interrogating the knowledge paradigm in Africa and to suggest a shift to what it calls the

---

[1] Nkrumah's famous position is cited in a number of works including Kwame Nkrumah (1957), *The Autobiography of Kwame Nkrumah*; Ama Biney (2011) *The Political and Social Thought of Kwame Nkrumah (USA: Palgrave Macmillan)*.

rational kingdom, defined as knowledge devoted to conceptual critical self-awareness driven by the vision to make innovation and constructivism a norm and a force in African social and intellectual life.

The paper is divided into three parts. I shall (i) articulate the idea of a rational kingdom by pointing out what it means, the reason and justification for its demand, the desired "kings" and "subjects" of this kingdom; the "constitutions" and "institutions" that should define this kingdom and the distinct mark of relevance that makes it urgent. Thereafter, I shall (ii) discuss the developmental imperatives of a rational kingdom and demonstrate how this justifies the need for a rational kingdom. I shall then (iii) discuss the place and role of culture in achieving this kingdom and the cultural gains of achieving this kingdom. To do this I shall discuss the various roles that culture plays in human society and how culture can be made developmental so as to play this role and how this can lead to the institution of a rational kingdom. I shall then (iv) conclude by rehearsing my claims and itemizing the implications of my positions.

I shall apply the method of inductive reasoning to advance my views. To do this, I will invoke selected but crucial areas of African life and how these demand a critical turn in African rationality. Through some critical considerations of these and how the nature of human reasoning could be said to re-enforce this need, I shall demonstrate how the idea of a rational kingdom fits into these demands. I shall rely on the views of a number of scholars in the area of culture, knowledge and development in the African context to demonstrate my claims, hoping that, as Isaac Newton once said, by "standing on the shoulders of these giants I shall see far" and probably say something desirably deeper and better.

2. The Idea of a Rational Kingdom

By rational kingdom I simply mean a cohesive self-constructed rational community where rationality would be marked by critical self-awareness in Africa along with self-invented and innovative options. Thus, the idea of a rational kingdom amounts to a rational community that admits or rejects forms of knowledge based on how far it supports the ethics of self-invention through conceptual and critical self-awareness and self-understanding. It is not a particular form of knowledge but a paradigm for sociology of knowledge and an ethics of knowledge and a knowledge process that directs the efforts and aspirations of a given community. Rather, it is one where rationality marked by constructivism and innovation assumes the center stage of African life and thought; where anti-rational or irrational forms of social interaction are to give way to a fresh paradigm that seeks to advance the best forms of rational expression desirable in Africa. My desired rational kingdom is one where different demands of reasoning will be realized in a complimentary manner as against one where a strand or an aspect of reasoning will function to dominate and destroy others; where productive rational ethics will enable Africans to move beyond the current state of thinking which amounts to rational medievalism to one where critical but resourceful culture of modernity marked by innovative rationality define Africa's rational ethics. A rational kingdom desirable in the African instance, in my view, is one where, by drawing from an array of social experiences that has defined social interaction between the African world and other geo-rational blocks of humankind, Africans are able to apply more relevant rational principles marked by innovation and creativity to their developmental needs to abstract from these and reduce the dependence of Africans on other blocks of humanity which leads to the subordination of the African will. Such a more critical and rationally grounded society will give a fresh but more forceful and impactful status to rationality in the African worldview and lead to what can be called a self-liberating religion of reason; one where what is most relevant and innovative becomes the most reasonable and desirable. By so doing, full freedom and autonomy which are twin cardinal demands of development will assume a dominant social ethics of life.

At the beginning of the African quest for independence, Kwame Nkrumah, the Ghanaian president widely known as the father of modern African political freedom project, is cited to have said "seek ye first the political kingdom and all other things will be added unto you." Regrettably, however, more than half a century after Nkrumah made this significant statement there is doubt on the merit of what has been added to Africa where many scholars would argue that "little has been achieved in the 50 years of Africa's independence which can be seriously described as developmental." (Prah 2011, p. 156). Many African states are nearly witnessing over sixty years of independence and the story is still the same. The poverty or outright failure of the development project in Africa is also strongly corroborated by the following strong claims of an African social scientist that;

> at the beginning of the new millennium, Africa was the poorest, most technology-backward, most politically unstable, most crisis-ridden, most-indebted, and most foreign-dominated and exploited as well as the most marginal continent in the world. Foreign debt represents up to 80% of GDP in net present value terms in most countries, inflation rates average between 12 and 45%, unemployment rates (excluding the informal sector) ranges between 12 and 25%, while the savings rate in Africa is the lowest in the world. As well, 15 of the world's 20 most impoverished nations are in Africa, with over 3 million refugees and 18 million internally displaced persons. It is estimated by international agencies that over 250 million Africans lack access to portable water, while over 200 million have no opportunities to access basic health services. More than 2 million children die before the first year, over 150 million youth are illiterate, and almost half of rural females do not attend formal schools. (Ihonvbere 2011).

I apply these positions to suggest that there is development failure in Africa and that the development failure in Africa has a deep cause which has not been seriously looked into—the failure of reason or the failure of the rational culture of Africans. I therefore allude to these claims and to Nkrumah's wisdom but in a reverse manner by saying that political kingdom is not even possible without the rational kingdom because the concept of polity or the state finds its root in the rational kingdom. So, I seek to institute another paradigm for an African future: "seek ye first the rational kingdom and all other things will be added unto you."

The desire for a rational kingdom in Africa does not in any way allude to contestation of the positive qualities, capability and potentials of African rational culture as can be found in many racist texts such as those of Hegel (1956), Levy-Bruhl (1923, 1926, 1975), Westermann (1934), Carothers (1972), etc. It rather amounts to the need to advance Africa's rational culture by way of locating and balancing the deficiencies in this rational culture in order to seek the best forms of reasoning that will secure the African future among the competing forces of rationality in the world today.

This desire finds strong corroboration and justification in the theory of difference held by the socio-political theorist Samuel Huntington. In his influential work, *The Clash of Civilizations*, Samuel Huntington presents an important theory of difference in which he argues that human civilizations are basically different and that the differences are justifiable, reliable and legitimate because they are born out of a conception of life. For this reason, they assume the stature of beliefs and articles of faith among diverse peoples of the world. According to Huntington (1993, p. 25):

> Civilizations are differentiated from each other by history, language, custom, tradition, and most important, religion. The people of different civilizations have different views on the relations between God and man, the individual and the group, the citizens and the state, parents and children, husband and wife, as well as differing ways on the relative importance of rights and responsibilities, liberty and authority, equality and hierarchy.

On the strength of the above claims, Huntington recognized eight major civilizations of the world, namely: Western, Islamic, Orthodox, Latin America, Indic, Japanese and African .A possible interpretation of the claims of Huntington that deserves to inform our project of rationality is that there are different concepts that define the core principles that drive human society and that these lead to different values that are found cogent and reliable within different cultures. The other implication is that any assumption of life and value that is not grounded on critical rationality is weak, false and dubious and it is only a matter of time before it presents these as the outcome. This is because critical rationality is necessary to sustain and strengthen social values especially among different competing social paradigms that present themselves as options for social growth. Huntington provides another view that supports the conceptual and rational foundations of human beliefs, ethics and civilizations when he argues against the very notion that there could be "universal civilization" (ibid., p. 41). He argues that this is basically a western assumption and argues that "western concepts differ from those prevalent in other civilizations" (ibid., p. 40). Another position that can be derived from Huntington is the need to question whether Africans should take Huntington seriously by protecting the gains of their civilizations and defending the values it promotes.

When Nkrumah theorized on the need for a political kingdom in what can now be called weak states, he had a false assumption of the kind of challenge implied by this because he thought that African self-rule would attract the consent of African elites on the agreeable intellectual paradigm to run the state and the best way to manage the project of freedom implied. As a result of this, he proceeded by drafting ideologies that would lead to this in what Nnamdi Azikiwe, his Nigerian counterpart, has called "renascent Africa." But ideologies are not the first and best paradigm to advance human reasoning because ideologies do not often harbor an inborn potential to meet the vagaries of change which is an aspect of life. Kwasi Wiredu (1980, p. 66) and Archie Mafeje (cited in Nabudere 2011) have done some significant work to point out the dangers of applying ideology as the sure route to proper development. This position does not need to be repeated here; it suffices to know that ideology amounts to preparing a ready-made answer for problems, many of which will be (re)defined by the future and this is strongly exemplified by the critical turn (rather than ideological option) that African thinkers have shown in a number of their works. This critical turn is well illustrated in the number of philosophers who have jettisoned the ideological orientation in favor of critical rationalism in the practice of their profession numbering from pioneers such as Kwasi Wiredu, Peter Bodunrin, Kwame Gyekye to several others too numerous to mention here.

As arising from the failure of rationality the very gain of African freedom is lacking. This is because freedom is not an asset unless and until the terms and goals of its operation are spelt out through a critical and constructive rational process. Nkrumah probably forgot that the principles and values that the new African states are meant to defend are considerably different from those of the states that find their origin in the African endogenous world and this would mean a whole task of self-definition in rational terms without which political kingdom will suffer grievously. This has nearly become the case at least from the social lens of the post-independent sub-Saharan Africa where the people's quality of life does not match that of their counterparts in other parts of the world. Although all states claim to function for the common good of their citizens, the political goods and the framework through which they are meant to be realized are considerably different and this means that no state anywhere is desirable without first articulating these terms and the role to be assigned to the state in their socio-historical context. But this rational self-invention has been neglected as a result of which duties are entrusted to states that have not been properly constructed. Although Nkrumah made some proposals in this regard by his ideology of 'consciencism,' the problem is that the ideology is basically a social ideology with no strong implication for the epistemological ordering of the African mind.

Paradoxically, it is almost as if what has been wrongly done in the political sphere is what is taking place in the intellectual sphere illustrated by the weakness of the African academy and the failure of the African intellectual industry to invent, theorize, and insist on a paradigm shift in the intellectual governance of African minds through the ideas, policies and practices that should direct the African academy or at least the impact of these polices in the African intellectual industry. It is almost as if the case in Africa has been: set up universities and academic institutions and your knowledge will become powerful. But how powerful the African academy has been can now be seen from the enormity of challenges confronting African universities where a sizeable number of the intellectuals have left their universities in what is now known as brain drain. These self-exiled academics are often inspired by the conducive spaces in other parts of the world to explore and exploit their talent more than anything else. Because of the challenges of the African academy, many of which lack funds for basic research, it is almost as if Africa is at the moment so dependent that African peoples import even how to laugh, as they seem to lack the confidence to accept and advance their aesthetics of laughter, owing to nothing but the rational culture directing these institutions.

A host of African scholars such as Chinweizu (1978, 2010), Ngugi wa Thiongo (1980, 1981), J. M. Ela (1994), F. B. Nyamnjoh (2004, 2012), A. Rwomire (1992), P. T. Zeleza (1997), P. Hountondji (1995) and T. Mkandawire (2005) have highlighted this point and pointed out the need to critically re-think the kind of knowledge which the state project through the academy in Africa is promoting as option for African humanities. Against the blurring forces of globalism, these scholars remind us that Africans should urgently think for themselves so that they do not become mere robots or pawns at the hands of those who think for themselves and insist on thinking for Africans without encouraging Africans to think for themselves. The reminder and lesson from these scholars is that in the same manner of Nkrumah's proposed political kingdom, the African academy if not properly directed might also lead the African intellectual world the wrong way as the African state is doing at the moment by manufacturing poverty both of the mind and of the body. Thus, a rational kingdom in an African contest would also mean not just one in which the rule or law of reason becomes dominant but one where ideas, ideals and values are favorable to the demands of African modernity by way of enabling the African worldview to generate and provide the basis for intellectual and social and political belonging. This task—that is, the need to re-arm the modern African with significant tools for national and international social belonging by generating the forms of knowledge that make Africans accountable agents of change for themselves, their nations and the international human community—cannot be ignored. Thus, it must cause a critical turn in the manner of knowledge generated and distributed in the African knowledge academy. The respected African thinker Achile Mbembe (2001) has raised relevant issues in favor of this position in his well-known book on the Post-Colony where he addresses a number of issues including Africa's pattern of self-narrative.

To demonstrate the need for a rational kingdom let me invoke at the least two positions to demonstrate my claim. The first is the philosophical position that defines man basically as a rational animal. The second is the psycho-philosophical position that holds that the manifestation of human intellect, regarded as intelligence, differs in different areas of life and from one person to the other. I wish to advance this position further by arguing that the manifestation of human reasoning differs from one social and cultural community to the other because of the social forces and challenges that define their societies. The implications of this is that reason can only be found valid when it is held to be a social project directed by the other or at least accountable to the other. The American philosopher Donald Davidson has applied this to argue that rationality is a form of co-existential project which cannot be held to have been so done without the co-operation of the other. I further apply this to urge a critical re-think of the rational culture of Africans in different aspects of life.

The view that man is a rational animal owes its formal adoption, at least in written form, to ancient Greek philosophers such as Aristotle. Philosophy—the peculiar love of wisdom and indeed the pursuit of how best to apply reason—has worked on this assumption that the faculty of human reasoning can be cultivated, refined and developed to serve the cause of humanity better. But while the human is a rational animal, what reason amounts to and the fundamental measure of reason has remained contentious. When Descartes, the French philosopher, provided his influential theory of reason with the view that rationality is the very basis for a claim to existence, he defined reason broadly as all of what we do—emotion, feeling, reasoning, etc. The implication is that thinking is basically all of what we do even when we do not know. This definition of thinking puts a crucial question mark on the specific mark of reasoning. Indeed, it was Edmund Husserl who later advanced this theory of rationality by saying that thinking must amount to thinking something. So, reason and its nature is about the person and the form. It might not be cogent to elaborate these claims further but it is urgent to submit that what man makes of reason has much to do with a fundamental disposition to this idea than the idea itself and that reason is basically a self-demanding project. What I mean by this is that rationality or "reasonability" is only a potentiality which can be validated by the outcome of its application. Thus, while human beings everywhere are fundamentally rational animals and reasoning can be applied to suite any desired project found to fall within the demand of human nature, human beings must deliberately seek to develop the "science of reason" (Ugwuanyi 2010, p. 8) to construct some desirable ends within the social demand of their world without which the faculty of reason that unites the human community will serve any poor, narrow, or dangerous end. In the African context, this makes it relevant to deliberately seek to apply the project of reason to produce the kind of human beings desirable within the demands of our world and to re-locate the African society from a society of conflicting ideals and values to one that is properly ordered and directed through a deliberate rational project. This, in essence, is what the idea of a rational kingdom is all about.

The second reason for a rational kingdom is the psycho-philosophical position which arises from what I call the peculiar demand of reason in the African world. Here I defend the view that, while all people are capable of same kind of intellection and while all social groups are capable of the same kind of reasoning, the results of rational engagements differ because they need different factors to manifest themselves. Among these factors are the psycho-social disposition of people and the form of knowledge desirable within a given community, the value that can be attached to knowledge (gained) at the exclusion of others, and to the individual or group that possess them. For instance, a society with strong disposition to traditional beliefs will not achieve a strong scientific culture unless science itself assumes a form of that tradition for the people. This is because of the rigors of scientific reasoning and the non-rigorous demand of belief ethic. This position can be better understood by inferring from the theory of multiple intelligence credited to Howard Gardner. Gardner (1983) identifies nine different forms of intelligences, namely;

> *naturalist intelligence* defined as "the human ability to discriminate among living things (plants, animals) as well as sensitivity to other features of the natural world (clouds, rock configurations)"; *musical-rhythmic intelligence*—"the capacity to discern pitch, rhythm, timbre, and tone … "; *logical-mathematical intelligence*—"the ability to calculate, quantify, consider propositions and hypotheses, and carry out complete mathematical operations … to perceive relationships and connections and to use abstract, symbolic thought; sequential reasoning skills; and inductive and deductive thinking patterns"; *existential intelligence* defined as "Sensitivity and capacity to tackle deep questions about human existence, such as the meaning of life … " *interpersonal intelligence*—the ability to understand and interact effectively with others. … bodily—*kinesthetic intelligence*—"the capacity to manipulate objects and use a variety of physical skills … "; *verbal-linguistic intelligence*-the ability to think in words and to use language to express and appreciate complex meanings … ; *intrapersonal intelligence*—the capacity to understand oneself and one's thoughts and feelings … ; and *spatial intelligence*—the ability to think in three dimensions.

I find Gardner's thesis attractive and would wish to apply it in locating the failure or perhaps challenges of rational creative freedom in Africa. This is anchored on my belief that intelligence summarily amounts to applied rationality. However, the view I hold is that several of the intelligences identified by Gardner could be united by the singular term *creative intelligence or innovative intelligence and artistic intelligence*. The position implied here is that not only are intelligences different among human beings but that social and environmental conditioning also gives rise to *different intellectual histories and hierarchies* (defined as valued different expressions of reason) which inform and influence the direction of the growth of the intellect. Thus, the social disposition of a society to an application of reason differs, perhaps as encouraged or discouraged by a particular cultural belief. Thus, just as the manifestation of human intelligence differs in different areas of life from one person to the other, this is also the case with a human community and this is based on different intellectual histories and hierarchies. What is desired of a particular community is to attempt to locate where it can be held that the manifestation of reason is deficient among them and seek to advance reason in that direction by deliberately creating values that promote rational growth in this direction.

It is in the light of this that I intend to locate the need for a rational kingdom that will address the failure or weakness of creative intelligence in Africa at the moment. Such creative intelligence (defined as applied reason) should be rooted in a notion of reason that is self-critical enough to amount to creative rationalism. By creative rationalism I mean the enlarged capacity of reason to adjust and respond to the demands of re-ordering the African world with the kind of ideas that can address the immense developmental crises of the society in all aspects of life as Africa interacts with the wider world some of which have had longer histories and cultures as well as formal and installed knowledge production and consumption. Thus, for me, the array of problems and crisis in Africa today is nothing but an indication of the failure of innovation and creativity in making Africa through thinking and in particular creative intelligence. Here, I do not limit creativity to literal creativity but broadly to intellectual creativity that locates the limits of what is held to be problems in Africa through desirable alternatives and solutions. The view suggested here, therefore, is that reason should innovate by locating the gaps in the existing ethics and science of reason so that creative intelligence will expand to address these needs and desires.

There is often the urge to look at Africans as people who are negatively special in the world, as a result of which the least problem in the continent is held to be caused by non-Africans against Africans. This ideology of victimhood is held in a vast literature on African studies. But these positions often ignore the fact that what is special about Africa is the positively special—that is, the fact that Africans naturally inhabit the best part of the earth and the most conducive positions of the world and the comfort of these zones have negatively affected their disposition to creative (and perhaps aggressive) intelligence as a social group. Thus, given the forceful nature of environmental and social conditioning to resourceful and creative thinking, it is doubtful the extent to which Africa would have been otherwise and developed such values as are different from what she has today. However, some of the values of African life no longer serve the cause of securing their world and there is again the need to begin to re-think these values and to seek the best ways to institute a whole process of rational re-ordering of the African world because the force of living in a global world means that Africans cannot survive without discarding these values through creative understanding. Thus, my view is that a form of *creative and critical rationalism* is demanded by the African society but is lacking and this makes urgent the desire for a rational culture where reasoning that will promote constructive rationalism should be promoted.

3. The Nature of a Rational Kingdom

To attempt to capture the nature of the rational kingdom desired for Africa, I shall appropriate the ideas of Plato as found in *The Republic*. Plato, it should be recalled, proposed a state where citizens were to be categorized into three—the auxiliaries, the soldiers and "philosopher-kings" and held that justice in the state could come by each of the three playing its role. In a similar vein, I hold that the rational kingdom desired in Africa should amount to a society dominated by reason and moderated by three categories of "rational citizens"—the kingmakers; the kings themselves and the subjects.

Let me begin with the subject (citizens) of the kingdom. The subject of the proposed rational kingdom desirable for Africa is everybody. This is because every member of the African society suffers the effect of the uncritical mass that dominates our society and the deficient African self-understanding at the moment. So, the kingdom in question is where everybody is rationally ruled by everybody—that is, the social governance of reason or a dominating ethics of critical reasoning. It is as if everybody were to say to everybody—'we have decided to advance our rational culture in a manner that will strengthen our society and give us a worthier place in human history by making us much more critical and constructive as individuals and as a society. We shall now seek to make all we do reasonable enough to be so done or rejected and attempt to do this by locating the foreseeable outcome of our actions in the far future. To do this, then, we shall eliminate such outstanding enemies of reason, especially those that human nature promotes such as emotion, prejudice and narcissistic application of force and unenlightened self-interest.'

The justification of the egalitarian desire for a rational society in Africa stems from what has been identified to be strong characteristics of reason in Africa but which do not favor the ethics of constructive and creative reasoning. The first is the authoritarianism of African society and its over reliance on tradition which discourages rational justification of beliefs. Kwasi Wiredu (1980) has done much to capture the traditionalism of African thought culture and the need to shift the paradigm from the ethics of belief to the ethics of critical reasoning. The desire of Wiredu, which falls in line with my view here, is that there is the need to advance the society from traditional authoritarianism to rational authoritarianism with stronger appeal to reason in African life.

The second position comes from the Senegalese philosopher Leopold Sedar Senghor. In his theory of negritude, Senghor characterizes reason in Africa as one directed by emotion or what again can be characterized as emotive rationalism. Senghor's position is that the African manner of thinking is dominated or significantly influenced by emotion. Senghor suggests that that the African principle of reasoning is reasoning by touch. For him;

> It is not reasoning eye of Europe, it is the reason of touch, better still, *the reason of the embrace*, the sympathetic reason, more clearly related to the Greek *logos* than to the Latin *ratio*.

Senghor goes further to argue that while the European views the object at a distance, analyses, and domesticates it in order to use it, the African gets wedded into the object and gets assimilated into it to know it more deeply (cited in Abanuka 2011, p. 83). At the surface, it might look as if Senghor has denigrated the African and indeed there are reasons to hold that he is often held to have done so. For instance, he routes thinking to the time "when animals and plants and even elements of nature were interwoven with man's life and were familiar to him in an environment which is imprisoned in memories." The thesis here is, if reasoning has such universal genealogy as implied by this claim, then why would the manifestation of reason become different in the African instance? I would not wish to further this debate here, but it is important to note that human geographical and environmental conditioning has significant influence on the manifestation of human reason and that the notion of reason that Senghor attributed to the African shares the same features with Aristotle's idea of wonder as the defining principles of wisdom. The Greek *logos* which he likened to a mode of reasoning is clearly a deepening ethics of wonder which leads more to engaging and appreciative wisdom than the Latin *ratio* which leads to interpretative wisdom. However, it is in the act of interrogating or understanding nature herself as an act of judgement that the social advancement that Africa needs at the moment lies. I apply this to argue that there is need to institute a more critically disposed society that understands the world "instrumentally" than one that understands the world admirably.

The third position that captures the need for an egalitarian project of reason is one that locates the African theory of thinking as a desire to acquire vital force. This theory is found in the influential book of Placide Tempels, entitled *Bantu Philosophy* (Tempels 1959). According to this theory, Africans perceive reality in terms of force; "force is even more than a necessary attribute of beings: force is the nature of being, force is being, and being is force." (ibid., p. 35) Thus, in the light of this, all the African does is "to acquire life, strength or vital force ... ." (ibid.) This theory of vital force finds its justification and collaboration in the patriarchal nature of the African society and in the fact that the "gods of African traditional religions were often gods of bravery, hence, the warrior values of Africa—courage, endurance, manhood and even purposeful ruthlessness." (Mazrui 1979–1980, p. 52) These views, properly interpreted, imply that a forceful impact on the society has more value than a rational impact. But a forceful ethics of social engagement does not make for the flowering of the human mind, especially in the light of the different potentials of intelligences we have identified.

Drawing from the positions identified above, it can be seen that the African world significantly needs an egalitarian or an all-citizen social ethics of reason in a rational kingdom because neither the force of tradition, the lure of emotion or the compulsion implied by force can make a people productively rational, given the fact that analytical and deductive principles should direct productive rationality. Although it could be debated whether the idea of kingdom can promote the emergence of an egalitarian society it should be borne in mind that the idea of kingdom implied here rules against raw force or power in favor of cooperative ethics of reason. These positions therefore suggest the need for a critical and constructive in-put into the project of reasoning. Thus, a certain disposition becomes urgent for a form of rationality that will meet the demand of resourceful and creative life in modern Africa.

After the attempt to demonstrate the subject of our proposal, let me proceed to locate who the kingmakers of this kingdom are and why. The kingmaker of this kingdom is *Reason*. By reason, I mean the effort towards an evidence-based exercise of brains with a fundamental disposition to justification and accountability. Reason as the king-maker of rational kingdom is defined as evidence based, justifiable and applicable thought; one that connects thoughts to ends and filters wrong assumptions to make way for cogency and reliability ion acceptance of positions. Furthermore, I find it cogent to anchor the power to make and direct the desired rational kingdom in Africa on applied reason because most human institutions are anchored on a form of authority (defined as certainty or the force of certainty). Virtually, all of what is considered as legitimate human conduct are those that are anchored on a form of authority defined as the right to act or the right to carry out a certain action with a reciprocal right of an action to be carried out but this agent must be given or at the least deduced from somewhere. Thus, the right to authority often comes from necessity and it is right to hold that, to a large extent, there was the force of necessity in what we consider to be the forces affecting African modernity. Even the minutest social legacy in Africa, from within or without was prompted by reason. Thus, it is important to filter the same through a form of rationality. Secondly; it is important to note that the idea of rational kingdom suggested is motivated by challenges affecting Africa which to a large extent has to do with a shift from a culture of belief to a culture of evidence based rationality. Reason as king-maker in a rational kingdom should be one that functions based on respect for principles; one that should function against solipsism and extend the culture of reason to a synthetic evaluation of the social self. It should also be one that avoids the internal contradictions that affect weak rational cultures by ensuring that the exercise of reason leads to measured worth and meaning and minimizes the conflict of values that arise from false and wrong claims to logic and reason.

Finally, let me attempt to locate those who are desired to be kings of my proposed rational kingdom. Here I adopt Plato's view to argue that the desired kings of the dream rational kingdom in Africa are the academic intellectuals in Africa. By academic intellectuals I mean those who seek to produce knowledge that do not just account for state of things but who by doing this apply a certain vision to direct their project. Giroux (2014) has argued that "while academics plough through a narrow disciplinary concern ... (and) are merely interested in ideas, intellectuals seek to bring ideas to an entire culture." Intellectuals often theorize by way of questioning the knowledge produced and how relevant it could be and if it should not be produced in another way. Thus, given the corporate demand of my dream rational kingdom in Africa, it becomes necessary to argue that the form of leadership desirable in Africa would amount to how one can connect an array of issues in Africa by way of demonstrating how their disconnection stands at the root of the poor quality of social organization and rational ordering in Africa. Such broad insight into issues and the ability to produce a desired link between them can best be expected of intellectuals who are also academics, not mere academics. Such academics will extend their creativity to formulating concepts that match the demands of the African world. Such intellectuals will realize that the desires of intellectual production in Africa should amount to a form of conceptual Africanization. By conceptual Africanization, I mean the re-negotiation of concepts through modern African experience—the effort to apply modern African experience to interpret, formulate or reformulate concepts, especially those that have the capacity to produce significant impact on African life and thought; the attempt to give ideas a distinct African interpretation and seek to forge and empower concepts to carry the weight of African experience; a sort of scientific knowledge of concepts that demands their social accountability within the African world to ensure that their desired relevance in the African world could be felt. This demands the questioning of concepts from within and the need to apply the minor differences in the African worldview as the basis to empower and enlarge and develop concepts for their adoption and use.

After the effort to illustrate the meaning and implication of rational kingdom let me next proceed to articulate the development demands of this proposal. This is because knowledge fundamentally amounts to a form of developmental humanism, thus, it is urgent to demonstrate how it can be held that this proposal has a developmental promise and effect.

4. Developmental Imperatives of a Rational Kingdom

One of the significant indices for a proper exercise of reason is the quality of development that can be attributed to a person or society. But the theory or notion of development must be reliably and rationally grounded for it to be relevant and developmental enough. If this is not the case it will only amount to movement without growth or what can be called development of underdevelopment. It does much seem that this is the case in several development literatures which have been applied in Africa. Development, to define it, amounts to "the qualitative improvement in the nature of an object or change in the status or state of a person, organ or body marked by advancement or improvement over some primitive status" (McGurk, cited in (Ikpe 1999)); or " . . . any change which has continuous direction in the qualitatively new . . . a directional cumulative change that either terminates in an event marked off by a recognized qualitative novelty or which exhibits in its cause a perceptible pattern of growth" (Sidney Hook, cited in (Ikpe 1999)); or, again as the Economic and Social Council of the United Nations (1962) defined it, "growth plus change." But the patterns of change and growth must be determined for development to serve as a proper end.

Development, in the human context, can be individual, collective or social. It can be applied to structures, human beings and institutions, etc. Individual development is the growth in the biological, emotional and rational features of a person, the proper expression of the germ of life embedded in the chromosome of the individual or the practical nurturing of skills and talents embedded in the individual. In the social context development is the advancement of different dimensions of social life—societal, economic, political, etc. In economic terms, development is the ability of an individual or group to provide or create wealth and resources to provide their basic needs and basic necessities of life and to address all desires that relate to their economic well-being. Political development amounts to the improvement in the quality of rights and gains of state belonging while social development refers to the quality of social control, social security and social services available within a social group, the advancement of strong and reliable norms, values and policies that a social group demands and needs to function as a human community. These aspects imply qualitative development in the idea of right and wrong that operate in a society because it is how the ethics of the society responds to the demand of right and wrong that could lead to happiness, which high minds like Aristotle have defined as the goal of the ethical life (for details see Aristotle's *Nichomachen Ethics*).

However, notwithstanding these diverse aspects of development, all development is aimed at the improvement of a people's life and should be judged by how it affects the people. Ade Ajayi (1999) puts it that, "development is about people," just as Julius Nyerere, former president of Tanzania and a foremost African thinker, provides strong positions that suggest this view. According to Nyerere:

> Roads, buildings and increase of the crop output, and other things of this nature, are not development: they are tools of development. A new road extends a man's freedom if he travels upon it. An increase in the number of school buildings is development only if those buildings can be, and are used, to develop the minds and the understanding of the people. An increase in the output of wheat, maize or beans is only development if it leads to the better nutrition of the people. An expansion of the cotton, coffee or sisal crop is development only if these things improve the health, comfort and understanding of the people. Development which is not development of the people may be of interest to historians in the year 3000: it is irrelevant to the future which is being created. (Nyerere, cited in (Oladipo 2006, p. 96)).

But there is a distinct challenge of development in Africa which spells out the gains of a rational kingdom. This can be located in the models through which development has been conceived in Africa. Christopher J. Koroneos and Dimitri Rokos (Koroneos and Rokos 2012) submit that "the historical model of industrialized societies in the 19th and 20th centuries served as the central notion of what constitutes development in both the cost-effectiveness and equity perspectives." This model of development, I submit, has been applied in Africa, but has affected other demanding areas of development as a result of which development in its contemporary demands is narrowed almost exclusively to imply and apply to economic development. When emphasis is narrowed to one aspect of development to the detriment of others then a fundamental harm is being done because of the complimentary quality of the human nature and society. Similarly, when development is so conceived that it creates a crisis of self-worth and personality then a fundamental damage is already done to the person for whom development is conceived. For instance, when we apply the term human resource development there is tendency to make the human being a reliable commodity for economic ends only not in the wide sense of resources or value. While a people might assume that they are developing and attempt to justify their claim by the length of period spent in their chosen direction they might just be developing underdevelopment because their development paradigm is in a wrong way.

Although the development discourse is now gradually recognizing a more encompassing notion of development to include wellbeing, it is important to note that the idea of wellbeing is still seen in the light of physical wellbeing or in terms of meeting the material needs of man more than the spiritual and mental needs. For example, when the idea of sustainable development captures such concerns as economic development, social development, and environmental protection the issue arises as to why moral development is not emphasized even as the idea of morality determines how these could and should be valued. This problem and others implied illustrates the need to allow the notion of development to benefit from a paradigm shift through the idea of a rational kingdom. This shift can be achieved in three ways. The first (i) is to achieve a notion of development favorable to the African worldview; one that would advance the potentials of this worldview without undermining the capacity of Africans to participate in development gains elsewhere. The second (ii) is to seek to determine the specific areas of African life that are developed and re-enforce the gains and values achieved here. The third (iii) is to see how this idea of development can influence the entire development paradigm globally. By doing these it would be seen that a deliberate effort has been made to involve and apply reason to appropriate the idea of development to an African advantage in its modern demands.

Let me proceed to elaborate on these positions beginning with the first (i). The first demand of the rational kingdom in relation to development paradigm is to seek to achieve a notion of development that is favorable to the provisions of the African worldview. At the moment, the development discourse in Africa is marked by "the dominance of foreign thoughts in the conceptualization and implementation of development . . . " and the penchant for Africa leaders " . . . to depend on imported theories and ideas on what constitutes development" (Gumede 2014). This importation is often from the Western world; notwithstanding the fact that for nearly half a century development strategists and social scientists of the developing world have detected a fault with the Western paradigm for development, which is largely exogenous to the non-western world (Yogesh Atal cited in Sang-Bok Han (2009, p. 1)). This has led to a growing interest in endogenous development[2]. But while the idea of endogenous development is gradually gaining root, at least in Africa as evident in a growing literature on endogenous knowledge and studies, there are reasons to believe that those who have embraced the idea and are applying alternative models of development are countries outside Africa. Furthermore, there are still noticeable deficiencies in the application of these terms in that they do also suffer the north-bound gaze on development in terms of narrowing development to the economic

---

[2]   Current literature on the subject include the following: (Apusigah and Millar 2010; Haverkort 2008; Haverkort and Reinjntjes 2006; Haverkort and Rist 2007; Haverkort et al. 2002; Hountondji 1997; Millar et al. 2006a, 2006b; Marianela Lafuente 2014; Han 1997).

aspect while neglecting other corporate demands of development in relation to the human person and society. These are strong bases for demanding for a deliberately constructed rational process in Africa as implied by the idea of a rational kingdom. Such a kingdom will lead to a specific articulation of the concept of endogenous development as it should be upheld through the African worldview and seek to apply the term to capture various aspects of development.

It is in the light of this that the need arises to locate specific areas of African life that are developed and re-enforce them as implied by (ii). To do this we shall now turn to locate these aspects of African life. There is often the assumption that Africa has lacked quality growth and development but the meaning of this term has not achieved a desirable African gain by way of locating the specific areas that is captured by this term. The charge that Africa is un/under/de-developed ignores the fact that there are certain specific aspects of life where the African world has (deliberately or not) advanced qualitatively and reliably. One of this is in the area of human relations and the social gains implied. There is a strong basis to hold that the African worldview harbors very strong potentials to provide the basis for interaction that would foster the good life in the total demand of the term because it lays strong emphasis on fostering same values for others as basis for realizing that for the agent. Pedro Tabensky (2002) provides a valuable link between happiness, person and the human community in such a manner that it would be seen that it can be validly upheld that these are interlinked as it obtains in the African worldview. This is a strong indicator that the African world harbors much potentials in developing the human person in the spiritual demands of the term given that happiness is significantly a spiritual principle. This is also evident given the fact that cases of suicide are less in Africa than in other parts of the world can be attributed to the virtue of empathy that significantly shapes African social life. Although the rarity of suicide is not necessarily the strongest indicator of a happy life, it nevertheless provides some reliable indices in that direction.

Latest discourse on development shows that efforts are made to develop what Koroneos and Rokos (2012) has called "worth-living integrated development" as a more desirable notion of development and this will demand an account of how values such as peace and solidarity have been inserted into the development discourse. This is also validated by the view that what should matter to a people is not just Gross Domestic Product (GDP) but Gross Domestic Happiness (GDH); because while GDP might delineate a higher productivity among a people, it is doubtful the extent to which it can represent what amounts to proper and valuable development among a people in terms of their total wellbeing. Indeed, the implication for my claim here is that economic development, however significant, cannot suffice for the totality of all that development means and that when this is applied as the sole measure of development danger stands knocking. If a rational kingdom is achieved in Africa, it will be discovered that the singular economic gaze on development through which Africa has been vilified all this while is not correct and that an aspect of development has been upheld by the African worldview; one which insists that the quality of human belonging should be characterized as development.

The effort to locate the distinct mark of development that is implied and upheld by the African worldview and the need to apply endogenous African perspective on development to influence development literature globally and serve as Africa's own contribution to global modernity is what I consider to be the third desirable gain for a rational kingdom in Africa. Indeed, I tend to think that, given the organic nature of human beings who constitute the human society, it is doubtful the extent to which a narrow view of development that lays emphasis on structures at the expense of persons and relegates corporate wellbeing of individuals (interpreted to mean mental and spiritual well-being and the availability of such values that will promote the social, moral and psychological capital of a person or group) will be upheld in a rational kingdom that aligns development to whole human ends. Thus, in view of the potentials of the concepts available in African thought in constructing a viable alternative to development for the larger portion of humanity, a rational kingdom is desirable in the African context. Such rational kingdom should seek to interrogate concepts such as freedom, responsibility and rights which are strong virtues that drive development. By critically evaluating and applying ideas and values like freedom, it will be seen that the cooperative and communal principle of African world should re-enforce each other and that principles like freedom should be applied to re-inforce the ethics of responsibility and accountability. In Africa, a rational kingdom with an emphasis on critical rationality would locate the fact that, in an African context, it is not acceptable to deliberately aim at creating wealth by undermining the contributory principle and capacity of other members of the society whose social and economic well-being help to foster peace and cooperate communalism. Such a position as this adds to emphasize the developmental imperatives of rational kingdom and its demand in Africa.

5. The Cultural Imperatives of a Rational Kingdom

In the effort to institute a rational kingdom in Africa, this work will next invoke the idea of culture and illustrate how the idea of culture re-enforces this demand. By this is implied the gains of the idea of the rational kingdom in cultural advancement. This is because, as part of what served to define, determine and yet undermine human civilizations generally, there is no better way to achieve a worthier future for Africa than by critically re-instating, refining and advancing culture in its modern African demands. In social discourse, no concept has commanded more attention than culture and development. This, perhaps, is because all thinking, including thinking about culture, "occurs in cultural and socio-cultural context" (Mafeje in Nabudere 2011, p. 74). J. H. Bodley (cited in (Ukpokolo 2004, p. 20)) holds that culture carries a wide range of meanings and definitions—"typical, historical, behavioral, normative, functional, mental, structural and symbolic," just as Clyde Kluckholn provides the following wide range of meanings that can be applied to culture:

"the total way of life of a people"

"the social legacy the individual acquires from this group"

"a way of thinking, feeling and believing"

"an abstraction from behavior"

"a theory on the part of the anthropologist about the way in which a group of people in fact behave"

"a storehouse of pooled learning"

"a set of standardized orientations to recurrent problems"

"learned behavior"

"a mechanism for the normative regulation of behavior"

"a set of techniques for adjusting both to external environment and to other men"

"a precipitate of history"

"a behavioral map, sieve, or matrix". (for details, see (Ukpokolo 2004, pp. 18–19)).

The wider and broader implication of these is that culture amounts broadly to a second nature in terms of and through which one adapts oneself in the world and negotiates his or her presence in the world. In the light of this, it becomes necessary to look at how culture influences human lives individually and socially so as to appraise its import and significance in the African context from which we can map out how it could be better influenced through a fresh rational culture implied by the desire for a rational kingdom.

The Ghanaian philosopher, Abraham (2015, pp. 16–21) identifies four main functions of culture each of which points to culture "as an integrative instrument" (ibid.). According to Abraham, society demands sufferance and co-operation and "culture is an instrument for making such sufferance and co-operation natural" (ibid., p. 19).Secondly, "it creates the basis of the formulation of a common destiny and co-operation in pursuing it" (ibid.)."A third use of culture is to make events intelligible and significant (ibid., p. 20). "A forth aspect of culture is to control change" (ibid., p. 21). Similarly,

Ali Mazrui (1979–1980, p. 47) enumerates seven functions of culture. According to Mazrui, culture (i) provides a worldview for a people; (ii) provides standards of evaluation; (iii) conditions motivation; (iv) is a medium of communication; (v) is the basis for stratification in the society; (vi) is the agent that determines the production pattern of a people; and (vii) defines the identity of a people.

If we examine the African culture in the light of these functions, we shall find out that the African culture has not been able to perform these functions properly and that it is questionable the extent to which African culture has functioned to secure the social demands of life in the contemporary terms. A cursory look at the modern African society reveals a predominant feature of instability and weakness. This state of affairs is clearly evident in the dependent nature of African society (Ugwuanyi 2003), the poor quality of life and social services, and the general state of insecurity in Africa results arguably from the absence of a strong and reliable cultural pattern to meet the many challenges of cultural development of the contemporary African. By strong cultural pattern, I mean a cultural pattern "that provides a coherent framework within which norms and behaviors are articulated" (Serageldin 1992, p. 19) and by a reliable cultural pattern I mean one that allows for the "incorporation of new elements" (ibid.). The absence of these two significant qualities, which constitute an important item in cultural development, has given rise to a certain crisis, which can be adequately characterized as the crisis of cultural identity in Africa. For instance, in Africa, we notice a prevalent culture of disorder, absence of harmony, and inability to manage change as well as make significant use of African experience of modernity. To illustrate this position, it should be noted that, given the fact that Africans have suffered the worst form of brutality in human history, it is curious to see how they treat each other with the same principle at the moment and to wonder whether they have gained anything from that experience. A strong view held to account for this is the disastrous ethics of violence through which modernity was introduced to Africa (slavery, imperialisms, colonialism).but the charge is why Africa has not negotiated herself from this inhuman culture. Thus, the need arises to determine the current state of culture in determining social interaction and whether it should be held that African problems are normal and usual enough as held by Patrick Chabal and Jean-Pascal Daloz (Chabal and Daloz 1999), in their infamous book *Africa Works* (Chabal and Daloz 1999). I do not accept Chabal's thesis but hold that it would be useful to measure the quality of pain that the African condition has attracted to Africans, those who truly feel the pains and why, how or whether African culture has defined and defended the African experience meaningfully, and critically motivated the quest for a worthier alternative.

In the light of the above positions the idea of rational kingdom promises a more relevant and productive role to cultural advancement in Africa. This role is twofold. The first is to create a social atmosphere where significant aspects of African life that are weak will be strengthened through a form of culture engineering. The second is to foster rational ideals that will serve as the defining mark of African modernity so as to promote the quest for a distinct version of modernity in Africa. Let me further attempt to elaborate on these recommendations and by so doing further illustrate the gains of rational kingdom in Africa in relation to cultural growth.

To do this, I submit that there are specific aspects of life that deserve crucial attention in African cultural industries and formations. By cultural industries I mean the domain of African arts where culture is produced and by cultural formations I mean the institutions that promote and foster desires and values for the society. An aspect of this is in the area of production and consumption. There is urgent need to apply the cultural industries of Africa to institute a consumption pattern that benefits from the productive capacity of Africans and limits the dependency of Africa on other regions of the world. These dependencies range from food, music, clothing to modes of communication such as language, transportation, etc. In these areas, the importance of culture is being under-applied in Africa and this undermines the desired confidence and autonomy of the people. For instance, much of what Africans consume at the moment is not produced by Africans, the implication of which is that a culture of dependency is being perpetuated among the people and this affects the emergence of self-willed development. Africa's maximum dependence on the non-Africans at the moment ridiculously undermines African self-worth and pride and a relevant culture of production needed to urgently address and reverse this trend. This deepening dependence, especially in the area of economic need, has served in strong ways to moderate the emergence of autonomous self-will on the part of Africans. For instance, in 2014, Uganda had her economic aid cut by the United States of America when the country enacted a law outlawing same-sex relationships. This measure which disregards the gains of social autonomy which the USA may ironically be exercising has another implication; this is, that Uganda's autonomy as a nation of people with values that bind them was being questioned and that the Ugandan people are being sanctioned for refusing to abandon certain values that make them one and cohesive.

But there is also another curious challenge implied by this and this is the gain in developing strong rational ethics as suggested by the idea of a rational kingdom. It is that of questioning the productive capacity of Ugandans and why they should remain dependent on aids and how long they intend to run their country on international aids. This is a crucial worry given the popular saying that a beggar has no choice. It is that of asking the Ugandans to work out how to live within their means and to administer their society so as to produce what they can consume and consume what they can produce.

This need is what I think is being emphasized, in a dubious and ironic manner, by the attempts of foreign and aid-giving countries when they try to enforce certain laws and customs onto African countries in furtherance of these foreign countries' own morals, ethics, and of course markets.

Africa's dependence on non-African or alien forms of thought is not just on economic matters. They span through political, moral and, aesthetic aspects of life. In politics, the dependence on the Western pattern of majoritarian democracy, and 'the winner takes it all' syndrome that is inherent in this mode of democracy, has caused the continent enormous harm given the industrial hate, acrimony, and bitterness that arise from this method of democracy. Yet the maximum loss in social capital which arises from this has not generated enough concern or caused a significant shift in political ethics and paradigm. In aesthetics, notions of beauty and taste significantly alien to African cultures has made it such that the African notion of beauty is gradually being eroded and that much of African wealth is spent shoring up foreign wealth in the effort to 'buy' beauty. These are crucial areas of cultural concern that a rational kingdom can address. They urge for a creative expansion of culture and the need to apply the potentials and provisions of African cultural capital to address these needs. This does not mean that Africans can manufacture machines overnight but that they can eliminate those wants that are deliberately created by the productive machines of non-Africans that seek to expand the African taste and desire for what they are not yet in a position to produce at the moment. It is about how not to want what is not available; except it is a necessity and how to use what is available within the cultural provisions of a given world to seek what is desirable but is not available within this world.

The second gain of cultural advancement which emphasizes the need for a rational kingdom is the need to institute a distinct version of modernity in Africa, one which will foster the desire of a distinct modern worldview significantly applied to some instruments of modernity that are desirably human. Many of these instruments of modernity have been achieved through scientific thinking and technological innovation which are inspired by alien cultures but while these achievements were propelled and produced through a particular culture of thinking, it does not mean that their application and the human value that should be attached to them should emanate from the same culture through which they were produced. For instance, if guns have been found to be desirable weapons to arm the security agencies and protect the society at large, there is no need for guns to be made a desirable item of social value such that toy guns are marketed to children. This is because the implication of this is that a whole worldview of violence is being inspired and constructed for the future. In essence, the second cultural gain of a rational kingdom in Africa is that it has the potential to lead to the humanization of science and technology in Africa by way of ensuring that science and technology are made to lead to a worthier human community in Africa. To do this it should seek to infuse and foster these ideals through the instrumentality of cultural institutions in Africa.

6. Conclusions

In this paper, I have to interrogate the demands of development in the African cultural con. I did this with the assumption that the very beginnings of western modernity in Africa did provide not a rational culture that will favor development. I did not criticize development or reject development as a concept because there is obviously what amounts to the natural origins of the concepts at least abstracting from the nature of human biology where the human nature functions better and worthier when it advances from one state or state to the other. I therefore chose to focus on advancing the idea of development by problematizing development in the African context. My effort in this direction is what have led to a proposal on the idea of a rational kingdom as a desirable alternative. I articulated the idea of the rational kingdom by pointing out what it means, the reason and justification for its demand and the distinct mark of relevance that makes it urgent. From a theoretical engagement with the idea of rational kingdom I attempted to articulate its practical gains. I discussed the gains of the kingdom in relation to development and culture. This proposal has vast disciplinary implications for the humanities in Africa. It has enormous demands for the arts, culture, heritage and commerce in Africa. It implies the need to critically re-articulate the knowledge desired by these disciplines—that is, the distinct desires of African people in relation to these disciplines and how by the knowledge gained in these areas the desire and need to be African in its modern demands are promoted and protected. For the historian, linguist, the writer or literary theoretician, it demands a deliberate attempt to produce knowledge in the areas, the type that by consuming it the force and cogency of reason will be felt, inspired and achieved. For the scholar of African religion, it demands interrogating the modern philosophy of religion in Africa and the forms of religious thought desirable at the moment; that is, how to ensure that demands of African rational re-awakening are not overrun by religious ideals that abhor or detest a rational ethics. All these should be able to lead to sustainable development which in the African context demands the application of reason to articulate, advance and secure worthy human ends which should lead to the development of the human person. In practical terms, this means promoting a culture of development that can sustain the developmental values of African ethics; that is, the form of development which while addressing the demands of socio-economic and political growth will defend the idea of a distinct African worth and value.

Conflicts of Interest: The author declares no conflicts of interest.

References

Abanuka, Batholomew. 2011. *A History of African Philosophy*. Enugu: Snaap Press.

Abraham, William Emmanuel. 2015. *The Mind of Africa*. Ghana: Sub-Saharan Publishers.

Ade Ajayi, Jacob. 1999. Development is About People. *Viewpoint: A Critical Review of Culture and Society* 1: 9–17.

Apusigah, Agnes A., and David Millar, eds. 2010. *Endogenous Knowledge and African Development: Issues, Challenges and Options*. Kumasi: University Press.

Biney, Ama. 2011. *The Political and Social Thought of Kwame Nkrumah*. New York: Palgrave Macmillan.

Carothers, John Colin. 1972. *The Mind of Man in Africa*. London: Tome Stacey.

Chabal, Patrick, and Jean-Pascal Daloz. 1999. *Africa Works: Disorder as Political Instrument*. London: The International African Institute, Bloomington: Indiana University Press.

Chinweizu. 1978. *The West and the Rest of Us*. Lagos: NOK Publishers.

Chinweizu. 2010. Education for Liberation in Black Africa. Paper presented at the CODESRIA Conference on 50 Years of African Independence, Legon, Ghana, September 27–29.

Ela, Jean-Marc. 1994. *Reconstruct the History of African Societies: Promoting the Social Sciences in Black Africa*. Paris: Harmattan.

Gardner, Howard. 1983. *Overview of the Multiple Intelligences Theory*. Alexandria: Association for Supervision and Curriculum Development. Cumbria: Thomas Armstrong.com.

Giroux, Henry A. 2014. Noam Chomsky and the Public Intellectual in Turbulent Times. Available online: www.truth.org (accessed on 24 March 2014).

Gumede, Vusi. 2014. Thought Leadership, Thought Liberation, and Critical Consciousness for Africa's Development and a Just World. Paper presented at the Inaugural Lecture Delivered at the University of South Africa, Senate Hall, Pretoria, 0002, South Africa, March 19. Dakar: CODESRIA Bulletin, April.

Han, Sang-Bok. 1997. The Role of Endogenous Culture in Socio-Economic Development of Korea. In *Integration of Endogenous Cultural Dimension into Development*. New Delhi: Indira Ghandi National Center for the Arts.

Han, Sang-Bok. 2009. The Role of Endogenous Culture in Socio-economic Development of Korea. Available online: http://www.vanhoahoc.vn/nghien-cuu/tai-lieu-tieng-nuoc-ngoai/other-cultures/1435-sang-bok-han-the-role-of-endogenous-culture-in-socio-economic-development-of-korea.html (accessed on 24 March 2018).

Haverkort, Betrus. 2008. Challenges for Endogenous Development and Biocultural Diversity. In *Endogenous Development and Bio-Cultural Diversity*. Zurich: Center for Development and Learning.

Haverkort, Bertus, and Coen Reinjntjes, eds. 2006. *Moving Worldviews: Reshaping Sciences, Policies and Practices for Endogenous Sustainable Development*. Leusden: ETC/Compas.

Haverkort, Bertus, and Stephan Rist, eds. 2007. *Endogenous Development and Bio-Cultural Diversity: The Interplay of Worldviews, Globalization and Locality*. Zurich: Center for Development and Learning.

Haverkort, Betrus, Katrien Van't Hooft, and Wim Hiemstra. 2002. *Ancient Roots, New Shoots, Endogenous Development in Practice*. Sachse: Compas.

Hegel, Katrien van't. 1956. *The Philosophy of History*. New York: Dover Publications, Inc.

Hountondji, Pauline J. 1995. Producing Knowledge in Africa Today: The Second Bashorun M.K.O. Abiola Distinguished Lecture. *Africa Studies Review* 38: 1–10. [CrossRef]

Hountondji, Pauline J. 1997. *Endogenous Knowledge: Research Trails*. Dakar: CODESRIA.

Huntington, Sameul. 1993. The Clash of Civilization. *Foreign Affairs* 72: 22–49. [CrossRef]

Ihonvbere, Julius. 2011. Reinventing Africa for the Challenges of the Twenty-First Century. Paper presented at the 2010 Annual Public Lecture of the Center for Black and African Arts and Civilization (CBAAC), CBAAC Occasional Monograph, Lagos, Nigeria, July 22.

Ikpe, Ibanga. 1999. The Culture of Development and the Development of Culture. *Viewpoint: A Critical Review of Culture and Society* 1: 1–8.

Koroneos, Christopher J., and Dimitri Rokos. 2012. Sustainable and Integrated Development—A Critical Analysis. *Sustainability* 4: 141–53. [CrossRef]

Levy-Bruhl, Lucien. 1923. *Primitive Mentality*. Boston: Beacon Press.

Levy-Bruhl, Lucien. 1926. *How Natives Think*. London: Allen and Unwin.

Levy-Bruhl, Lucien. 1975. *Notebooks on Primitive Mentality*. Oxford: Basil Blackwell.

Marianela Lafuente, Carlos Genatios. 2014. Science and Technology, for Endogenous Development. Available online: http://www.voltairenet.org/spip.php?page=recherche&recherche=Carlos%20Casimiro%20Salvador%20Armend%C3%A1riz&lang=en (accessed on 24 March 2018).

Mazrui, Ali. 1979–1980. *The African Condition*. London: Heinemann.

Mbembe, Achille. 2001. *On the Post-Colony*. Berkeley: University of California Press.

Millar, David, Stephan Bugu Kendie, Agnes Atia Apusiga, and Bertus Haverkort, eds. 2006a. *African Knowledge and Sciences: A Potential for Endogenous Development*. Ghana: COMPAS&UDS.

Millar, David, Stephan Bugu Kendie, Agnes Atia Apusiga, and Bertus Haverkort, eds. 2006b. *African Knowledge and Sciences: Understanding and Supporting the Ways of Knowing in Sub-Saharan Africa*. Ghana: COMPAS&UDS.

Mkandawire, Thandika, ed. 2005. "The Social Sciences in Africa: Breaking Local Barriers and Negotiating International Presence": The Bashorun MKO Abiola Distinguished Lecture presented to the 1996 African Studies Association, Annual Meeting. *African Studies Review* 40: 15–36.

Nabudere, Dani. 2011. *Afrikology, Philosophy and Wholeness: An Epistemology*. Pretoria: Africa Institute of South Africa, February.

Nkrumah, Kwame. 1957. *The Autobiography of Kwame Nkrumah*. Edinburgh and New York: Thomas Nelson and Sons.

Nyamnjoh, F. B. 2004. A Relevant Education for African Development—Some Epistemological Considerations. *African Development* 23: 161–84. [CrossRef]

Nyamnjoh, F. B. 2012. "Potted Plants in Greenhouses": A Critical Reflection on the Resilience of Colonial Education in Africa. *Journal of Asian and African Studies* 47: 129–54. [CrossRef]

Oladipo, Olusegun. 2006. *Philosophy and Social Reconstruction in Africa*. Ibadan: Hope Publications.

Prah, Kwesi. 2011. Culture: The Missing Link in Development Planning in Africa. In *Philosophy and Development: Theory and Practice*. Edited by Lansana Keita. Dakar: CODESRIA.

Rwomire, A. 1992. Education and Development: African Perspectives. *Prospects* 22: 227–39. [CrossRef]

Serageldin, Ismail. 1992. The Challenge of a Holistic Vision: Culture, Empowerment and the Development Paradigm. In *Culture and Development in Africa, Proceedings of an International Conference Held at the World Bank, Washington, DC, USA, April 2–3*. Edited by Ismail Serageldin and June Taboroff. Washington: World Bank.

Tabensky, Pedro Alexis. 2002. *Happiness: Personhood, Community, Purpose*. London: Ashgate.

Tempels, Placid. 1959. *Bantu Philosophy*. France: Presence Africaine.

Ugwuanyi, Lawrence Ogbo. 2003. Mind and Liberation: Towards a Theory of African Cultural Renewal. Ph.D. thesis, Department of Philosophy, University of Ibadan, Ibadan, Nigeria.

Ugwuanyi, Lawrence Ogbo. 2010. An Insight into the Dilemma of African Modernity and a Theoretical Response. Paper presented at the 7th Iberian Congress of African Studies, Hosted by ISCTE/Lisbon University Institute, Lisbon, Portugal, September 9–11. Available online: http://cea.iscte.pt/ciea7/ (accessed on 10 March 2018).

Ukpokolo, I. 2004. *Philosophy Interrogates Culture*. Ibadan: Hope Publications.

wa Thiongo, Ngugi. 1980. *Decolonising the Mind: The Politics of Language in African Literature*. Nairobi: Heinemann.

wa Thiongo, Ngugi. 1981. *Home Coming: Essays on African and Caribbean Literature, Culture and Politics*. London: Heinemann.

Westermann, D. 1934. *The African To-Day*. London: Oxford University Press.

Wiredu, Kwasi. 1980. *Philosophy and an African Culture*. Cambridge: Cambridge University Press.

Zeleza, Paul Tiyambe. 1997. *Manufacturing African Studies and Crisis*. Dakar: CODESRIA.

religions

MDPI

Article

From Dis-Enclosure to Decolonisation: In Dialogue with Nancy and Mbembe on Self-Determination and the Other

Schalk Hendrik Gerber

Department of Philosophy, Stellenbosch University, Stellenbosch 7602, South Africa;
schalk.gerber101@gmail.com

Received: 26 January 2018; Accepted: 10 April 2018; Published: 13 April 2018

Abstract: What might a sense of decolonisation (not)/be? Or, what comes after the logic of the coloniser? This question is at the centre of many debates in South Africa and extends to all countries worldwide who are faced with the challenge of self-determination by rethinking the world we live in after the domination of the world by the so-called "all *enclosing* Western world-view" incarnated in various oppressive political, economic, social and intellectual practices. The challenge of rethinking the world following the demotion of the West from its centre, as will be argued, is not only for those who are particularly living in a previously colonised world, but also for those who were/ still are in the position of dominance, which is a universal task. It is at this point where the various philosophical traditions meet, more precisely that of continental philosophy of religion and African philosophy. Accordingly, this article seeks to explore the question in two parts by way of an inter-cultural approach. Part one retraces the critique of (a certain) Western metaphysics in terms of its onto-theological constitution. Subsequently, this onto-theological constitution is discussed in relation to the notions of identity and political to outline what a sense of decolonisation might not be, that is a re-enforcement of the *logic of the coloniser*, which denies the full existence of an-other. In part two, four suggestions are made on what a sense of decolonisation might be in dialogue with Jean-Luc Nancy and Achille Mbembe. The suggestions include a two-sided attitude of reticence/dissidence against falling back into the problematic logic. A move to consider decolonisation as the *dis-enclosure* of the world, which in turn, opens up a space for an alternative ontology that acknowledges our existence as always being-in-the-word *with* others. The fourth suggestion concerns the implications of this alternative ontology regarding a non-substantialist notion of identity as *mêlée*, which is the action of constant struggle within the re-opened space for what it means to live in the world. Finally, it is concluded that the alternative ontology of decolonisation as dis-enclosure implies a universal task of taking responsibility for the reparation of the dignity of the whole of humanity within our shared world.

Keywords: dis-enclosure; decolonisation; self-determination; identity; onto-theology; African philosophy; continental philosophy of religion; intercultural philosophy; Jean-Luc Nancy; Achille Mbembe

---

1. Introduction

One of the main themes in post-colonial thought, including the post-apartheid world of South Africa[1] concerns self-determination. Intertwined with the challenge of determining the meaning of

---

[1] Hermeneutically speaking the article is inspired by the 2015–2016 student protests and the subsequent call for decolonisation of the university and society at large, which for the first time has resulted in the question of decolonisation and self-determination within South Africa taking centre stage. Although the discourse concerning decolonisation itself is not

the world one lives in is interpreting otherness or making sense of the stranger. This challenge of determining the self and at the same time interpreting the other may be formulated into the classic philosophical question that is concerning the relationship between the particular and the universal. Take, for example, the debate outlined in the African philosophical tradition regarding the quest for self-identity. On the one side, as Fayemi (2011) describes, you have the ethnophilosophies[2] that focus on the particularity of African cultures to the point of cultural relativism. On the other side, you have the anti-ethnophilosophies that attempt to account for cultural universalism.[3] Within the South African context, the question concerning self-determination and the interpretation of otherness includes eras of colonisation (an overemphasis of the universal character of Western identity), apartheid (an overemphasis on particular differences), and democracy (the attempt to rethink the relationship between the universal and particular). In short, problems arise when either the universal or the particular is overemphasised and it dictates the meaning for its counterpart.

Important here is to ask how these events have shaped the relationship between the so-called Western subject and the African other? Firstly, through the domination and *enclosure* of the world by the "all *enclosing* Western worldview", i.e., a (pseudo) universalist perspective that became incarnated in various oppressive political, economic, social, and intellectual practices and institutions. Secondly, by the call for *decolonisation*, which in South Africa has become a "buzz word", especially after the 2015–2016 student protest at universities across the country. This call seems to appeal to the particularity of African cultures translated into the ethnocentric ideology[4] advocated as Afrocentrism or Pan-Africanism, which has dominated African philosophy in recent decades[5], and may be understood as responses that aim to liberate Africa and African personhood from Western epistemic oppression (Eze 2015; Mudimbe 1988; Appiah 1992; Mbembe 2002a, 2002b). In other words, it is an attempt at self-determination in the midst of a world that is enclosed by a dominating Western worldview. The problem, however, with this position, outlined by Mbembe (2002a) in *African Modes of Self-Writing*, is that often manifests as the logic that it seeks to overcome and thereby it merely reverses or redirects the *logic of the coloniser*. The tables are simply turned, where everything "African" is seen as positive. In turn, everything "Western" is regarded as negative. This leads to a sense of decolonisation as destruction. The *de-* of decolonisation refers to an emptying out or exclusion of anything Western. Moreover, no critique against this position is considered; hence, one is left with cultural relativism (Wiredu 2004, p. 12).

The challenge thus may be formulated in the following question: What comes after the logical of the coloniser? Or, put differently, what might a sense decolonisation be, that does not reinforce the same dominating and oppressive thought system it proclaims to overcome? Attempts at formulating an alternative sense of decolonisation[6] to that of destruction only, are to be found. These attempts

---

new, nor is it restricted the South African context, the engagement thereof within the broader South African philosophical tradition has only recently been taken seriously—twenty plus years after the fall of apartheid. Hence, these events act as the background and rationale to take up the question concerning decolonisation once more by learning from the established discourse and imagining possible steps forward by being based in the particular, and in conversation with the universal project.

[2] Scholars that form part of this group according to Fayemi (2011, p. 260) include: Abraham (1966); Mbiti (1969); Sodipo (1973); Anyanwu (1983); Tempels (1959); and Senghor (1991).

[3] Philosophers that are included in this classification according to Fayemi (2011, p. 260) are: Bodunrin (1985); Hountondji (1983); Appiah (1992); Towa (1991); and Wiredu (1980). Although Mbembe has a complex relationship with African philosophy and is influenced by a wide range of authors from Fanon and Cesaire to Foucalt and Nancy, for the purpose of this paper Mbembe could also be placed among these thinkers that aim at rethinking the relation of the universal and the particular. See Mbembe (2017).

[4] Ideology understood here according to Hutchens' (Hutchens 2005, p. 40) definition: "thought that does not critique or think through its own provenance and its relation to reality".

[5] For a brief outline of the history of the African intellectual development and some of its important figures, see Eze (2015, p. 408). For a brief outline of the history of the African intellectual development and some of its important figures, see Eze (2015, p. 408); Ramose (2005, pp. 1–9); and Wiredu (2004, p. 1–28).

[6] Other forms and themes within the decolonisation and broader African discourse include not only the conceptual decolonisation but also religion, politics, literature and gender. For an overview of the different themes see Wiredu (2004).

have a double *modus operandi*. First, to critique the negative aspects of the colonial heritage. Second, to attempt to engage with aspects of the colonial past and the rest of the world that may be beneficial to humankind. A notable thinker in this category is Wiredu (1998, p. 17) who defines decolonisation as follows:

> By decolonisation, I mean divesting African philosophical thinking of all undue influences emanating from our colonial past. The crucial word in this formulation is "undue". Obviously, it would not be rational to try to reject everything of a colonial ancestry. Conceivably, a thought or a mode of inquiry spearheaded by our erstwhile colonisers may be valid or in some way beneficial to humankind. Are we called upon to reject or ignore it? That would be a madness having neither rhyme nor reason.

For Wiredu (1998, p. 17), the "emptying out" lies especially with the conceptual heritage of the colonial past with its binary categories that are promoted by language, for instance, English. But, at the same time, there is also an element of self-critique. Another thinker that takes up this position is Ramón Grosfoguel. Grosfoguel (2011, p. 3) holds that the aim of decolonisation that is not only an essentialist and fundamentalist anti-European critique, but "it is a perspective that is critical of both Eurocentric and Third World fundamentalisms, colonialism and nationalism". It is in this line of thought that aims at a double critique, which the current piece aims to engage with the question in an inter-cultural fashion addressing the problem on an ontological level.

Accordingly, the article is divided into two parts. Part one will attempt to outline what a sense of decolonisation might not be, by firstly formulating the problem concerning colonisation in terms of the critique of the so-called Western world-view, i.e., Western metaphysics, which will also be called *the logic of the coloniser*. More specifically, the discussion will focus on what is meant by the end or closure of (a certain) Western metaphysics[7] by referring to Martin Heidegger's (Heidegger [1956] 2006b) analysis of the onto-theological constitution of this system of thought and the implications and critique thereof relating to the notion of identity. Next, the question concerning the political that is intertwined with this system of thought will be explicated via the writings of Lacoue-Labarthe and Nancy (1997a, 1997b). Subsequently, with the help of Mbembe (2002a, 2002b), these critiques of the political and identity may be translated in terms of the question concerning African subjectivity, or *the colonised*, in this instance. The final remarks in the first part consider the challenge of rethinking what it means to live in South Africa, where decolonisation would not mean a reinforcement of the logic of the coloniser through an African world-view that simply aims to replace that of the West as the ultimate reference point. Part two of this paper will explore what a sense of decolonisation might be. Firstly, a two-sided attitude of reticence and dissidence following the analyses in part one will be suggested. Next, Mbembe's (Mbembe 2010) use of Nancy's (Nancy 2008) notion of *dis-enclosure* as decolonisation will be investigated. Additionally, the discussion of dis-enclosure as decolonisation will be expanded in terms of Nancy's rethinking of the question of being as being-*with* or what Mbembe advocates as the complexity and plurality of reality, which is an alternative ontology and way of creating the world, as the shared world we live in, anew. This section will also consider the implications of the alternative ontology for a notion of identity that is non-substantialist to counter the metaphysical notion of identity as A = A. Finally, the implications of the alternative ontology are considered as the universal task of taking responsibility for the reparation of humanity as a whole in the one world that we share.

For a discussion of the link between decolonisation and feminism in South Africa see Wilkinson (2005): *South African women and the ties that bind*.

[7] With the notion of 'a certain Western metaphysics', the author aims to acknowledge the debate concerning the onto-theological constitution of metaphysics within contemporary continental philosophy of religion and that one should be hesitant to simply place the whole tradition in one group. See, for instance, the work of Marion (2001) and Smith (2014) on the Radical Orthodoxy movement. Both claim that onto-theology is a modern phenomenon only, see also Schrijvers (2011, p. 188) for an outline of the different positions.

2. What a Sense of Decolonisation Might Not Be: The Reinforcement of the Enclosure

Adorno (2005, p. 365) once stated that the task of thinking should aim not to repeat what happened in Auschwitz. In order to do so, one has to understand the thought system that constituted it. It is in this spirit that I suggest turning to Heidegger to attempt to outline the problem concerning colonisation in terms of identity and the political by rehearsing his analysis of the question concerning the constitution of (a certain) Western metaphysics, as outlined by Gerber and Van der Merwe (2017). For Heidegger (Heidegger [1956] 2006b, p. 64), this system of thought asks two questions, namely: What are beings? and How do they fit into a greater whole? This system has however not asked the question of Being—what it means to exist (Heidegger [1956] 2006b, p. 3). Meaning as the *Being* of beings has instead been conceptualised as a double ground: a grounding, or German: *ergründenden*, ground of the general unity of things that accounts for the *onto-* of the phrase onto-theology. Simultaneously, a grounding, or German: *begründenden*, ground that signifies the highest principle or first ground that unifies the whole and accounts for the *theo-* of onto-theology. Hence, it is this logic or onto-theo-logic, which accounts for the figuration of the *Being* of beings. Moreover, the space of the figure named and held by the *Being* of beings in this schema have in the history of Western thought subsequently been held and replaced by figurations like God, History, the Subject, Man, and most recently National Identities and Race. Restated, the figure, also being understood as substance or essence, acts as the double ground that provides meaning to beings and the system they fit into as a whole.[8]

How, then, does the notion of identity—or what may be better named as the metaphysical identity of the subject; or as Lacoue-Labarthe and Nancy (1997a, p. 111) formulate identity as the homogenisation of the social body that operates in the same manner—relate to the logic of onto-theology? Heidegger (Heidegger [1956] 2006b, p. 33) helps to start unpacking this question in *Identity and Difference.* Herein, Heidegger explicates that the metaphysical formulation of identity that reads A = A, reformulated by Fichte in the Enlightenment period as I = I, and in turn, by Schelling as "the indifference of subject and object" (Stambaugh 2001, p. 10), is constituted by the mediating syntheses of object to subject according to, of course, onto-theo-logic. In other words, concurring with the onto-theo-logic of the Subject, the world including objects and others, are synthesised back into the unity of the Subject as highest and grounding reference point. The world is understood according to the categories of the Subject[9]. Once more, the colonised other is synthesised into the categories of the Western Subject. Mbembe (2017, p. 1) re-emphasises this point when he writes in the introduction of *Critique of Black Reason:* "[...] we need first to remember that, throughout its history, European thought has tended to conceive of identity less in terms of mutual belonging (cobelonging) to a common world than in terms of a relation between similar beings—of being itself emerging and manifesting itself in its own state, or its own mirror".

Next, we may ask: How does the metaphysical or onto-theological constitution of identity relate to the question concerning the political (French: *Le politique* in contrast to *La politique*, translated as politics)? Lacoue-Labarthe and Nancy outline the result of the Western metaphysical tradition in what they term the domination of the political and the loss of transcendence as alterity[10], as incarnated in the various totalitarian regimes of the twentieth century, including apartheid. Which, echoing Sartre's formulation of Marxism, is the unsurpassable horizon of our times (Lacoue-Labarthe and Nancy 1997b, p. 126). Totalitarianism, Lacoue-Labarthe and Nancy (1997b, p. 126) argue, may be understood here in two senses. Firstly, following the analysis of Arendt (1966, pp. 437–59) regarding the term, totalitarianism is a state where no political question has any chance to emerge that may correspond to the transformation of the world. Political questions may only arise from within the

---

[8] See also Derrida's (Derrida [1978] 2005) critique of Western metaphysics the plots an *archai* point of reference at the centre of the structure, which relation to colonisation would be the Western identity.

[9] See also Emmanual Levinas' critique of Western Metaphysics, wherein he argues that the other is synthesised into the Same, i.e., the knowing subject par excellence (le Moi connaissant) (Levinas 1996, p. 89).

[10] For a discussion on the relation of transcendence and the political, see Gerber and Van der Merwe (2017).

ideological phraseology that is accepted, for example, from within the ideology of class; the nation; the State; the meaning of history; or in our instance the West.

The second sense is to be understood against Lefort (1988, p. 17) definition of democracy, that denotes "the empty space of power", which was previously occupied by a figuration and results in the so-called "democratic crisis" (Lacoue-Labarthe and Nancy 1997b, p. 127), through, for instance, the disembodiment of power. "In a word: totalitarianism is here each time thought as the attempt at a frenzied re-substantialisation—a re-incorporation or re-incarnation, a re-organisation in the strongest and most differentiated sense—of the 'social body'" (Lacoue-Labarthe and Nancy 1997b, p. 127). Democracy is accordingly understood as keeping empty, or in tension, the space that was previously held by the onto-theological figuration. This will-to-figure, which is a defining characteristic of the Western metaphysical tradition, comprises, on the one hand, the effacement of the figure of God, Man, History, etc., and on the other, the constant urge to replace the empty space with another figure, most recently, that of the National identity, or in terms of colonisation, the Western identity. The figuration of the identity of the "social body", of course, operates in the same fashion as the metaphysical identity of the subject, i.e., all other areas of reference are excluded and the world is synthesized into the figuration of the "social body", with the renewed telos and utopia of a homogenous society. One voice dictates the meaning for society, and thereby we have the completion or closure as the enclosure of the world. Mbembe (2017, p. 35) also outlines how the formation of race[11] is a product of this logic: "Historically, race has always been a more or less coded way of dividing and organizing a multiplicity, of fixing and distributing it according to a hierarchy, of allocating it to more or less impermeable spaces according to a *logic of enclosure*. Such was the case under the regimes of segregation".

More importantly, the overhanging consequence of such an onto-theological figuration of the subject or the social body is a matter of exclusion (Nancy 2000a, p. 24). That is the exclusion of everything that does not fit into the identity of the Subject or Social body, or in a reversal of terms, included as excluded. The exclusion proceeds ultimately in the denial of alterity, of difference, i.e., the existence of the other. Restated in terms of colonisation, according to the onto-theo-logical figuration of the Western identity as the highest and grounding reference point, which constitutes the logic of the coloniser, the colonised other is excluded and their existence regarded as a problem to justify in the same manner as that of the coloniser.

In the same vein of thought, Mbembe (2002b) discusses the critique of Western metaphysics and the effects of the denial of the African subjectivity most famously in *On the Post-Colony*. One might understand the effects of colonisation as described by Mbembe as the experience of the excluded other in a state of totalitarianism—"colonial discourse ends up producing a closed, solitary totality that it elevates to the rank of a generality. So reality becomes enclosed within a pre-ordained madness" (p. 178)—where the existence of the African subject, who is the other of the Western metaphysical subject or social body, is a problem to justify. Or as Mbembe (p. 2) writes:

> We should first remind ourselves that, as a general rule, the experience of the Other, or the *problem of the "I" of others and of human beings we perceive as foreign to us*, has almost always posed virtually insurmountable difficulties to the Western philosophical and political tradition. Whether dealing with Africa or with other non-European worlds, this tradition long denied the existence of any "self" but its own.

Hence, in this specific instance, the African subject, who is the other to the Western metaphysical subject, is thought of in two ways. Firstly, as the negative or opposite of the Western identity forming a binary opposition through the synthesis into the categories of the Western subject. Here, Mbembe

---

[11] For a discussion on the creation of race and Blackness see Mbembe (2017, pp. 10–77) and Eliav-Feldon et al. (2009) *The origins of racism in the west*. Important to note is that Blackness has not always had a fixed meaning. For a discussion on how Blackness has been rethought in a liberating sense within the African philosophical tradition see Mbembe (2017, pp. 151–78).

evokes the thematic of the animal, which stands in opposition to the rational human, exemplified in, for example, the text of Hegel, dealing with Africa in his *Reason in History* (Mbembe 2002b, p. 173).

Secondly, if the Western metaphysical identity of the subject constitutes the existence of a human being, or in Heidegger's words, *Dasein*, then what is excluded and denied is correspondingly seen as less than a non-being, an empty figure (Mbembe 2002b, p. 173). Restated, the other, or African subject, is nothing:

> In the colonial principle of rationality, however, there is a clear difference between being and existing. Only the human exists, since the human alone can represent the self as existent, and have a consciousness of what is so represented. From the standpoint of colonialism, the colonised does not truly exist, as person or as subject (Mbembe 2002b, p. 187).

This denial according to Mbembe (2002b, p. 182), defines the violence *par excellence* of colonisation.[12] Moreover, it is the role that language plays in constituting reality through constant repetition that allows the coloniser to deny the existence of the colonised and the colonised's subjectivity (Mbembe 2002b, p. 181). These identities are also linked to the creation the of race, that is the creation of being black and being white. Ultimately, the creation and categorising of peoples were fuelled by capitalism[13] to serve the purpose of producing a relation of subjugation. The African subject, or "Black man", was resultantly only exploited for his/her labour, and was not allowed to take part in creating the world amongst other humans.

To recapitulate, the problem of the logic of the coloniser in terms of identity and the political becomes apparent when unpacking the critique of Western metaphysics as a system of thought that is constituted by onto-theo-logy that produces figurations, such as the Subject or Social body, which serve as ultimate reference point. The consequence of these figurations is the exclusion and ultimate denial of the existence of the other as human, who becomes categorised as nothing or less than human. The problem is situated on an ontological level, producing a negative epistemology concerning the other or African colonised subject. *Injustice* as the denial of the existence of the other as fully human.

To briefly then sketch what a sense of decolonisation would not be: If at the heart of the problem of colonisation lies the logic of the coloniser that constitutes the Western worldview and forms the enclosure as the closed totality for the colonised, thereby not permitting or acknowledging the existence of anything that may contradict this totality, then decolonisation would not aim to reinforce the logic of the coloniser. In other words, a sense of decolonisation would not be a re-figuration of a highest and grounding reference point, even that of an African worldview or identity, which would, in turn, deny the existence of anything that contradicts the totality structured around this viewpoint or identity as the centre in a totalitarian fashion. Put more plainly, decolonisation thought along these lines, would not be more just than that which it aims to replace. Paradoxically, it would rather reinforce the logic of the coloniser. Injustice will be followed by more injustice.

Restated: In endeavouring the task of decolonisation, one might aim to avoid simply falling back into the temptation of a new onto-theological figuration. For even if the African identity may take the place of its Western counterpart as the highest and grounding reference point for making sense of the world, it has still not, Mbembe argues, addressed the question of what it means to be an African, i.e., the lived everyday experience of what it means to live in Africa. It is falling back into the same onto-theo-logic that constituted the original binary oppositions of difference, which Mbembe (2002a) calls the falling back into the *metaphysics of difference*, which has not been overcome thus far in the struggle concerning the question of African identity, but rather reinforced. Moreover, according to Mbembe, the violence sprouting from this logic of subjugation, i.e., the logic of the coloniser, is

---

[12] See also Césaire (2000) and Fanon (1967).
[13] See Mbembe (2017, pp. 10–37, 179) for a discussion of the birth of the racial subject as constituted by capitalism.

thereby re-appropriated by post-colonial regimes after Independence. In Syrotinski's (Syrotinski 2012, p. 415) words:

> The relations of subjection are perpetuated by a process of the indigenization of the State that colonialism had set in motion. This can be seen, for example, in the ways in which elements of ancestral tradition are appropriated and "reinvented" by African potentates in order to consolidate their power. Governance and the exercise of violent power are thus indissociable, and a logical extension of the violent origins from which they have emerged.

In post-colonial Africa, there are plenty examples of this phenomena. The attempts of Africanism, Afrocentrism, and most prevalently, Pan-Africanism seem to fall prey to the temptation of onto-theological figuration. Or, as Nganang (2007, p. 45), writing on the Rwandan genocide states, this kind of essentialist or "identitarian thinking" informed the rationale for motivating mass killing. This is nothing other than the injustice of the denial of the existence of the other. Specifically in the South African context, one might consider that apartheid, itself being the result of a project of decolonisation and self-determination, took over the logic of the coloniser with the difference that the world was not structured around the imposed universal identity as with British colonialism. But, rather on the particular differences with the White Afrikaner Christian identity forming the highest reference point and double ground. The problem with this variety of discourses from Afrocentrism to Afrikaner Nationalism is not the desire for self-determination itself, but rather, as I attempted to outline above, how the conception of a particular identity in this process is constituted in relation to the totality or the universal and the ethical and political consequences of such a move.

3. What a Sense of Decolonisation Might Be: The Dis-Enclosure of the World

We now turn to the second part of the article, as an attempt to outline what is to be done at the closure of this Western metaphysical tradition, or what a sense of decolonisation might be. If the analysis of the problem holds, that is we are faced with the challenge of rethinking the ontological status of the self in relation to the other, and more specifically here, the colonised other, then I would like to suggest the following remarks on what a sense of decolonisation might be.

(1) Decolonisation would entail the act or attempt to avoid an onto-theo-logical re-figuration or re-substantialisation, thereby keeping open "the empty space of power". This attempt at eluding totalitarian thinking may be translated into a two-sided attitude. On the one side, the attitude of reticence (Nancy 1991, p. 83), of reserve and generosity not to choose to fill the "empty space of power" with a new figuration. For instance, with a new myth of a lost African identity, which is detached from lived experience. On the other side, the attitude of dissidence (Syrotinski 2014), which is to fight and resist the prevailing enclosure of the world, which takes the form of a nostalgic remanence of the lost mythologies of Afrikaner identity with its distinction between "God's chosen people" versus the "*goddeloses*" (godless), or the British colonial distinction between the civilised and barbarians. The two-sided attitude echoes the modus operandi of the double critique regarding thinkers like Wiredu and Grosfoguel discussed above.

(2) In turn, this two-sided attitude opens a space where the category of being "nothing" or less than human that denoted the colonised, may be rethought, and one's place as a being in the world can be reclaimed through an alternative ontology. In one of Mbembe's more recent writings namely, *Sortir de la grande nuit: Essai sur l'Afrique décolonisée (Emerging from the Dark Night: Essay on Decolonized Africa)*, he takes up the question by exploiting Nancy's lexical innovations, most notably the notion that is translated as *dis-enclosure*[14] (of the world), from the French *la déclosion*, which Nancy (2008) articulates in the book entitled *The Deconstruction of Christianity* (Syrotinski 2012, p. 410). The notion of *dis-enclosure*

---

[14] The German translation of the term *dis-enclosure* taken over by Mbembe (2016, p. 85) is *Welterschließung*, which includes the reference to world, hence making it the *dis-closure of the world*.

for Nancy indicates "the act of opening up something that is not only closed but also enclosed, such as an enclosure" (Syrotinski 2012, p. 416). What is enclosed, at the closure of the political, is of course, the other, or in this case, the colonised. Enclosed in the enclosure of Western metaphysics. The action of dis-enclosure is, and I again quote Syrotinski (p. 416): "thus a profoundly transformative action, that is at the same time a coming into being, or *eclosión* (literally: hatching)". Or, as Mbembe (2010) puts it: "The idea of *déclosion* includes that of *eclosión*, of an eruption, or advent of something new, of an opening out" (p. 68). Here, "the term *déclosion* is thus adopted by Mbembe as a paronomastic link-word joining together *eclosión, déclosion* and *décolonisation*"[15] (Syrotinski 2012, p. 416). Thus, the hatching of something new, that is the dis-enclosure of Western metaphysics, is the second remark concerning what a sense of decolonisation might be taken in contrast to a sense of decolonisation as only destructive.

(3) What may be thought as the dis-enclosure? As analysed in part one, what is to be thought is an alternative ontological status of and relation to the other as colonised that breaks with the onto-theological tradition. Keeping in mind the two-sided attitude mentioned above, one may turn to Nancy's reformulation of Heidegger's *Dasein* analyses, as renewing the analyses where *Dasein*, that is to be in the world, is to be thought as *Mitsein*, or being in the world *with* others. For Nancy (2000a), "Philosophy is, in sum, the thinking of being-with; because of this, it is also thinking-with as such" (p. 31). Consequently, the existence of the other in relation to the metaphysical subject or even *Dasein* does not need justification and escapes the synthesis into the categories of the knowing Western subject, because it is given before the constitution of the subject. In other words, the Subject as the onto-theological figuration of modernity is decentred, and it is no longer considered as the highest and grounding reference point. However, Nancy does not uncritically follow Heidegger's analysis in 1927 of *Dasein* in *Sein und Zeit (Being and Time)*. Although Heidegger aimed to break with the Western metaphysical tradition by asking what it means to exist in the world, which means always already existing with others, Heidegger's *Dasein* is critiqued as constituting a solipsistic subject whose relation to others is still problematic. Accordingly, for Nancy, the analysis of *Mitsein* (being-with) in *Sein und Zeit* remains nothing more than a sketch, and although *Mitsein* is coessential with *Dasein*, it remains in a subordinate position (p. 93). *Mitsein* is subordinate due to the focus that falls on *Dasein's* choice of being authentic or inauthentic, resulting in the dissimulation of *Mitsein* under the notion of *Das Man*. Hence, "as such, the whole existential analytic still harbours some principle by which what it opens up is immediately closed off" (Nancy 2000a, p. 93). Nancy calls for a re-opening of the analysis of *Mitsein*, which would neither lead to a completion thereof nor setting up *Mitsein* as a principle. For, in principle, being-with escapes completion and the taking up of the place of a principle.

What is necessary, then, according to Nancy "is that we retrace the outline of its analysis and push it to the point where it becomes apparent that the coessentiality of being-with is nothing less than a matter of the co-originarity of meaning—and that the 'meaning of Being' is only what it is (either 'meaning' or, primarily, its own 'precomprehension' as the constitution of existence) when it is given as with" (Nancy 2000a, p. 93). Hence, differing from Levinas[16], Nancy does not place the emphasis on a reversal of the position of the preoccupation from the Subject to the Other. Or, for that matter, the replacement of the Western with the African. Rather, the decentering of the subject lies in the move to co-originality of the subject and the other, in being-*with*. The essence of *Being*, re-appropriating Heidegger (Heidegger [1927] 2006a, p. 42), is not a substance but rather "to exist" (*Zu-sein*), which for Nancy is being-with, existing with others as *being singular plural*.

To re-emphasise the point: With this re-appropriation of Heidegger into his own terminology, Nancy aims to avoid onto-theology, "because none of these three terms precedes or grounds the other, each designates the co-essence of the others" (Nancy 2000a, p. 37). Correspondingly, every other is seen as an origin, from where the world is co-created; the world occurs at each moment of the world,

---

[15] Apart from identifying the task of thinking the dis-enclosure of the world within in Nancy's thought, Mbembe (2016, p. 86) also outlines how the thought Franz Fanon is an attempt dis-enclosure of the world as self-determination.
[16] See Gerber and Van der Merwe (2017).

as each time of Being in the realm of being-with of each time with every other time (Nancy 2000a, p. 20). Consequently, there is no set example, origin, or identity, according to which to model others. What it means to exist is not given or enforced on someone by another in reference to an abstract principle or identity. Rather, each time of Being constitutes a singularly unique origin of the world, making up the plurality of origins.

Furthermore, the *with* of being-*with*, which lies between the I (subject) and the other, belongs to neither. No one possesses the monopoly on the question of existence with others. The *with*, instead, exposes one to an-other. The *with* or *cum* in Latin is nothing as in no-thing (Nancy 2000a, p. 36), not a substance; identity; history; value; and, so on, that may be made into a figuration. Nor is it a category of the subject. It is rather the exposure to our ontological mode of existence as *Mitsein*, of one to an-other.[17] This program of re-opening ontology to its complexity is also to be traced in the agenda Mbembe (2002b), which is formulated on thinking in the post-colony:

> What a certain rationality, claiming to be universal but in reality mired in the contingent and the particular, has never understood is that all human societies participate in a complex order, rich in unexpected turns, meanders, and changes of course, without this, implying their necessary abolition in an absence of centre (p. 8).

It is this complexity of what it means to exist that Mbembe (p. 17) seeks to address in what he, in turn, names the *emerging subject*, and I quote him in full:

> [...] the *subject* emerging, acting effectively, withdrawing, or being removed in the act and context of *displacement* refers to two things: first, to the forms of "living in the concrete world," then to the subjective forms that make possible any validation of its contents—that objectify it. In Africa today, the subject who *accomplishes the age* and validates it, who lives and espouses his/her contemporaneousness—that is, what is "distinctive" or "particular" to his/her present real world—is first a subject who has an *experience* of "living in the concrete world." She/he is a subject of experience and a validating subject, not only in the sense that she/he is a conscious existence or has a perceptive conscious-ness of things, but to the extent that his/her "living in the concrete world" involves, and is evaluated by, his/her eyes, ears, mouth—in short, his/her flesh, his/her body.[18]

The *emerging subject* is a subject that understands who he/she is in relation to the world, in participation in the creation of the meaning of that world, not isolated, nor by subjugation. But, in relation to the other.

(4) The notion of identity after the decentring of the metaphysical subject as the reference point—understood according to the alternative ontology of Nancy, or the emerging subject of Mbembe—would no longer be a search for an essence, an identity that is reduced to a fixed set of attributes a person should possess. Rather, identity is to be thought according to the plurality of singular beings, that is the complex reality of the context that we live in. Identity, hence, may be thought of in terms of what Nancy (2000b) refers to as a *mêlée*[19] (French), also melee in English,

---

[17] One may also compare this ontological move to the exposure of being-with, to Magobe Ramose's (Ramose 2003) discussion of Ubuntu, which "disposes every person to encounter every other person as human" (Eze 2015, p. 416).

[18] In this citation, Mbembe introduces the question of embodiment that regretfully cannot be addressed here. For an overview of the question of embodiment and its various interpretations in the contemporary phenomenological tradition see (Fotiade et al. (2014); Kearney (2015); Manoussakis (2015); Pretorius (2016)).

[19] To understand the difficulties of translating the word from French to English and comprehending its full meaning, I refer here to the translators of Nancy's text, namely Robert D. Richardson's and Anne E. O'Byrne's footnote on the translation of *mêlée*: "The French word *mêlée* has entered the English language in an impoverished form. Throughout this piece, it should not be read as meaning only a confused fight, a fray, scrap, skirmish, or scuffle, that is, as a word in English. Rather, it remains an untranslated French word meaning a fight, but also a mingling of a more sexual nature. In addition, as its connection to the verbs *mêler* and se *mêler* ('to mix') make clear, the ideas of mixture, mixing, motley, and variegation are also implied" (Nancy 2000b, p. 205).

which is an action rather than in substantive terms from where attributes may be named and collected. Moreover, the *mêlée* has a double meaning or form, namely "that of combat and that of love"—"the melee of Ares to that of Aphrodite" (Secomb 2006, p. 456), which emphasises that *both need each other*. Thus, the idea of a "pure" identity is challenged (p. 149). There is no such thing as a "pure" Western, nor "pure" African identity, which somehow exists apart from other identities in a vacuum, or outside the world from where it then mixes with the other. Rather, as Nancy argues, identities need each other: "Identity is by definition not an absolute distinction, removed from everything and, therefore, distinct from nothing: it is always the other of an-other identity" (Nancy 2000b, p. 149). Furthermore, this move from substance to action implies that there is no absolute origin from where a pure identity could sprout (Nancy 2000b, p. 151). Instead, each identity is always already a multi-identity, each culture a multi-culture, that is in a continuous *mêlée* not only within the space its own identity demarcates, but also with other identities or cultures that form each other, and need each other, to be an-other. Or, again in Nancy's words:

> Cultures, or what are known as cultures, do not mix. They encounter each another, mingle, modify each other, reconfigure each other. They cultivate one another; they irrigate or drain each other; they work over and plough through each other, or graft one onto the other. (Nancy 2000b, p. 151).

Therefore, when we would speak, for instance, about the South African culture, following Nancy (Nancy 2000b, p. 153), we would speak about the different voices that make up style or tone of the culture and "the various different voices and aptitudes (*portées*) for interpreting this tone" (Nancy 2000b, pp. 152–53). But, this style or tone is nowhere present in a person, or subject. One would rather say that it is between persons. Moreover, breaking with the Western-metaphysical notion of identity, i.e., A = A, identity is never simply identical with itself in terms of time duration. Again, this line of reasoning resonates in Mbembe's thought on African identity:

> There is no African identity that could be designated by a single term, or that could be named by a single word; or that could be subsumed under a single category. [. . .] Neither the forms of this identity nor its idioms are always self-identical. And these forms and idioms are mobile, reversible, and unstable. Given this, they cannot be reduced to a purely biological order based on blood, race, or geography. Nor can they be reduced to custom, to the extent that the latter is constantly being reinvented. (Mbembe 2002a, p. 33).

4. Towards a Universal Task of Responsibility and Reparation

To summarise, what a sense of decolonisation as the quest for self-determination might not be, is simply reinforcing the same logic of the coloniser, i.e., taking an essentialised identity (A = A) and making it the ultimate reference point that transcends our lived experience and ontological condition of existing with others. According to this logic, the identity of the self that is taken as the highest reference point dictates the meaning for the other. The construction of race and the Black man as less than human in relation to slavery, the colony, and apartheid (Mbembe 2017, p. 78) is an example of this logic. A variety of decolonising projects from Afrikaner Nationalism to Pan-Africanism also fall into the trap of reinforcing the logic of the coloniser.

To ask then what comes after the logic of the coloniser and its construction of racial identities is to attempt to open a space where responsibility for both the past and the future can be taken and wherein reparation can be enabled. For if the logic is continuous, one construction replaced by another, it simply leads to the perpetuation of oppression through the misrecognition of our given ontological condition of being-with others, and the other as fully human. But, the space that may be opened by the (1) double attitude of reticence and dissidence allows for one to (2) rethink anew therein what it means to (3) co-exist in our shared world, and conceive of (4) identity beyond race. The space can only be kept open if the responsibility for reparation is taken up by all in the *mêlée*. Hence, if we need each other to be an-other, then the task of reparation is not only that of a particular context that is doomed to self-determination in a vacuum, but rather a universal one.

Or, to turn around the order of discussion, by rethinking our sense of identity in terms of an ontology of a shared world would entail taking responsibility for both the past, and also making sure that this kind of logic regarding race and the ontological status of the other does not continue in new forms in the future. It is then that the question of reparation can start to take place, of restoring the dignity of the other who co-exists in our shared world. To take responsibility for the past then is to take part in the reparation of the other in relation to the self in the future by thinking what it means to share the world, of being-in-the-world *with* others. According to the ontological given of being-with, this may also entail the reparation of the self, itself an-other. Stated differently, we all share the desire to be a full human being. In order for this desire to be met in our shared world, "we must restore the humanity stolen from those who have historically been subjected to processes of abstraction and objectification" (Mbembe 2017, p. 187).

In conclusion: With no abstract, transcendental, or otherworldly starting point, like a substantialised Western or African subject, identity or worldview, which implies standing outside of the world in an onto-theological fashion, our thought rather extends from the concrete world itself, i.e., from being-in-the-world. In other words, it starts from the *mêlée* as a struggle between all of the various voices that make up the style and tone of the world that we find ourselves in. It is the struggle for self-determination itself that is important, and therefore the space for this struggle should be kept open and not be filled. There is not one voice that may impersonate and fill-up the space that is named South Africa, but rather there exists the plurality of singular voices that make up the South African melody. Restated, self-determination would thus take place within the *mêlée*, in the struggle for meaning, that allows for a new emerging subject, rather than being imposed from the outside by the other misrecognising your being-with in the world. Again, as Mbembe (2017, p. 183) reminds us, the desire for self-determination that is the "proclamation of difference is not necessarily the opposite of the project of the *in-common*". Rather, the particular is to be thought in relation to the universal project, that is the project of what Mbembe (2017, p. 162) finds in Fanon, called *the rise of humanity*. Justice would then be co-creating the meaning of the world we live in. Once more, in the words of Mbembe (2017, p. 177):

> Until we have eliminated racism [the logic of the coloniser] from our current lives and imaginations, we will have to continue to struggle for the creation of a world-beyond-race. But to achieve it, to sit down at a table to which everyone has been invited, we must undertake an exacting political and ethical critique of racism and of the ideologies of difference. The celebration of difference will be meaningful only if it opens onto the fundamental question of our time, that of sharing, of the common, of the expansion of our horizon.

We are thus called to think our being-with in the world, or again: to take up the universal responsibility for reparation in the active struggle, with the attitude of reticence and dissidence, for the creation of a world dis-enclosed and decolonised.

Conflicts of Interest: The authors declare no conflict of interest.

References

Abraham, Willie E. 1966. *The mind of Africa*. Chicago: The University of Chicago Press.

Adorno, Theodor W. 2005. *Negative Dialectics*. London and New York: Continuum International Publishing Group.

Anyanwu, K. Chukwulozie. 1983. *The African Experience in the American Market Place*. New York: Exposition Press.

Appiah, Kwame A. 1992. *In My Father's House*. New York: Oxford University Press.

Arendt, Hannah. 1966. *The Origins of Totalitarianism*. New York: Harcourt Brace.

Bodunrin, Peter O. 1985. Introduction. In *Philosophy in Africa: Trends and Perspectives*. Edited by Peter O. Bodunrin. Ile-Ife: University of Ife Press, pp. 1–14.

Césaire, Aimé. 2000. *Discourse on colonialism*. New York: NYU Press.

Derrida, Jacques. 2005. *Writing and Difference*. London: Routledge & Kegan Paul Ltd. First published 1978.

Eliav-Feldon, Miriam, Benjamin H. Isaac, and Joseph Ziegler, eds. 2009. *The Origins of Racism in the West*. Cambridge: Cambridge University Press.

Lefort, Claude. 1988. The Question of Democracy. In *Democracy and Political Theory*. Oxford: Polity Press, pp. 9–20.

Levinas, Emmanuel. 1996. Transcendence and Height. In *Basic Philosophical Writings*. Edited by Adriaan T. Peperzak, Simon Critchley and Robert Bernasconi. Bloomington: Indiana University Press, pp. 11–32.

Eze, Chielozona. 2015. Decolonisation and its Discontents: Thoughts on the Postcolonial African Moral Self. *South African Journal of Philosophy* 34: 408–18. [CrossRef]

Fanon, Frantz. 1967. *Black Skin, white Masks*. New York: Grove.

Fayemi, Ademola K. 2011. A Critique of Cultural Universals and Particulars in Kwasi Wiredu's Philosophy. *Trames: A Journal of the Humanities & Social Sciences* 15: 259–76.

Fotiade, Ramona, David Jasper, and Oliver Salazar-Ferrer, eds. 2014. *Embodiment: Phenomenological, Religious and Deconstructive Views on Living and Dying*. Farnham: Ashgate Publishing Limited.

Gerber, Schalk, and Willie L. Van der Merwe. 2017. On the Paradox of the Political/Transcendence and Eschatology: Transimmanence and the Promise of Love in Jean-Luc Nancy. *Religions* 8: 28. [CrossRef]

Grosfoguel, Ramón. 2011. Decolonizing Post-Colonial Studies and Paradigms of Political-Economy: Transmodernity, Decolonial Thinking, and Global Coloniality. *Transmodernity* 1: 1–37.

Heidegger, Martin. 2006b. *Identität und Differenz (1955–1957)*. Frankfurt: Vittorio Klostermann. First published 1956.

Heidegger, Martin. 2006a. *Sein und Zeit*, 19th ed. Hameln: Niemeyer. First published 1927.

Hountondji, Paulin J. 1983. *African Philosophy: Myth and Reality*, 2nd ed. Indianapolis: Indiana University Press.

Hutchens, Benjamin C. 2005. *Jean-Luc Nancy and the Future of Philosophy*. Montreal: McGill-Queen's University Press.

Kearney, Richard. 2015. The wager of carnal hermeneutics. In *Carnal Hermeneutics*. New York: Fordham University Press, pp. 15–56.

Lacoue-Labarthe, Philippe, and Jean-Luc Nancy. 1997a. Opening Address to the Centre for Philosophical Research on the Political. In *Retreating the Political*. Edited by Simon Sparks. London: Routledge, pp. 107–21.

Lacoue-Labarthe, Philippe, and Jean-Luc Nancy. 1997b. Retreating the Political. In *Retreating the Political*. Edited by Sparks Simon. London: Routledge, pp. 122–34.

Manoussakis, John P. 2015. On the flesh of the word. In *Carnal Hermeneutics*. New York: Fordham University Press, pp. 306–15.

Marion, Jean-Luc. 2001. *The Idol and Distance: Five Studies*. New York: Fordham University Press.

Mbembe, Achille. 2002a. African Modes of Self-Writing. *Public Culture* 14: 239–73. [CrossRef]

Mbembe, Achille. 2002b. *On the Postcolony*. Berkeley: University of California Press.

Mbembe, Achille. 2010. *Sortir de la grande nuit: Essai sur l'Afrique décolonisée*. Paris: La Découverte.

Mbembe, Achille. 2016. *Ausgang aus der langen Nacht: Versuch über ein entkolonisiertes Afrika*. Berlin: Suhrkamp Verlag.

Mbembe, Achille. 2017. *Critique of Black Reason*. Johannesburg: Wits University Press.

Mbiti, John S. 1969. *African Religions and Philosophy*. London: Heinemann.

Mudimbe, Vumbi Y. 1988. *The Invention of Africa*. Indiana: Indiana University Press.

Nancy, Jean-Luc. 1991. Shattered Love. In *The Inoperative Community*. Edited by Peter Connor. Minneapolis: University of Minnesota Press, pp. 82–109.

Nancy, Jean-Luc. 2000a. Being Singular Plural. In *Being Singular Plural*. Stanford: Stanford University Press, pp. 1–100.

Nancy, Jean-Luc. 2000b. Eulogy for the Mêlée. In *Being Singular Plural*. Stanford: Stanford University Press, pp. 145–58.

Nancy, Jean-Luc. 2008. Dis-Enclosure. In *Dis-Enclosure: The Deconstruction of Christianity*. New York: Fordham University Press, pp. 158–62.

Nganang, Patrice. 2007. *Manifeste d'une Nouvelle Littérature Africaine: Pour une Écriture Pré-emptive*. Paris: Homnisphères.

Pretorius, Helgard. 2016. Reading 'blackface': A (narrative) introduction to Richard Kearney's notion of carnal hermeneutics. *HTS Theological Studies* 72: 1–9. [CrossRef]

Ramose, Magobe B. 2003. The Ethics of Ubuntu. In *The African Philosophy Reader*. Edited by Pieter H. Coetzee and Abraham P. J. Roux. London: Routledge, pp. 379–86.

Ramose, Magobe B. 2005. Introduction: The struggle for reason in Africa. In *The African Philosophy Reader*. Edited by Pieter H. Coetzee and Abraham P. J. Roux. London: Routledge, pp. 1–9.

Schrijvers, Joeri. 2011. *Ontotheological Turnings? The Decentering of Modern Subjectivity in Recent French Phenomenology.* Albany: SUNY.

Secomb, Linnell. 2006. Amorous politics: Between Derrida and Nancy. *Social Semiotics* 16: 449–60. [CrossRef]

Senghor, Leopold. 1991. Prayer to the masks. In *The Collected Poetry*. Charlottesville: University Press of Virginia.

Smith, James K. A. 2014. *Introducing Radical Orthodoxy: Mapping a Post-Secular Theology*. Grand Rapids: Baker Academic.

Sodipo, John O. 1973. Notes on the concept of cause and chance in Yoruba traditional thought. *Second Order: An African Journal of Philosophy* 11: 12–20.

Stambaugh, Joan, ed. 2001. Introduction. In *Identity and Difference*. Chicago: University of Chicago Press.

Syrotinski, Michael. 2012. Genealogical Misfortunes': Achille Mbemibe's (Re-)Writing of Postcolonial Africa. *Paragraph* 35: 407–20. [CrossRef]

Syrotinski, Michael. 2014. Between 'God's Phallus' and 'The Body of Christ': The Embodied World of Contemporary African Literature in Achille Mbembe and Jean-Luc Nancy. In *Embodiment: Phenomenological, Religious and Deconstructive Views on Living and Dying*. Edited by Ramona Fotiade, David Jasper and Oliver Salazar-Ferrer. Farnham: Ashgate Publishing Limited.

Tempels, Placide. 1959. *Bantu philosophy*. Paris: Presence Africaine.

Towa, Marcien. 1991. Conditions for the affirmation of a modern philosophical thought. In *African Philosophy: The Essential Readings*. Edited by Tsenay Serequeberhan. New York: Paragon House.

Wilkinson, Jennifer R. 2005. Introduction: South African women and the ties that bind. In *The African Philosophy Reader*. Edited by Pieter H. Coetzee and Abraham P. J. Roux. London: Routledge, pp. 402–22.

Wiredu, Kwasi A. 1980. *Philosophy and an African Culture*. Cambridge: Cambridge University Press.

Wiredu, Kwasi A. 1998. Toward Decolonizing African Philosophy and Religion. *African Studies Quarterly* 1: 17–46.

Wiredu, Kwasi A., ed. 2004. Introduction: African Philosophy in Our Time. In *Companion to African Philosophy*. Oxford: Blackwell Publishing Ltd., pp. 1–27.

![religions logo] *religions*

MDPI

Article
The Freedom of Facticity

Abraham Olivier

Department of Philosophy, University of Fort Hare, Alice 5201, South Africa; aolivier@ufh.ac.za or
abrahamolivier@gmail.com

Received: 8 February 2018; Accepted: 30 March 2018; Published: 4 April 2018

Abstract: "Here I am—Jew, or Aryan, handsome or ugly, one-armed, etc. I am all of this for the Other
with no hope of changing it." Thus wrote Sartre in his *Being and Nothingness*. But was not Sartre
the major advocate of existential freedom, with the tenet that "we are condemned to be free"—no
matter what our situation might be? The question hence arises: How free are we from the facticity
of situations, particularly ones in which we are subject to collective identification? How free are we
to change the situations—places, environments, histories, others—that we inevitably belong to and
which subject us to collective identities? How free are we from identification in terms of others? How
free are we to transform such identification? These questions are of particular relevance given the
harmful effects of collective ascriptions and the currently pressing demand to transform them. In
an attempt to address these questions, I offer as alternative to Sartre's concept of the "facticity of
freedom" what I would like to call the "freedom of facticity".

Keywords: Sartre; facticity; freedom; collective identification; liberation

1. Introduction

"The most decisive argument which is employed by common sense against freedom consists in
reminding us of our powerlessness. Far from being able to modify our situation at our whim, we seem
to be unable to change ourselves. I am not 'free' either to escape the lot of my class, of my nation, of my
family, or even to build up my own power or my fortune or to conquer my most insignificant appetites
or habits. I am born a worker, a Frenchman, a hereditary syphilitic or a tubercular" (BN p. 503).[1]

Thus spoke Sartre in his *Being and Nothingness*. On an even gloomier note, he adds:

"Here I am—Jew, or Aryan, handsome or ugly, one-armed, etc. I am all of this for the Other
with no hope of changing it." (BN p. 544)

But was not Sartre the major advocate of existential freedom, with the tenet that "we are
condemned to be free"—no matter what our situation might be?

The question hence arises: How free are we from situations, particularly ones in which we
are subject to collective identification? More exactly, how free are we from the situations—places,
environments, histories, others—that we inevitably belong to, and which subject us to collective
identities? How free are we from identification in terms of others? How free are we to transform
such identification?

This question is of particular relevance given the harmful effects of collective ascriptions and the
currently pressing demand to transform them. In his response to Sartre, among others, Appiah offers a
striking contemporary analysis of the effect and nature of collective identification in terms of what he
calls "labelling" (Appiah 2003).[2] Labelling includes what Du Bois[3] called "badges of colour" such as

---

[1] Henceforth Sartre's *Being and Nothingness* (Sartre 2003) is referred to as BN.
[2] See also Appiah's more recent 2016 BBC Reith Lectures, entitled *Mistaken Identities*.
[3] Du Bois (1975, pp. 116–17) as referred to by Appiah.

"African", "Negro," "coloured race", "black", "Afro-American", or "Jewish-", "Italian-", "Japanese-", "Korean-American", "gay", "lesbian", "straight". Labels or badges, so Appiah points out, collectively shape the way people conceive of themselves and their projects (Appiah 2003, pp. 436–37). Quoting Hacking (1992), Appiah shows how " ... numerous kinds of human beings and human acts come into being hand in hand with our invention of the categories labelling them".[4] Labelling has the harmful effect of imposing a set of committed criteria, which perpetuate a prejudiced ascription of collective identity, and involuntarily shape people's actions, plans, projects and lives altogether (Appiah 2003, pp. 438–39). Indeed, as Sartre put it, such collective identification has the effect of defining me in my "being-for-others"—I am put in a situation in which I become the Other-as-object; I become something I have not chosen to be (BN p. 545).[5]

Sartre offers one of the most radical and challenging but also most sophisticated classical philosophical notions of freedom and its primacy over and above the facticity of situations.[6] This pertains particularly to situations of collective identification. Sartre's view of freedom has elicited a host of responses inside and outside philosophical literature, particularly within the framework of postcolonial discussions on ethics and politics, including contemporary scholars such as Taylor (1994), Appiah (2003), Alcoff (2006), Bernasconi (2007) and Gordon (1997, 2015), among others. Less attention has been paid to Sartre's phenomenological approach to freedom, and, actually, his key respondent still remains his own contemporary, Maurice Merleau-Ponty.[7] My focus is on the phenomenological analysis of Sartre's view of freedom. Although I analyse Sartre's position in considerable detail and pay attention to, among others, Merleau-Ponty's response to Sartre, this paper is not primarily an attempt to revisit Sartre's work and add footnotes to the existing scholarly literature—as important as such an endeavour might be. Rather I aim to address the question concerning the relation of freedom to facticity by using Sartre's position in order to introduce an alternative to his concept of freedom.[8] I argue that it is not as much despite, but rather *because* of the facticity of situations that there is what Sartre calls the freedom of choice. This alternative, so I contend, puts the discussion of freedom on another plane—at least within the framework of phenomenology.

The first part examines Sartre's view of "the facticity of freedom", while the second part introduces as alternative what I'd like to call "the freedom of facticity".

2. Part 1: The Facticity of Freedom

2.1. The Freedom of Choice

Common sense holds that the most decisive argument against freedom is our powerlessness against the adversities of circumstance. As Sartre puts it:

> "Much more than he appears to 'make himself' man seems 'to be made' by climate and the earth, race and class, language, the history of collectivity of which he is a part, heredity, the individual circumstances of his childhood, acquired habits, the great and small events of his life." (BN p. 503)

Sartre rejects both classical responses to the common-sense view—libertarianism and determinism. He rejects both the idea that the will is infinite and therefore free to rule over circumstances and the notion that we are completely determined by circumstantial causes (BN pp. 458, 503). Sartre does not

---

[4] Quote taken from Appiah (2003, p. 438).
[5] Appiah accuses Sartre for not taking the theoretical commitments of collective identification seriously enough—I discuss his critique in Section 2.3.
[6] See Webber (2011, 327ff).
[7] Merleau-Ponty (1962). See the discussion of Webber (2011).
[8] To be sure, I shall give a relatively lengthy discussion of Sartre's position first in order to make my use of and difference from his position clear. This discussion is also meant to help introduce the non-specialist to Sartre, while the specialist might prefer to glance at the first part of my paper and advance to the second part.

deny that freedom has circumstantial adversities; however, he argues that such adversities actually only arise because of the limits and ends that freedom itself posits. A crag, for instance, will manifest a profound resistance if I want to replace it, or else it can be a valuable aid if I want to climb upon it to look over the countryside (BN p. 504). Although brute things can limit our freedom of action from the start, it is only because of freedom that these things manifest as limits or ends (BN 504). This means, a subject is principally free to choose to determine its own limits and ends. Sartre thereby introduces what can be called a concept of autonomous freedom—the freedom of agency, of a subject to choose its own limits and ends of action; in short, the freedom of choice.

A common misreading of Sartre's position, so Webber (2011) points out, is that it comes down to some sort of "staccato voluntarism", meaning we decide capriciously how to respond to the world we encounter or how to make it appear.[9] Sartre rather thinks of choice as an act of deliberation towards limited ends, that is, within the framework of projects (BN p. 505). As Webber notes, Sartre is not entirely clear on what is meant by "project". The term project is both a verb and noun and most basically refers to actions undertaken towards particular ends or possibilities.[10] An example is a book project, the choice of the act of writing with the set possibility to complete a book. In its most general sense, a project encompasses life itself, including all our actions toward realising the possibilities of our choice. This resembles in core Heidegger's notion of a project as the projection of our "ownmost" possibilities, as described in *Being and Time* (Heidegger 1962, 183ff, BN pp. 482ff.). Thus, one can say, it is by choosing our "ownmost" possibilities that we are free; however, our choices are not whimsical but embroil limits between options as framed by projects.

Sartre's contention, that it is by choosing that we are free, does not mean that we choose to be free (p. 506). This distinction is at the heart of Sartre's phenomenology of freedom at the core of his monumental *Being and Nothingness*. Due to limited space, I confine myself to a rough outline of what seems to be the major thrust of his argument in the following.[11]

Sartre argues that freedom is not the product of choice, something we can choose to be or not to be, because it is rather a characteristic of what we are, as choosing conscious beings. What belongs to being conscious is to be free to turn what is given as mere thing, as non-conscious being, or what Sartre calls, "being-in-itself" (*être-en-soi*), into "being-for-itself" (*être-pour soi*)—into what this being means to oneself as subject (BN p. 19). Sartre follows Husserl's phenomenological view of consciousness as being structurally intentional, as being about and directed to things that are not itself. To be a subject means that, prior to any reflection or thetic decision, one is conscious of things, free to turn whatever thing one is conscious of into what this thing is not in-itself, thus into an object of consciousness (BN p. 53). Sartre argues that consciousness is thus directed toward a thing in a way free to "nihilate" it, to make out of it a thing "for" consciousness, which is in effect "nothing". Hence it is "nothing" but contents of consciousness.[12] Consequently, consciousness turns everything into "nothing", nothing but meaning, which is the reason why Sartre equates consciousness with "nothingness" as opposed to "being".

This does not mean that consciousness turns everything into its own interiority, its inside project. As consciousness is intentional, it always transcends itself towards what is outside itself, so consciousness is actually out there in the world, abandoning itself to whatever it is directed to. In fact, as Sartre already argues in *The Transcendence of the Ego*, even the attempt of consciousness (the cogito) to conceive of itself as consciousness consists in turning itself into its own object (the ego) such that it will transcend its interior operations to become an exterior object among objects for itself outside

---

9   Webber refers, among others, to Føllesdal (1981) charge against Sartre.
10 See, for instance, BN pp. 457 and 475. See also the key to special terminology in *Being and Nothingness*.
11 For a very basic but concise introduction to Sartre's theory of consciousness and freedom, see Cerbone (2006) and also Moran (2000).
12 BN pp. 40ff, 46ff, 99ff.

itself in the world.[13] As such, consciousness, as it were, remains in free flow, being constantly drawn beyond itself to whatever exterior objects it is directed. These things are, however, phenomenologically reduced to what they mean to the conscious subject. Hence, Sartre refers to objects in the outside world as the transcendental field of conscious awareness—they are out there but as what they mean to subjects.

Sartre's phenomenology of consciousness reverberates Heidegger's famous claim in *Being and Time*, which is that the human being is such that its being is an issue for itself. More particularly, humans are directed to things primarily as far as these things concern their own being and its possibilities. In a way similar to Heidegger, Sartre's phenomenology can be characterised as existential. This means that the human subject is directed to objects because of the possibilities it takes objects to have within the framework of its own projects (BN p. 502). A subject is free by choosing its own projects, thus by choosing what to make of its world and itself. In his *Existentialism is a Humanism*, Sartre confirms this point emphatically by stating the "first principle of existentialism"—or subjectivity—to be that "Man is nothing else but what he makes of himself" (Sartre 1965, p. 36). Sartre thus advocates what one can call the existential autonomy of freedom—the freedom to choose how to shape one's own being.

As a result, one can argue that, in Sartre's phenomenology, the subject's intentional focus on the object is ultimately played out in terms of existential meaning. "Intentional" thereby assumes a twofold meaning. It refers to the fact that (a) subjects direct themselves to objects (b) because of the envisioned projects of their choice. As far as consciousness consists in the autonomous freedom to nihilate objects by giving them existential meaning, one can also speak of it as existential freedom.

To summarise, I have shown that, in Sartre's view, freedom belongs to the nihilating capacity of consciousness to choose the meaning of things and so determine the way they appear (BN p. 53). To be conscious means to be directed to things other than ourselves with the freedom to act upon them, to nihilate them towards their possible meaning in our experience and for the sake of our own projects. It is in this sense that we qua subjects do not choose to be free, but rather, as conscious beings, we cannot but be free to choose to act upon the objects to which we are intentionally directed. In Sartre's words: "In fact we are a freedom which chooses, but we do not choose to be free." (BN p. 506). The intentional structure of consciousness renders us free to choose whatever meanings we attribute to them, whatever projects we make out of them, and we do not choose to be free in this way.

Sartre emphasises the contention that we do not choose our freedom by his famous claim that "we are condemned to freedom" (BN 506). We are condemned to be free and thus to make choices. The fact that we are bound to be free is actually the primary meaning of what he calls our facticity.

2.2. The Facticity of Freedom

Sartre's contention that we are condemned to be free—thus, to make choices—implies that we are bound to choose between options, and in this way set to meet the limits of our choices. He consequently defines freedom in terms of facticity. The "facticity of freedom" most basically means that one cannot but be free to choose; in short, that one is condemned to be free (BN p. 508). Facticity includes contingency. Contingency means that one cannot but exist, which means one is only free in relation to existents, to circumstances, to the given, to things and others in a particular situation, with regard to which one makes choices.[14] In this extended sense, facticity means that one cannot but be free in relation to things and others in specific situations (BN p. 508).

Facticity thus manifests in terms of what Sartre calls a "situation" (BN p. 509). He illustrates what he understands by a situation by using the example of considering whether a rock will lend itself to scaling. One is free to climb it, but this is contingent upon the limits the choice incurs. One is free to

---

[13] Sartre (1957, pp. 93ff); BN pp. 97ff. See also Cerbone (2006, pp. 84ff).
[14] Sartre maintains that facticity and contingency are really one (BN p. 508). Mostly he speaks of facticity, thereby including contingency. I shall follow his practice and use facticity in its extended sense including contingency.

consider climbing it, or just admiring it; but one is bound to choose to view it in one way or the other. Depending on our choice, the rock will show particular limits either to our view or movement, which demonstrates how one's freedom is contingent upon circumstances (BN pp. 509–10). Because of my choice, there is a situation in which things will limit me and show me my limits, but it is from within these limits that I realise my freedom. Quoting Sartre:

> "Thus we come to catch a glimpse of the paradox of freedom: there is freedom only in a situation, and there is a situation only through freedom." (BN p. 511)

Sartre concludes that human reality has a lot of obstacles and resistances not created by humans, but that these obstacles and resistances have their *meaning* only through the free choice which human reality is. To quote him:

> "Thus our freedom itself creates the obstacles from which we suffer." (BN p. 516)

Conversely, freedom can only exist as restricted since freedom is choice. Every choice supposes elimination and selection, thus every choice confines options and therefore is a choice of finitude. This is what the facticity of freedom is exactly about: that we cannot but choose between finite options (BN p. 516). As Sartre puts it succinctly:

> "Without facticity freedom would not exist—as a power of nihilation and of choice—and without freedom facticity would not be discovered and would have no meaning." (BN p. 517)

Sartre proceeds to discuss specific examples of a situation and its various structures—they are my place, my body, my past, my position, and my fundamental relation to the other (pp. 511ff.). I shall briefly discuss his view of the other, which he calls "my neighbour", in order to address the question as to how free we are from collective identification.

2.3. Freedom and Identification

It would be easy, Sartre says, if I would just belong to a world whose meanings were revealed simply in the light of my own ends. I would be the one by whom meanings would come to reality in itself. However, " . . . there exist objective meanings which are given to me as not having been brought to light by me." (BN p. 531) I find myself engaged in a world which reflects to me meanings I have not put into it (BN p. 501). For example, rocks appear to be brutal things without any meaning, but we all learn that rocks are there to be climbed, or to build with, or to be admired; moreover, there are buildings out of rock with particular meanings and signs leading us to them, without us deciding their meanings (BN p. 532).

The question is, then, as Sartre puts it: "Am I not going to find in all this strict limits to my freedom"? (BN p. 532). How far do these meanings limit my freedom? Sartre states that clearly we cannot survive without submitting to a world with technically organised meanings (BN p. 532). I take collective ownership of instruments and techniques that organise my world. The world offers this countenance to everybody. Directions, instructions, orders, prohibitions, billboards organise a world to which I submit in order to realise my own specific projects (BN p. 532). As such, they make the facts of my facticity in its contingency. I cannot but be free, but I am free by adhering to given meanings others have attributed to reality (BN pp. 532–33).

The technical world that we share with others is clearly a defining feature of my own being and my freedom.[15] As Sartre puts it:

---

[15] In this sense, the typical accusation that Sartre's early work is overwhelmingly modernist and individualist, not allowing constitutive connections with others, as made by Alcoff (2006, p. 69), is not quite justified.

"Belonging to the human species is defined by the use of very elementary and very general techniques. To know how to walk, to know how to take hold, to know how to pass judgment on the surface and the relative size of perceived objects, to know how to speak, to know how in general to distinguish the true from the false, etc." (BN p. 533)

A seminal feature of such techniques is the way they manifest in modes of speech. Speech is not universal but demarcated by a national collective language. And a national language, in turn, is not simply defined by academic dictionaries and grammars but practiced in particular regions, bound to the lingo of provinces, professions and families (BN p. 534). Consequently, so Sartre claims, the reality of speech is language and the reality of language is dialect, slang, jargon etc. Moreover, such language is imbedded in a reality of customs. For instance, to be French is not only to speak French, but is in reality to be a Savoyard, and to be a Savoyard implies a thousand of techniques to appropriate the world, for instance, skiing in the winters, and having very specific techniques of skiing needed specifically for the particular slopes of the valleys of Savoy. Using Heidegger's language, Sartre thus makes the point that one is always "thrown into" a world framed by collective technical meanings of some sorts—a French world, a workers' world, the world of the Savoy, etc.:

"I am not thrown only face to face with the brute existent. I am thrown into a worker's world, a French world, a world of Lorraine of the South, which offers me its meanings without my having done anything to disclose them." (BN p. 535)

Sartre concludes that I am free only in a particular place in the world, a situation in which I choose between existing options offered by collective techniques as shared with others in such a situation. Although I choose to take my own place in the world, I have no choice but to be in some place together with others (BN p. 541).

However, this does not mean that I simply have to submit to the existence of others and adopt existing meanings. On the contrary, one is compelled by one's condemnation to be free to make the other's existence manifest to oneself in the form of choice. In order to understand this point, it is important to consider Sartre's distinction between the choice to apprehend "the-Other-as subject" or "the-Other-as-object" (BN p. 541).

The Other-as-object manifests particularly in terms of collective identification.[16] Through the upsurge of the other certain determinations arise, which I am without having chosen them. To repeat my initial quote:

"Here I am—Jew, or Aryan, handsome or ugly, one-armed, etc. I am all of this for the Other with no hope of changing it." (BN p. 544)

With this passage, Sartre clearly emphasises the limits to freedom set by objectifying forms of collective identification. Once again, such identification inevitably defines me in my "being-for-others"; in short, I become the-Other-as-object (BN p. 545). In this sense, I am something I have not chosen to be.

What is the result of such objectification for my freedom? Sartre argues that actually the limit imposed upon me by labelling does not *per se* come from the *action* of others. This limit does not as such dispossess us from our freedom. When we give in, we choose to do so, and it is an act of freedom (BN 545). Prohibitions like "No Jews allowed here, or Jewish restaurant. No Aryans allowed" refer to collective techniques which have meaning only on and through the foundation of my free choice. To quote Sartre:

---

[16] This goes back to Sartre's famous analysis of the "Other-as-a-look" (BN pp. 276ff.) which I confine to my discussion of collective identification.

"In fact, according to the free possibilities which I choose, I can disobey the prohibition, pay no attention to it, or, on the contrary, confer upon it a coercive value which it can hold only because of the weight which I attach to it." (BN p. 545)

The prohibition is based on a structure in which I am taken to be an object. Still, it loses its force within the limits created by my own choice not to attach weight to it (BN p. 545).

So how free are we really from being objectified by the other through labelling? On the one hand, Sartre makes clear our limits:

"The true limit of my freedom lies purely and simply in the very fact that an Other apprehends me as the Other-as-object and in that second corollary fact that my situation ceases for the Other to be a situation and becomes an objective form in which I exist as an objective structure." (BN p. 546)

This alienating process of objectification is a constant and specific limit of my situation, a way in which my "being-for-itself" is made a "being-for-others". Thus, I come to exist in a situation which has a dimension of alienation, which I can in no way remove from the situation any more than I can act directly upon it (BN p. 546).

Nevertheless, Sartre insists that the limit of my freedom exists fundamentally in my condemnation to choose, and when we include the other's existence, my freedom finds its limits also in the existence of the other's freedom. Sartre's argument comes down to the following: If the other chooses to make me an object, then this is because I choose to view the other as subject, free to make me an object; I choose to view the Other-as-subject. I can however choose to view the Other-as-object, not free to be a subject that can make me an object (BN pp. 546/7). As he puts it:

"It is only by my recognising the freedom of anti-Semites (whatever use they make of it) and by my assuming this being-a-Jew that I am a Jew for them; it is only thus that being-a-Jew will appear as the external objective of the situation." (BN p. 547)

So, the freedom of the other is what confers limits on my situation, but I can experience these limits only if I choose to take myself to be a being-for-others, that is, if I choose to give meaning to it. The question still remains, to put it in Sartre's words:

"How then shall I experience the objective limits of my being: Jew, Aryan, ugly, handsome, king, servant, untouchable, etc.—when will language have informed me as to which of these are my limits?" (BN p. 548)

Sartre argues that it cannot be in the way I intuitively, through non-thetic or prereflective conscious perception, apprehend my qualities or project myself within the limits of my projects. Prereflectively, I am not for myself a waiter in the café, or a writer, or handsome or ugly. I do not spontaneously experience myself in this thetic way as somebody such as a waiter, or as handsome or ugly. In fact, I am not anything, I am nothing, unless I make myself an ego and object of reflection. So, even though we are lured by reflection into giving ourselves static identities such as in the case of labelling, our spontaneous experience will as such always escape any such objectification.

Alternatively, one can appropriate labelling in bad faith, that is, through self-denial, by taking toward oneself the point of view of the other (BN p. 549). But bad faith is also a choice, a choice to have meaning conferred on me. Others might, for instance, categorise me as Black, but I have the choice as to what I make of such a category; if I do nothing, I act in bad faith and actually choose to deny myself (BN p. 549). Ultimately, so Sartre claims, a Jewish or a black person chooses to be a Jew or a Black and this being a Jew or Black is nothing more than the free manner of adopting it (BN p. 550).

Sartre's conclusion is that, on the one hand, I cannot but assume my-being-for-Others, and in this sense we are condemned to the facticity of freedom; that is, we cannot but choose to be ourselves for others. Even if we abstain from or refuse to choose, we still make a choice, thus "whether in fury, hate, pride, shame, disheartened refusal or joyous demand", it is impossible for me not to choose to be what

I am for others (BN p. 550). On the other hand, so Sartre emphasises his view, the only limits which freedom ultimately bumps up against at each moment are those which it imposes on itself (BN p. 552). In the final instance, one remains free not to allow the other to subject oneself to the imposition of his or her freedom on oneself through objectification (BN p. 552).

Let me point out some important critique of Sartre's position before moving on to the second part. Merleau-Ponty agrees with Sartre that I cannot but assume my being for others, and am not free to ignore them, but that I have the choice between being an object of disapproval or disapproving of others (Merleau-Ponty 1962, p. 505). However, Merleau-Ponty critically points out that this depends on the situation; for instance, a slave who succeeds in making his/her master an object cannot be really free if remaining a slave (Merleau-Ponty 1962, p. 507). Appiah makes a similar point. Following Hacking, he argues that Sartre does not take seriously enough the gravity of oppressive situations of collective labelling such as racism or sexism. Appiah confines himself to referring to Sartre's famous example of the waiter in the café, who has the choice to just play the role of a waiter without any strong commitments to identify with his role. Appiah argues that, in other settings, people lack such a choice; for instance, when a Feudal serf puts food on "my lady's table", he can no more choose to be a garçon de café than he can choose to be lord of the manor (Appiah 2003, p. 438). My contention is that the waiter is an overemphasised example of Sartre's view of the denial of either the limits of our situations or autonomy of freedom. Sartre offers several more serious examples of the binding effects of labelling. One such example is the issue of labelling people as Jews as discussed above. In fact, Sartre would agree with Appiah's point that when a Feudal serf puts food on "my lady's table", he can no more choose to be a garçon de café than he can choose to be lord of the manor. However, I agree with Merleau-Ponty and Appiah that, ultimately, Sartre does not adequately account for the need of oppressive situations to change as a condition of the possibility for subjects to be free. I discuss this point in the next part, particularly in the final Section 3.3 on "freedom and liberation".

3. Part 2: The Freedom of Facticity

3.1. Autonomous and Heteronomous Freedom

To resume, this paper raises the question as to how free we are from the situations—places, environments, histories, others—that we inevitably belong to and which subject us to collective identities. Sartre's claim is that we are condemned to freedom. Freedom always manifests in a situation, but firstly, it is because of freedom that we have a situation with its limits, and secondly, one can always be freed from a situation through the nihilating power of consciousness. Sartre thus resists the libertarian concept of absolute freedom by making it bound to a situation, but he also resists determinism by taking freedom to be the source of limits and options.

I want to put the discussion of freedom on another plane. I shall argue that it is not, in the first place, through freedom that we have a situation with limited options, but rather it is on the basis of a situation and the limits of its options that we are set free to have choices.

I have argued that Sartre contends that freedom is based on the nihilating ability of consciousness to choose what meaning objects (things or also others) take for the sake of our projects. Consciousness is always directed to objects in a situation. So, freedom always manifests in a situation in which we qua subjects direct ourselves to objects by giving them meaning within the framework of our projects. Sartre claims that consciousness is directed to objects. In effect, however, he reverses the direction of focus from the object back to the subject. The subject, which is claimed to be intentionally directed to the world outside itself, is in effect absorbed by projects concerning its own being in the world. Hence, objects ultimately assume existential meaning. In other words, our freedom is based on the autonomy of subjects to give objects the meaning of their existential choices. So, one can say Sartre advocates a concept of the existential autonomy of freedom.

I argue instead for a notion of what I call the intentional heteronomy of freedom. I agree with Sartre that freedom is based on and manifests in choice; however, I argue that choices are not in the first place the manifestation of the nihilating power of consciousness, but rather that they are originally based on and shaped by the options offered in particular situations. This argument will address the critique that Sartre does not adequately account for the need of oppressive situations to change as a necessary condition of the possibility of freedom.

In the remaining section, I aim to argue that we need to revert the intentional focus back from the subject to the object. My claim is that intentionality means to be originally directed by, rather than to, objects in particular situations because of their effect on us, and that objects will shape our choices, actions, and projects accordingly.

I argue this claim in two steps: first, I illustrate how choices between options are directed by objects in particular situations and their enabling conditions; second, more particularly, how choices between available options are learned in situations shared with others.

1. As a first step, I'd like to illustrate the above claim that choices are directed by objects and situations by taking Sartre's very own life as a sample case. In his autobiography *Words* (*Les mots*), Sartre wrote: "I began my life as I shall with no doubt end it: amidst books." (Sartre 1964, p. 40). According to his memoir, life began for Sartre in his grandfather's library. He recounts in detail how he developed a passion for books, specifically literature, during the ten years that he stayed in his grandparents' home after his father's death, and notably, his autobiography focuses on reflections on these years. He seems to have spent all his time in the library even before he could read. His grandfather, Charles, was a lycée professor of German and Sartre profited much from his grandfather's guidance. Charles held him in high regard, apparently as a prodigy,[17] which prompted him to read and write novels. Despite critical intimations on Charles' intimidating authority, he ends his autobiography stating "I was saved by my grandfather." (Sartre 1964, p. 135) Sartre serves as a life-example of how someone was affected by certain objects: the books in his grandfather's library, in a specific enabling situation, the tutelage of his grandfather, which incited him to dedicate his life to projects of writing. His writing was as such influenced throughout by situations in his life. The events of the Second World, for instance, incited him to write a War trilogy with the significant title *Roads to Freedom*. The same can be said about the way his writings would then also come to reflect trends in Marxism in *Marxism and Existentialism*. Quite ironically, one can argue that Sartre's own life presents an anti-thesis to his theory that man creates himself; instead, he was shaped by objects (books) absorbing his attention and options given to him in particular situations (tutoring in the library), which formed and informed his choices and projects (to write particular books).

There are numerous other examples to demonstrate the same point, of how people are directed by specific objects in particular situations and their enabling conditions to choose to act exactly as they do and to pursue the projects around which their lives revolve—I point out some of these in the next step of the argument. At this point, one can argue that it is not that (a) subjects are directed *to* objects (b) *because* of the intended projects of their choice, but rather that (a) subjects are directed *by* objects (b) *towards* the intended projects of their choice. This means, freedom arises primarily from the options that objects in particular situations and their enabling conditions make us choose rather than from choices that are autonomously made. In a way, we can say our situation chooses us first before we choose it.[18]

2. The first step of my argument was to illustrate how choices between options are directed by objects in particular situations and their enabling conditions; the second step is to show, more particularly, how choices between options are learned in situations shared with others. The second step of my argument will consequently show that a seminal feature of the object-directed way to understand freedom is that choices are not primarily understood as self-made or autonomous but rather as other-made or *heteronomous*.

---

[17] See Gordon (2015, p. 1).
[18] This alludes to Merleau-Ponty's statement that the world chooses us and we choose the world, in his critical discussion of Sartre's concept of freedom in *The phenomenology of perception*. I come back to Merleau-Ponty's view in Section 3.2.

As pointed out in the previous section (Section 2.3), Sartre rightly states that the "technical world" of meanings established by others is a defining feature of our own being and freedom. Belonging to the human species is defined by and requires that we learn to use elementary and general techniques. So, we learn to know how to walk, how to take hold, what to believe, how to pass judgment on perceived objects, how to speak, etc. (BN p. 533)—or, so one can add, how to choose to dedicate one's life to books like Sartre himself did under the tutelage of his grandfather. Actually, Sartre himself could just as well have argued that we learn that we have options to choose from, and more importantly, that we learn how to choose between options; therefore, that it is on this basis, on the basis of other-made options in a given situation, that choices are learned to be made in situations shared with others.

Many examples of what Sartre calls the "world of technical meanings" actually demonstrate this point. We learn in school to choose the right behaviour, to choose the right subjects for career purposes, we learn how to speak a language by choosing the right words, what to believe or how to reason, and we learn skills taken from the toolbox of logic to choose the best arguments; in short, we learn how to make choices between available options. We learn how to choose to take collective options while talking and acting in many different individual ways. Hence, the actions and projects of our choice are not, as Sartre argues, primarily autonomous, self-made, and as such projected within a given situation, but rather originally other-made, heteronomous, thus shaped by choices between options that others offer and that we learn to make in the enabling conditions of a situation.

This also goes for what seem to be original projects. So, for instance, any scientific project formulates its research question and aim or hypothesis of choice in response to options arising from the standing field of research. This is demonstrated by the expectation to offer a literature review and theoretical framework of major contributions to a given research field, and one's research project is required to address a lacuna in or contribute something new to the state of the art. One's choice of research is thus not originally self-made, it is in the first place other-made, no matter how original its approach and results might turn out to be. The same goes for the artist's choice of art works, which are always created in a way that responds to options that aesthetic traditions or their contemporaries have created. Consequently, one can say, I, the first-personal subject, do not primarily project meanings of my own choice into the world, but rather I learn to choose from options made available to me. Situations which I am thrown into enable me to have options from which I learn to choose.

We are in a position to draw the two steps of the above argument together into a conclusion now. The first step shows how choices between options are directed by objects in particular situations and their enabling conditions, the second step how one learns from others to choose between available options in such situations. In conclusion, one can say freedom is primarily heteronomous and consists of the way objects shared by others in specific situations form and inform our choices between options. In other words, it is not the autonomy but rather the heteronomy of choice that makes us free in the first place. Not my choice in a situation, but the situation itself, with the enabling conditions it offers in the form of options which it instructs me to take, is what primarily sets me free. One can thus say, it is on the basis of other-made choices alone that the freedom of self-made choices can exist. Thus, heteronomous choice has ontological priority to autonomous choice. Heteronomous choice does not exclude autonomous choice but precedes it.

3.2. The Freedom of Facticity

The argument is not yet complete. The question remains: how can one be really free if the options are all given and we have to learn how to take them?

In the following section, I address this question by briefly pointing out how far I agree with and differ from Merleau-Ponty's concept of freedom, which he develops as a critique of Sartre, and in this way show why exactly I speak of the "freedom of facticity".

In his famous chapter on freedom in his *Phenomenology of Perception*, Merleau-Ponty writes:

"What then is freedom? To be born is both to be born of the world and to be born into the world. The world is already constituted, but also never completely constituted; in the first case we are acted upon, in the second we are open to an infinite number of possibilities. But this analysis is still abstract, for we exist in both ways at once. There is, therefore, never determinism and never absolute choice, I am never a thing and never bare consciousness. In fact, even our own pieces of initiative, even the situations which we have chosen, bear us on, once they have been entered upon by virtue of a state rather than an act. The generality of the 'rôle' and of the situation comes to the aid of decision, and in this exchange between the situation and the person who takes it up, it is impossible to determine precisely the 'share contributed by the situation' and the 'share contributed by freedom'." (Merleau-Ponty 1962, p. 527)

Merleau-Ponty opposes the extremes of both determinism and libertarianism (or as he calls it, "idealism"), of admitting absolute priority to either facticity or freedom. According to him, facticity (the situation) and freedom are like magnetic poles kept in the tension of constant exchange. As he puts it, " ... even the situations which we have chosen, bear us on" (Merleau-Ponty 1962, p. 527). Hence, " ... it is impossible to determine precisely the 'share contributed by the situation' and the 'share contributed by freedom.'" (Merleau-Ponty 1962, p. 527). I am neither determined nor absolutely free, it is impossible to say whether I choose because of my situation or because I am free to decide. I am a project of the world that I project myself (Merleau-Ponty 1962, pp. 499–500).

Contrary to Sartre, Merleau-Ponty argues that it is not due to choice that we experience the world with limits and options, but rather we are "born into" experiencing it with its limits and options. Consider Merleau-Ponty's example of a worker deciding to become proletarian (Merleau-Ponty 1962, p. 514). A worker neither chooses to be a proletarian, nor is he born into the proletarian movement, but rather in dealing with his situation and others in his situation, the worker adopts his situation as his existential, proletarian project. Freedom arises through such an existential project, through which, together with others with whom I share a past and present, I give my life direction.

Merleau-Ponty puts more emphasis than Sartre on the share that the situation contributes to freedom, but as for Sartre, the situation ultimately remains an existential project for him too, one in which subjects deal in a way with the world that makes it their project, one in which they are primordially free to direct their lives. The fact that the subject inhabits—or, as Merleau-Ponty says, embodies—a situation as its existential project admits the priority of its freedom over and above the facticity of the situation.

My position differs from Merleau-Ponty's in two respects:

Firstly, instead of thinking of the facticity of the situation and freedom in terms of two poles in tension, I argue that the situation as such entails freedom by virtue of the way it offers us choices and shapes the way we choose. If we claim that choice constitutes freedom, and that a situation enables and teaches us to choose, it follows that the situation must entail choice and consequently freedom. To return to Merleau-Ponty's example: instead of saying a worker becomes part of the proletariat by dealing with other workers, one can rather say the worker is directed by social conditions to start dealing with other workers and consequently to be brought to understand and make the choice to join the proletarian movement, thus to deliberately decide to become a proletarian, and to play his/her individual role as part of this collective project.

Secondly, by taking facticity to entail freedom in a way that originally directs choice, my own position to some extent inverses this priority of freedom over facticity. This comes down to setting a difference in ontological priority. I agree that freedom coincides with choice but argue that facticity gives rise to choice in the first place. Like Sartre, albeit in a more moderate way, Merleau-Ponty prioritises the autonomy of choice. I prioritise the heteronomy of choice. In this sense I speak of the *freedom of facticity*.

In order to be clear on why I think facticity entails freedom, it is important to consider the meaning of what we might take to be the limits of situations. It is helpful to view limits in terms of the Greek term for limit, πέρασ (*peras*), which, as Heidegger insightfully showed, bears the meaning of "opening" (Heidegger 1971, p. 154).[19] Limits in this sense can assume various meanings and it will require a study of its own to explore these meanings. Take the example of a game: limits in many ways "open the game", making it possible by, for instance, outlining the borders of the playfield or sportsground, making divisions between teams, prescribing rules, restricting movement, navigating manoeuvres, charting chances and altogether by demarcating its beginning and end. Limits are in this sense essentially part of the condition of the possibility to play, they, as it were, open the game by delineating its options. One can say, they define rather than confine a game. In other words, limits can be said to delineate and direct the options of choice by virtue of which situations make freedom possible. Hence, contrary to Sartre, one can say, it is not in the first place because of the freedom of choice that situations have limits, but rather situations give choices the limits that define our freedom.

However, as should be clear, this argument should not be mistaken to deny the autonomy of freedom. On the contrary, while it is necessary for subjects to have learned to choose between options offered by situations, for freedom to unfold sufficiently, it is obvious that subjects must actually make their own choices between such options or choose to create new options of their choice. Consider a situation like a game again: while the game primarily gives subjects the options (tactics, manoeuvers, etc.) to choose and thus grant them the necessary freedom to play, one still needs individuals making their very own choices between these options for the game not to be manipulated but to allow what is typically called free play.

In conclusion, one can say, freedom has a heteronomous origin with an autonomous dimension. Primarily, a situation enables us to have heteronomous freedom; we are driven, drawn in, pushed by objects and situations like, for instance, in the case of games, to make choices. In this sense, one can say, a situation and the options it offers is the fulfilment of the necessary condition for heteronomous freedom. Secondarily, we have autonomous freedom, which manifests in our choosing between the options situations offer, or choosing to change or create new options in given situations. Ultimately, one can say, a situation as such is a necessary but not sufficient condition of the possibility to be free. The freedom of the situation and its other-made choices require the freedom of self-made choices to sufficiently fulfil the condition of the possibility of freedom.

3.3. Freedom and Liberation

Ideally, the limits of situations, rather than to confine, will disclose possibilities of choice. But this is ideally the case, for there are some situations that can seriously oppress possible options of choice. One of these is the limitations set by collective labelling. The concluding question is how the notion of heteronomous freedom can help address the problem of collective identification. How free are we really from situations that subject us to collective identification?

Sartre has a fascinating suggestion: do not allow the other to be free to subject you to objectification. But how free are we to do this? His suggestion assumes that people principally always have the possibility to autonomously make their own, self-made or "authentic" choices, choices to be made no matter what the situation is. The privation of authentic choices is what Sartre famously calls "bad faith", self-denial (BN pp. 70ff). As we are condemned to be free, Sartre believes that we always have a choice not to submit to labelling, no matter what the situation might be. Even to surrender oneself to a situation, to resign, or not to choose, manifests the freedom of choice. Sartre's belief in the condemnation to autonomous freedom is, no doubt, fascinating, but, as Merleau-Ponty indicates, suffers from an idealistic overemphasis of the autonomy of freedom despite, and over and above, the facticity of the situation.

A situation can narrow down our options of choice to a bare minimum, to a point such that we can hardly speak of authentic choices without resorting to idealism. What options remain to choose from authentically, for instance, for soldiers condemned to death in a train to the concentration

---

[19] See also the discussion of Malpas (2006, p. 254).

camps, as Sartre describes in poignant detail at the end of *Troubled Sleep* (Sartre 1986), the second novel in his trilogy, *Roads to Freedom*? Closer to home, what authentic choices remain in a place like a township, an informal settlement consisting of shacks, with a serious unavailability of basic options in terms of protection, nourishment, water supply, education, and medical resources? In a recent paper, "Heidegger in the township", I have attempted to demonstrate in extensive detail how people in a township, specifically so called "shanty towns", are faced with a disenabling rather than enabling situation, deprived of the most basic options and possibilities of choice (Olivier 2015). Only in rare, exceptional cases will people have the extraordinary ability to be free, or to escape, despite their limits in such a situation. So, if collective identification translates into laws that enforce the badge of colour on people to the extent that they are expulsed to disenabling places, like shack towns, bereft of possibilities, the heteronomy of freedom in such a situation makes the autonomy of freedom impossible. Then, to insist that we are condemned to be free seems to result in existentialist idealism.

If the heteronomous freedom offered by situations is the necessary condition of the possibility for autonomous freedom, then a situation must fulfil this condition for autonomous freedom to be. If a situation cannot satisfy this condition, there will be no autonomous freedom; thus, for freedom to be, such a situation will have to be transformed as a whole. In the case of an oppressive situation such as collective labelling, freedom only manifests if the situation itself is transformed in a way that heteronomous choices become collectively available. For instance, to release an individual such as Mandela from jail was of seminal importance, not so much because the confines of imprisonment were removed and he was offered individual liberty, but rather because his release was a symbol of the collective liberation of the majority of the people suffering under collective labelling under apartheid legislature.

At this juncture, it is perhaps helpful to recall Fanon's distinction between liberty, as the removal of individual constraints, and freedom, as taking collective responsibility for one's choices in a situation.[20] In his *Existentialism is a Humanism*, Sartre actually seems to argue along the same lines that individual choice necessarily implies collective responsibility. Using this distinction, one can argue that it is not enough to guarantee the liberty of some individuals in order to obtain freedom, but rather a whole situation, which people collectively bear, needs to be transformed for freedom to be possible. Decolonisation is, according to Fanon, an example of such transformation needed for the liberation of the situation of colonial oppression (Fanon 2004, p. 11).[21] In this sense, one can usefully distinguish between liberty and liberation as between removing individual constraints and transforming a collective situation. Liberation, the transformation of the situation, is needed if a situation oppresses rather than offers options of choice. Thus liberation, rather than liberty, is needed for freedom to exist. Only such liberation can meet the necessary condition of the possibility of heteronomous freedom, the other-made choices that enable us to have self-made choices.

Some questions remain: How do we recognise and also change situations of oppression? How do we avoid such transformation to become a form of oppression itself, as scholars such as Freire (2000), Appiah (2003) or Alcoff (2006) challenge us to ask? What role does power or education play in such transformation? Due to limited space, these questions will have to be addressed in another study. Such a study will require more focus on Sartre's later works and the idea of resocialisation, such as developed in his *Critique of Dialectical Reason* (Sartre 1982), and a discussion of works such as Freire's idea of educating transformation in his book *The pedagogy of the oppressed*. But that will need to wait for another time.

---

[20] Lewis Gordon helpfully points out this distinction (Gordon 2008, p. 83).
[21] Fanon explicitly refers to liberation in terms of the transformation of the situation, particularly, the decolonisation of the situation (Fanon 2004, p. 2) versus the liberties taken by the colonisers (pp. 33, 50).

4. Conclusions

I agree with Sartre that freedom is defined by choice, but I disagree that freedom is based on autonomous choice in a given situation. I argued that, primarily, we have heteronomous freedom by virtue of situations enabling us to have options of choice. Secondarily comes autonomous freedom, which manifests in what we make of situations, how we choose options by taking or changing them or by creating new ones. Consequently, individuals cannot be sufficiently free if oppressive situations that legitimise collective labelling, such as racism, are still allowed to exist. Some individuals free themselves from such situations because they obtain exceptional options or have extraordinary abilities, but if these situations are not changed, individual actions do not necessarily constitute freedom. Conversely, a situation as such is a necessary but not sufficient condition of the possibility for freedom. The freedom of the situation and its other-made choices requires the freedom of self-made choices to qualify sufficiently as freedom. But we are in bad faith if we deny that we need situations to set us free to make autonomous choices, and that if we do not have such situations, they need to be liberated first. Thus, heteronomous freedom is the necessary but not sufficient condition of the possibility for autonomous freedom.

Acknowledgments: All sources of funding of the study should be disclosed. Please clearly indicate grants that you have received in support of your research work. Clearly state if you received funds for covering the costs to publish in open access. Research work for this paper was done during a Sabbatical in 2017. I received travel grants in support of the presentation of my research work from projects funded by the Social Sciences and Humanities Research Niche Area at Fort Hare, Leverhulme Trust at the London School of Economics, DAAD (German Academic Exchange Service) at the Institute of African Studies (Afrikanistik) at the University of Bayreuth, and as keynote at the conference this special issue is based on.

Conflicts of Interest: The author declares no conflict of interest.

References

Alcoff, Linda Martín. 2006. *Visible Identities: Race, Gender, and the Self*. Oxford: Oxford University Press.

Appiah, Kwame A. 2003. Race, culture, identity. In *The African Philosophy Reader*. Edited by P. H. Coetzee and A. P. J. Roux. New York: Routledge, pp. 373–91.

Bernasconi, Robert. 2007. *How to Read Sartre*. London: Granta Books.

Cerbone, David R. 2006. *Understanding Phenomenology*. Chesham: Acumen.

Du Bois, William Edward Burghardt. 1975. *Dusk of Dawn: An Essay toward an Autobiography of a Race Concept*. Milwood: Kraus-Thomson Organization Limited.

Fanon, Frantz. 2004. *The Wretched of the Earth*. New York: Grove Press.

Føllesdal, Dagfinn. 1981. Sartre on Freedom. In *The Philosophy of Jean-Paul Sartre*. Edited by P. A. Schilpp. La Salle: Open Court, The Library of Living Philosophers.

Freire, Paulo. 2000. *Pedagogy of the Oppressed*. London: Continuum, New York: Continuum.

Gordon, Lewis R. 1997. Black Existential Philosophy. In *Existence in Black: An Anthology of Black Existential Philosophy*. Edited by L. Gordon. New York: Routledge.

Gordon, Lewis R. 2008. *An Introduction to Africana Philosophy*. Cambridge: Cambridge University Press.

Gordon, Lewis R. 2015. Sartre. In *The Encyclopedia of Political Thought*, 1st ed. Edited by Michael T. Gibbons. Somerset: John Wiley & Sons, Ltd.

Hacking, Ian. 1992. Making up People. In *Forms of Desire: Sexual Orientation and the Social Constructionist Controversy*. Edited by Edward Stein. New York: Routledge, pp. 69–88.

Heidegger, Martin. 1962. *Being and Time*. Translated by J. Macquarrie and E. Robinson. Oxford: Blackwell.

Heidegger, Martin. 1971. *Poetry, Language, Thought*. Translated by A. Hofstadter. New York: Harper and Row.

Malpas, Jeff. 2006. *Heidegger's Topology*. Cambridge: The MIT Press.

Merleau-Ponty, Maurice. 1962. *Phenomenology of Perception*. Translated by C. Smith. London and New York: Routledge.

Moran, Dermot. 2000. *Introduction to Phenomenology*. London and New York: Routledge

Olivier, Abraham. 2015. Heidegger in the Township. *South African Journal of Philosophy* 34: 240–54. [CrossRef]

Sartre, Jean-Paul. 1957. *Transcendence of the Ego*. Translated by F. Williams and R. Kirkpatrick. New York: Noonday Press.

Sartre, Jean-Paul. 1964. *Words*. Translated by B. Frechtman. New York: Braziller.

Sartre, Jean-Paul. 1965. *Essays in Existentialism*. Edited by W. Baskin. Secaucus: Citadel Press.

Sartre, Jean-Paul. 1982. *Critique of Dialectical Reason*. Translated by A. Sheridan-Smith. London: Verso.

Sartre, Jean-Paul. 1986. *Troubled Sleep*. Translated by E. Sutton. London: Penguin.

Sartre, Jean-Paul. 2003. *Being and Nothingness*. London: Routledge.

Taylor, Charles. 1994. *Multiculturalism and 'The Politics of Recognition'*. Princeton: Princeton University Press.

Webber, Jonathan. 2011. Freedom. In *The Routledge Companion to Phenomenology*. Edited by S. Luft and S. Overgaard. New York: Routledge, pp. 327–35.

religions

MDPI

Article

Existential Choice as Repressed Theism: Jean-Paul Sartre and Giorgio Agamben in Conversation

Marcos Antonio Norris

English Department, Loyola University Chicago, Chicago, IL 60660, USA; mnorris4@luc.edu

Received: 26 January 2018; Accepted: 30 March 2018; Published: 2 April 2018

Abstract: This article brings Sartre's notion of existential authenticity, or sovereign decisionism, into conversation with the work of contemporary political theorist Giorgio Agamben, who argues that sovereign decisionism is the repressed theological foundation of authoritarian governments. As such, the article seeks to accomplish two goals. The first is to show that Sartre's depiction of sovereign decisionism directly parallels how modern democratic governments conduct themselves during a state of emergency. The second is to show that Sartre's notion of existential authenticity models, what Agamben calls, secularized theism. Through an ontotheological critique of Sartre's professed atheism, the article concludes that an existential belief in sovereign decision represses, rather than profanes, the divine origins of authoritarian law. I frame the argument with a reading of Sartre's 1943 play *The Flies*, which models the repressed theological underpinnings of Sartre's theory.

Keywords: Jean-Paul Sartre; Giorgio Agamben; existentialism; contemporary continental philosophy; authenticity; sovereignty

---

When Orestes, the protagonist of Jean-Paul Sartre's 1943 play *The Flies*, returns to the city of Argos to avenge his father Agamemnon, Zeus commands King Aegistheus, Agamemnon's murderer, to incarcerate Orestes before he acts. Fearing for his life, Aegistheus implores Zeus to kill Orestes with a thunderbolt, but Zeus no longer has the power to do so because Orestes discovers his own god-like ability to make self-originating choices. "Once freedom lights its beacon in a man's heart, the gods are powerless against him," Zeus laments; "It's a matter between man and man, and it is for other men, and for them only, to let him go his gait, or to throttle him" (Sartre 1989, p. 102). Orestes's newfound freedom disrupts the socio-political order of Argos by threatening the sovereign control that Zeus exerts over King Aegistheus and his people. If left to his own devices, Orestes will usurp the throne and reclaim his true identity as the ruler of Argos—or so believes his sister, Electra, who has long expected her brother's return to force out imposters like Aegistheus and restore the kingdom to its rightful state. But Orestes kills Aegistheus and their mother, Queen Clytemnestra, only to abandon Electra and the citizens of Argos to fend for themselves. "I shall not sit on my victim's throne or take the scepter in my blood-stained hands. A god offered it to me, and I said no. I wish to be a king without a kingdom, without subjects," Orestes declares, for true authenticity lies not in one's destiny or ontological essence, for Sartre, but in freedom, which makes humanity what it is—the sovereign (though, perhaps, unwitting) bearers of pure, unencumbered choice (Sartre 1989, p. 123). The people of Argos are liberated from the oppressive weight of divine authority, but, as I will attempt to show, they do not escape the deleterious effects of sovereignty, even as a kingdom without a king. For true authenticity, in Sartre's vocabulary, refers to the practice of a divine-like freedom that renders the gods "powerless" against Orestes and anyone else capable of conscious, self-originating choice.

This episode from Sartre's stage adaptation of the Electra myth highlights a problematic notion at the center of Sartre's philosophical enterprise that this paper attempts to unravel. As Electra would have it, Orestes rebuffs his ontic vocation as the king of Argos, but this essentialist depiction of personhood, to which Electra is militantly committed, is seriously at odds with Sartre's own doctrine of authenticity. Sartre insists that there is no pre-given nature, or set of essential properties, that constitute human identity as such, meaning that there are no restrictions on the human will, and therefore no way to violate or act according to the contours of an essential self. Rather, human identity is radically free—where the potential to be (a negative ontology that Sartre calls "nothingness") actualizes through choice—so authentic behavior, as Sartre defines it, can only be accomplished through self-originating acts of volition that manifest identity *ex nihilo*, just as the Judeo-Christian God is believed to have created the cosmos *out of nothing*. For this reason, Sartre describes selfhood as "a lack of being" that, he asserts, "is not to be distinguished from choice," or the "desire" to be, a potentiality that is always in the process of actualizing (Sartre 1953, p. 725). Sartre derives from this logic his famous dictum that "existence precedes essence" and, in this formulation, we are given two models of personhood that structure the content of this article (Sartre 1953, p. 725). The first of these casts human nature as a pure essence, or a set of essential properties; the second, by contrast, sees human nature as paradoxically natureless, an absolute freedom that strives to become an essence through the power of sovereign, self-originating choices. Sartre attributes the latter to his exemplary model of existential authenticity, Orestes, who, in profaning the gods, defiantly states that "I *am* my freedom" (Sartre 1989, p. 117). But unlike the vast majority of people who strive, in Sartre's view, to become an essence, Orestes refuses the ontic vocation to which he is supposedly destined in order to retain his freedom.

Electra, however, remains committed to an essentialist model of personhood and gives up her freedom as a result, similar to the cafe waiter in Sartre's *Being and Nothingness*, who roots his identity in the vocation that he performs. "What I attempt to realize is a being-in-itself," the waiter reports, "as if it were not my free choice to get up each morning at five o'clock or to remain in bed ... As if from the very fact that I sustain this role in existence I did not transcend it on every side ... as one *beyond* my condition" (Sartre 1953, p. 103). Sartre contrasts this "being-in-itself", which he likens to an inkwell, a drinking glass, and other inanimate objects, with the conscious subject, or "being-for-itself," who strives to unify with the former to achieve autonomous self-presence. Kate Kirkpatrick argues in *Sartre and Theology* that the perfect union of consciousness and being is impossible, representing, in Sartre's study, an unrealizable goal to become God. She compares the self-identical subject of Sartre's analysis with the Jewish divinity of the Torah who identifies himself to Moses as "I am that I am" (Kirkpatrick 2017a, p. 90). Indeed, Sartre himself writes that "the best way to conceive of the fundamental project of human reality is to say that man is the being whose project is to be God. ... To be man means to reach toward being God. Or if you prefer, man fundamentally is the desire to be God" (Sartre 1953, p. 724). But striving to become a self-identical essence similar to God is to live in bad faith, according to Sartre, who argues that all people should learn by virtue of their freedom to live authentically without God and without the impulse to deify themselves. Indeed, to embrace the absolute "nothingness" of one's identity is to profane divine authority for Sartre, who would otherwise locate God, in line with Judeo-Christian orthodoxy, as the ontological foundation of the universe.

It is therefore easy to read Orestes as analogous to Sartre, who, according to Noreen Khawaja, saw himself as "the primary representative" of a distinctly atheistic version of existentialism that "emphasized the total isolation of the human being and the total responsibility of each person for his own existence" (Khawaja 2016, p. 2). According to Khawaja, Sartre's idea of "nothingness" grew directly out of his atheism, so to consciously embrace freedom was to simultaneously profane God. It was to demonstrate, in other words, that God doesn't exist through the sovereign creation of one's identity and moral values. This is why Orestes, in contrast to his sister Electra, does not experience guilt after killing their mother. Electra feels herself bound by a transcendental moral law; Orestes does not. "I am doomed to have no other law but mine," Orestes states; "For I, Zeus, am a man, and every man must find out his own way" (Sartre 1989, p. 119). By first appearances, then, it would seem that Sartre advances a philosophical position that profanes the sovereign authority of God and political leaders alike, for every individual is sovereign over himself by virtue of the "little God which inhabits" him, Sartre writes, the power that each of us possesses to freely decide on the meaning and value of our own life apart from the dictates of a divine or political authority (Sartre 1953, p. 81).

This article brings Sartre's notion of existential authenticity into conversation with the work of contemporary political theorist Giorgio Agamben, who argues by contrast that self-originating choice is the repressed theological foundation of authoritarian governments. In doing so, the article seeks to accomplish two goals. The first is to show that Sartre's depiction of sovereign decisionism directly parallels how modern democratic governments conduct themselves during a state of emergency. The second is to demonstrate that Sartre's notion of existential authenticity models what Agamben calls secularized theism, or the ontotheological foundation of law. It will be shown, in fact, that Sartre's atheistic critique of ontotheology—what he describes as an unconscious desire to be God—is itself ontotheological from Agamben's perspective, for Sartre replaces the essential nature of being-in-itself with a divine-like freedom to create moral values *ex nihilo*. So while the ontotheological desire to be God results in a loss of freedom, for Sartre, for Agamben, it results in the absolute freedom to dictate the metaphysical value of one's chosen behavior at will. This is the very definition of sovereign power for Agamben, who identifies God not with being, as Sartre does, but with nothingness, or a total lack of being, the negative ontology upon which Sartre builds his notion of existential authenticity. As I will show, both philosophers level a critique against ontotheology, but they begin their critiques with opposing notions of what constitutes the nature of God.

1. On Sartre and God

Jerome Gellman argues in a 2009 article that Sartre walks the line of mystical Christianity but fails to establish a relationship with God. "[W]hen Sartre asserts that a person has no *self*-substance," he writes, "Sartre is seeing through glass darkly what the Christian mystic has [already] discovered—that a person has no distinct self being, because he exists only in the encompassing being of God" (Gellman 2009, p. 131). According to Gellman, the believer of mystical Christianity experiences a complete breakdown of ontic distinctions and becomes aware of the single divine nature to which everything belongs. In the mystic tradition, as in the Augustinian tradition, a proper relationship with God results in the believer's ontological becoming, whereas the absence of God obversely results in the individual's ontological privation, or loss of being, which Sartre describes as the negative ontology of being-for-itself. For this reason, "Christian mystics exemplify bad faith at its worst," Gellman writes, for they "pretend[] to have discovered that they belong to the substance of God sufficiently so as to receive for themselves a substantive, in-itself form of being" (Gellman 2009, p. 129). Sartre's notion of the divine therefore embodies what Christina Howells calls "Absolute being," an essentialist view of ontology that precludes the subject's capacity for self-originating choice (Howells 1981, p. 550). As Howells writes, "the only plausible idea of God" for Sartre is "an impossible idea of God: a synthesis" of oppositional views that conceals the for-itself within a fixed ontological essence (Howells 1981, p. 550).

In a two-part series published in *Sartre Studies International* between 2013 and 2014, John Gillespie argues that Sartre wanted to develop a truly atheistic philosophy, but Sartre remained preoccupied with religious questions throughout his life and constantly referred to God in his writings, as a result. This preoccupation began with Sartre's youthful rejection of religious belief, for in rejecting God, Sartre became obsessed with God, forging his most important philosophical ideas around the deity's ostensible disappearance. Gillespie writes that Sartre "rejects God and incorporates the concept of God into his thinking. God is paradoxically both absent and present" (Gillespie 2014, p. 46). As Sartre explains in his 1963 autobiography *The Words,* he exchanged his nominal Christianity very early in life for a deeply felt religion of letters. Pouring himself over the books in his grandfather's study, he came to regard the publications as religious artifacts that would nourish his spiritual life in the decades to come. "Christian belief provide[d] an interpretive structure" for Sartre that was "transposed by Charles [Schweitzer, Sartre's grandfather,] into a secular form and transmitted to his more radical grandson" (Gillespie 2005, p. 244). Because of this, Sartre remained partial to a Christian framework throughout his life, and, as Adrian van den Hoven writes, Sartre "struggle[d] to develop a theology on an atheistic basis," which is to say in other words that Sartre struggled to develop a political philosophy bereft of moral absolutes (van den Hoven 2010, p. 81). Much later in his career, Sartre criticized his earlier work for being too individualistic, and though he remained an atheist to his death,

Sartre became fascinated with Judaism toward the end of his life because of its "ethical concern for the other as the basis on which to fulfill revolutionary goals" (Gillespie 2014, p. 53). Gillespie concludes the study with the suggestion that, had Sartre lived longer, he might have adopted a theistic position and, with it, the possibility of a "metaphysically based universal morality" (Gillespie 2014, p. 55). But the death of God meant the end of moral absolutes, for Sartre, who tied the transcendental authority of "universal morality" to the metaphysical nature of God's ontological essence. Therefore, it is not the sheer notion of God that Sartre rejects, but, if Gillespie is right, the orthodox God of the scholastic tradition, the ontological foundation of being.

In fact, it would seem that the God of Sartre's atheism is thoroughly Augustinian, for, as Kate Kirkpatrick argues in her 2017 publication *Sartre on Sin: Between Being and Nothingness*, Sartre was influenced by French theological and literary figures who themselves fell under the pervasive influence of Pierre de Bérulle, the Catholic mystic of nothingness whose Augustinian view of sin profoundly shaped the intellectual topography of 17th century France. René Descartes, Blaise Pascal, and François Fénelon were among Sartre's philosophical predecessors in this regard, and they argued, similar to Bérulle, that sin was the absence of being. Under this theological paradigm, all being-in-itself, to borrow Sartre's terminology, is contingent upon God, who "perpetually wills being into being," so to violate God's will is to violate one's God-given nature and return quite literally to nothingness, or the negative ontology of being-for-itself (Kirkpatrick 2017b, p. 33). Sartre secularizes Augustine to fit his atheistic worldview, professing the death of God at the same time that he advances a traditional (though secularized) theological idea. In Kirkpatrick's view of Sartre, God is the positive ground of ontology, and the source from which all other essences derive their being. Emptying the Augustinian system of its divine center, Sartre deprives humanity of its essence, and thereby reveals the absolute freedom of the for-itself in a world without God. But there are other theological traditions through which to read Sartre's idea of nothingness, and, as I will show in the following sections, different theological readings for Sartre and Agamben result in opposing critiques of ontotheology.

2. Sartre's Critique of Ontotheology

The theoretical death of God resulted for Sartre, as it did for Friedrich Nietzsche a century before, in the transvaluation of society's most sacred and authoritative values. Without God, there are no eternal moral principles, no inherent meaning to life, and, most significantly for Sartre, no pre-given human nature to which our actions must remain faithful. Indeed, it is precisely because human beings lack the *imago Dei*, precisely because "there is no God to conceive" of their nature, that we possess sovereign control over our identities and levy the power of self-originating choice through volitional acts of signification (Sartre 2007, p. 22). The freedom upon which Sartre founds his notion of existential authenticity logically emerges in a world without God, so the philosopher is critical of secular positions that base their metaphysical theories on what he calls the desire to be God. "This exultant atheism demonstrates that Sartre's liberty is a freedom *without* God," Gillespie writes; "His theoretical writings seek to refute the idea of God, but they also, returning as they frequently do to the notion of the divine, both reject it and incorporate it" (Gillespie 2013, p. 85). To this end, Sartre describes human consciousness, or the for-itself, as a lack of being that naturally strives to become an ontological essence, or the in-itself, writing that:

> The for-itself is the being which is to itself its own lack of being. The being which the for-itself lacks is the in-itself. ... Thus human reality is the desire of being-in-itself. ...
> The fundamental value which presides over this project is exactly the in-itself-for-itself; that is, the ideal of a consciousness which would be the foundation of its own being-in-itself by the pure consciousness which it would have of itself. It is this ideal which can be called God. (Sartre 1953, pp. 723–24)

The nothingness, or lack of being, upon which human consciousness is founded strives to become a self-identical essence that Sartre identifies with the Judeo-Christian God, as Kirkpatrick had noted earlier. Sartre is critical of this metaphysical stance because it endows ontology with a divine-like authority which itself is derived from the theological presupposition that God is the foundation of being. Thus, for Sartre, to be "in-itself-for-itself" is to be like God, meaning that any philosophical stance that prioritizes the metaphysical authority of pure essence is, at its core, a sublimated theological belief. This ontotheology disguises the for-itself as the in-itself, concealing nothingness, or non-being, within an absolute essence. But, as Gellman writes, it "is not possible for anything to be both the in-itself and a for-itself," in Sartre's view, and Sartre concludes on this basis that "God does not exist" (Gellman 2009, p. 132).

In a brief description of the *ancien régime*, Agamben observes that, prior to the French Revolution, the king's sovereignty was "divinely authorized" (Agamben 2017, p. 106). In this sense, the legal system enforced under the king of France was actually decreed by God, whose sole ability to establish transcendental moral laws placed him, rather than the king, at the top of a political hierarchy. Theoretically speaking, then, God was the origin of power; the king was his political representative. The distinction that Agamben draws here between legislative power and executive power broadens in scope and utility as the study progresses, but, for now, readers should note how the king's executive powers merely enforced transcendental laws that under a theocratic monarchy were thought to originate with God, who retained the sole capacity to create or abolish laws. Agamben describes the executive power of the king as a "force of law without law," which is to say, in other words, that the king enforces not his own will but the will of a sovereign God, from whom the king's authority is derived (Agamben 2017, p. 199).

This distinction between executive power and legislative power—between the power to enforce laws and the power to create them—is similarly depicted by Sartre in *The Flies*. As Zeus says to King Aegistheus, "You may hate me, but we are akin; I made you in my image" (Sartre 1989, p. 100). Unlike Orestes, who shirks the ontic responsibilities of a king, Aegistheus lacks sovereign control over his identity and enforces not his own will but the will of the deity who made him. In other words, the actions of Aegistheus are, to quote Agamben, "divinely authorized," while the free choices of Orestes derive their authority from Orestes alone. For Sartre, these contrasting models of personhood represent, as before, the sovereign subject, who as the paragon of authenticity takes full responsibility for his freedom, as well as by contrast the essential subject, who, expressing an unconscious desire to become like God, acts according to the nature of his ontic vocation. This is why freedom for Sartre is thought to profane divine authority. Aegistheus performs his identity as one exercising the executive powers of a king, while Orestes, fully equipped with both executive and legislative capabilities, exercises sovereign control over his identity though volitional acts of free will. He states, "I am doomed to have no other law but mine" (Sartre 1989, p. 119). This freedom to create laws that run counter to and exert authority over the eternal laws of God represents, for Sartre, a profane challenge to ontotheology. But it also models how authoritarian governments conduct themselves during a state of emergency, as I will demonstrate shortly.

It is therefore important at this juncture to make explicit where Sartre and Agamben are in agreement, as it will help to clarify, in the coming pages, where exactly their theories diverge. To begin, both Agamben and Sartre share the distinction between executive power and legislative power, but Sartre uses a different terminology to communicate these ideas. For Sartre, executing a law is the same as performing by acting in accordance with the laws of nature, just as a theocratic king, in both his and Agamben's accounts, acts according to nature by enforcing the divine laws handed down to him from above. Likewise, both Agamben and Sartre share an understanding of legislative power, though Sartre describes this law-making capacity as a negative ontology that gives humanity the power to make sovereign, self-originating choices. However, as the previous analysis has shown, many human beings utilize this power in bad faith and conceal the freedom of the for-itself within the absolute essence of a fixed, ontological identity. For Sartre, this represents the sublimated desire to become a pure essence similar to God. Though Agamben will give a very different account of the divine nature, he agrees with Sartre that theological beliefs are sometimes sublimated, or repressed, in ontotheological form. He gives an account of the political implications of theological repression in his 2007 book *Profanations*:

> Secularization is a form of repression. It leaves intact the forces it deals with by simply moving them from one place to another. Thus the political secularization of theological concepts (the transcendence of God as a paradigm of sovereign power) does nothing but displace the heavenly monarchy into an earthly monarchy, leaving its power intact. Profanation, however, neutralizes what it profanes. Once profaned, that which was unavailable and separate loses its aura and is returned to use. Both are political operations: the first guarantees the exercise of power by carrying it back to a sacred model; the second deactivates the apparatuses of power and returns to common use the spaces that power had seized. (Agamben 2007, p. 77)

Sartre's atheistic stance would appear to profane, rather than merely secularize, the sovereign authority of God. He describes the subject's attempt to become a pure essence as an ontotheological tendency in human beings who, in the very manner described above by Agamben, sublimate their desire to become God by concealing within their feigned ontological essence a capacity for sovereign, self-originating choice. But it is precisely his legislative powers as a free subject that makes the authentic individual most like God for Agamben, whose account of sovereign decisionism also comprises his political theory of the state.

Therefore, Sartre's atheism does not profane the metaphysical authority of God but redirects it from the deity to mankind (Gillespie 2013, p. 82). For this reason, I agree with Agamben scholar Colby Dickinson that modern atheistic thought "has not removed God from the scene," but has rather "intensified theology's hold on humanity" by turning, as it has, "to a repressed form of secularity" (Dickinson and Kotsko 2015, p. 130). In the following section, I examine Agamben's account of nothingness to show how self-originating choice models the repressed theological foundation of Sartre's theory. In doing so, I work toward the conclusion that Sartre's atheistic critique of ontotheology is itself the result of sublimated theological views, for "[t]he key consequence of not believing in God," Gillespie writes, is tantamount, in Sartre's philosophy, to "be[coming a] God for oneself;" it is assuming the power, in the aftermath of God's disappearance, to create moral laws in much the same way that a sovereign political leader creates new laws during a state of emergency (Gillespie 2013, p. 82).

3. Agamben's Critique of Ontotheology

To understand Agamben's critique of ontotheology, I turn to his 1991 publication *Language and Death: The Place of Negativity*, where he develops a theory of language that profoundly informs his political analyses in the decades to come. It is also here that Agamben begins building a critique of sovereign decisionism that, in the following sections, will help me draw out the violent political consequences of Sartre's philosophy. Agamben traces the key existential concept of *nothingness* back to the scholarship of ancient Greek grammarians, who significantly informed the theological perspectives of St. Thomas Aquinas, St. John of Damascus, and Alain de Lille, in Agamben's view. Noting the influence of the grammarians on medieval theology, Agamben proposes a linguistic understanding of God's nature, writing that:

> *The link between grammar and theology is so strong in medieval thought that the treatment of the problem of the Supreme Being cannot be understood without reference to grammatical categories. In this sense, despite the occasional polemics of theologians opposed to the application of grammatical methods to sacred scripture* (Donatum non sequimur), *theological thought is also grammatical thought, and the God of the theologians is also the God of the grammarians.* (Agamben 1991, p. 27)

The origin of grammar, according to Agamben, was attributed by the ancient grammarians to Plato and Aristotle, who believed that language was inseparable from the categories of being. "A decisive event in this context came," he writes, "with the connection of the pronoun to the sphere of the first substance (*prote ousia*), made by Apollonius Disculus, an Alexandrian grammarian from the second century A.D." (Agamben 1991, p. 20). The connection took on an even greater currency with grammarians in the second half of the fifth century who identified the pronoun with "pure being in itself, before and beyond any qualitative determination" (Agamben 1991, p. 20). The basic idea was that pronouns remained indeterminate until entering discourse, where they could be attributed to a particular identity, or determinate meaning, in context.

This "privileged status of the pronoun" would reemerge in modern linguistic theories by Roman Jakobson and Émile Benveniste, who described the pronoun as an empty signifier that pointed to the very event of language itself, which is to say, the mere fact of existence before any determinate meaning is given to it (Agamben 1991, p. 20). Pronouns "become 'full' as soon as the speaker assumes them in an instance of discourse. Their scope," Agamben writes, "is to enact 'the conversion of language into discourse' and to permit the passage from *langue* to *parole*" (Agamben 1991, p. 24). According to Agamben, the grammatical distinction between entities and the mere fact of existence, between signification and language as an abstract system of potential meanings also plays a role in the history of Christian thought. It is here that the ontological category of nothingness takes on ontotheological significance.

To better understand the theological underpinnings of Sartre's theory, I shift the focus to ancient Hebrew and medieval Christian theologians who saw the divine nature, according to Agamben, as a kind of *nothingness*, an originary potential that passes into actuality through divisive, signifying acts of creation. As Agamben explains, the capacity to create *ex nihilo* cuts to the heart of the divine nature which, as the "*negative foundation of human discourse*," is paradoxically natureless—a realm prior to signification and the representational divisions that bring intelligibility to our world (Agamben 1991, p. 30). Agamben traces this belief back to the secret and unspeakable name of God, the Tetragrammaton, which St. Thomas Aquinas, St. John of Damascus, and Alain de Lille all identified with God's pre-linguistic nature, the originary potential from which all determinate entities would finally emerge. "[A]t *this extreme fringe of ontological thought*," Agamben writes, "*where the taking-place of being is grasped as shadow, Christian theological reflection incorporates Hebrew mystical notions of the* nomen tetragrammaton, *the secret and unpronounceable name of God*" (Agamben 1991, p. 30). On this basis, the ancient Hebrews would conclude that God was "*no longer an experience of language but language itself, that is, its taking place in the removal of the voice*" (Agamben 1991, p. 30).

In other words, God, or "the taking place of language", as Agamben refers to him, "appears thus as the negative ground on which all ontology rests, the originary negativity sustaining every negation. For this reason, the disclosure of the dimension of being is always already threatened by nullity," which is to say, in other words, that nothingness, or the unbound potential at the heart of existence, lies within and thus renders contingent every ontic reality, or positive instance of being (Agamben 1991, p. 36). As Agamben writes in *Potentialities*, "To be potential means: to be one's own lack, *to be in relation to one's own incapacity*. Beings that exist in the mode of potentiality *are capable of their own impotentiality*; and only in this way do they become potential. They *can be* because they are in relation to their own non-Being" (Agamben 1999, p. 182). God, then, for these theologians and religious believers, was not an essence, as Sartre imagined him, but the nothingness that precedes our ontological becoming.

One can certainly see, then, striking parallels in how Sartre and Agamben formulate their conceptions of freedom, which is to say, the negative ground of ontology that both refer to as nothingness. This nothingness is ontologically prior to essence and therefore holds the capacity, as an indeterminate consciousness, to construct the world *ex nihilo* through the power of decision, just as the Judeo-Christian God is believed to have created the cosmos *out of nothing*, and just as the sovereign leader of the state is thought by Agamben to dictate the boundaries of legal behavior during a state of emergency. Articulating these parallels more explicitly, we have the for-itself and what Agamben calls a divine potentiality under the heading of *existence*, whereas, under the heading of *essence*, we have what Sartre calls the in-itself and what Agamben calls the actualization of ontological entities. Existence precedes essence as a potentiality that precedes actuality. The parallels between their theories bear a striking resemblance.

The crux of their disagreement, on which my own argument depends, concerns what both philosophers describe as a sublimated desire to become God. As we have already seen, Sartre argues that the for-itself strives to become a fixed entity in order to mimic the self-identical nature of God. As a result, the for-itself is concealed within the in-itself, and the free subject goes on to behave, in bad faith, as if he lacked the freedom to act in violation of the purportedly fixed boundaries of his ontic vocation. In a direct reversal of this order, Agamben casts the divine nature as a pure potentiality, not as a fixed ontological essence. So, humanity's desire to become God does not result in the vanishing of the for-itself for Agamben, but by contrast in the reformulation of the in-itself, which takes on a drastically different mold. For, in Agamben's depiction of ontotheology, the in-itself is made contingent upon the for-itself, which dictates the boundaries of a mutable but no less authoritative ontic reality through the power of self-originating choice. Thus, "pure potentiality and pure actuality are [made] indistinguishable" from each other, Agamben writes, giving way to a "zone of indistinction" that founds the sovereign subject in addition to the sovereign authority of the state (Agamben 2017, p. 42).

This is why free choice, for Agamben, like the divine nothingness at the heart of language, "is that through which Being founds itself *sovereignly*, which is to say, without anything preceding or determining it (*superiorem non recognoscens*) other than its own ability not to be" (Agamben 2017, p. 42). Self-origination is thus the highest expression of ontotheology for Agamben, who argues that sovereign leadership operates under this metaphysical paradigm during a state of emergency to justify its violation of constitutional law. Executive powers and legislative powers—actuality and potentiality—combine as a single force in this "zone of indistinction" to police the laws that it alone has the ability to create. Thus, while Aegistheus performs his identity as one exercising the executive powers of a king, Orestes exercises the sovereign control of a divinity as one fully equipped with both executive and legislative capabilities. From Agamben's perspective, then, it is Orestes, rather than Aegistheus, who models a sublimated desire to be like God. Agamben's take on secularized theism can be more widely applied to Sartre's philosophy as a whole, as I will demonstrate in the following section. Of particular importance to this analysis is the role that language plays in Agamben's study, for human decision-making activates the transition from *langue* to *parole*, from potential meaning to articulated meaning, and gives birth to juridical divisions that dehumanize the non-citizen members of society in accordance with the sovereign structures of signification.

4. Sovereign Decisionism and the Death of God

Sartre famously states that "man is condemned to be free" (Sartre 2007, p. 29). As we have already seen, he believes that people lack an immutable human nature that would otherwise condition their actions, but there is another element to this claim that seems to go unnoticed—namely, Sartre's insistence that choice must by necessity take place, that potentiality *must* pass into actuality through its constant activation of the will. "[W]hat is impossible is not to choose," Sartre writes; "I can always choose, but I must also realize that, if I decide not to choose, that still constitutes a choice" (Sartre 2007, p. 44). As he states elsewhere: "No limits to my freedom can be found except [for] freedom itself, ... to be is to choose oneself; nothing comes to it either from the outside or from within ... it is entirely abandoned to the intolerable necessity of making itself be" (Sartre 1953, pp. 567–68). Sartre's formulation is peculiar in that it rules out the possibility of indecision, or *non-being*, the defining aspect of potentiality for Agamben, who writes that the "potential to be or to do something is always also [the] potential not to be or not to do" something; otherwise "potentiality would always already have passed into actuality and would be indistinguishable from it" (Agamben 1999, p. 245). But potentiality is precisely that which exists prior to choice and, for that reason, it always contains its opposites, or the potential to choose differently. In fact, it is only after a decision takes place—eliminating, as a natural consequence, all other possible choices—that potentiality passes into actuality and assumes the form of an ontological entity. Before that moment takes place, however, potentiality as such remains undecidable, caught between the potential to be and the potential not to be. This, as we have already seen, marks the presence of *langue* before its conversion into *parole*, the sheer fact of existence before its differential signification as an ontic reality.

Therefore, what Sartre describes as the necessary passing of potentiality into actuality directly mirrors what Agamben identifies as the zone of indistinction in his critique of ontotheology. The desire to be God, you will no doubt remember, does not result in the vanishing of *langue*, or the for-itself, for Agamben, but rather in the transformation of the in-itself from an unchanging essence into a mutable ontic substance. Actuality—which we could extend, in this context, to include the laws of nature and, by that same right, the normative laws of the state—is rendered contingent upon self-originating choice in the zone of indistinction during a state of emergency. As Agamben explains it, a sovereign political leader will suspend normal constitutional procedures—which are based on the *fixed* laws that protect its citizens' *essential* human rights—if the nation faces a hardship or unique international threat. President Barack Obama's use of the "War on Terror" to legitimize the assassination of U.S. citizens suspected of terrorism is a recent, more shocking example of this in the modern democratic West. Since the United States government was facing a "unique" threat to national security, its Commander in Chief granted himself the freedom to act outside of constitutional laws that otherwise protect the rights of American citizens. In doing so, he assumed both executive and legislative responsibilities, enforcing new laws that he alone has the ability to create. In this zone of indistinction, *langue* becomes identical with *parole*, because *parole*, as the taking place of differential signification, summons *langue* into being. At the same time, however, *parole* always implies its opposites, or the potential to choose differently, so every ontic expression of *parole* in the zone of indistinction is inherently unstable. Thus, the necessary passing of potentiality into actuality during a state of emergency ensures that every decision the sovereign makes automatically turns into law. "That the sovereign is a living law can only mean that he is not bound by" any previous laws, Agamben writes, "that in him the life of the law coincides with a total anomie," or lawlessness, the freedom to create, at will, the legal path of his choosing. For there is no transcendental law to which the sovereign is bound; there is only the nothingness of *langue*—which is to say, the living law of the sovereign exception—that, in the zone of indistinction, takes on the metaphysical authority of *parole*, or ontological essence (Agamben 2017, p. 225).

The state of emergency therefore results for Agamben in much the same way that God's death results for Sartre: in the suspension of laws authorized by humanity's essential, *God-given* rights, for with God's "disappearance," Sartre writes, "goes the possibility of finding values in an intelligible heaven. There could no longer be any *a priori* good, since there would be no infinite and perfect consciousness to conceive of it" (Sartre 2007, p. 28). As in Plato's famous account of Euthyphro's dilemma, the question is raised by Sartre as to whether moral laws are independent of God (as they are thought to be in modern democratic societies that base their constitutional laws on essential human rights) or determined to be morally valuable by the fact of God's choosing them (just as the "divinely authorized" laws of the *ancien regime* were thought to be handed down to the French monarchy from above). Sartre concludes, contrary to Euthyphro, that morality is legitimizable only in relation to God, such that God's death must result in the de-authorization of morality as such. But Sartre's logic takes an unexpected turn at this juncture, and he appears to adopt a contradictory stance. Sovereign free choice, he argues, ratifies its own goodness, such that the object of choice *becomes* valuable by there mere fact of its being chosen. "Choosing to be this or that is to affirm at the same time the value of what we choose," he writes, "because we can never choose evil. We always choose the good" (Sartre 2007, p. 24). Just as moral laws are thought by Sartre to derive their authority from the deity who chooses them, the good, in Sartre's account, derives its authority from the freely made choices of the sovereign subject. So, while ethical decisions lack final authorization in a world without God, they are also at the same time inherently good in Sartre's view, despite his claim to the contrary. "[I]f I have eliminated God the

Father, there has to be someone to invent values," he writes, but in replacing God with the sovereign subject, Sartre secularizes a theological idea, "moving" divine authority, as Agamben had charged, "from one place to another" (Sartre 2007, p. 51; Agamben 2007, p. 77). Sartre's stage adaptation of the Electra myth suggests this reading, for Orestes does not profane the gods but becomes their equal—an act that models, for Sartre, the core idea of existential authenticity: sovereign power begins with self-originating choice.

Sartre draws our attention to the subject's *lawmaking* capacity and, with it, the universalizing tendencies of differential signification. Every person, he writes, is a "legislator" whose decisions standardize what it means to be human (Sartre 2007, p. 25). Sartre asserts that individuals should preserve their authenticity by rejecting the definitional categories imposed on them by other people, but then he claims—in almost the same breath, in fact—that every individual is responsible for defining human nature and projecting that definition onto the rest of mankind. The first task of existentialism, he writes, "is to make every man ... solely responsible for his own existence" (Sartre 2007, p. 23). Immediately after, though, he appears to contradict himself: "when we say that man is responsible for himself, we do not mean that he is responsible only for his own individuality, but that he is responsible for all men. . . . In choosing myself," Sartre writes, "I choose [all of] man[kind]" (Sartre 2007, pp. 23–25). This paradoxical change of heart would be inexplicable if not for the unconscious assumption in Sartre's philosophy that non-being is always in the process of actualizing through choice. For in this process, the for-itself is made indistinguishable from the in-itself, such that free decision, as a signifying apparatus, takes on the metaphysical authority of universal truth, despite its fundamental instability and capacity for change. The sovereign subject creates human nature *ex nihilo* by speaking it into being, just like the divine nothingness in Agamben's critique of ontotheology, so the desire to be God does not result in a loss of freedom, as Sartre had argued, but, by contrast, in the absolute freedom to dictate, *at will*, the ontic nature of human identity. It would appear then that Sartre's critique of ontotheology is itself ontotheological in Agamben's view, for, in the wake of God's death, and against Sartre's better judgment, the for-itself, as the *living law*, would seem to take on the metaphysical authority of the divine.

5. Sovereign Choice as Political Violence

Like Sartre, Agamben recognizes the representational nature of sovereign decision, which marries *langue* to *parole*, and potentiality to actuality through divisive significations of human identity. The problem for Agamben, which Sartre fails to address, is that representational acts of this kind humanize those under the ban of normativity at the same time that they animalize the culturally aberrant in the form of a political sacrifice, for *"that which is excluded from the community,"* Agamben writes, *"is, in reality, that on which the entire life of the community is founded"* (Agamben 1991, p. 105). Every sovereign decision, as a signifying act, divides the human from the non-human because language, in its articulation as *parole*, operates according to a differential logic. Thus, there will always be members of society who are not granted the rights of a citizen because they lack human identity in the eyes of the state, just as the *muselmann* lacked a human identity in Nazi Germany, and just as the African slave lacked a human identity in the antebellum South. The more a person deviates from sovereign determinations of the *imago Dei*, the less valuable and, indeed, the less human that person becomes. Agamben identifies this individual with the *homo sacer*, an ancient figure of Roman law who, by virtue of the sovereign decision, was stripped of his citizenship and deprived of legal protection, animalized and forced outside of the law, where he was subject to be killed with impunity.

Agamben directs our attention here to the problematical nature of law and, with it, the problematical nature of justice, traditionally conceived. For it is only by concretizing human identity in the zone of indistinction, and thereby attributing to all people an identical set of inherent rights, that one may standardize what it means to be treated equally and, by these means, administer a system of legal, compensatory justice. Our analysis has shown, however, that no choice can be made, or system of justice administered, without bastardizing alternate accounts of human rights and morally just behavior. As Agamben's interlocutor Jacques Derrida observes, "[n]o justice is exercised, no justice is rendered, no justice becomes effective nor does it determine itself in the form of law, without a decision that cuts and divides" the human from the non-human, the lawfully protected citizen from the condemned outlaw (Derrida 2002, p. 252). Since there is no God in Sartre's world to conceive of human nature, and, consequently, no essential human rights upon which to ground constitutional laws, self-originating choice can only ever be just, in Sartre's eyes. This is why "politics would seem to be an almost religious ritual of sorts, a continuous reenacting of the exclusive inclusion performed upon the self in order to constitute some sense of sovereign being in relation to," what Dickinson calls, the sacrificial other (Dickinson 2011, p. 72). In Sartre's profane universe, the sovereign can do no evil, which is why his every bloody action is already justified under the law.

6. Orestes and the State of Emergency

Returning by way of conclusion to *The Flies*, let us recall the state of emergency with which the play begins: King Agamemnon, the ruler of Argos, is betrayed by Queen Clytemnestra and murdered by her lover Aegistheus, who usurps the throne. Similar to the sovereign leader of the *ancien regime*, Aegistheus is divinely authorized by God; so, when Orestes returns to avenge his father, he challenges the authority of both a king and a deity. Zeus says to Orestes: "in the fullness of time a man was to come, to announce my decline. And you're that man" (Sartre 1989, pp. 119–20). Much like the suspension of normative laws in a state of emergency, the death of God transfers authority, as Agamben will charge, "from one place to another." Thus, unlike Aegistheus, who executes the divine laws handed down to him from above, Orestes assumes both executive and legislative responsibilities. He acts "[o]utside [of] nature," Sartre writes, and is "doomed to have no other law" but his own (Sartre 1989, p. 119). This is why, as the true king of Argos and sovereign leader of the state, Orestes does not feel remorse after committing murder. "I am no criminal," he says to Zeus, "and you have no power to make me atone for an act I don't regard as a crime" (Sartre 1989, p. 113).

However, the reason that Zeus lacks moral authority over Orestes is not because Orestes stops believing in the gods. On the contrary, it is because Orestes, as a truly authentic individual, believes himself to be their equal. "Your whole universe is not enough to prove me wrong," he says to Zeus; "You are the king of gods, king of stones and stars, king of the waves of the sea. But you are not the king of man. . . . you blundered; you should not have made me free" (Sartre 1989, p. 117). Orestes lacks remorse because, like the gods, he determines his own morality. He therefore models what Agamben calls a secularized theological belief, for, in proclaiming himself to be commensurate with the gods, Orestes seeks to deify the rest of humanity. As Sartre writes: "a man . . . who realizes that he is not only the individual that he chooses to be, but also a legislator choosing at the same time what humanity as a whole should be, cannot help but be aware of his own full and profound responsibility" (Sartre 2007, p. 25). Leaving the city of Argos, Orestes abandons his people in a veritable war zone, where every individual, newly awakened to his freedom, must bid for sovereignty over the rest of mankind as a god unto himself (Sartre 1989, p. 123). Orestes grows indifferent to the gods because, like them, he possesses the divine capacity for sovereign, self-originating choice. But "[t]here is no God," in Sartre's view, and, likewise, "no moral values, but, even if God existed," as he clearly does for Orestes, "nothing would change," for Sartre's "key doctrine [is] man's radical freedom," Gillespie writes, and this is the one true source of metaphysical authority for Sartre (Gillespie 2013, p. 82). The sovereign subject, similar to God, creates human nature *ex nihilo*; he is the living law in Sartre's universe and the primary target of Agamben's ontotheological critique.

But one need not accept the particularities of this argument wholesale to discover the value of reading Sartre in light of Agamben, whose critique of the grammarian God illuminates the violent political consequences of existential authenticity. After all, Sartre advances his own critique of unconscious theism, which he bases on the in-itself-for-itself of the orthodox Augustinian tradition, so if Sartre were, in fact, repressing any unconscious theological views of his own, they would most likely show themselves, as multiple Sartre scholars have already noted, in the form of humanity's fixed ontological essence. What readers *should* take away from the article is the extent to which Agamben's ontotheological critique mediates the philosophical inconsistencies of Sartre's thought. For Orestes appears to deify himself at the same time that he profanes divine authority, just as Sartre declares the end of morality while defending the metaphysical value of sovereign, self-originating choice. These philosophical inconsistencies are unexplainable outside of what Agamben calls the zone of indistinction, where ontic reality is made contingent upon choice, and legislation is made contingent upon its execution by the metaphysical presupposition that potentiality is always in the process of actualizing. Agamben's critique of ontotheology would appear to illuminate otherwise murky paths in Sartre's philosophical universe, whether by sheer coincidence or by virtue of an unacknowledged theological element in Sartre's work—what he refers to, ironically, as the "little God which inhabits" him and "possesses [his] freedom as a metaphysical virtue" (Sartre 1953, p. 81). Beyond this, I hope that readers appreciate the rich parallels I have drawn between two thinkers who, before now, have not been compared in an official capacity, for there is no doubt much more to be learned from an extended comparison of Sartre and Agamben.

Conflicts of Interest: The author declares no conflict of interest.

References

Agamben, Giorgio. 1991. *Language and Death: The Place of Negativity*. Translated by Karen. E. Pinkus, and Michael Hardt. Minneapolis: University of Minnesota Press.

Agamben, Giorgio. 1999. *Potentialities: Collected Essays in Philosophy*. Edited by Daniel Heller-Roazen. Palo Alto: Stanford University Press.

Agamben, Giorgio. 2007. *Profanations*. Translated by Jeff Fort. New York: Zone Books.

Agamben, Giorgio. 2017. *The Omnibus Homo Sacer*. Palo Alto: Stanford University Press.

Derrida, Jacques. 2002. *Acts of Religion*. Edited by Gil Anidjar. Abingdon: Routledge.

Dickinson, Colby. 2011. *Agamben and Theology*. London: T&T Clark.

Dickinson, Colby, and Adam Kotsko. 2015. *Agamben's Coming Philosophy: Finding a New Use for Theology*. London: Rowman & Littlefield International.

Gellman, Jerome. 2009. Jean Paul Sartre: The Mystical Atheist. *European Journal for Philosophy of Religion* 1: 127–37. [CrossRef]

Gillespie, John. 2005. Les Mots: Sartre and the Language of Belief. *Sartre Studies International* 11: 234–48. [CrossRef]

Gillespie, John H. 2013. Sartre and God: A Spiritual Odyssey? Part 1. *Sartre Studies International* 19: 71. [CrossRef]

Gillespie, John H. 2014. Sartre and God: A Spiritual Odyssey? Part 2. *Sartre StudiesInternational* 20: 45–56. [CrossRef]

Howells, Christina. 1981. Sartre and Negative Theology. *Modern Language Review* 76: 549–55. [CrossRef]

Khawaja, Noreen. 2016. *The Religion of Existence: Asceticism in Philosophy from Kierkegaard to Sartre*. Chicago: University of Chicago Press.

Kirkpatrick, Kate. 2017a. *Sartre and Theology*. London: T&T Clark.

Kirkpatrick, Kate. 2017b. *Sartre on Sin: Between Being and Nothingness*. Oxford: Oxford University Press.

Sartre, Jean-Paul. 1953. *Being and Nothingness*. Translated by Hazel E. Barnes. Unknown place: Washington Square Press, Inc.

Sartre, Jean-Paul. 1989. *No Exit and Three Other Plays*. New York: Vintage Books.

Sartre, Jean-Paul. 2007. *Existentialism is a Humanism*. Edited by John Kulka. Translated by Carol Macomber. New Haven: Yale University Press.

van den Hoven, Adrian. 2010. Sartre and Atheism: An Introduction to the Round-Table Discussion of Ronald Aronson's Living without God. *Sartre Studies International* 16: 75–84. [CrossRef]

![religions logo] *religions*

MDPI

Article

Adam Smith, the Impartial Spectator and Embodiment: Towards an Economics of Accountability and Dialogue

Mark Rathbone

Faculty of Economic and Management Sciences, North-West University, Potchefstroom 2531, South Africa;
Mark.Rathbone@nwu.ac.za

Received: 29 March 2018; Accepted: 4 April 2018; Published: 8 April 2018

Abstract: This article argues that Adam Smith's notion of sympathy and the impartial spectator in his work *The Theory of Moral Sentiments* [1759] connects the individual to society. In this work, Smith's economics are far more complex than mere self-interest as a driver of commerce. Self-interest functions within a socio-ethical framework that limits excess and narcissism. However, morality was not based on normative assumptions for Smith and Hume. Morality was directly linked to social and cognitive processes in which the approbation of others was important. In other words, behaviour was based on the perceptions of others; therefore, action was to be adjusted to obtain sympathy. The impartial spectator refers to the cognitive process in which moral assessments are made. Therefore, the empiricism of Smith differs from determinism as related to physical causation because it operates through habituation and/or socialisation that can accommodate change and variation. Clearly, the socio-cultural presupposition of society directly influences the moral judgment of the individual. However, this deterministic tendency may result in an uncritical assessment of moral behaviour. To address this potential limitation of determinism, the embodied phenomenology of Merleau-Ponty is explored as an alternative theory which attempts to move beyond a dualism rooted in materialism/idealism. This perspective may expand on Smith's economics by adding a more inclusive assessment of behaviour. Specifically, Merleau-Ponty's corporeality provides a theory of behaviour that goes beyond a particular society's perceptions of acceptable behaviour. This framework may provide the impartial spectator with a more encompassing perspective on moral assessment that may also be beneficial for sustainable commerce. It will be proposed that Merleau-Ponty's embodied phenomenology and the hyper-dialectic of the flesh highlights the role of accountability and dialogue in moral assessment that may contribute to responsible economics in the South African context.

Keywords: Adam Smith; Merleau-Ponty; sympathy; impartial spectator; determinism; embodiment; accountability; dialogue

1. Introduction

The economic philosophy of Adam Smith is usually associated with his work *An inquiry into the Nature and Causes of the Wealth of Nations* (WN) (Smith [1776] 1950). However, his earlier work, *The Theory of Moral Sentiments* (TMS) (Smith [1759] 2004), is equally important because it explains how self-interest is embedded in a socio-ethical framework in which sympathy plays a crucial role (Wells 2014, pp. 90–91; Gonin 2015, pp. 221–22). Sympathy refers to the mode of moral development in which the impartial spectator is a mental construction which serves as a means of assessing events and behaviour. Hühn (2017) notes that Smith's contribution to social science was his linking of the individual with society through the impartial spectator. Smith [1759] (2004, p. 100) highlights this connectivity between individual and society in TMS by stating that "human society stand in need of each other's assistance, and are likewise exposed to mutual injuries".

This paper argues that Adam Smith's notion of sympathy and the impartial spectator in TMS connects the individual to society. In this work, Smith's economics are far more complex than mere self-interest as a driver of commerce. Self-interest functions within a socio-ethical framework that limits excess and narcissism. However, morality was not based on normative assumptions for Smith and Hume. Morality was directly linked to social and cognitive processes in which the approbation of others was important. Behaviour is based on the perceptions of others; therefore, action is to be adjusted to obtain sympathy. Therefore, the empiricism of Smith differs from the determinism of physical causation because it operates through habituation and/or socialisation that can accommodate change and variation (Berry 1997). It is clear that the socio-cultural presupposition of society directly influences the moral judgment of the individual.

Unfortunately, this deterministic tendency may result in an uncritical assessment of correct moral behaviour. To address this potential limitation of determinism, the embodied phenomenology of Merleau-Ponty is explored as an alternative that attempts to move beyond a dualism rooted in materialism/idealism. In this article, embodiment is understood from the perspective of phenomenology and intentionality. In this regard, embodiment incorporates a physical form that embraces the role it plays in the creation of meaning. As such, the reception of sensory information is not limited to mental or cognitive constructions in which the subject becomes a third person observer. The physicality of the perceiving subject is not bracketed or of no consequence to the construction of meaning. The pre-reflective subject is part of meaning creation and connected to reality. This perspective may expand on the economics of Smith by adding a more inclusive assessment of behaviour rooted in Merleau-Ponty's corporeality which goes beyond a particular society's perceptions of acceptable behaviour. This may provide the impartial spectator with a more encompassing perspective on moral assessment that may also be beneficial for sustainable commerce. Accordingly, the impartial spectator is not a cognitive or imaginative construction that assesses a situation based on the assumptions of a homogeneous group or society; rather, the embodied subject is part of a corporeality that is heterogeneous and diverse. It will be proposed that Merleau-Ponty's embodied phenomenology and the hyper-dialectic of the flesh highlights the role of accountability and dialogue in moral assessment that may contribute to responsible economics in the South African context.

In this article, I will firstly argue that Smith's understanding of self-interest is more nuanced than how it has been popularly viewed in contemporary literature. I will also argue that self-interest is contained by the notion of sympathy. However, the social determinism involved in the assessment of the impartial spectator requires further exploration to avoid moral judgement based on the singular perceptions of a particular society. Secondly, it will be proposed that Merleau-Ponty's embodied view of the subject and corporeality may address the limitations of determinism. Embodiment has the potential to deal with problems associated with determinism without falling prey to idealism. Thirdly, the implication of accountability and dialogue for responsible business decisions and actions of individuals will be discussed with particular reference to the South African context.

2. Adam Smith, Sympathy and the Impartial Spectator

It is commonly argued that the notion of self-interest in WN (Smith [1776] 1950, p. 16) is the driving force of economics. Stigler (1971, p. 265) refers to WN as " ... a stupendous palace erected upon the granite of self-interest" that guides "resources to their most efficient uses, stimulates laborers to diligence and investors to splendid new divisions of labor—in short it orders and enriches the nation which gives it free rein". Recent research has highlighted that Smith presents a far more nuanced view of self-interest in WN (Sen 1999; Wells 2014; Paganelli 2008; Gonin 2015; Rathbone 2015). Werhane (1989, p. 670) notes that Smith's self-interest cannot be associated with selfishness or greed; that "self-interest is both driven and restrained by the desire for approval" and therefore "economic self-interest makes sense only in the atmosphere of mutual cooperation" (Werhane 1989, p. 670).

However, Smith's work has often been misused to justify selfishness: "It is not from the benevolence of the butcher, the brewer or the baker, that we expect our dinner, but from their regard to their own self-interest. We address ourselves, not to their humanity but to their self-love, and never talk to them of our own necessities but of their advantages" (Smith [1776] 1950, p. 16). Nowhere in the above-mentioned quote does Smith condone selfishness. Instead, he argues that, in a society of free people, we do not "address" ourselves to the "humanity" of others to make a living. A person does not rely on the charity of others; rather, an individual works in a co-operative manner by providing goods and/or services another requires to satisfy his/her "self-love". Heath (2013, p. 241) notes that self-interest is not a motive for economic activity; rather, it is an orientation regarding human interaction. It is a positive ethic of freedom, self-realization, and production.

Smith's contemporaries such as Jean-Jacques Rousseau and others noted that the growth of commerce would undermine natural benevolence (Folbre 2009, p. 85). It is often misunderstood that Smith was against benevolence. For Smith, benevolence was not a mature economic expectation. This should not suggest that Smith supported a notion of egoistic economics. Werhane (1989, p. 674) highlights that, for Smith, greed "prevents good economic performance". However, recent research on TMS has gone a step further and has highlighted how sympathy and the impartial spectator play a crucial role in connecting the individual and society (Paganelli 2008, 2010; Gonin 2015; Hühn 2017). The natural impulse of self-interest is embedded in a system with important moral, ethical, and societal dimensions.

The opening chapter of TMS clearly highlights that sympathy is a natural instinct: "How selfish so ever man may be supposed, there are evidently some principles in his nature, which interest him in the fortunes of others, and render their happiness necessary to him, though he derives nothing from it … " (Smith [1759] 2004, p. 3). Smith refers to this instinct as "fellow-feeling" that is evident in the "sympathy" which may arise when the pain and suffering of others is witnessed (Smith [1759] 2004, p. 13). For Smith, sympathy does not refer to pity, compassion, or empathy; instead, Smith uses it as a technical term, referring to the cognitive and psychological processes which connect people. Although Smith generally believed that most people possess this natural ability (except for some people with possible anti-social disorders), he did not believe that the mere sight of the passions of others leads to action.

Smith [1759] (2004, p. 15) argued that action is always a matter of context. For example, the suffering of a criminal may not necessary lead to acts of kindness. Any act of kindness is a matter of prudence and propriety as perceived by others based on contextual variables. Not all acts of kindness may gain the sympathy of others and not all situations that require philanthropy may lead to action. Therefore, only action which is considered both acceptable and that may gain the sympathy of others is deemed appropriate and lead to the joy of mutual sympathy (Smith [1759] 2004, p. 17). According to Smith, mutual sympathy is one of the motivational aspects of morality, leading to harmonious societal relations (Smith [1759] 2004, p. 17).

To arrive at a state of mutual sympathy, people instinctively develop the cognitive mechanism to assess behaviour and events. Smith refers to this cognitive mechanism as the impartial spectator (Smith [1759] 2004, p. 28). The function of the impartial spectator is to assess a situation based on the potential acquired sympathy of others. To do this, the subject imagines him/herself as a spectator to an event in which his/her action may be assessed by others. This imaginative construction is based on previous events which serve as an analogical construction. According to Smith, the subject accordingly avoids being swayed by personal or impulsive presuppositions and/or passions. Events are judged in an "impartial light" (Smith [1759] 2004, pp. 27–28). Action is therefore based on the degree of approbation that may be received from others. Accordingly, moral development is the ability of the subject to act in accordance with the assessment of the impartial spectator that may enhance prudence and propriety. The irony of this subject's impartial perspective is that societal perception dictates what is acceptable or not.

In context of business, sympathy is crucial to avoid excessive self-interest and maintain societal harmony (Smith [1759] 2004, p. 24). Moral behaviour is directly linked to the socio-cultural system that condones behaviour, resulting in the joy of "fellow-feeling" or mutual sympathy. Smith [1759] (2004, p. 29) acknowledges that " . . . virtues of self-denial, of self-government, of that command of the passions which subjects all the movements of our nature to what our own dignity and honour, and the propriety of our own conduct require, take their origin from the other". For Smith, self-interest and virtue are inseparably linked to the wellbeing of society, "The wise and virtuous man (*sic*) is at all times willing that his own private interest should be sacrificed to the public interest or his own particular order of society" (Smith [1759] 2004, p. 346). Clearly, the accusation that Smith's reference to self-interest is a precursor to *homo economicus* is misguided. Sen (1999, p. 23) notes that these integral moral dynamics related to economics "tended to be lost in the writings of many economists championing the so-called 'Smithian' positions on self-interest and its achievements".

However, the limitation of Smith's view of sympathy and the impartial spectator is linked to the empiricist roots of his work. The determinism that is embedded in his view of moral development and his later economics has a negative impact in that the partiality of a particular society dictates moral assessment and behaviour. Although Smith steers clear of idealism, our globalized world requires a more encompassing and inclusive view of moral assessment. For example, showing kindness to a suffering criminal may not result in sympathy from other people. This assessment of the impartial spectator may be the result of an analogical reconstruction based on similar situations, for example, one in which kind action towards someone judged deserving of suffering resulted in rejection by others. However, the question remains as to what social presuppositions is the judgement of society based? That someone is viewed as a criminal may support specific social biases and perceptions. For example, framing a person as a criminal may be justified in some societies; however, in other societies, a criminal could be reframed as a freedom fighter. This ties into a broader question to the extent the impartial spectator is equipped to deal with competing and even conflicting moral dilemmas.

A possible solution from Smith's perspective may be found in the role that strangers play in moral development. Smith notes that contact with strangers results in restraint and control of passions because the subject knows that the stranger does not have knowledge of his/her circumstances, "We expect still less sympathy from an assembly of strangers, and we assume, therefore, still more tranquillity before them, and always endeavour to bring down our passion to that pitch, which the particular company we are in may expect to go along with" (Smith [1759] 2004, p. 28). The unfamiliarity of strangers and their view of the subject leads to a cautious evaluation at the moment of contact. This concern may result in action that avoids unnecessary offence and/or conflict with strangers. It is important to note that strangers can eventually become acquaintances and even friends with continued contact. However, strangers may remain outsiders in a society and consequently are not able to influence the dominant presuppositions of that society. A potential consequence of this is behaviour which fosters the oppression of strangers, given the slow process of social change. Therefore, the deterministic basis of the impartial spectator is not able to provide a sufficient critical perspective on moral assessment.

The limitations of determinism are made manifest in the discussion of the gender stereotyping of women in TMS. Smith [1759] (2004, p. 34) notes that to "talk to a woman as we would to a man is improper: it is expected that their company should inspire us with more gaiety, more pleasantry, and more attention; and an entire insensibility to their fair sex, renders a man contemptible in some measure even to the men". Although the impartial spectator would propose an adjustment of tone of man's voice in the presence of a woman based on the fact that she is "fair", this assessment is based on culturally determined gender stereotyping.

The limits of determinism may have inadvertently contributed to the emergence of an economic system and culture infused with rationalism, greed, and exploitation known as *homo economicus or* the money-making animal (Ingram 1915). Although the term was developed in John Stuart Mill's works entitled *Essays on Unsettled Questions of Political Economy* (Mill 1844) and later *Principles of Political*

Economy with Some of Their Applications to Social Philosophy (Mill 1848), it is largely attributed to Adam Smith and the WN. Mill (1844) describes *homo economicus* as someone who "desires to possess wealth, and who is capable of judging of the comparative efficacy of means for obtaining that end". The main tenants of *homo economicus* are self-interest and instrumental rationality. Therefore, *homo economicus* refers to a reductionist view of people as economic beings with the ability to make rational decisions in all circumstances based on the self-interest of the individual or group. Although Smith attempted to avoid excess and injustice, the idea of sympathy can be applied using deterministic methodology. A person is reduced to a data-gathering subject who is guided by analogical experiences, without the ability to create meaning through a wider horizon of meaning creation.

Therefore, although Smith cannot be held responsible for *homo economicus*, determinism has limitations in which the impartial spectator cannot critically scrutinize the societal presuppositions that inform assessment of situations. To address this limitation, the next section will explore the embodied phenomenology of Merleau-Ponty which attempts to move beyond the empiricism/idealism dichotomy.

3. Embodiment and the Impartial Spectator

Merleau-Ponty's phenomenology is part of an intellectual tradition that dates to the philosophy of Husserl. Phenomenology attempts to overcome the distinction that Immanuel Kant made between *nouma* (real world) and phenomena (perception of reality). To bridge this separation, the phenomenological reduction or *epoche* is an attempt to bracket questions relating to reality and transcendence (Cobb-Stevens 1994, p. 13). Thus, the focus is on immanence and the subject's creation of meaning by opening oneself to the world, a process that Husserl referred to as intentionality. The subject cannot be reduced to a container which gathers sensory data of the world. Rather, the subject gives meaning to sensory information in a constructive process of meaning creation. Later, Heidegger (a student of Husserl) took the phenomenological project further by exploring the ontological aspect of meaning or *Dasein* (Taminiaux 1994, p. 42). Heidegger's work was a clear existential turn that related meaning to existence and authentic being. Sartre continued this line of thinking but was far more pessimistic as to the possibility of arriving at any meaning in itself (Flynn 1994, pp. 73–104). The work of Merleau-Ponty provides a clear departure from Husserl, Heidegger, Sartre, and others by asserting that the body/mind binary is false and instead proposes an embodied intentionality.

One of the major implications of Merleau-Ponty's phenomenology is that the body, perceived by empiricists and idealists from a third-person perspective, is embedded in the interpretative process. That the body is embedded in the interpretative process is significant because it implies that the mind and its power of perception is an incarnate reality and is situated or contextual (Merleau-Ponty 1964, pp. 1–11). Therefore, the situated subject, consciousness, and intentionality cannot be separated from the perceived environment or other people. Embodied perception also emphasizes that other people are not mere objects but perceiving subjects. The mind is part and parcel of "corporeality" which refers to the ambiguous relationship we have with our body and perceived things (Merleau-Ponty 1964, p. 4). Our bodies are involved in the way we perceive ourselves and the way others perceive us.

The self cannot be viewed from the Cartesian perspective as a personal reflective subject because the self is a pre-reflective embodied subject in the world. This pre-reflective or tacit position in the world is linked to others and is not mere materiality or rationality. Rather, it is a unified perspective in which we all "participate as anonymous subjects of perception" (Merleau-Ponty 1962, p. 369). This participatory relationship with others is the basis of the subject's identity from which individual differences and individuality are established. The participatory perception can suggest that the freedom of the individual may be compromised. However, for Merleau-Ponty (1962, p. 379), although the other is linked to the identity of the individual, the perception of difference (that which distinguishes the subject from others) is a pre-reflective perception, what is known as the violence of perception.

The views of others or circumstances are not determinate. The intentionality of the subject remains in control of perceptions.

Empiricism is a theory of knowledge which attempts to determine the cognitive processes involved in perception. One implication of this theory is that the subject is turned into a third-person gatherer of data (Matthews 2010, p. 22). This empiricist presupposition is clear in the case of the impartial spectator: one which is a function of the cognitive processes involved in assessing appropriate moral behaviour. Empiricism fails to assess the primary perceptions involved with our engagement with the world. Our primary engagement is intentional in the process of the creation of meaning. We do this as embodied subjects who are aware of others and the perception of difference (Matthews 2010, p. 116). The perception of others assists the self to understand its identity but this does not mean we only socially constructed identities.

This is also true of materialism. Merleau-Ponty (1964, p. 12) notes that matter is pregnant with form. Perception is not limited to the mind; rather, it is a pre-conscious activity of the body-subject. That the body-subject is pre-conscious implies that we are born with prescribed perceptions of reality and therefore the subject does not simply react to external stimuli as proposed by behaviourists. On the other hand, the idealist assumption that cognition is an imposition on the material body is also problematic. Rather, the organism is involved in "prospective activity" which is influenced by the complex contextual interrelations that connect the subject, body, and the world (Merleau-Ponty 1964). Material reality does not dictate how we make sense of the world because we make sense of reality based on our embodied perception. This is a complex network of perceptions of both the environment and others, one which has implications for how we view ourselves and our recognition that we are different from others.

The awareness of difference highlights the possibility of other perceptions; because our perception of the world and others is inexhaustible and is not completely accessible to our consciousness and its intentionality, we remain free individuals. This freedom to act does not go beyond the existence of intersubjective relations between people; therefore, freedom goes hand in hand with accountability. The facticity of existence makes it impossible for empiricism to give way to idealism. We cannot be free in our minds with our self-determining consciousness if not also as bodily perceptive beings. For Merleau-Ponty, to escape self-determining consciousness, unlike Sartre's view that the consciousness is undetermined or "nothing", perceptions and freedom is always dependent on a particular situation. We are not determined to be an object in this world; however, there are limits to our freedom which require that we confront a situation and our assessment of it. We choose between various possibilities within a situation. There is no absolute freedom or absolute determinism, no idealistic norms for behaviour or behaviour that will gain approbation by others as envisioned by the impartial spectator. Rather, we are always embodied subjects within a particular situation and historical context provides the motivation for specific action. This is not a historicist reduction because the self remains different from others and the situation and can therefore act with freedom.

Operative intentionality or the "world lived by me" refers to this paradox of facticity and freedom (Merleau-Ponty 1962, vol. xviii). The lived experience of the subject is crucial to understand Merleau-Ponty's phenomenology because it highlights that intentionality can never be reduced to either environmental and/or cognitive processes. Rather, lived experience returns philosophy to the complex interconnection of self/other and mind/body. Therefore, the possibility for the impartial spectator to achieve an accurate assessment of appropriate behaviour first is based on the embodied intentionality of the subject. The first response may not be the desire to conform to social conventions. Rather, the opposite may be true; that is, that any act of meaning creation has an effect on others and the environment. The freedom to act as mentioned assumes accountability because the implication of "operative intentionality" is that the subject is connected to others, "It is precisely my body which perceives the body of another, and discovers in that other body a miraculous prolongation of my own intentions . . . as parts of my body together comprise a system, so my body and the others are one whole, two sides of one and the same phenomenon" (Merleau-Ponty 1962, p. 354).

We perceive the presence of others as perceptive beings with whom we might be able to communicate and therefore create a potential bridge between people. According to Merleau-Ponty, this bridge is language. Language embodies a culture and therefore relates to my being in the world as an embodied intentional being (Matthews 2010, p. 121). Communication is not the means of engagement but rather an intentional embodied experience. It is a shared operation and the reality of coexistence. In this regard, solitude and communication are two moments of the same phenomenon (Merleau-Ponty 1962, p. 359). The implication is that action is not *determined* but *motivated* by our shared world or flesh.

Merleau-Ponty (1968, p. 94) notes that a constant dialectic between the subject and the world takes place, what is known as a "hyper-dialectic of the flesh". This is dialectic without synthesis in which the state of being is not limited to the interior or exterior; rather, being is always in a state of flux at the border between inside and outside. The border is the "body" because it is part of the world and has a sensory capacity to observe the world. Sensory capacity is not based on the supposed disinterested relationship of the subject relative to objects of consciousness. The opposite is true: the body is part of the environment in which the perceiving body exists. The body is both seen and seer or both visible and invisible—*la chair* (flesh in French). Merleau-Ponty (1968, p. 248) states that my " . . . body is made of the same flesh as the world . . . and shared by the world". The implication is that open and inclusive dialogue is one of the characteristics of embodied phenomenology.

To conclude, Merleau-Ponty's embodied intentionality addresses the possible determinism present in the functioning of the impartial spectator. In TMS, Smith highlights the cognitive processes by which an individual assesses behaviour and possible action bases on the functioning of the impartial spectator. The approbation of others informs the behaviour adopted. According to Merleau-Ponty, the focus on studying cognitive processes in moral development results in the objectification of the subject who is relegated to the third person. The embodied perception of the subject is paramount and highlights that the subject is both contextual and relational and also differentiated from the perceived situation and others. Therefore, embodied intentionality assumes that any process of meaning creation assumes accountability. Accountability highlights freedom and presence in the world with others. Secondly, accountability also presupposes the possibility of communication and engagement with others. This form of communication is not unilateral but open and dialogical.

4. Embodied Economics: Accountability and Dialogue

The implications of Merleau-Ponty's embodied phenomenology are clear in terms of its critique of determinism. The role of accountability and dialogue may reveal new perspectives on economics. The subject is intentional and contextually located. On the one hand, the individual is free to pre-reflexively interpret reality based on presuppositions. On the other hand, the subject has facticity which implies that interpretation is also a physical act with a range of possibilities influencing the choices available; it also indicates that the environment and other people are connected to the subject. The presence of others implies that the subject cannot simply act without recognition of others and accountability. Accountability is extended through multi-lateral dialogue. This is specifically relevant to the South African context which has rampant unemployment, poverty, and economic inequality perpetuated by legacy issues related to colonialism and apartheid. Another aspect is that dialogue is crucial to confront the cultural diversity of South Africa by creating the possibility of co-operative meaning creation.

Smith highlights the role of self-interest and sympathy as well as the individual and community. Unfortunately, the implied spectator is not involved in meaning creation and the subject is disembodied. The determinism involved in the calculation of the implied spectator therefore creates the impression that social constraints are paramount. Another problem is that the subject is viewed as neutral and the material and social space become determinants. This is problematic in the South African context where liberal economic principles and African culture need to co-exist (Nussbaum 2009). Nussbaum (2009, p. 239) notes that many African business leaders experience "internal conflicts" because the "dominant capitalist pattern is the exact opposite of the more equitable imperatives and economic justice called for by *Ubuntu*". In Africa, the self is integrated into the community and also is specifically connected to geographical space (Munyaka and Motlhabi 2009, pp. 70–73).

Merleau-Ponty's phenomenology highlights that individuals in commerce are involved in meaning-creating activities. Different people will find different purposes in business, some with a profit motive and others philanthropic. However, embodiment assumes that people are socially connected implying meaning and accountability are linked. Therefore, unethical activities in business are self-destructive. The reality of limited resources which enables the system of supply and demand to function cannot be abused without damaging yourself. Finally, business is more than just mere calculation; it is also dialogue, which recognises interdependence. In this regard, Merleau-Ponty's embodied phenomenology resonates with African moral theory and *Ubuntu* because both focus on shared identity and human dignity (Metz 2009; Mbiti 1969).

4.1. Accountability and the Economy

Accountability derives from the Latin word *accomptare* (to account) and is also related to the word *computare* (to calculate). From its earliest usage, accountability referred to the blameworthiness of the individual. Any decision or action has a corresponding liability. Roberts (1991), with reference to Merleau-Ponty, notes that embodied perception identifies the self in relation to others which may lead to greater accountability in accounting practices. Roberts argues that accountability from a compliance perspective reduces the self to a solitary and singular position which has the possibility of moral failure. Embodied intentionality moves beyond this perspective to highlight inter-subjectivity. In such a view, organisations consist of a collective workforce or interconnected individuals where each person is accountable to co-workers, management, and society. For example, if a company is involved in practices that are unethical, each member of the business is accountable for his or her actions.

This principle of blameworthiness is prominent in contemporary governance practices which require business to comply with certain laws and/or business regulations. Naidoo (2009, p. 3) notes that corporate governance "regulates the existence of power (that is, authority, direction and control) within a company in order to ensure that the company's purpose is achieved ... ". Governance is a means to achieve accountability that incorporates all stakeholders. To achieve this, codes of corporate governance are continually developed to respond to the ever-changing business environment. In South Africa, governance was first institutionalised with the first King Report in 1994. With the release of King IV Report on Corporate Governance for South Africa (2016), it has become a business standard in South Africa. King IV may also be regarded as an extension of *Ubuntu* which endeavours to keep organisations accountable.

As Roberts noted (1991), the problem is that accountability retains a sense of compliance; a company that does not comply would probably not attract the same investment as those that do. This is clear from the results of the McKinsey Investor Opinion Survey (2002) that highlighted that investors value good corporate governance: 85% of investors agreed that there is a link between good governance and financial performance. Additionally, 73% of investors would pay a premium for shares of a company that is well governed. However, this view of compliance is limited to individual responsibility and well-governed companies still find themselves in the midst of corporate scandals and incur staggering financial losses as a result. A good example in the global context is the Nestlé Indonesian Palm oil scandal in which Greenpeace used social media to raise awareness that one of Nestlé's palm oil suppliers was using unsustainable methods that threatened the indigenous orangutan population (Ionescu-Somers and Enders 2012). This widely published case study highlights the failure to consider the environmental impact of the supply chain of a company and the negative publicity it can cause. However, it also highlights the role of inter-subjectivity and accountability of an embodied phenomenology through the Greenpeace media campaign.

Social media has become a fast and effective channel for communication and awareness, i.e., corporeality. Therefore, accountability goes far beyond individuals complying to rules; it suggests that no act of business can be separated from either the society or the environment and that each individual involved in business is accountable for their actions. As this case study highlighted, failure to recognise this transformation of consciousness could be devastating for business and the environment. In the article, *The Business Case for Corporate Social Responsibility: A Review of Concepts, Research and Practices* (Carroll and Shabana 2010), Carroll and Shabana highlight the importance of accountability as a core business value. They support the notion of accountability as inherent to a business's identity based on its presence in the world. The identity of business is based on its relation to society; accordingly, any damage to society also damages business.

Something is clearly missing from contemporary perspectives of governance that result in failures of good governance. Naidoo (2009, p. 4) notes that corporate governance should be a way of life. In other words, corporate governance should not be a matter of compliance. The high occurrence of corporate scandals is probably related a move beyond individual responsibility. Singularity is required for intra- and inter-subjectivity within business and beyond or, as Merleau-Ponty's highlights, a hyper-dialectic of the flesh. In South Africa, individual accountability has been eroded as a result of the many corruption scandals that have become endemic of our politics, economics, and socio-cultural fibre. According to the *Corruption Perception Index* compiled by Transparency International (2017), South Africa has a corruption score of 43 (zero indicating maximum corruption and 100 no corruption). Accordingly, although a multitude of governance policies may be adopted, accountability must start with each individual to change the culture of corruption.

4.2. Dialogue and the Economy

For Merleau-Ponty, dialogue refers to self-understanding and meaning creation through communication. Embodied phenomenology and linguistics are related as a function of inter-action and dialogue. In this way, the hyper-dialectic of the flesh becomes evident through an intersubjective communication network—responsible action is based on the ability to listen and not instruct. This is a challenge because it involves active engagement to understand my identity as someone doing business. Singularity and unilateral communication must be exchanged for open dialogue if the individual is to remain a responsible business person as well as a member of society. For the individual to be part of business innovation and creativity, a transformation is required from instrumentalist logic, exclusivity and singularity to dialogue. *Homo economicus* has perpetuated extraction capitalism, in which individuals are part of a business model that emphasises the singularity and the reduction of employees, natural and other resources to means for personal wealth creation. Instead of being part of a corporeality that can be the basis of a flourishing society, singularity has led to individuals who are engaged in business in a unilateral and rationalistic that contributes to the chaos of exploitation, environmental disasters, poverty, and unemployment.

Stakeholder engagement is a popular business theme of management and governance which attempts to move beyond *homo economicus*. Stakeholder theory is associated with the work of Freeman (1984) and highlights the network of an organisation's internal and external stakeholders. The strength of this theory is that an organisation is viewed as a network of relationships and that responsible business practices and governance requires engagement. Unfortunately, this engagement may be prioritised according to the strategy of the company to achieve singular goals and not greater responsibility through dialogue. This prioritisation may result in blind spots and oversight or it may perpetuate a *homo economicus* mindset of individuals in business. The individual as embodied subject is not given priority. As a result, dialogue, not inter-subjectivity, can then become part of the company strategy.

A stark example of such failures of communication is the 2012 Marikana Massacre where, during an extended wage dispute, communication broke down and violent clashes erupted between workers and the South African Police Service (SAPS), leaving 44 dead and 70 injured. An investigation into the event revealed that one of the workers' allegations against the management of Lonmin was that they were not open to dialogue. The Marikana Commission of Inquiry (2015, p. 542) found that the complaint from workers regarding housing had not been addressed, leaving them to live in unacceptable conditions and that this " . . . created an environment conducive to the creation of tension, labour unrest, disunity among its employees or other harmful conduct." In this context, listening could have probably averted the massacre.

Listening is also related to the ability to address legacy issues related to colonialism and apartheid. Currently, one of the most important South African issues relates to land and repatriation without compensation. Listening and dialogue is critical for the emergence of a new corporeality that is inclusive, just, and sustainable. An important factor in these issues are the diverse cultural presuppositions which highlight the difference between liberal views of ownership of private property and *Ubuntu* which fosters an interconnection amongst the individual, community, and land (Munyaka and Motlhabi 2009, pp. 70–73).

Another example that highlights the urgency of dialogue from the corporate environment is the 2017 announcement of the possible retrenchment of 8500 workers by AngloGold Ashanti in South Africa. The stated reason for the company's offer of a retrenchment was to protect the long-term sustainability of the business and the jobs of the majority of their workforce (Fin24, 29 June 2017). Retrenchment is part and parcel of business and it is understandable that a company facing staggering losses must react and do the responsible thing to protect the future of the business. However, individuals in business usually communicate intentions unilaterally, not multi-laterally. Further, such a claim is based on rationality (profitability and saving jobs), not on listening to the affected employees. *Ubuntu* is consultative, engaging, and multi-lateral which is a crucial aspect that Merleau-Ponty's embodied phenomenology perpetuates.

Listening implies that each individual is part of corporeality and participates in the hyper-dialectic that is crucial for sustainable societies. On the other hand, without sustainable societies, there will be no sustainable businesses. This requires trust, creativity, and innovation, all of which start with each individual's ability to contribute to the creation of a sustainable future.

5. Conclusions

This paper discussed the role of TMS as the socio-ethical basis for self-interest with special reference to the role of sympathy and the impartial spectator in Smith's philosophy. It was shown that Smith cannot be reduced to a *homo economicus* view of the individual. However, the empiricist mode of the impartial spectator can give rise to determinism in moral decisions. This perspective fails to take account of the pre-reflectivity of the subject and intentionality. Although Smith does envision a socio-ethical framework for business, he fails to move beyond reducing the individual to the third person. This failure may be the reason why *homo economicus* remains part of the fabric of the business world.

To address this failure, the embodied phenomenology of Merleau-Ponty was explored to provide alternative perspectives for responsible business practices. Merleau-Ponty regards the subject as part of corporeality and presentness in the world. The subject is part of a hyper-dialectic of the flesh which highlights relational self-understanding. Embodiment implies that the physical presence of the subject cannot be bracketed; therefore, the gender, ethnicity, possessions, and other physical aspects impact the creation of meaning. Further meaning is always in a process of creation through engagement with the world, a process also reflected by African moral theory and *Ubuntu*. This inter-subjective perspective or being part of corporeality implies that the subject is always accountable for decisions and action in business. Accountability has direct relevance in governance which may drift into a state of compliance. Embodied phenomenology also highlights that communication is a dialogical process and uses the hyper-dialectic of the flesh as a basis for responsible business practices. This understanding of dialogue implies that the starting point of any form of stakeholder engagement should begin with the responsibility of the individual as part of business and society.

Acknowledgments: All sources of funding of the study should be disclosed. Please clearly indicate grants that you have received in support of your research work. Clearly state if you received funds for covering the costs to publish in open access.

Conflicts of Interest: The author declares no conflict of interest.

References

Berry, Christopher. 1997. *Social Theory of the Scottish Enlightenment*. Edinburg: Edinburgh University Press, chp. 4.

Carroll, Archie B., and Kareem M. Shabana. 2010. The Business Case for Corporate Social Responsibility: A Review of Concepts, Research and Practices. *International Journal of Management Reviews* 12: 85–105. [CrossRef]

Cobb-Stevens, Richard. 1994. The beginning of phenomenology: Husserl and his predecessors. In *Continental Philosophy in the 20th Century*. Edited by Richard Kearney. Cornwell: Routledge.

Flynn, Thomas R. 1994. Philosophy of existence 2: Sartre. In *Continental Philosophy in the 20th Century*. Edited by Richard Kearney. Cornwell: Routledge.

Folbre, Nancy. 2009. *Greed, Lust and Gender. A History of Economic Ideas*. Oxford: Oxford University Press.

Freeman, R. Edward. 1984. *Strategic Management: A Stakeholder Approach*. Boston: Pitman.

Gonin, Michael. 2015. Adam Smith's Contribution to Business Ethics, Then and Now. *Journal of Business Ethics* 129: 221–36. [CrossRef]

Heath, Eugene. 2013. Adam Smith and self-interest. In *The Oxford Handbook of Adam Smith*. Edited by Christopher J. Berry, Maria Pia Paganelli and Craig Smith. Oxford: Oxford Press.

Hühn, Matthias P. 2017. Adam Smith's Philosophy of Science: Economics as Moral Imagination. *Journal of Business Ethics*. [CrossRef]

Ingram, John Kells. 1915. *A History of Political Economy*. New and Enlarged Edition with a Supplementary Chapter by William A. Scott and an Introduction by Richard T. Ely; London: A. and C. Black.

Ionescu-Somers, Aileen, and Albrecht Enders. 2012. How Nestlé Dealt with a Social Media Campaign against It. Available online: https://www.ft.com/content/90dbff8a-3aea-11e2-b3f0-00144feabdc0 (accessed on 15 September 2017).

King IV Report on Corporate Governance for South Africa. 2016. *Institute of Directors Southern Africa*. Available online: http://c.ymcdn.com/sites/www.iodsa.co.za/resource/resmgr/king_iv/King_IV_Report/IoDSA_King_IV_Report_-_WebVe.pdf (accessed on 15 September 2017).

Marikana Commission of Inquiry. 2015. *Report on Matters of Public, National and International Concern Arising out of the Tragic Incidents at the Lonmin Mine in Marikana, in the North West Province*. Available online: http://www.gov.za/sites/www.gov.za/files/marikana-report-1.pdf (accessed on 3 August 2015).

Matthews, Eric. 2010. *Merleau-Ponty: A Guide for the Perplexed*. London: Continuum International Publishing Group.

Mbiti, John Samuel. 1969. *African Religions and Philosophy*. London: Heinemann.

McKinsey Investor Opinion Survey. 2002. Available online: http://www.eiod.org/uploads/publications/pdf/survey_mckinsey.pdf (accessed on 15 August 2017).

Merleau-Ponty, Maurice. 1962. *Phenomenology of Perception*. Translated by C. Smith. London: Routledge & Kegan Paul.

Merleau-Ponty, Maurice. 1964. *The Primacy of Perception and Other Essays on Phenomenological Psychology, the Philosophy of Art, History and Politics*. Edited by J. M. Edie. Evaston: Northwestern University Press.

Merleau-Ponty, Maurice. 1968. *The Visible and the Invisible*. Edited by C. Lefort. Translated by A. Lingis. Evaston: Northwestern University Press.

Metz, Thaddeus. 2009. Africa moral theory and public governance: Nepotism, preferential hiring and other partiality. In *African Ethics: An Anthology of Comparative and Applied Ethics*. Edited by F. M. Murove. Pietermaritzburg: University of KwaZulu-Natal Press.

Mill, John Stuart. 1844. *Essays on Some Unsettled Questions of Political Economy*. London: Longmans, Green, Reader, and Dyer.

Mill, John Stuart. 1848. *Principles of Political Economy with Some of Their Applications to Social Philosophy*. London: Longmans, Green and Co.

Munyaka, Mluleki, and Mokgethi Motlhabi. 2009. Ubuntu and its Socio-moral Significance. In *African Ethics: An Anthology of Comparative and Applied Ethics*. Edited by F. M. Murove. Pietermaritzburg: University of KwaZulu-Natal Press.

Naidoo, Ramani. 2009. *Corporate Governance: An Essential Guide for South African Companies*, 2nd ed. Durban: LexisNexis.

Nussbaum, Barbara. 2009. Ubuntu and Business: Reflections and Questions. In *African Ethics: An Anthology of Camparative and Applied Ethics*. Edited by F. M. Murove. Pietermaritzburg: University of KwaZulu-Natal Press.

Paganelli, MariaPia. 2008. The Adam Smith Problem in Reverse: Self-interest in the Wealth of Nations and the Theory of moral sentiments. *History of Political Economy* 40: 365–82. [CrossRef]

Paganelli, Maria Pia. 2010. The moralizing distance in Adam Smith: The Theory of Moral sentiments as possible praise of commerce. *History of Political Economy* 42: 425–41. [CrossRef]

Rathbone, Mark. 2015. Love, money and madness: Money in the economic philosophies of Adam Smith and Jean-Jacques Rousseau. *Southern African Journal of Philosophy* 34: 379–89. [CrossRef]

Roberts, John. 1991. The possibility of accountability. *Accounting, Organisations and Society* 16: 355–68. [CrossRef]

Sen, Amaryta. 1999. *On Ethics and Economics*. London: Blackwell.

Smith, Adam. 2004. *The Theory of Moral Sentiments*. Cambridge: Cambridge University Press. First published 1759.

Smith, Adam. 1950. *An Inquiry into the Nature and Causes of the Wealth of Nations*. Edited with Introduction, Notes, Marginal Summary and an Enlarged Index by Edwin Cannan; London: Methuen & Co. Ltd. First published 1776.

Stigler, George J. 1971. Smith's travel on the ship of state. *History of Political Economy* 3: 265–77. [CrossRef]

Taminiaux, J. 1994. Philosophy of existence 1: Heidegger. In *Continental Philosophy in the 20th Century*. Edited by Richard Kearney. Cornwell: Routledge.

Transparency International. 2017. *Corruption Perception Index*. Available online: https://www.transparency.org/news/feature/corruption_perceptions_index_2017 (accessed on 28 March 2018).

Wells, Thomas R. 2014. Recovering Adam Smith's ethical economics. *Real-World Economics Review* 68: 90–97.

Werhane, Patricia H. 1989. The role of self-interest in Adam Smith's Wealth of Nations. *The Journal of Philosophy* 86: 669–80. [CrossRef]

religions MDPI

Article

Encountering Transcendence: Žižek, Liberation Theology and African Thought in Dialogue

Anné Hendrik Verhoef

School of Philosophy, North-West University, Potchefstroom 2520, South Africa; anne.verhoef@nwu.ac.za

Received: 21 October 2017; Accepted: 7 December 2017; Published: 12 December 2017

Abstract: The concept of transcendence has been described by various academic disciplines like philosophy, theology, art and literature, but also by various religions and cultures. This has also been the case with the three traditions that are brought into dialogue in this special issue, namely critical theory, African thought and Liberation theology. In this article I will focus on transcendence as it is 'encountered' by the philosopher Slavoj Žižek as a postmetaphysical thinker and as a voice from critical theory. Žižek's emphasis on the 'gap in immanence' and its implications for freedom will then be brought into dialogue with African thought and Liberation theology. Transcendence as an entry point in this dialogue has the potential not only to give more insight into these traditions, but also to advance the concept of freedom, which is central in all these traditions.

Keywords: transcendence; liberation theology; critical theory; African thought; Slavoj Žižek; immanence; freedom Gilles Deleuze; religion; metaphysics; gap in immanence

---

1. Transcendence as Point of Departure for Dialogue

The concept *transcendence* will be taken as the point of departure to initiate and facilitate a dialogue between the three diverse traditions: critical theory, African thought and Liberation theology. The reason is that transcendence is closely connected to the concept of freedom, which is central in each of these traditions. This will be explicated after the concept of transcendence has been clarified.

The word *transcendence* is composed of the prefix *trans-* (from the Latin *trans*, 'across') and the action verb *to ascend* (from the Latin *scandere*, 'to climb across, surmount'), indicating a type of 'crossing over', the 'exceeding of boundaries'. Transcendence can thus refer to 'some place above or outside the world'—an ascension to an 'outside'—or to a crossing of borders 'within this world'—depending on what is being transcended. Epistemological transcendence, for example, refers to whether objects of knowledge transcend the consciousness. It also refers to the boundaries of our knowledge—to enigmas, the unknown, the incomprehensible. This in turn coheres with ontological transcendence: the question whether reality transcends consciousness or whether it is immanent in it (Stoker 2016, p. 1). In monism, for example, various ontological areas are reduced to one principle (Spinoza), while for Plato, transcendence is dominant. Other types of transcendence (or rather boundaries that are crossed) are described as anthropological (how human subjects transcend to other fellow human subjects) or psychological (which refers to "something greater than ourselves, which we should respect and work for" (Layard 2005, p. 91) or self-transcendence). Transcendence as an ascension to an 'outside world' or 'place above' is described as religious, metaphysical or existential transcendence. In this case the crossing over is from the sensorial observable to the supersensorial; from historical time and place to a future utopia; from the temporary imperfect world to the eternal perfect world. The yearning (or escape from our imperfect world) for fulfilment, salvation, and completion (as that which the true outside world offers) is connected in religious terms to God as the transcendent. In metaphysical terms it can refer to Plato's true world 'outside' the cave, or in existential terms our awareness of moral values 'outside' ourselves. In sum: Transcendence is correlative with immanence and its meaning depends on the context in which it is used.

In African thought[1] the concept *transcendence* is mostly used in the context of the religious or spiritual. Transcendence in African Traditional Religions (ATR) can refer to the fact that human beings "continually surpass themselves in all they are, all they wish and all they have" (Rakotsoane 2010, p. 2)— a type of self-transcendence. Self-transcendence is, however, discouraged in ATR because conformity and uniformity are prioritised: "the ideal person, in relation to nature, is relatively passive fitting himself or herself into the given rhythms" (Cumpsty 1991, p. 120). Transcendence in ATR also refers to God, "the object of their worship" (Rakotsoane 2010, p. 2). Although God's transcendence is very prominent in ATR, this God is not a *deus remotus* but immanent. The "root of ATR is belief in the existence of the mystical and mysterious power or energy (popularly known as *mysterium tremendum, manna*, the life force, the vital force, the life essence or dynamism)" (Rakotsoane 2010, p. 5). This life force is an impersonal power present in everything that exists—animate of inanimate; corporeal or spiritual (Turaki 2006, p. 24). All living beings are interconnected through this life force (Beyers 2010, p. 4) and the whole purpose of ATR is to "preserve and enhance this life force that everyone has received" (Magesa 2002, p. 51). In ATR, God as the Supreme Being "appears to be ontologically transcendent . . . but this transcendence and aloofness must not be interpreted in absolute terms" (Turaki 2006, p. 59). The transcendence (God, powers, spirits) is "just as much part of reality as the visible elements in the world" (Beyers 2010, p. 6) and not part of a different reality. There is a connectedness and unity in life—this life. ATR is "not concerned with metaphysics", but is "this-worldly" (Maluleke 1998, p. 127). It "hardly, if ever, looks beyond this world and age" (Henry and Malan 2017, p. 1) and salvation is here and now.

The above brief overview of transcendence in African thought—specifically in ATR—reveals that there is not an 'outside', not another world or place or time to yearn for, no existential or metaphysical transcendence.[2] Even God, as the Supreme Being, is transcendental only within this world. This seems like a contradiction, but it means that God as the highest "degree of mystical power . . . the mysterious power or vital force" cannot be approached directly (prayers need to be directed through ancestors and divinities) because going "too close to a being that is believed to be endowed with a massive vital force is considered fatal" (Rakotsoane 2010, p. 9). He (or It as Spirit) is, however, always part of this world.[3] It is the impersonal life force itself which creates life and unity. There is thus no differentiation between the sacred and the profane (Thorpe 1992, p. 3; Wernhart 2003, p. 269) and "all of nature is invested with a mystical, religious quality" (Thorpe 1991, p. 28). God's transcendence is thus completely found within the immanent—the absolute or transcendent is no longer sought outside mundane reality because both realities converge. The concept of transcendence has in effect become redundant. It has lost its power and meaning, and it has virtually disappeared into immanence. Stoker describes this type of 'transcendence' as "radical immanence" (Stoker 2012, p. 15). Even on an epistemological and ontological level there is no transcendence, because there is a holistic understanding of reality as one world, one reality.[4] Rakotsoane says "Africans have a monistic view of reality. For them, what is out there is a closed system of cause and effect" (Rakotsoane 2010, p. 3) and even chance is

---

[1] African thought or philosophy is of course not a single unified tradition of thinking and it remains difficult to define. Philosophers such as Bodunrin (1981, *The question of African Philosophy*), Momoh (1985, *African philosophy . . . Does it exist?*), Wiredu (2004, *A Companion to African Philosophy*) and Oruka (1990, *Trends in contemporary African philosophy*) all debate the concept of African Philosophy itself. Momoh says for example: "The attempt to stablish African Philosophy as a respectable discipline has been impaired by this thought that it is a traditional thought. Scholars are becoming increasingly aware that African pneumatological beliefs, metaphysical and moral doctrines, political and social principles, epistemology, logic, law, science and the scholars own theories and extractions from all of these should not be indiscriminately labelled 'African traditional thought'." (Momoh 1985, p. 79).

[2] I am aware of the danger of generalisation here, but the aim here is to only define transcendence in broad terms in order to start the dialogue with the other traditions and, not to work present a comprehensive understanding of it.

[3] Mbiti says: "For most part of their life, African people place God in the transcendental plane, making him seem remote from their daily affairs. But they know that he is immanent . . . Thus for them, God is in theory transcendent, but in practice immanent." (Mbiti 1970, p. 18).

[4] An African understanding of reality, however, implies more than a "mere clinical, scientific analysis of the material" (Turaki 1999, p. 122) because part of reality is invisible—the transcendental life force.

ruled out, because "everything that happens is understood to have a specific cause in the system" (Rakotsoane 2010, p. 3).[5] With such a strong understanding of reality as a closed system of cause and effect, the possibility for freedom and an ethical life are two issues that immediately come to the fore. Du Toit points out in this regard that "For Africans the aim of life is to experience and enhance life force and become part of it. Anything that diminishes this force is evil and anything that increases it is good." (Du Toit 2009, p. 109) Turaki adds that "[t]he pursuit of cosmic harmony is an ethical principle in traditional Africa" (Turaki 1999, p. 122). This indicates partly how the question of an ethical life is answered, but the question of freedom remains because of the univocity of being and the monistic view of reality. I will return to this question after the discussion of Žižek's concept of transcendence.

In the discussion of Critical Theory (broadly defined as social theory oriented toward critiquing and changing society as a whole) I will focus mainly on the philosopher Slavoj Žižek. His first book published in English, *The Sublime Object of Ideology* (1989), develops a materialist conception of ideology that draws heavily on Lacanian psychoanalysis and Hegelian idealism. In his overview of Žižek's huge oeuvre, Depoortere observes that Žižek not only returns to Marxist orthodoxy, but also increasingly to Christianity (Depoortere 2008, p. 96). This leads to the interesting question of whether there is any room for transcendence in Žižek's work, and if so why he regards it as necessary. To answer this, I will focus on Žižek's essay "The Descent of Transcendence into Immanence, or, Deleuze as a Hegelian" (Žižek 2004).[6] This essay also brings Deleuze's concept of the 'plane of immanence' into the conversation, which further develops the ideas on transcendence and its link to freedom. Deleuze's radical immanence has salient similarities with the immanence and univocity of African thought and the critique Žižek raises to Deleuze will have some relevance for African thought and the question of freedom as well.

In Liberation theology[7] the liberation of the poor and oppressed in society is a main concern. Christian theology is reinterpreted in practical terms to criticise 'sinful' socioeconomic structures that cause social inequities, but also to actively participate in changing those structures. Liberation theologians were often criticised as naive purveyors of Marxism and advocates of leftist social activism (clearly linking it with Critical Theory), but their focus were uncompromisingly on the needs and liberation of the poor and oppressed. This involved the political struggle of the poor against wealthy elites, firstly based on the Bible, and not necessarily on Marxist ideas. They emphasised that the voice of the poor should be heard—others cannot speak on their behalf—and that God's voice can be heard through the poor, and that "God, in a world full of injustice and enmity, is in a special way the God of the destitute, the poor and the wronged" (Belhar Confession 2006).[8]

The focus of Liberation theology is "on action and justice more than on those of belief and truth" (Ogden 1979, p. 21) and allows "Christian faith in God and the contemporary concern for freedom to interpret one another" (Ogden 1979, p. 14). It is a theology of praxis, a political and public theology in which the emancipation and freedom of all people, especially the oppressed and poor, are of main importance. A "transformed Christian vision of religious transcendence" (McCann 1981, pp. 199–200) takes place in this process in which God is not seen as remote or distanced, but 'within human touch'. In her engagement with Liberation theology Mayra Rivera, for example, develops a concept of God "as transcendent within" (Rivera 2007, p. 170), where transcendence is seen as a relationship

---

[5] Tempels, for example, says about the African world view that "[n]othing moves in this universe of forces without influencing other forces by its movement. The world of forces is held like a spider's web of which no single thread can be caused to vibrate without shaking the whole network" (Tempels 1969, p. 60).

[6] In this essay Žižek highlights the link between transcendence and freedom which I will appropriate in the dialogue between the three traditions in this article. However, it is not possible to discuss his work in detail within the scope and limits of this article.

[7] As with African thought, Liberation theology is not a simple concept that refers to a single unified tradition or set of beliefs. Liberation theology is a diverse and dynamic 'movement' and the discussion here only pertains to one aspect—transcendence—within the broader understanding of Liberation theology, without attempting any generalisations.

[8] This is a translation of the original Afrikaans text of the confession that was adopted by the synod of the Dutch Reformed Mission Church in South Africa in 1986.

which describes how humans can touch God through others. To find the 'transcendence within', an 'extraworldly transcendence' is seemingly rejected. This world is important, and not an 'outside' world. God is within this world, incarnated in Jesus. He emptied Himself (the Spirit in kenotic form), and is therefore found within the world itself, within humanity as the body of Christ. The biblical term 'Kingdom of God' is interpreted as to refer to the presence of God as immanent universal Spirit, and there is a general move to the "absence of the God of pure transcendence" (Altizer 1980, p. 50). In this world, freedom, emancipation and justice are sought by Liberation theology. The emphasis is on the immanent and not on the transcendent. The transcendent is not necessarily rejected,[9] but the move is toward immanence which raises the questions: Is transcendence still needed and why? To what extent will the 'project of emancipation' (liberation) be furthered or hindered with the complete rejection of transcendence?

Žižek's critique on Deleuze's radical immanence, and his pursuing of transcendence (or rather the gap in immanence) for the sake of freedom itself, will shed some light on the above questions. The aim of this article, however, is not to argue for an uncritical rehabilitation of transcendence, especially not as a power, logos or authority. Too many dangers of and problems with transcendence have been exposed and experienced through history to endeavour such an argument. Some of these problems will be discussed next, before the discussion proceeds to Deleuze and Žižek.

2. Dangers and Problems of Transcendence

The concept *transcendence* signals what is beyond—beyond what can be known, represented or experienced—but it "has also been linked to unfashionable concepts like presence, being, power, an argument beyond recourse, an authority beyond reason, the tyranny of the most excellent, the hegemony of the west, and of course a totalitarian deity" (Schwartz 2004, p. vii). The problem and danger with transcendence is that "crimes have been committed in the name of transcendental principles—principles held beyond question, beyond critique—and even in the name of a transcendent God" (Schwartz 2004, p. vii). This is why it is argued today that transcendence is a relic of former mistakes.

Especially the metaphysical understanding of transcendence (as God, the Supreme Being, the divine, something outside this world, the cause of being) was immensely criticised in the modern period, by amongst others Immanuel Kant, Friedrich Nietzsche and Martin Heidegger. They all argued in different ways that there is no 'true' foundation, no ontotheology, no other reality that determines our reality. Nietzsche, for example, indicated clearly that the concept of a transcendent world (separated from this world) and the concept of God as being radical transcendent are very problematic, because it may lead to a devaluation of this world, and of this life. Other problems with transcendence (apart from the critique of metaphysics) include that it creates a 'too distant' transcendent (an unknowable, unreachable, and eventually irrelevant transcendent); it creates a nihilistic world because it is 'the other/outside' world which has true meaning; it devalues the immanent on a bodily level (only the spiritual becomes important as it connects with the transcendent); and it locates the transcendent in brief moments of experiences (with the rest of our lives doomed as being less important). It is some of these problems which African thought and Liberation theology address (and overcome) in their more immanent concept of transcendence.

The aim of this article is not to re-establish transcendence in a 'remote', ontotheological, authoritarian form as a ground for oppression, but the opposite. It is to explore transcendence as a potential and even a condition for human freedom. It is to conceive of transcendence as "the ground of

---

[9]   There remains a tension in Liberation theology between emancipation (liberation in the political sense) and redemption (as that which God alone can do). In Liberation theology there are long standing debates and different interpretations concerning these issues (see Davis 1980; Hennelly 1979) and my intention is merely to introduce the problem of transcendence in this tradition.

humility: epistemological, ethical, aesthetic, and political" (Schwartz 2004, p. vii).[10] The philosophical line that runs from Spinoza to Deleuze stands for absolute immanence and it suggests a freedom in its break from transcendence. The restricted 'absoluteness' of this immanence, however, is exposed by Žižek, amongst others.[11] In response to the radical immanence of Gilles Deleuze, he argues that a gap in immanence is needed to maintain our human freedom.

3. The Radical Immanence of Deleuze

Absolute immanence means a 'closed world' with no escape to the 'outside', no 'crossing over', a denial even of the limits or boundaries itself. A radical immanence renders the concept of transcendence redundant, because it virtually disappears into immanence:[12] all transcendence is completely within this world, within our experience, within our grasp, and there is nothing 'more'. It positively acknowledges our interconnectedness as human beings with the material world we find ourselves in, and our connectedness to nature. In this regard the philosopher Deleuze represents one of the most radical positions of immanence with his concept of 'the plane of immanence'.[13] Žižek argues that "[i]f there ever was, in the twentieth century, a philosopher of absolute immanence, it was Gilles Deleuze, with his notion of life as 'the immanence of immanence, absolute immanence: it is sheer power, utter beatitude'" (Žižek 2004, p. 235).

Deleuze defended the notion of immanence explicitly and passionately. He considered immanence not as a concept but as the pre-philosophical horizon against which thinking can be creative and productive. He calls this horizon the "plane of immanence" (Deleuze 2007, p. 386). With his passionate acceptance of immanence, Deleuze rejects any form of transcendence, connecting it with "the poisonous logic of representation" (Deleuze and Guattari 1991, p. 35). With his notion of pure immanence, he wishes to move beyond the dualism of form-matter that brings with it a transcendent judgement of mind over matter.[14] Deleuze rejects not only epistemological transcendence, but also all types of transcendence, and of the metaphysical in particular. The reason is that Deleuze believes that 'Being' should be liberated from the chains of representation and that we must relocate ourselves on the plane of immanence, where we will discover that "Being necessarily only expresses Itself in all beings, because Being is all there is" (Justaert 2012, p. 98).

Because Being is all there is, Deleuze argues that there is no antonym (like transcendence) for immanence and that immanence should be thought of independently: "Absolute immanence is in itself: it is not in anything, nor can it be attributed to something; it does not depend on an object or belong to a subject. [...] Only when immanence is immanent to nothing except itself, can we speak of a plane of immanence." (Deleuze 2007, p. 389). In other words, for Deleuze, the world of representation is "a site of transcendental illusion" (Deleuze 2004, p. 334); it is "a fake dualism, albeit a very persistent one" (Justaert 2012, p. 102). Deleuze connects the absolute/infinite with pure immanence, and this immanence, according to him, allows or calls one to be creatively ethical and not to be bound to a prescribed morality (Smith 2001, p. 178). In order to do so, one must discover the true power and beauty in immanence, in Being, and live a life not divided in categories or hierarchies. For

---

10   This transcendence is not a recovery of previous figures of transcendence. It is rather a "delirious rupture in immanence, an erotic claim made by it, a gap in the Real, a question put to subjectivity, a realm of the impossible that breaks into possibility" (Schwartz 2004, p. xi).

11   John Milbank argues for example for the recovering of the relation between the sublime and the beautiful, because in absolute immanence there is a sundering of the sublime from the beautiful. There remains a 'gap' in immanence because the sublime is "that *within* representation which nonetheless *exceeds* the possibility of representation" (Milbank 2004, p. 212).

12   Some philosophers argue that radical immanence is basically similar to atheism and that it is philosophically a move to nihilism. See, for example, Jonkers's (2012, p. 33) analyses of Jacobi's critique of philosophy's annihilation of transcendence in the wake of the pantheism controversy of 1785 and the atheism controversy of 1799. Jonkers discusses these two controversies in detail.

13   My discussion of Deleuze here follows my previous work on him in, "Embodied religion's radicalization of immanence and the consequent question of transcendence" (Verhoef 2013).

14   For Deleuze, transcendence implies a superiority of thinking over Being and he wants to unify these two poles and to "let Being speak loudly and clearly through thought and life once more" (Justaert 2012, p. 97).

Deleuze, this immanent life is impersonal—"life is Being itself, a power that runs through every being" (Justaert 2012, p. 97); not divided into categories—"a human being's life is literally equal to a life of a rock" (Pearson 2001, p. 141), and has the state of mind of beatitude—the realisation that it is not we who think, but "Being (God) who thinks through us; Being has absorbed us as it were: our life has become a Life, an expression of Being." (Justaert 2012, p. 97).

To live on this plane of immanence intends to be liberating (free from the illusion of transcendence, hierarchy and dualism, free to be truly creative and ethical), but the question is whether this position is philosophically tenable. A paradox in Deleuze's philosophy in that his plane of immanence somehow transcends the world of representation. The plane of immanence is indeed wholly other than this world.[15] Deleuze hereby creates a new dualism between the 'old world of representation' and the 'new world of the creative plane of immanence'. Deleuze's philosophy is still an "affair of transcendence" (Pearson 2001, p. 141), and the paradox in Deleuze's philosophy is that the plane of immanence becomes the 'transcendent'.[16]

So ironically, even in this radical plane of immanence there is no denial of transcendence, but rather a notion that the absolute empties itself in the mundane reality. 'God' is now the impersonal Being of the plane of immanence (Life itself). It is a move away from hierarchy and dualism to the creative life of pure immanence. Life itself seems to attain meaning/value on this plane, but not the personal life. The human being's life is literally like that of a rock, something completely physical, a body—and by implication determined by causality.

Žižek criticises Deleuze's plane of immanence for its inability to allow for human freedom. Again this is ironic, because freedom is exactly what Deleuze intends to promote with his plane of immanence and critique on representation. Žižek does not want to restore or argue for some metaphysical transcendence or God in his critique against Deleuze, but emphasises the need for epistemological and ontological transcendence, for a 'gap in the immanence' in *immanence*. This gap implies that immanence is not completely closed off, not all totalising, but that there is space for something 'more', a 'transcendental dimension', and an "immanent transcendence" (Žižek 2001b, p. 99) within immanence. To clarify this, I will first explicate Žižek's understanding of transcendence in Christianity (his rejection of radical or metaphysical transcendence) and then move to his critique on Deleuze.

4. Žižek: Transcendence and Freedom

In Žižek's understanding of Christianity the incarnation of God in Christ should be understood as the complete abolishment of God's transcendence.[17] In this regard there are some similarities between Žižek and Liberation theology to which I will return in the last section. Žižek argues that Christianity rejects the 'God of the Beyond' and thus can be described as a radical desublimation, "in the sense of the descendence of the sublime Beyond to the everyday level" (Žižek 2001b, p. 90). For him, Christianity makes the transition from God "as the wholly Other Thing to the Divine as barely nothing" (Žižek 2001b, p. 89). *Barely* nothing is not 'nothing', because "the imperceptible something" (Žižek 2001b, p. 90) remains. He points out that since the coming of Christ "there is no longer any transcendent God with whom to communicate" and that "God has passed into the Holy Spirit as

---

15 Justaert says for example: "The radically immanent can be understood as transcending our lives, because the whole interpretation of the plane of immanence as a goal to strive for, away from the world of representation, pictures this form of immanence as quasi unattainable. To reach it, we have to transcend our own ego, give up our own personality." (Justaert 2012, p. 102).

16 According to Justaert transcendence does have a meaning in Deleuze's philosophy, namely as "the dynamic meaning of transcending as an act of human beings [...] Their static form transcends towards a more dynamic constellation in which they can be creative, in which they can produce again. This is what happens on the plane of immanence: all these moving lines produce different intensities of Being" (Justaert 2012, p. 102).

17 Žižek says Christianity accepts God "as just another human being, as a miserable man indiscernible from other humans with regards to his intrinsic properties" (Žižek 2001b, p. 90). See also Depoortere's "The End of God's Transcendence? On Incarnation in the Work of Slavoj Žižek" (Depoortere 2007).

the (spirit of the) community of believers" (Žižek 2001a, pp. 50–51)—to the everyday level. Here the "split between man and man-Christ [is a] minimal difference" (Žižek 2004, p. 246).

There is no 'Divine Thing' as something transcendent, or 'God as the wholly other Thing' left for Žižek. Following the Lacanian psychoanalysis, he argues that such a notion is part of our 'tragic desire' or 'stubborn attachment' to the impossible object. The coming of Christ implies for Žižek the death of this Divine Thing and consequently of our tragic desire. The 'Divine' is rather that what we find in the immanent that makes us 'more' than animals. It is that "imperceptible something", the "X or excess of human life" (Žižek 2001b, p. 89), that distinguishes human beings from animals. It is not something beyond the world of visible phenomena, but the 'surplus' human life in this world. Žižek explains that divinity is "that unfathomable X, on account of which man cannot ever fully become MAN, self-identical" (Žižek 2001b, p. 90), because "God is the unique case of full humanity" (Žižek 2001b, p. 91). God is thus not the God of the Beyond in the transcendent sense, but the "coincidence, identity even, between the sublime and the everyday object" (Žižek 2001b, p. 92). God, or Christ-man, is what makes man hu-man. God is just the immanent imperceptible X: the X which makes man (animal) X-man (human). It is not a substantial property, but the excess of human life—an example of the *gap in immanence*.

This transition of God from the 'sublime to the everyday object' corresponds for Žižek (in the Lancanian sense) to the transition from desire to drive. Desire for the impossible Thing (for the God of Beyond) is tragic because the impossible Thing is placed in an inaccessible Beyond. Desire becomes an endless movement, from one substitute to the next, without reaching it. With 'the coming of Christ' the domain of 'tragic desire' is, however, left behind[18] and the 'domain of drive' is entered.[19] Drive is orientated towards some particular object: an "object that is also the support of something in the object that is more than the object itself" (Depoortere 2008, p. 113). That the object can be 'something more' than the object itself, has to do with the gap in immanence for Žižek.

Žižek's emphasis on the gap in immanence brings an important point of critique on Deleuze's radical immanence to the fore: the question whether absolute immanence abolishes freedom. Žižek explains that Deleuze follows Spinoza as the philosopher of 'Substance'. Substance means that there is no mediation between attributes and only a *univocity of being*—the "motif on which Deleuze insists so much" (Žižek 2004, p. 235). Spinoza understands this univocity of being as purely positive: "all that he admits is a purely positive network of causes and effect in which, by definition, an absence cannot play any positive role" (Žižek 2004, p. 236).[20] There is no absence, gap or crack in the Real for Spinoza.

This strong assertion of Spinoza of the positivity and univocity of Being grounds his equation of 'power' and 'right' in a radical way. A 'right' is for Spinoza to act upon things according to one's nature. In other words "justice means that every entity is allowed to freely deploy its inherent power-potentials, that is, the amount of justice owed to me equals my power" (Žižek 2004, p. 236). In a closed network of cause and effect, my power equals my right. This is an anti-legalistic notion of rights as not something which one has, but something one 'does' according to one's nature. Spinoza uses this, for example, as his key argument for the 'natural inferiority' of women. He contends that "…women have not *by nature* equal right with men" (Spinoza 1951, p. 387; my emphasis). What this equation of rights and

---

[18] In contrast, both "pagans and Jews … share the belief in a sublime beyond. To put it differently, they both believe in God as the Thing and thus both share the fantasy that the Divine Thing is far too sublime, far too elevated for human beings to be able to handle direct confrontation with it" (Depoortere 2008, p. 111). This link to the concept of 'Supreme Being' in ATR which Rakotsoane describes as something that cannot be approached directly because going "too close to a being that is believed to be endowed with a massive vital force is considered fatal" (Rakotsoane 2010, p. 9).

[19] For Žižek, Christ figures as the exemplary figure which frees us from the Divine Thing (and our tragic desire for it) and this liberation must lead to the abolishment of all superior transcendences (and consequence tragic desires). Radical 'desublimation' in all forms is thus necessary.

[20] For Spinoza reality is what we can positively describes with causes and effects. Any absence, any negativity, should not be filled by a notion that merely fills the lacunae within our knowledge. Such negativity is 'imaginary' and "the result of our anthropomorphic, limited, false knowledge that fails to grasp the actual causal chain" (Žižek 2004, p. 236). Žižek, however, disagrees and says there are always some lacks with regard to positive measures—it can be a generative absence.

power eventually culminates to in Spinoza's work, is the radical suspension of any 'deontological' ethical dimension (norms that prescribe how we should act when we have a choice). He proposes an ethic of 'is' and not of 'ought'. Ethical laws have only been given, he argues, because of our limited connection to see the true causal connection in things (or in our acts), because of our lack of knowledge. There is, however, only necessity involved and not freedom and choice: "... in reality God acts and directs all things simply by the necessity of His nature and perfection, and that His decrees and volitions are eternal truths, and always involve necessity" (Spinoza 1951, p. 65).

In such a universe of necessity which Spinoza portrays, there is only pure positivity of forces—no life-denying negativity, but only the joyful assertion of life. True freedom is here "not the freedom of choice, but the accurate insights into the necessities which determine us" (Žižek 2004, p. 237). With the suspension of the ethical dimension ("of commandment, of the Master Signifier" (Žižek 2004, p. 238), Spinoza leaves us only with 'accurate insight' or knowledge into cause and effect to determine our actions. This very indifference and pure assertion of life can be described in the psychoanalytic language of today as the superego (Žižek 2004, p. 239). Žižek construes that the superego (who is on the side of knowledge) wants nothing from you when you decide about actions, but only informs you of the causal link. The health warnings printed on a cigarette packet may serve as an example: the superego (as an awareness or knowledge about causal links) has an indifference about human interests and is elevated above feelings of guilt and moral outrage.

In this purely positive network and universe of causes and effect, of necessity, of closed immanence, the first question for Žižek is whether we really can have 'accurate insight' or 'full knowledge'; and secondly whether this knowledge will restrict our freedom rather than enhance it. Put differently: Is there not a gap in the One-Whole Real of Spinoza, in this 'closed immanence'? And is a gap not perhaps necessary to uphold our human freedom? It is on this point that Žižek examines Kant's break with Spinoza. Kant argues that the Spinozan position of knowledge, without the deontological 'ought', is impossible to sustain. Kant says that there are some things we cannot know: there is a gap between appearance (phenomena) and reality (noumena). For Kant, as Žižek formulates it, there is "an irreducible crack in the edifice of Being, and it is through this crack that the 'deontological' dimension of 'Ought' intervenes—the 'Ought' fills in the incompleteness of 'Is', of Being" (Žižek 2004, p. 239). The substantial order of being is for Kant inaccessible (out of bounds for reason), but this opens up the space for morality, religious faith and ethical freedom.

Kant is anti-Spinozist, because from Kant's perspective "Spinoza's position appears as a nightmarish vision of subjects reduced to marionettes" (Žižek 2004, p. 239); a loss of our human freedom. To have full knowledge (as Spinoza envisions) will mean that we have access to the 'ding an sich', to the *noumenal*, as Kant formulates it. Such knowledge is not only impossible according to Kant, but it will be knowledge that will change us into mere mechanisms or puppets because:

> ... instead of the conflict which now the moral disposition has to wage with inclinations and in which, after some defeats, moral strength of mind may be gradually won, God and eternity in their awful majesty would stand unceasingly before our eyes ... Thus most actions conforming to the law would be done from fear, few would be done from hope, none from duty ... The conduct of man, so long as his nature remained as it is now, would be changed into mere mechanism, where, as in a puppet show, everything would gesticulate well but no life would be found in the figures. (Kant 1956, pp. 152–53)

For Kant, direct access to the noumenal would mean that we would be deprived of "the very 'spontaneity' which forms the kernel of transcendental freedom" (Žižek 2004, p. 239). We will become lifeless automata, thinking machines or mere mechanism with no autonomy and freedom. In other words, we need the space, the gap or crack, between the noumenal and the phenomenal. Kant's argument is that we are only free (autonomous agents) insofar as "our horizon is that of the phenomenal, insofar as the noumenal domain remains inaccessible to us" (Žižek 2004, p. 240). The Kantian Real thus remains the noumenal Thing beyond phenomena, and it is here where Deleuze (following Spinoza and Hegel) proposes an alternative, a more open, dynamic and free 'Real' than the noumenal Real that Kant describes, as well as the closed system of causality of Spinoza's immanence (a One-Whole all totalising Real).

Deleuze follows Hegel's critique of Kant in emphasising the absolute immanence that underlies the experiential appearances of the difference between noumenal and phenomena. Hegel argues that it is in the immanence of our thought that we experience the distinction between the way things appear to us and the way they are in themselves. This inherent-immanent refraction (or contradictory) experience of a Thing is for Hegel what brings us into direct contact with it (instead of denying us access to it, as Kant argues). Hegel hereby asserts the univocity of being and effectively abolishes the tension "between the ordinary phenomenal reality and the transgressive Excess of the Real Thing" (Žižek 2004, p. 243). Deleuze develops this idea further with his 'plane of immanence', and with his insistence on the univocity of being. This plane of immanence implies a 'flat ontology'—in line with Spinoza—in which all heterogeneous entities can be conceived at the same level, without ontological exceptions or priorities. The question is, however, whether this is not a move back to the Spinozan One-Whole totalizing Real. How, in this plane of immanence and univocity of Being, does Deleuze find space for freedom, an escape from the implied deterministic closed network of causality?

Deleuze, following Hegel, leaves the opposition of epistemology and ontology behind and does not see reality as something 'out there' (as something fully constituted and given) that we as subjects should investigate by gradually approaching it (the Kantian noumenal). Rather, we as subjects and the objects are both constituted by each other; both are 'becoming' in this univocity of being. What "seems to *separate* us from the way reality really is out there—is already the innermost constituent of reality itself" (Žižek 2004, p. 244). That we cannot ever fully know reality, is not a sign of the limitation of our knowledge, but "the sign that reality itself is 'incomplete', open, an actualization of the underlying virtual process of Becoming" (Žižek 2004, p. 244). There is thus an openness, a dynamic 'becoming' on this 'plane of immanence', within this univocity of Being. This differentiates Deleuze from Spinoza—but does this allow for freedom, for a non-totalising One-World?

Žižek would respond that it at least allows more freedom than Kant's noumenal 'Real' as the full and exhaustive ontological domain. Significantly, Hegel did not fill the gaps in the Kantian system (closed it in that sense), but shifted the perspective from the Kantian impossibility of 'knowing everything' to 'absolute knowing', as the "path towards Truth is already Truth itself" (Žižek 2004, p. 245). This is crucial for the notion of freedom, because of the short circuit between epistemology and ontology. With a strict epistemology we reduce our process of knowledge to a process external to the thing itself (and an endless approximation of the thing). Reality is then conceived of as a completed, inaccessible ontological domain. Because we do not have access to this completed noumenal Real, we will never know if we really have freedom (on the noumenal level). Kant accepts that we are free on the noumenal level in that space between the noumenal and phenomenal—but because the phenomenal is always only as it appears to us, it is still possible that we may not be free and that we may indeed be 'puppets' on the noumenal level (in 'reality'), without knowing it. This inconsistency of Kant is overcome by Hegel and Deleuze, who "transpose the incompleteness and openness . . . *into the thing itself*" (Žižek 2004, p. 245). The Thing is not closed—to fill the Kantian gap will be too Spinozan—but incomplete in itself. Being itself is incomplete. The Kantian gap is not the problem but the solution. Žižek maintains that this is what Hegel's motto means: "one should conceive the Absolute not only as Substance, but also as Subject", where *subject* refers to "the name for a crack in the edifice of Being" (Žižek 2004, p. 242).[21]

---

[21] To conceive the Absolute as Subject means that the split that is found within the subject—as an inner-worldly entity (the empirical person, the object) and the transcendental subject (the constitutive agent of the world itself)—is also found within the Absolute. The 'crack' is in Being itself. Žižek says the 'split of the subject' (in the modern philosophy of subjectivity) and the pre-Kantian metaphysical problem or 'split of humankind' (between the particular/sensual/animal and the universal/rational/divine) are something that should be insisted on, because this is what is missing from Spinoza's Substance. The split of the Subject acknowledges that there is more in the Real (the Absolute), more than Substance, and more to humankind than the animal/sensual. This 'more' is, however, not outside immanence, outside the

While Hegel and Deleuze are both philosophers of immanence, Hegel emphasises the 'crack' in Being (with his notion of Subject), while Deleuze emphasises the 'Substance', the univocity of Being. Žižek describes the difference between them as culminating in Deleuze's emphasis of the continuous *flux* of pure becoming as absolute immanence; whereas for Hegel there is an "irreducible *rupture* of/in immanence" (Žižek 2004, p. 245). This difference between 'flux' and 'rupture' (gap) is significant for Žižek, who sides with Hegel in terms of insisting on this 'gap or crack' in immanence. This gap is, however, not a gap to transcendence. The gap in immanence is for Hegel something that is present in the phenomena themselves. It is an *immanent* gap and transcendence is only the "illusory reflection of the fact that the immanence of phenomena is ruptured, broken, inconsistent" (Žižek 2004, p. 245). It is a gap in immanence not in the sense that some 'outside' transcendence (a superior transcendent; final truth; ultimate Being) can shine through, but a crack in immanence *as immanence*. Žižek explains that the gap in immanence is not that "phenomena are broken" or that "the transcendent Thing eludes our grasp", but rather that "the spectre of this Thing is the 'reified' *effect* of the inconsistencies of the phenomena" (Žižek 2004, p. 245). Transcendence is not on the other side of the gap, but in immanence, in the 'inconsistent' phenomena. The experience of the gap in immanence is not a pointing to a transcendent Beyond—such an understanding is just a "fetishized misperception-effect of the gap in immanence" (Žižek 2004, p. 246)—but to immanence, the gap is within phenomena itself.

While Deleuze emphasises the continuous flux of becoming in radical immanence, Žižek emphasises Hegel's gap in immanence because it allows for a greater understanding of the Real and consequently for possible freedom. To explain: For Deleuze the continuous flux of pure becoming involves a 'flat ontology', it takes place on the 'plane of immanence', on the 'plane of consistency'. With this absolute immanence, there is a univocity of being. It is, however, dynamic and everything is 'becoming'—an openness which aims to avoid the deterministic, all-totalising, Spinozan One-Whole Real. Žižek argues that this dynamic Real of Deleuze is still restrictive and reductive because it is exclusive. Deleuze's plane of immanence implies consistency between all entities without ontological exceptions and priorities. Žižek counters this with the Lacanian Real, which "is precisely that which resist inclusion within the plane of consistency, the absent Cause of heterogeneity of the assemblage" (Žižek 2004, p. 242). If something is excluded from this plane of consistency, it becomes all totalising. This is the problem with Deleuze's 'flux' in contrast to Hegel's 'rupture': Deleuze 'limits' the Real with his insistence of 'consistency', whereas Hegel broadens the Real (and by implication freedom) with his acceptance of the irreducible *rupture* of/in immanence which is in phenomena themselves and which amounts to an *inconsistency* within phenomena. By accepting this inconsistency within phenomena and the inconsistency within immanence itself, a gap or crack is allowed (albeit immanent) which disturbs the 'plane of consistency', the 'flat ontology'. In this way the all totalising Real is 'ruptured', becomes more inclusive for the transcendental dimension, and allows for the 'transcendent Beyond' (as immanence) to 'shine through'. In other words, it allows for the Truth, the Symbolic,[22] the Sublime, the Beyond—that imperceptible something in the immanent *as the immanent*—to show itself, to 'shine through'. There is not only a flux in immanence, but a gap, because of the inconsistencies of phenomena. This more radical openness of and within immanence is important for freedom, because it moves away from an all totalising One-Whole Real. It always allows for more. Truth, for example, is not a big metaphysical truth, posited as the inaccessible Beyond, and neither is it in the 'slip of the tongue' (in a flat ontology), but 'truth itself speaks'.[23] To have such a notion of truth, the transcendental dimension

---

empirical/temporal/finite, because the split (Kantian transcendental) is "the trans-phenomenal *as it appears within the finite horizon of temporality*" (Žižek 2004, p. 241). The split is within the noumenal itself, within the real, within immanence, within Being. It is a transcendental dimension that Hegel accepts, but which Deleuze (like Spinoza) does not, thereby moving back to a totalising One-Whole (deterministic) Real.

22 This is an important point for Žižek because of the fundamental thesis of Lacan: "the Real is not simply external to the Symbolic, but, rather, the Symbolic itself deprived of its externality, of its founding exception" (Žižek 2004, p. 243).

23 Žižek follows Lacan by saying truth can only be half-spoken, and that "the inconsistencies and slip of my speech directly connect to the inconsistencies and the non-all of the Truth itself" (Žižek 2004, p. 247).

(or gap in immanence) needs to be maintained. The same applies for what humankind is. What makes us different than animals is not that we are divine; but neither are we just animals. There is something more; there is an "imperceptible X" that differentiates us, a minimal difference. This minimal difference separates Deleuze's immanence (as a flat ontology) from Hegel and Žižek's gap in immanence (as still being immanent). The importance of this minimal difference (gap in immanence)[24] is that it avoids a completed full totalising Real (plane of consistency), which can be interpreted as the deterministic Spinozan One-Whole Real.

5. Žižek's Gap in Immanence, Liberation Theology and African Thought

The notion of transcendence in Liberation theology is in many ways attuned to Žižek's gap in immanence. A first resemblance is the emphasis on the incarnated nature of God in the world. Žižek argues that in Christianity the 'God of the Beyond' is left beyond and that a radical desublimation takes place, "in the sense of the descendence of the sublime Beyond to the everyday level" (Žižek 2001b, p. 90). While this is perhaps not the case in all the different Christian theologies, it is one of the accents of Liberation theology. McCann, for example, speaks of the "transformed Christian vision of religious transcendence" (McCann 1981, pp. 199–200) of Liberation Theology; and Mayra argues that God is not seen as remote or distanced, but 'within human touch'. With Liberation theology's emphasis on social justice and on the emancipation of the poor and oppressed, it focuses less on the 'beliefs and truths' of Christianity and the transcendence superiority of God, but more on social action. The 'Thing Beyond' and the 'tragic desire' for it are thus, in Žižek's terms, left behind, and the transition has taken place to the drive towards the object. In Liberation theology, however, this object is not closed because, for example, God's voice is still sought, but now through the voices of the poor that should be heard. In Žižek's terms it means that the gap in immanence is maintained, the 'excess', the 'symbolic', the 'voice of God' is found within the immanent—the voices of the poor. God's voice, though, is not heard as a final truth from Beyond, but within this reality, within immanence.

If Liberation theology gave up completely on the transcendence of God as a superior 'outside' being—transcendence in the metaphysical sense—it does not mean that there is only radical immanence left. It does not necessarily imply a move to the One-Whole deterministic Real of Spinoza, or the flat ontology with continuous flux of Deleuze's immanence. In its quest for freedom, Liberation theology can find in Žižek's 'gap of immanence' a space to keep on insisting on the 'more', the excess, the 'imperceptible something', the 'minimal difference' between Christ-man and man. The insistence is needed in order not to close off this world as pure consistency, as a flat ontology. If God is not described as the God of the Beyond in the transcendent sense in Liberation theology, all is not necessarily lost. God—as the gap in immanence—is the "coincidence, identity even, between the sublime and the everyday object" (Žižek 2001b, p. 92) and the "unique case of full humanity" (Žižek 2001b, p. 91). Such an immanent understanding of God (in Žižek's sense) allows for a move away from the radical transcendence of God—which Liberation theology by nature tends to do—but it is also not a move to an absolute immanence where freedom—that which Liberation theology prioritises—is put at risk.

The univocity of being which is emphasised in African thought (highlighted in ATR) has strong similarities with Deleuze's plane of immanence. For both, life is Being itself, a power that runs through every being. Deleuze will say we have a flat ontology with no division into categories—"a human being's life is literally equal to a life of a rock" (Pearson 2001, p. 141), and it is Being "who thinks through us; Being has absorbed us as it were: our life has become a Life, an expression of Being" (Justaert 2012, p. 97). ATR will in similar vein say that the Supreme Being is transcendental only in this world, as the highest "degree of mystical power ... the mysterious power or vital force"

---

[24] Žižek describes this gap in immanence also as the Symbolic gap. Myers says that in Žižek's work, the "Symbolic and the Real are intimately bound up with each other. The Symbolic works upon the Real; it introduces a cut into it, as Lacan claims, carving it up in a myriad different ways. Indeed, one of the ways in which you can recognize the Real is by noting when something is indifferent to Symbolization" (Myers 2003, p. 24).

(Rakotsoane 2010, p. 9). The life force is always part of this world. It is an impersonal life force which creates life and unity. There is no differentiation between the sacred and the profane and "all of nature is invested with a mystical, religious quality" (Thorpe 1991, p. 28).

Whereas Deleuze emphasises the flux of continuous becoming on the plane of immanence, in ATR there is a stronger affinity to Spinoza's immanence of One-Whole Real. This difference inhibits the possibility of human freedom in African thought. Africans have a monistic view of reality, which means that "what is out there is a closed system of cause and effect" (Rakotsoane 2010, p. 3). Even chance is ruled out, because "everything that happens is understood to have a specific cause in the system" (Rakotsoane 2010, p. 3). Reality as a closed system of cause and effect is—as indicated with Spinoza—a restriction to autonomous human freedom, because it is all totalising and deterministic. All that is left in such a world is to find your place in this system of causality, or as Du Toit points out, "[f]or Africans the aim of life is to experience and enhance life force and become part of it" (Du Toit 2009, p. 109). Turaki adds that "[t]he pursuit of cosmic harmony is an ethical principle in traditional Africa" (Turaki 1999, p. 122). With no real transcendence in a metaphysical sense, Žižek's notion of the gap in transcendence may create space in such a closed world of causality for freedom, though. There are some pointers to this Žižekean 'gap in immanence' in ATR, for example the references to the mysterious dimension in reality, the spiritual, and even the transcendent nature of the Supreme Being. The problem is that the univocity of Being seems to be getting such strong priority that the gap in immanence is lost.

6. Conclusions

In this article, the concept *transcendence* was used as a departure point for a dialogue between the three traditions of Critical theory, African thought and Liberation theology. The aim was not to offer a detailed discussion of the notion of transcendence in all these traditions, but rather to see how transcendence in African thought (ATR) and in Liberation theology can be understood from Žižek's critique on Deleuze's absolute immanence and from his own concept of the 'gap in immanence'. It was pointed out that the aim was not to achieve a re-establishment of transcendence, and some dangers and problems associated with transcendence were indicated. Neither was the aim to uncritically move to a notion of radical immanence. Deleuze's radical transcendence was discussed in order to indicate some problems with this position.

Although Žižek's gap in immanence is not a return to transcendence—since it remains an immanent gap—it was discussed in more detail to elucidate the relation between freedom, transcendence and immanence. Žižek follows Hegel in maintaining a gap in immanence; whereas Spinoza and Deleuze opt for a univocity of Being and a flat ontology. The Spinozan position is problematic for autonomous human freedom, though, because it understands reality as a closed network of cause and effect. In such a world, human actions are only part of bigger forces of causality; and the deterministic all-totalising character of this Spinozan One-Whole Real is threatening human freedom. African thought (specifically ATR) has many similarities with Spinoza's univocity of being and tends to move toward the same deterministic outcome. Hegel's insistence on the 'inconsistencies of phenomena' allows Žižek to understand immanence not as a flat ontology, but as one with a gap or crack. This remains a gap in *immanence*, but it allows for a disruption of the flat ontology. In other words, everything is not simply reduced to causality—'something imperceptible', a transcendental dimension, is allowed for within immanence. This gap in immanence is needed to allow for more human freedom. The concept of immanence in Liberation theology has similarities with Žižek's gap in the immanence. These similarities actualise the concept of freedom in Liberation theology: not to move back to complete immanence (a move into a relentless eternal deterministic process of liberation), but neither to move to radical transcendence (with its tragic desire for the Thing in an inaccessible Beyond), with no connection to the emancipation of the poor and oppressed.

Although Žižek is a postmetaphysical thinker (or perhaps because of this) his concept of the 'gap in immanence' served well as an entry point for the dialogue with traditions that include apparent

Religions **2017**, *8*, 271

notions of transcendence. This entry point gave more insight into these traditions, and into the conditions that are necessary to advance freedom in these traditions. The concept of transcendence is therefore of the utmost importance in the continuation of this dialogue.

Acknowledgments: This work is based on a research project supported by the National Research Foundation (NRF) of South Africa (Grant Number KIC170405225838). The grant holder acknowledges that opinions, findings and conclusions or recommendations expressed in any publication generated by the NRF-supported research are those of the author(s), and that the NRF accepts no liability whatsoever in this regard.

Conflicts of Interest: The author declares no conflict of interest.

References

Altizer, Thomas J. J. 1980. *Total Presence: The Language of JESUS and the Language of Today*. New York: Seabury Press.

Belhar Confession. 2006. *Text and Commentary*. Bellville: Convent for Unity.

Beyers, Jaco. 2010. What is religion? An African understanding. *HTS Theological Studies* 66: 1–8. [CrossRef]

Bodunrin, Peter O. 1981. The question of African philosophy. *Philosophy* 56: 161–79. [CrossRef]

Cumpsty, John S. 1991. *Religion as Belonging: A General Theory of Religion*. Lanham: University Press of America.

Davis, Charles. 1980. *Theology and Political Society*. Cambridge: Cambridge University Press.

Deleuze, Gilles. 2004. *Difference and Repetition*. Translated by P. Patton. New York: Continuum.

Deleuze, Gilles. 2007. *Two Regimes of Madness: Texts and Interviews 1975–1995*. New York: Semiotext(e).

Deleuze, Gilles, and Félix Guattari. 1991. *Qu'est-ce que la Philosophie?* Paris: Les Éditions de Minuit.

Depoortere, Frederiek. 2007. The End of God's Transcendence? On Incarnation in the Work of Slavoj Žižek. *Modern Theology* 23: 497–523. [CrossRef]

Depoortere, Frederiek. 2008. *Christ in Postmodern Philosophy, Gianni Vattimo, René Girard and Slavoj Žižek*. London: T&T Clark.

Du Toit, Cornel W. 2009. *African Challenges: Unfolding Identities*. Pretoria: Research Institute for Theology and Religion, University of South Africa.

Hennelly, Alfred T. 1979. *Theologies in Conflict: The Challenge of Juan Luis Segundo*. Maryknoll: Orbis Books.

Henry, Desmond, and Jacques Malan. 2017. Considering the This-worldly religious focus of the African traditional worldview as found in South Africa. *Verbum et Ecclesia* 38: 1–12. [CrossRef]

Jonkers, P. H. A. I. 2012. The Death-Defying Leap from Nihilism to Transcendence: F H Jacobi's Idea of Transcendence. In *Looking Beyond? Shifting Views of Transcendence in Philosophy, Theology, Art, and Politics*. Edited by Wessel Stoker and Willie L. van der Merwe. Amsterdam: Rodopi, pp. 31–46.

Justaert, Kristien. 2012. Gilles Deleuze and the Transcendence of Immanence. In *Looking Beyond? Shifting Views of Transcendence in Philosophy, Theology, Art, and Politics*. Edited by Wessel Stoker and Willie L. van der Merwe. Amsterdam: Rodopi, pp. 76–87.

Kant, Immanuel. 1956. *Critique of Practical Reason*. New York: MacMillan.

Layard, Richard. 2005. *Happiness: Lessons from a New Science*. New York: Penguin.

Magesa, Laurenti. 2002. *African Religion: The Moral Traditions of Abundant Life*. Maryknoll: Orbis Books.

Maluleke, Tinyiko Sam. 1998. African Traditional Religions in Christian mission and Christian scholarship: Re-opening a debate that never started. *Religion and Theology* 5: 121–37. [CrossRef]

Mbiti, John S. 1970. *Concepts of God in Africa*. London: SPCK.

McCann, Dennis P. 1981. *Christian Realism and Liberation Theology: Practical Theologies in Creative Conflict*. Maryknoll: Orbis Books.

Milbank, John. 2004. Sublimity: The Modern Transcendent. In *Transcendence, Philosophy, Literature, and Theology. Approach the Beyond*. Edited by R. Schwartz. New York: Routledge, pp. 211–34.

Momoh, Campbell S. 1985. African philosophy . . . Does it exist? *Diogenes* 130: 73–104. [CrossRef]

Myers, Tony. 2003. *Slavoj Žižek*. New York: Routledge.

Ogden, Schubert. 1979. *Faith and Freedom: Toward a Theology of Liberation*. Nashville: Abingdon Press.

Oruka, H. Odera. 1990. *Trends in Contemporary African Philosophy*. Nairobi: Shirikon Publishers.

Pearson, Keith Ansell. 2001. Pure reserve: Deleuze, philosophy and immanence. In *Gilles Deleuze and Religion*. Edited by Mary Bryden. London: Routledge, pp. 141–55.

Rakotsoane, Francis. Transcendence in African Traditional Religions. Paper presented at the 16th Conference of the South African Science and Religion Forum (SASRF) of the Research Institute for Theology and Religion,

University of South Africa, Pretoria, 2–3 September 2010; Available online: http://uir.unisa.ac.za/handle/10500/4282?show=full (accessed on 15 August 2017).

Rivera, Mayra. 2007. *The Touch of Transcendence: A Postcolonial Theology of God.* Louisville: Westminster John Knox Press.

Schwartz, Regina M. 2004. *Transcendence, Philosophy, Literature, and Theology. Approach the Beyond.* New York: Routledge.

Smith, Daniel W. 2001. The Doctrine of Univocity. In *Gilles Deleuze and Religion.* Edited by M. Bryden. London: Routledge, pp. 167–83.

Spinoza, Benedict. 1951. *A Theologico-Political Treatise and a Political Treatise.* New York: Dover Publications.

Stoker, Wessel. 2012. Culture and transcendence: A typology. In *Culture and Transcendence—A Typology of Transcendence.* Edited by Wessel Stoker and Willie L. Van der Merwe. Leuven: Peeters.

Stoker, Wessel. 2016. Transcendence and Immanence. In *Vocabulary for the Study of Religion.* Edited by Robert A. Segal and Kocku von Stuckrad. Leiden: Brill, Available online: http://dx.doi.org/10.1163/9789004249707_vsr_COM_00000343 (accessed on 4 October 2017).

Tempels, Placide. 1969. *Bantu Philosophy.* Paris: Presence Africaine.

Thorpe, Shirley Ann. 1991. *African Traditional Religions: An Introduction.* Pretoria: University of South Africa.

Thorpe, Shirley Ann. 1992. *Primal Religions Worldwide: An Introductory Descriptive Review.* Pretoria: University of South Africa.

Turaki, Yusufu. 1999. *Christianity and African Gods: A Method in Theology.* Potchefstroom: Potchefstroom University for Higher Christian Education.

Turaki, Yusufu. 2006. *Foundations of African Traditional Religion and Worldview.* Nairobi: World Alive.

Verhoef, Anné. 2013. Embodied religion's radicalization of immanence and the consequent question of transcendence. *Acta Academica* 45: 173–94.

Wernhart, K. R. 2003. Ethnische religionen. In *Handbuch Religionswissenschaft: Religionen und Ihre Zentrale Themen.* Edited by Johann Figl. Innsbruck: Tyrolia-Verlag.

Wiredu, Kwasi, ed. 2004. *A Companion to African Philosophy.* Malden: Blackwell.

Žižek, Slavoj. 2001a. *Did Somebody Say Totalitarianism? Five Interventions in the (Mis)Use of a Notion.* London: Verso.

Žižek, Slavoj. 2001b. *On Belief.* London: Routledge.

Žižek, Slavoj. 2004. The Descent of Transcendence into Immanence, or, Deleuze as a Hegelian. In *Transcendence, Philosophy, Literature, and Theology. Approach the Beyond.* Edited by Regina Schwartz. New York: Routledge.

religions

MDPI

Article

Marx, the Praxis of Liberation Theology, and the Bane of Religious Epistemology

Malesela John Lamola

Department of Philosophy, University of Fort Hare, Alice 5700, South Africa; jlamola@mweb.co.za

Received: 4 February 2018; Accepted: 2 March 2018; Published: 8 March 2018

Abstract: Can religious epistemology aid in the transformation of the world to the same effect as Marxist Theory? Utilizing an approach derived from Louis Althusser's isolation of the radical implications of the epistemological break of Karl Marx, from his Feuerbachain theological thought to a materialist epistemological tradition, we probe the relationship between the mystical intent of Christian theology and the appearance of praxis as a category derived from the Marxist lexicon, within the *modus cogitans* of Latin American theology of liberation. We problematise the transcendentalism that liberation theology places on social practice, in its retention of a spiritualist Weltanschauung as the preeminent framework for the critique of socio-historical reality. Far from being a materialist-transformative "epistemological break" from orthodox theology, this putative theology of revolution is thus exposed as being a brand of a Hegelian theosophy, which is discontinuous with the dialectical understanding of the socio-material basis of human relations that emerges around Marxist Theory, namely *praxis*. Our leitmotif is therefore a claim that political theology, qua theology in general, and the Latin American Theology of Liberation in particular, have a limited efficacy as a theoretical tool for socio-political transformation, due to its inherent transcendentalist and rationalistic orientation.

Keywords: Althusser; epistemological break; Feuerbach; liberation theology; Marx; political theology; praxis; religious epistemology; philosophy of religion; philosophical theology

1. Introduction

In *The Future of Liberation Theology: Essays in Honor of Gustavo Gutierrez*, Leonardo Boff points out that with his publication of *Teologia de la Liberación, Perspectivas* (Gutierrez 1973), Gutierrez "helped to create a new epistemological field within Christian thought" (Boff 1989, p. 38). Admiring Gutierrez, he observes that "creators of an epistemological break—that is, of a new possibility of interpreting reality—are rare", and proceeds to quote from Gutierrez's classic:

> The theology of liberation offers us not so much a new theme for reflection, but a new way of doing theology. Theology as critical reflection on historical praxis is a liberating theology . . . This is a theology which does not stop with reflecting on the world but rather tries to be part of the process through which the world is transformed (quoting Gutierrez 1973, p. 15)

Liberation theology is here represented as an epistemological break, in which the new in its character is captured in the category of praxis, as derived from the Marxian lexicon. The rationalization of this transversal foray of Marxian consciousness into theological practice was encapsulated in the title of Argentine Methodist theologian José Míquez Bonino's book, *Christians and Marxists: The mutual challenge to revolution* (Bonino 1976), and in Jon Sobrino's *The True Church and the Poor* (Sobrino 1981), in which Sobrino seminally posits that liberation theologians consciously set out an "epistemological break" (Sobrino 1981, p. 35) from the Euro-American theoretical way of doing theology. Sobrino's text sought to read classical religious texts, and do theology through the epistemological lens of the poor. To this "anti-abstract-theorization" emphasis, Bonino added "revolutionary commitment and practice" (Bonino 1975, p. 38) as the new element arising out of this epistemological break. Praxis was thus conceptually consummated as a disavowal of abstract theologizing that does not engage and seek to change unjust societal structures. This brought liberation theology into an epistemological affinity with the historico-materialist tradition of Western philosophy, as Aidon Nicholas' "The story of praxis, liberation theology's philosophical handmaid" (Nicholas 1989, pp. 45–58), as well as Nikolaus Lobkowicz's (Lobkowicz 1984) study, *Theory and Practice: History of the Concept from Aristotle to Marx* both remind us.

With the publication of a collection of essays titled, *For Marx* (Althusser 1969), Louis Althusser inaugurated an episodic development in the debate on the periodization and evolution of Karl Marx's thought in his insistence that Marx performed an "epistemological break" that delineates the "humanistic" early Marx from the "materialist-scientific" later Marx, when he penned his eleven theses on Feuerbach in 1845 (Althusser 1969, p. 220). In an essay entitled "On the Materialistic Dialectic", Althusser went on to outline the meaning and implications of an epistemological break as a notion derived from the philosophy of science (ibid., pp. 219–47). He pointed out that properly conceived, an epistemological break is a paradigm-shifting, an installation of a new scientific field and a new mode of thinking. Originally conceived by French philosopher of science, Gaston Bachelard (1884–1962), *la coupere épistémologue* was deployed to refute the empiricist view that the history of science is an incremental accumulation of knowledge. Contradicting this view, Bachelard insisted that science develops through a series of discontinuous raptures, cuts (coupere). These "breaks", given the need to avoid the fallacies contained in their preceding phases, are by nature radical and irreversible. As a necessity, the "new" rejects the preceding problematique and its concepts, and replaces these with revamped theoretical constructs. An epistemological break, "thus entails not simply the addition of new knowledge, but the reorganization of the very possibility of knowledge. It changes the conditions of what is and can be known."[1]

What is the nature of the epistemic break that liberation theology performed on Christian thought, and what is the new scientific field (Leonardo Boff uses "epistemological field" (Boff 1989, p. 39)) it inaugurated? The re-conceptualization of theology "as critical reflection on historical praxis", a phrase incorporating a concept ("praxis") introduced in the "Theses on Feuerbach" as part of Marx's protestation that "hitherto philosophers have only interpreted the world in various ways, the goal now is to change it" (Althusser 1969) appears as the consequence of this epistemological break constitutive of liberation theology. Or does it? What are the ramifications of this praxis in theology, given that it arose out of Marx's epistemological break from speculative and contemplative thought typical of Hegel and Feuerbach during his discovery of dialectic-historical materialism? Paul J. Davies and Johannes Reimer's (Davies and Reimer 2015) recent review of Bonino's theology resurrects the theme of praxis as a product of an epistemological break, in a manner that frames the problematique of this paper–namely, the question of the revolutionary efficacy of this theological praxis as an epistemic framework, as it remains mediated through a fidelity to biblical reflection and ecclesiastical orthodoxy.

Obviating the broader debate on the nature of the dialectical materialism conceived by Marx, in relation to that later postulated by Frederick Engels and Vladimir Lenin, our paper focuses exclusively on the character of the Feuerbachain epistemology that Marx appraises in the "Theses on Feuerbach", and on how this post-Feuerbach materialism relates to the embrace of Marxian epistemology in political theology, as experimented by Latin American theologians of liberation. Our mission is not an evaluation of the general use of Marx by liberation theologians; neither is it a critique of the apparent

---

[1] *A Dictionary of Critical Theory*. Oxford University Press, vid. 'epistemological break', http://www.oxfordreference.com/view/10.1093/oi/authority.20110803095755104, (accessed on 25 January 2018).

affinity of liberation theology with Marxism, nor an assessment of how liberation theology deals with Marx's ontological critique of religion.

Our specific focus is on the content and value of the concept of praxis as the interpretive frame of reference that emerged from the post-Feuerbachian Marx, and the implications of this frame for theology as a discipline and mode of knowledge that is premised on transcendence. We shall therefore delineate the two dimensions of praxis, as the "coincidence of the changing of circumstances and of human activity" (Marx and Engels 1968, p. 29) on the one hand, and as pertaining to its relationship (as parallax) to theoria, or reflection and rationalization, on the other. As we discuss liberation theology, we turn the spotlight on the latter—that is, the examination of the nature and the epistemic role of theoretical reflection in a theology that deliberately claims praxis as its hermeneutical compass. Consequently, our bibliographical point of reference shall be centered around Marx's "Theses on Feuerbach" (Marx and Engels 1968, pp. 28–30) as well as "The German Ideology" (Marx 1977), and not on the sociological application of praxis as an elaboration on the socio-historical modus vivendi of human existence as summarized by Marx in his "Preface to the Contribution to a Critique of Political Economy" (1859).

Following a brief explicative review of the embrace of Marxist philosophy in liberation theology, against the background an Althusserian introduction of Feuerbach, we counter-pose Marx's thought on praxis against the inherent epistemic nature of theology. This exposes what we highlight as the contemplative character of liberation theology's praxis. Towards our conclusion, we provide by way of illustration, the treatment of a selection of doctrines (on sin, history, poverty, and discipleship) in Latin American liberation theology, to demonstrate how this "contemplative materialism" as a religious epistemology, in fact, assumes a form of a pre-Feuerbachian Hegelian theosophy.

2. Marx, Feuerbach and Althusser

The theological and philosophical work of Ludwig Feuerbach (1804–1872) represents a historical watershed, which marks a point of distinction between two major systems of Western philosophical thought—on the one hand, the absolute idealism of post-Kantian German philosophy, as formulated into a teleological-dialectical idealism by Georg Wilhem Friedrich Hegel (1770–1831), and on the other, the latent historico-dialectical materialism of Karl Marx (1818–1883) and Frederick Engels (1820–1895). Besides his achievements on the critique of speculative idealism, Feuerbach distinguished himself as a philosopher in that he preeminently exposited the theological architecture of the epistemological framework of western philosophy. Memorably, he wrote in "Provisional Theses for the Reformation of Philosophy" that:

> The secret of theology is anthropology, but the secret of philosophy is theology; whoever fails to give up Hegelian philosophy fails to give up theology. The Hegelian doctrine that the nature of reality is posited by the Idea is merely the rational expression of the theological doctrine that nature is created by God, that the material essence is created by the immaterial, i.e., abstract essence ... (Stepelevich 1977, p. 156)

In a summative statement of his philosophy in *The Essence of Christianity* (Feuerbach 1957), Feuerbach famously postulated that in worshiping God, we are actually yearning for our alienated Self:

> In the object he contemplates, man becomes acquainted with himself since consciousness of the objective is the self-consciousness of man; consciousness of God is self-consciousness, knowledge of God is self-knowledge ... whatever is God to a man, that is his heart-soul; and conversely, God is the manifested inward nature, the expressed self of man ... (Feuerbach 1957, p. 12)

It is this Feuerbachian philosophy, particularly its assertion of the human subject as the point of departure in critical philosophical analysis, which mediated Karl Marx's move to his novel materialistic reformulation of the Hegelian dialectic, and his development of other fundamental socio-philosophical contentions (Gregor 1994, pp. 93–103). This move, which we shall appreciate as an epistemological break, is performed in the "self-clarificatory notes" (Marx 1977, p. 5) which were posthumously published in 1932 as "The German Ideology", and in the declaratory "Theses on Feuerbach", penned whilst he was working on the latter in 1845–1846.

Our examination of Marx's life writings puts us *ad idem* with Althusser, as far as he points out the radical nature of the methodological variation in the works following the "Theses on Feuerbach" (hereinafter, "Theses"), that reaches an apogee in the method of "Capital: A Critical analysis of Capitalist Production" [*Das Kapital*] (Marx 1954). We concur that this methodological break is of a nature that can rightly be characterized as an epistemological rapture, in the tradition of Bachelard's philosophy of science, and that the *differentia specifica* of this new epistemological framework is its disavowal of ideologically susceptible modes of thought in preference of knowledge, dialectically conceived as understanding-for-transformation, which arises from the ever-changing historico-contextual base (Benton 1984, pp. 24–26; Callinicos 1976, ad passim).

The key feature of the methodological position that Marx develops after 1845 is his establishment of a qualitative differentiation between ideology and science as theoretico-epistemological practices. Significantly, the context and derivative meaning of this ideology is expressed in the title of "The German Ideology" ("Deutsche Ideologie"). The latter is an excoriation of the theologico-philosophical methodology ("ideology") of the Left-Hegelians, or so-called "Young Hegelians", who had rallied around Feuerbach's influential critique of Hegel and Christian theology in an endeavor to recast Hegel's thought system into an anti-establishment mold. Arising out of his observations on the determining influence of socio-historical factors on intellectual output during his 1843–1844 exposure as a journalist and observer of the debates within the socialist movement in Paris (McLellan 1969, p. 74), Marx grew concerned about the theoretical integrity of the universe of ideas, as a realm that is detached from the material base of the human condition. He thus identified as "ideology" a theoretical practice that is either unconscious of the derivative nature of its formulations, or which deliberately seeks to conceal its awareness of this fact, in order to further partisan or subjective interests (Marx 1977, pp. 37–38). As a step leading away from this vulnerability of understanding (*Verstehen*) about corrupting reality (social institutions, as viewed by Hegel, as the incarnation of Absolute Reason, or *das Geist*), Marx devoted himself to cultivating a "scientific", non-ideological, and socially transformative way of analysis. This could only be done through his re-reading of Hegel, and the inversion of the idealist Hegelian dialectic—Hegel's elaboration of how history moves through Absolute Reason producing its own self-contradictions (see "Afterword" to 2nd Edition of *Das Kapital*, (Marx 1954, p. 29)). This inversion, as an epistemological act, would have as its hallmark, the adoption of a disciplined (dialectical) understanding of the socio-material basis of human existence, praxis, as the basis of historical progress. That is, instead of starting off from the abstracted level of ideas, the superstructure, focus would be on social reality, holding that this reality is the interpretive key and framework of super-structural phenomenon.

How does this Marxian maturation from the ideological/abstract to the scientific/dialectico-historical, as a fundamental epistemological posture, cohere with theology as a *modus cogitans*, being a "critical reflection on historical praxis"? (Is "praxis" not by definition "historical"?). We understand Marxism to be a theory, a scientific tool of interpretation, "a canon of historical interpretation" (Creco 1966, p. 22) formulated around the inversion of Hegel's dialectic, with an obsession with the human condition that emerged in the later Marx (Lamola 2013, pp. 187–96). This understanding alerted us to the non-consanguinity of Marxism with the mystical and rationalistic nature of Latin American liberation theology. Our concern was corroborated by Gutierrez's admission in the essay"Liberation Praxis and Christian Faith", in the collection *The Power of the Poor in History* (Gutierrez 1983, pp. 36–75) that "the rationalistic-theoretical is accorded significant prominence in liberation theology" (Gutierrez 1983, p. 67). We shall therefore problematise the transcendentalism that liberation theology places on social practice, through its retention of a spiritualist *Weltanschauung* as the preeminent framework for the critique of socio-historical reality. This mystical intent of Christian theology, and the simultaneous appearance of praxis within the *modus cogitans* of liberation theology caused us to question the notion of praxis as an antonym of *theoria*, in the sense the intrinsic rationalistic and transcendentalist nature of religious epistemology are emblematic of *theoria*. Can religious epistemology, as liberation theology, aid understanding for transformation of the world, to the same effect as praxis as conceived within Marxist Theory would?

3. The Triumph of Marx in Theology

In *The Militant Gospel: An Analysis of Contemporary Political Theologies* (Fierro 1977), Spanish theologian Alfredo Fierro asserts that the emergence of Christian political theology is chiefly a result of "the incorporation of dialectical reasoning and historical materialism into Western thought" (Fierro 1977, p. 2). In corroboration of this observation, in his seminal formulation of the systematic account of a theology of liberation as a political theology that emerged from Central and Southern America in the early 1970s, Gutierrez affirms that "it is to a large extent due to Marxism's influence that theological thought, searching for its own sources, has begun to reflect on the meaning of the transformation of this world and the action of man in history." (Gutierrez 1973, p. 9).

Beyond this affirmation of the fact of the service of Marxism as a significant catalyst in the search for an epistemological framework of analysis that would best exhaust the socio-historical relevance of the Christian faith in the contemporary world, we find that within liberation theology, Marxism is upheld as a theoretical tool, whose conscientious application is posited as the *conditio sine qua non* for the realization of the liberation that this theology envisions. This view, or rather conviction, was declared by, amongst others, Bonino, who in his *Revolutionary Theology Comes of Age* (Bonino 1975) stated that Marxist theory "has proved, and still proves to be, the best instrument available for an effective and rational realization of human possibilities in historical life … it is the unavoidable historical mediation of Christian obedience" (Bonino 1975, p. 97). Bonino buttressed this a year later in a book with a telling title, *Christians and Marxists: The Mutual challenge to Revolution* (Bonino 1976), where he states:

> As Christians confronted by the inhuman conditions of existence have tried to make their Christian Faith historically relevant, they have been increasingly compelled to seek an analysis and historical program for their Christian obedience. At this point, the dynamics of the historical process, both in its objective conditions and its theoretical development, have led them, through the failure of several remedial reformist alternatives, to discover the unsubstitutionable relevance of Marxism. (Bonino 1976, p. 19)

Poignantly, Bonino's analysis resonates with Gutierrez's concurrence with and endorsement of Jean-Paul Sartre's declaration that "Marxism, as the formal framework of all contemporary philosophical thought, cannot be superseded" (quoted in Gutierrez 1973, p. 9).

The apex of this embrace of Marxist philosophy in Christian theology would be the celebrated publication in 1985 of *Fidel and Religion: Fidel Castro in conversations with Frei Betto on Marxism and Liberation Theology* (Castro and Betto 2006). According to Betto, a Dominican friar who had endured imprisonment in his home country of Brazil because of his anti-government church work, the book became an instant international bestseller because "it was the first time that a communist leader in office had spoken positively about religion and admitted that it, too, could help change reality, revolutionize a country, overthrow oppression, and establish justice" (Castro and Betto 2006, p. 5).

Whilst Alberto Feirro completed his survey of the political theologies with a conclusion that could only be framed as a question as to whether "a materialist theology", which is what Marxist epistemology seems to adumbrate vis a vis theology, is possible (Fierro 1977, p. 10). In 1978, Mexican theologian José Miranda overtook Feirro's consternation with his *El Cristianismo de Marx*, published in English as *Marx Against the Marxists: The Christian Humanism of Karl Marx* (Miranda 1980).

Miranda's work served as a notable milestone within the intellectual struggle of liberation theology to define its relationship with Karl Marx. In it, Miranda went beyond the traditional position that Marxism and Christianity are compatible, and posits an argument that Marx's entire thought was essentially and consciously not only humanistic, in the sense of emphasizing the importance of the human subject in an epistemological process, but that actually, Marx's was a Christian humanism. Miranda wrote about "the Gospel roots of Marx's thought" (Miranda 1980, p. 197) and that Marx's philosophy is a "conscious continuation of early Christianity" (Miranda 1980, p. 224). In 1982, he released his exegetical *Communism and the Bible*.

Miranda's school of thought was to be fueled by the high-profile publication of *Fidel and Religion*. For our purposes, we note Frei Betto's lamentation in the introduction to the book's second edition in 2006, reflecting on the still-ambiguous fraternity between the Cuban Catholic church and the Cuban government since the euphoric détente occasioned by the publication of the book, and that "what the Cuban bishops lack is a theology that allows them to understand socialism as an absolutely necessary stage on the path toward the kingdom of God ... " (Castro and Betto 2006, p. 7).

4. Anti-Rationalism and Orthopraxis

As we noted in our introduction, according to Sobrino (supporting Leonardo Boff's view), the Latin American theology of liberation signifies a consciously initiated "epistemological break" (Sobrino 1981, p. 35) with the methodology of European theology, which he portrays as having as its hallmark a veneration of abstract thinking and idealism. Liberation theology, Sobrino explains, came about and remains a negation of this idealist form of thinking (Sobrino 1981, pp. 35–38). It is a conscious attempt at a materialist (practical) epistemology, in the sense of being a negation of a rationalism that fails to issue into social action. Sobrino set out to specifically emphasize that the entire motif of liberation theology derived its basis from a castigation of "speculative thought", and focuses on the importance of the social context of the thinking person as the point of departure of the theological process. He pointed out that it is absolutely necessary for self-authentication of whatever can be equated with Christian theology that it begins its activity with an analysis of the social conditions of those who are involved in the theological process, the *locus theologicus* (the materially-impoverished believers). This imperative to engage with the social and historical context of the *locus theologicus* is then conceptualized into a methodological category of praxis (Sobrino 1981, p. 16).

Furthermore, Sobrino, who the Vatican censored (issued a Notification against) in 2006 for "the methodological presuppositions on which [he] bases his theological reflections"[2], asserts that unlike in "European theology", in Latin American liberation theology it is the demands arising out of life experience that provide material for theological work, and not reasoning and logic (Sobrino 1981, p. 20). Not even the injunctions of this reason, as ecclesiastical orthodoxy, are the *point de départ* and goal of liberation theology. Instead and in negation of orthodoxy, Sobrino foregrounded "orthopraxis". The employment of orthopraxis, Gutierrez had already explained, was "to recognize the work and importance of concrete behavior, of deeds, of action, of praxis in the Christian life" (Gutierrez 1973, p. 10). It is significant that the doxological in orthodoxy is directly contrasted with orthopraxis. The right, or accepted way of worshiping God (orthodoxy as opposed to heterodoxy), is juxtaposed with the right way of living out one's faith, according to Gutierrez and Sobrino.

In parallel, in *Revolutionary Theology Comes of Age*, Bonino, a Protestant theologian, argues that liberation theology is founded on a "revolutionary commitment" (Bonino 1975, p. 38) to render the theological effort a cogent facilitator of the liberation of the poor. The participation in revolution, as an obedience to the Word of God, would, in Bonino's postulation, also translate in orthopraxis (Bonino 1975, p. 98).

This "revolutionary commitment", expressed as an anti-idealist attitude questing for a materialist theoretical framework, and the adoption of the predicament of the human condition in the oppressive

---

[2] http://www.vatican.va/roman_curia/congregations/cfaith/documents/rc_con_cfaith_doc_20061126_notification-sobrino_en.html, accessed on 28 January 2018.

and repressive political context of the Latin America of the 1970s and 1980s as a point of departure of theology, constitute the two epistemic pillars of the praxis of the Latin American theology of liberation. We are most fascinated by the first of the twin pillars of this praxis: the claimed rejection of and critique of speculative rationality, whilst at the same time endeavoring to be a theology that is grounded within the acceptable orthodoxy of the ecclesiastical regime. This contrast directs focus on the epistemological aspect of praxis, that is, the nature and content of its relationship with *theoria* as orthodoxy questing (*quaerens*) orthopraxis.

As a further tension between orthodoxy and Marxist-inspired "revolutionary commitment" as praxis, it is worth noting that the Peruvian Gutierrez appealed against the threat of excommunication by Cardinal Joseph Ratzinger's "Congregation for the Doctrine of the Faith" in 1984, successfully "proving his orthodoxy" (Torres 1989, p. 98). Gutierrez's writings after *A Theology of Liberation* veered toward themes of spirituality, with the most successful work since then being a theodicy, *On Job: God-Talk and the Suffering of the Innocent* (Gutierrez 1987). In the year 2015, he was invited to the Vatican, in what has variously been viewed as the eventual accommodation of his theology of liberation by the ecclesiastical authority. On the other end, there were liberation theologians who were persecuted by the Church, emblematic of whom was Nicaraguan Fernando Cardenal, who landed an appointment as Minister of Education in the 1979 government of the Marxist Sandinistan National Liberation Front (FSLN)[3]. It has thus to be admitted that there were some variations on the conceptualisation and actualisation of praxis across the diverse geopolitical contexts of South and Central American countries. Obviously, the Nicaraguan liberation theology movement offered an orthopraxis that varied from that of Gutierrez (Hindley 2015).

In terms of scholarly self-application, next to Gutierrez, Enrique Dussel was to distinguish himself as the Latin American theologian who would set himself up as a formal philosopher, a "philosopher of liberation", who laboured to decode the inter-disciplinarity in the meaning of concepts used in liberation theology for the non-religious world (Dussel 1985). Dussel would, in relation to praxis, emphasise "ethics", *inter alia* averring: "Liberation philosophy affirms that ethics (and therefore politics, as first horizon) is prima philosophia. Philosophy begins with reality, and human reality is practical, always a priori person-to-person relationships in a communication community (of language and life), presupposed in reality (objectively) and transcendentally (subjectively)" (Dussel 1996, p. 7). This theme emanated from his earlier theological *Ethics and Community* (Dussel 1986), in which ethics, as theoretical reflection on morality, is affirmed as *prima theologia* (Dussel 1986, p. 18).

The arrival at a formulation of praxis as a reasoned normative framework—how to live in community as exhorted in the Word of God (as orthopraxis)—as articulated by Dussel, crystallises our identified *status quaestionis* on the apparent affinity of liberation theology to the thought of Karl Marx—specifically, how the concept of praxis as applied in liberation differs from Marx's conception of 'ideology' and the *theoria* within praxis.

5. Marx's Theses on Praxis

The enlightenment that dawned on Marx's thinking as he penned the "Theses on Feuerbach", and the catalytic effect this has had on social science since is, in our consideration, comparable to the effect that Martin Luther's ninety-five theses posted on the door of the Wittenberg Castle church in 1517 had on western civilisation. A rapturous and new frame of reference, and a "scientific dispensation" of understanding how social structures rise and fall was inaugurated. From the first ("Thesis I") to the famous eleventh ("Thesis XI"), "The philosophers have only interpreted the world, in various ways; the point, however, is to change it" (Marx and Engels 1968, p. 30) the "Theses" are a critique of "all

---

[3] For a 2005 interview of Fernando Cardenal by Mathew Krain, distilling the fact that Nicaraguan liberation theology was 'a religious movement, and not a socialist movement' see http://liberationtheology.voices-old.wooster.edu/documents/document-7/.

previous materialism" as pertaining to the essence of the nature of human existence and the modus operandi of its self-interpretive capacity (consciousness).

Feuerbach, who had been the chief protagonist for the shifting of Hegel's philosophy from its foundation on transcendental Absolute Reason, or the Spirit (*das Geist*), to the realm of the human being ("Man"), since his publication of *The Essence of Christianity*, was castigated by Marx for confabulating religious thinking with the reality of the human essence as a self-subsisting ("labor") social existence. The apogee of the "Theses" became Marx's declaration that in changing their environment, human being are creating circumstances that in turn change them: "the coincidence of the changing circumstances and of human activity can be conceived and rationally understood only as revolutionary practice" ("Theses III", (Marx and Engels 1968, p. 30)). Here, the Marxian re-conceptualization of praxis, a concept dating back from Aristotle, is seminally enunciated. It is materialism newly conceived as an observation of human consciousness being modelled by labor, the development of forces of production (productive forces), and the resultant social relations, which in turn determine how that human labor power is expended. The emphasis upheld is that "the human essence is no abstraction inherent in each single individual. In its reality it is the ensemble of social relations" ("Thesis VI", (Marx and Engels 1968, p. 29)). Where one finds oneself socially in a stratified society is one's essence.

However, the value of the message of the "Theses", taken within the context of the juncture of Marx's intellectual development in which they were penned, does not yet rest on the active political meaning of praxis; it rests on the isolation, identification, and rejection of the Feuerbachian way of thinking about human reality. This is the *causa bellum*, the reason for his epistemological rupture from Feuerbach. This point is vitally important to our discussion of the putatively Marxian epistemology of liberation theology.

Here, Marx explicitly reckons that "in *The Essence of Christianity*, he [Feuerbach] regards the theoretical attitude as the only genuine attitude, while practice is conceived and fixed only in its dirty-juridical form of appearance. Hence he does not grasp the significance of 'revolutionary', of 'practical–critical', activity." ("Thesis I", (Marx and Engels 1968)). What he is addressing and disavowing here is the regard of *theoria*, "the theoretical attitude" as the primary epistemological-hermeneutical *modus cogitans*. Subsequent scholarship has generally interpreted *theoria* vis a vis praxis as simply meaning the employment of intellection over observed experience, or simply as "reflection" (Bin-Kapela 2011, p. xii). For Marx, thinking (reflection) is a dialectical material undertaking, an understanding-for-transformation of social reality. This subsumes *theoria* into the revolutionary practical–critical activity—that is, praxis.

Experienced reality, which Marx here refers to simply as human "practice", was viewed in Hegel as the self-estrangement of, interchangeably, Absolute Reason, Idea, Spirit, *das Geist*, or God, who is in all things—which in turn, during the thinking process (*verstehen*) is reconciled (*aufhebung*) with the thinking being (Hegel 1984, pp. 83–88). Feuerbach and the Left-Hegelians (Bruno Bauer and company) proposed a variation: the epistemological starting point must be reality, and not a fascination with the hypostasis of reason. This reason upon reality would be critique. The Left-Hegelians then developed this into a philosophical category named "critical criticism", or simply Critique (Kee 1990, pp. 69–76). Critique was conceived as a participation in the hypostasis of the Hegelian dialectic. It was reason functioning as the anti-thesis. It was progressive step from what Hegel had merely postulated as "understanding", and was thus fêted as a step into the Hegelian dialectic that Hegel himself had missed or neglected (Stepelevich 1977, pp. 451–63). Through critique, reality is saved from its self-alienation. In Feuerbach, this meant the retrieval of the human essence from its self-alienation that results from Hegelian theological thinking.

In the "Theses", at this stage of his intellectual development, Marx could only focus on his disavowal of this methodological standpoint of critique as an abstract mode of thought that leads to contemplative materialism. Sympathy with this theosophical mode of analysis is comprehensively buried in a joint publication with Engels, entitled *The Holy Family or Critique of Critical Criticism:*

against Bruno Bauer and Company (Marx 1977, pp. 1–221). When he settled in London two years later, Marx would read the history of human societies and economics with a new epistemic framework, the dialectic–materialist epistemology that reveals itself in the content of the 1848 *Manifesto of the Communist Party*.

The postulation of praxis as developed in the "Theses" is, therefore, the template against which we shed light on praxis as conceived in liberation theology.

6. Praxis as Contemplative Materialism

As noted, Gutierrez famously defined liberation theology as "a critical reflection on historical praxis" (Gutierrez 1973, p. 11). The terms "critical" and "reflection" are instrumentally significant against the background of what we just learned about the methodology and mission of the Left-Hegelians. Within this definition, it is clear that the rationalistic–theoretical approach is still accorded a significant measure of prominence, despite Sobrino's assertion that the method of liberation theology actively differentiates itself from rationalistic and speculative mainline European theology, and is thereby Marxian in its epistemological intentions (Sobrino 1981, p. 36). Archetypically, Gutierrez would ameliorate this anti-rationalism thus:

> Theology as a critical reflection on praxis in the light of the Word [of God] does not replace the other functions of theology, such as wisdom and rational knowledge; rather it presupposes them. (Gutierrez 1973, p. 13)

Similarly, with regard to Sobrino's revolutionary commitment and orthopraxis, Gutierrez would underline that during the course of Latin American liberation theology, "revolutionary activity simply became a new field for the application of theological reflection" (Gutierrez 1973, p. 17).

The central conception of theology as a logos in content, and as an act of religious reflection applying symbolic language on historical experience, is generally adhered to and preserved. Liberation theology is a "critical reflection on praxis in the light of the Word" (Gutierrez 1973, p. 13). In their critical appreciation of Bonino's theology, Davies and Reimer (2015) underscore how Bonino admirably grounded his thought on biblical precepts and hermeneutics. This invites attention to literature about the challenges of religious epistemology, such as Dan R. Stiver's *The Philosophy of Religious Language: Sign, Symbol, Story* (Stiver 1996). For our immediate purposes of a historico-philosophical review, however, we have to restrict ourselves to referencing the poignancy of Marx's appraisal of Feuerbach to the materialist revolutionary character of the *theoria* that is immanent in liberation theology.

In the opening thesis ("Thesis I"), Marx agonizes that, "The chief defect of all previous materialism (that of Feuerbach included) is that things, reality, sensuousness are conceived only in the form of the object of contemplation, but not as sensuous human activity, practice [praxis], not subjectively" (Marx and Engels 1968, p. 28). Marx takes up the charge further in "Thesis V", that "Feuerbach, not satisfied with abstract thinking, advocates sensuous contemplation ... " (Marx and Engels 1968, p. 28). In attempting to supplant Hegelian abstract idealism, Feuerbach posited a "contemplative materialism" ("Thesis IX" in (Marx and Engels 1968)). The word that Marx uses for "contemplative" or "contemplation" in the original German of the "Theses" is *Betrachtung*. This translates into English as "meditation" or "religious reflection". Marx came to the conclusion that Feuerbach's epistemology is nothing but a meditation seeking to be merely empiricist.

In considering the relationship between Marxism and liberation theology, and recalling that Gutierrez defined a theology of liberation as "an attempt at reflection, based on the Gospel and the experiences of men and women committed to the process of liberation, in the oppressed and exploited land of Latin America"' (Marx and Engels 1968, p. xi), we are therefore struck by the appearance of "reflection" as a proposition for a revolutionary cognitive practice. What are the epistemological features of this reflection based on the Gospel, and "reflection on praxis in the light of the Word of God" (Marx and Engels 1968, p. 13)? We can isolate only one—namely, what the phrase literally means: the abstraction of the theological schema, themes as well as dogma, and a use of these as a universalistic paradigm for interpreting concrete social reality. It is contemplative materialism, or *Betrachtung*. This is *theoria* with its primacy and paramount role affirmed. In confirmation of our observation, Gutierrez writes: "Theology . . . as linked to praxis, fulfils a prophetic function insofar as it interprets historical events with the intention of revealing and proclaiming their profound meaning" (Marx and Engels 1968, p. 13).

This is, precisely, an epistemological practice, whereby theology, which in Marx is a super-structural intellectual effort, is used to "give meaning" to the substratum of natural historical existence. This disregards the fact that the content and language of theology, according to historical-materialism, is generated and shaped by the substratum of the socio-economic relations of the historical and cultural context from which that theology emerges. This idea also contradicts Marx's method of starting with the material, given as the modicum of giving meaning to the theoretical. Therefore, by starting with, or basing itself on the theoretical, on the "Word" (*Logos*; Bible, John 1:1–14), liberation theology is open to the charge of being identified as an ideology, as understood in Marx. This, in fact, is what spurred Juan Luis Segundo to engage in what turned to be the unsuccessful project of *Faith and Ideologies: Jesus of Nazareth Yesterday and Today* (Segundo 1984).

Taken as a theology of the logos itself, that is, at how the historical Jesus of Nazareth is theologized and meditated away as the Word of God that subsequently becomes flesh and is then transfigured back into heaven, this contemplative materialism steps back into pre-Feuerbachian Hegelian idealism. Indeed, in the preface to the 1844 *Paris Manuscripts* Marx noted that:

> On close inspection theological criticism—genuinely progressive though it was at the inception of the movement—is seen in the final analysis to be nothing but the culmination and consequence of the old philosophical and especially the Hegelian transcendentalism, twisted into a theological caricature (quoted in Kee 1990, p. 69))

In order to corroborate and amplify our foregoing claims on the historico-epistemological location of liberation theology, as well as the quality of its revolutionary efficacy, we propose to proceed to demonstration, with a few illustrations to show how this contemplative materialism exhibits itself in this theological tradition.

7. Contemplative Epistemology Action

As one example of the "reflection" method of liberation theology, and the way this reveals "profound meaning" (Gutierrez 1973, p. 13), it is important that we note the critical theme of history in liberation theology, as this occupies a vital role in Hegel's philosophy and in Marxian materialism. Significantly, the full title of the English translation of liberation theology's primal classic by Gutierrez is *A Theology of Liberation: History, Salvation and Politics*. Here, Gutierrez proclaimed that: "We have recovered the idea that history is an intrahistorical reality. Furthermore, that, salvation—the communion of men with God, and the communion of men among themselves—orients, transforms, and guides history to its fulfilment" (Gutierrez 1973, p. 152). This Hegelian anti-Marxist statement emanates from Gutierrez's following definition of history:

> Human history is a political occupation through which man orients and opens himself to the gift which gives history its transcendent meaning: the full and definitive encounter with the Lord and other men. (Gutierrez 1973, p. 10)

How profound! Is this "transcendent meaning" not a mystification of human history, a transfiguration of human history into "History" the transcendental concept? This is similar to Feuerbach's apotheosisation of anthropology into a theologico-philosophical analytic concept of "Man", or Hegel's theosophical postulation of history as the teleological locus of Absolute Reason, through which human civilisation is oriented towards freedom.

In *The German Ideology*, Marx provided the following succinct analysis of Feuerbach's transcendentalist method, which we maintain will be applicable to theologies that claim a material socio-political *point de départ*, whilst at the same time venerating the supernatural dimension as the framework of interpretation:

> Feuerbach's 'conception' of the sensuous world is confined on the one hand to mere contemplation of it, and on the other to mere feeling; he posits 'Man' instead of 'real historical man' . . . in the contemplation of the sensuous world, he necessarily lights on things which contradict his consciousness and feeling . . . to remove this disturbance, he must take refuge in double perception, a profane one which perceives 'only the flatly obvious' and a higher, philosophical one, which perceives the 'true essence' of things. (Marx 1977, p. 39)

By applying theological categories on concrete socio-historical reality, and in positing these categories as determinative hermeneutical premises for explaining reality, liberation theology is actually constructing abstract notions out of socio-historical reality. In the least, which cannot be denied, liberation theology imposes an interpretative mantle of religion upon its object of analysis, and gives to social reality purely mythical meanings, which go beyond the acceptable role of a myth as being a hermeneutic aid. In the foregoing example, Gutierrez fetishizes history and reifies the idealized mythological–religious result/notion as the ultimate experience.

Liberation theology reduces social processes and experience into theological dogmas; the result is that praxis, transforming reality, is then left conceived as a riddled system of dogmatic inconsistencies, which are perpetually in search of some form of an esoteric resolution or another. The most pertinent example of this resultant theoretic confusion we find in the application of the doctrine of sin as *theoria*, an interpretive principle in political analysis. We encounter this analysis in Dussel's political ethics:

> . . . someone may be born wealthy, a member of the dominant class and a moneyed, bourgeois family. He or she is surely not responsible for having been born there. But just as surely, this individual inherits this institutional "originary" sin. Thus as Paul proclaims, it is possible for death to reign even over those who had not sinned by breaking a precept as did Adam (Rom 5: 14). (Dussel 1986, p. 21)

This, according to Dussel, is an analytical judgment on an exploitative class in capitalist society. The bourgeoisie—the ruling class—is a community of sinners, but most of them are sinners not by choice. They simply have the fortuitous misfortune of being born into families whose class location happens to produce, exploit, and oppress the poor.

Having characterized the moneyed bourgeois families in such biblical terms, where does Dussel's postulation leave the poor? He elaborates:

> The constitutive act of the 'poor' in the Bible is not lacking goods, but being dominated, and this by the sinner. The poor are the correlative of sin. As the fruit of sin, their formality as 'poor' constitutes the poor or oppressed, and as such, the just and holy . . . The poverty or want suffered by the poor is not the sheer absence of goods. No, the poverty of the poor consists in having been despoiled of the fruit if their labor by reason of the objective domination of sin. (Dussel 1986, p. 21)

The impoverished, who in Marx's historico-materialist analysis of capitalist social relations would be characterized as the exploited labor power, are poor simply because they have to mirror, signify, and actualize "the objective domination of sin"! Such is perhaps the inadvertent results of the logic of a theosophical praxis.

In the same vein, in their *The Bible, the Church, and Poor* Clodovis Boff and George Pixley hold that the poor, who struggle against structures of oppressive opulence, are a "sacrament of God" (Boff and Pixley 1989, p. 111). This theme is taken up by Bishop Moacyr Grechi in his foreword to the same book. He summarizes the message of the book with the singular theme that God is using the poor to save the Church, and thereby the world: "Without the poor, the church loses its Lord, who identified with them and elevated them into final judges of this world. Without the poor, the church is simply lost" (Boff 1989, p. 1).

This nebulous portrayal of victims of an unjust system, in terms that dissuade them from mobilizing themselves for their liberation, or an analysis which make it impossible for them to be made conscious of the causes of their domination in material-scientific terms is, according to Engels in *Ludwig Feuerbach and the End of Classical German Philosophy* ([1888] (Marx and Engels 1968, pp. 584–607)), exactly what Feuerbach's "neueren Philosophie" was about. Apart from this fallacious materialism, Marx had epistemologically defected by critically developing a new analytical approach, as Engels explains:

> [Feuerbach] is realistic since he takes his start from man . . . this man remains always the same abstract man who occupies the field of the philosophy of religion. For this man is not born of a woman; he issues, as a chrysalis, from the god of the monotheistic religions. He therefore does not leave in a real world historically determined . . . But from the abstract man of Feuerbach one arrives at real living men only when one* considers them as participants in history. And that is what Feuerbach resisted . . . But the step which [he] did not take had nevertheless to be taken. The cult of abstract man, which formed the kernel of Feuerbach's new religion, had to be replaced by the science of real men and of their historical development. This further development to Feuerbach's standpoint beyond Feuerbach was inaugurated by Marx in 1845 in The Holy Family. (Marx and Engels 1968, p. 604)

To subsume all reality into a religious cognitive system is a hallmark of Feuerbachianism, as being both a preservation of the theologism of Hegel, as well as the privileging of *theoria* over praxis.

The consequence of this idealist epistemology is logically—in the context of the fundamental intent of Marx's philosophy—exposed in the ultimate meaning of the "revolutionary commitment" that liberation theological practice is supposedly grounded upon. According to Gutierrez, Boff, and Bonino, the church's engagement and commitment to historical ("secular") liberation struggles is not an end in and of itself: "this commitment is [merely] the matrix for a discovery of the true meaning of discipleship", informs Bonino (Eagleson and Drury 1975, p. xxv). He then proceeds to quote from the final document "Christians for Socialism" (participants at the conference held in Santiago, Chile, in April 1972 under the same theme):

> The Christian committed to revolutionary practice discovers the liberating force of the love of God, of the death and resurrection of Christ. He discovers that his faith does not imply the acceptance of a world that is already made, or of a predetermined history, but rather that the very living of his faith involves the creation of a new and solitary world and leads to historical initiatives fertilized by Christian hopes. (Eagleson and Drury 1975, p. xxv)

Revolutionary participation in the transformation of history is interpretatively rendered subservient to the higher ideal of attaining and experiencing a more profound religious experience, the epiphany of the experience of the love of God. In other words, all forms of struggle, from the wider class struggle to the very political skirmishes that the oppressed occasionally mount against their oppressors, are acts of Faith. They are ritual. They are acts through which "the true meaning of discipleship" is discovered.

Latin American liberation theology itself is not, per se, an intentional development of a theoretical apparatus aimed at being used as a weapon for structural transformation, as Jon Sobrino explains:

> Latin American liberation theology is interested in the liberating of the real world from its wretched state since it is this objective situation that has obscured the meaning of faith. Its task is not primarily to restore the meaning of faith in the presence of the wretched conditions of the real world. It is to transform this real world and at the same time recover the meaning of the faith. The task, therefore, is not to understand the faith differently, but to allow a new faith to spring from a new practice. (Sobrino 1981, p. 20)

A fortiori, the primary goal of this new practice (praxis?) is religious: to transform the world so that it can be sanctified (evangelized) and serve as the script for further revelations. In the process, even Marxism as a social theory is transfigured into a religious artefact, an icon—an aid for religious contemplation. This is encapsulated in Bonino's epic pronouncement that Marxism is embraced in the program of liberation theology as "the unavoidable historical mediation of Christian obedience" (Bonino 1976, p. 98). It is out of this understanding that Frei Betto could state that, "what the Cuban bishops lack is a theology that allows them to understand socialism as an absolutely necessary stage on the path toward the kingdom of God . . . " (Castro and Betto 2006, p. 7).

8. Conclusions

What we have set out to demonstrate is that insofar as it sought to situate itself within the historico-epistemological milieu of Marxist thought, the Latin American theology of liberation has remained intractably trapped in a Hegelian religious transcendentalism, as expressed in a Feuerbachian contemplative materialism. It develops mystical constructs out of historical contradictions, and rationalistically uses this mystical matrix as an ethical imperative to resolve the same historical contradictions, which in turn results in a circuitous mystification of historical reality. The theorized mystical matrix—as theology, the "Word of God"—is paramount and reified. This is not praxis qua Marxian praxis. Even as *theoria*, its abstractive and ahistorical conceptualization or contemplation of the victims of social injustice ("the poor") disqualifies it as a theoretical tool for social revolution.

Conflicts of Interest: The author declares no conflict of interest.

References

Althusser, Louis. 1969. *For Marx*. Middlesex: Penguin Books. First published 1966.

Benton, Ted. 1984. *The Rise and Fall of Structural Marxism: Althusser and His Influence*. London: Macmillan.

Bin-Kapela, Victor. 2011. *The Dialectics of Praxis and Theoria in African Philosophy: An Essay in Cultural Hermeneutics*. Bamenda: Langaa Research.

Boff, Leonardo. 1989. The originality of the liberation theology. In *The Future of Liberation Theology: Essays in Honour of Gustavo Gutierrez*. Edited by Marc H. Ellis and Otto Maduro. Maryknoll: Orbis, pp. 38–48.

Boff, Clodovis, and George Pixley. 1989. *The Bible, the Church and the Poor*. Maryknoll: Orbis.

Bonino, José Miguez. 1975. *Revolutionary Theology Comes of Age*. London: SPCK.

Bonino, José Miguez. 1976. *Christians and Marxists: The Mutual Challenge to Revolution*. Grand Rapids: Eerdemans.

Callinicos, Alex. 1976. *Althusser's Marxism*. London: Pluto Press.

Castro, Fidel, and Frei Betto. 2006. *Fidel and Religion: Fidel Castro in Conversations with Frei Betto on Marxism and Liberation Theology*, 2nd ed. Translated by Mary Todd. Melbourne: Oceana Press. First published 1985.

Creco, Benedetto. 1966. *Historical Materialism and the Economics of Karl Marx*. New York: Russell & Russell.

Davies, Paul J., and Johannes Reimer. 2015. Faith Seeking Effectiveness: Missiological insights from the hermeneutics of Jose Miguez Bonino. *Missionalia* 3: 306–22. [CrossRef]

Dussel, Enrique. 1985. *Philosophy of Liberation*. Translated by Aquila Martinez, and Christine Morkovsky. Maryknoll: Orbis.

Dussel, Enrique. 1986. *Ethics and Community*. Oregon: Wipf & Stock.

Dussel, Enrique. 1996. *The Underside of Modernity: Apel, Ricoeur, Rorty, Taylor, and the Philosophy of Liberation*. Atlantic Highlands: Humanity Books.

Eagleson, John, and J. Drury, eds. 1975. *Christians and Socialism: The Christians for Socialism Movement in Latin America*. Marknoll: Orbis.

Feuerbach, Ludwig. 1957. *The Essence of Christianity, Trans. George Eliot*. New York: Harper & Row. First published 1841.

Fierro, Alfredo. 1977. *The Militant Gospel: An Analysis of Contemporary Political Theologies*. London: SCM.

Gregor, A. James. 1994. Marx, Feuerbach and the Reform of the Hegelian Dialectic. In *Karl Marx's Economics*. Edited by John Cummingham Wood. London: Routledge, pp. 93–103.

Gutierrez, Gustavo. 1987. *On Job: God-Talk and the Suffering of the Innocent*. Maryknoll: Orbis. First published 1985.

Gutierrez, Gustavo. 1983. *The Power of the Poor in History*. Translated by Robert R. Barr. Maryknoll: Orbis. First published 1979.

Gutierrez, Gustavo. 1973. *A Theology of Liberation: History Salvation and Politics*. Translated by Caridad Inda, and John Eagleson. Maryknoll: Orbis Books, Originally published as 1971. *Teologia de la Liberación, Perspectivas*. Lima: CEP.

Hegel, Georg W. F. 1984. *Lectures in the Philosophy of Religion*. Edited by Peter Crafts Hodgson. Los Angeles: University of California, vol. 1. First published 1831.

Hindley, John. 2015. Neo-Colonialism, Liberation Theology and the Nicaraguan Revolution. Available online: http://digitalcommons.providence.edu/research_prize/1 (accessed on 25 December 2017).

Kee, Alistair. 1990. *Marx and the Failure of Liberation Theology*. London: SCM Press.

Lamola, M. John. 2013. Marxism as a Science of Interpretation: Beyond Althusser. *South African Journal of Philosophy* 32: 187–96. [CrossRef]

Lobkowicz, Nikolaus. 1984. *Theory and Praxis: History of the concept from Aristotle to Marx*. Indiana: University of Notre Dame Press.

Marx, Karl. 1954. *Capital: A Critical analysis of Capitalist Production*. London: Lawrence & Wishart, vol. 1. First published 1867.

Marx, Karl. 1977. *Collected Works*. London: Lawrence and Wishart, vol. 5.

Marx, Karl, and F. Engels. 1968. *Selected Works in One Volume*. Moscow: Progress Publishers.

McLellan, David. 1969. *The Young Hegelians and Karl Marx*. London: MacMillan Press.

Miranda, José. 1980. *Marx against the Marxists: The Christian Humanism of Karl Marx*. Maryknoll: Orbis.

Nicholas, Aidon. 1989. The Story of Praxis: Liberation theology's philosophical handmaid. *Religion in Communist Lands* 17: 45–58. [CrossRef]

Segundo, Juan Luis. 1984. *Faith and Ideologies: Jesus of Nazareth Yesterday and Today*. Maryknoll: Orbis.

Sobrino, Jon. 1981. *The True Church and the Poor*. London: SCM Press.

Stepelevich, Lawrence, ed. 1977. *The Young Hegelians: An Anthology*. Cambridge: Cambridge University Press.

Stiver, Dan R. 1996. *The Philosophy of Religious Language: Sign, Symbol, Story*. London: Wiley.

Torres, Sergio. 1989. Gustavo Gutierrez: A Historical Sketch. In *The Future of Liberation Theology: Essays in Honor of Gustavo Gutierrez*. Edited by Marc H. Ellis and Otto Maduro. Maryknoll: Orbis, pp. 95–101.

religions · MDPI

Article

Kairos and Carnival: Mikhail Bakhtin's Rhetorical and Ethical Christian Vision

Ian Bekker

School of Languages, North-West University (Potchefstroom Campus), Potchefstroom 2520, South Africa;
Ian.Bekker@nwu.ac.za

Received: 1 February 2018; Accepted: 6 March 2018; Published: 12 March 2018

Abstract: The term *kairos* has been used to mean, alternatively, right timing or proportion in Ancient Greek rhetoric, by Jesus to refer to the Christian eschaton and by Paul Tillich and modern liberation theologians to refer to the breakthrough of the divine into human history. *Kairos*, unlike *chronos*, is an intrinsically qualitative time and implies a consciousness of the present as well as the need for responsive action. This emphasis on action provides the link between *kairos* and virtue, the particular virtue in question being that of prudence (phronesis in Greek). The aim of this article is twofold: to highlight and make explicit the connections between the notion of *kairos* and the Russian literary-theorist and philosopher Mikhail Bakhtin's rhetorical and ethical world, with particular emphasis on his notion of carnival; secondly, to further support a Christian reading of Bakthin's work by making explicit the connections between his carnivalesque vision and a Christian reading of the ethical importance of *kairos* and its links with incarnation.

Keywords: Bakhtin; carnival; kairos; rhetoric; liberation theology; Paul Tillich; Albert Nolan; phronesis; prudence; virtue; incarnation; the grotesque

---

> *In meinen Mauern bauen*
> *sich neue Zeiten auf,*
> *und alle Völker schauen*
> *mit kindlichem Vertrauen*
> *und lautem Jubel d'rauf!*
> *Der glorreiche Augenblick,*

Beethoven (op. 136)

1. Introduction

Traditionally, *kairos* has been opposed to *chronos*, the later referring to quantitative (measured or ordered) time, the former referring to qualitative time, or special time. From the beginning, there has been a clear link between *kairos* and what we could refer to, following Husserl (1992), as internal time consciousness[1]. *Kairos* is an intrinsically value-laden time; in Tillich's words it implies "a consciousness of the present and for action in the present" (Tillich 1957, p. 32). *Kairos* thus implies a sensitivity to the contingencies of a particular context.

The emphasis on action in this quote from Tillich also highlights the fact that there is, very often, an explicit or implicit link between *kairos* and virtue or ethics, the particular virtue in question

---

[1] Thanks go to Anné Verhoef for pointing out in response to an earlier version of this article that Ricouer makes a related distinction between private time and cosmic time—as discussed in Verhoef and van der Merwe (2015).

often being that of prudence (*phronesis* in Greek; *prudentia* in Latin; often also referred to as practical wisdom), which is a virtue that is also characterized by sensitivity to context. The link between *kairos* and *phronesis* has been clear right from its Ancient Greek beginnings, very often mediated by the concept of *paideia*, the education of the citizen. More recently, for example, Benedikt (2002, p. 226) attempts to "create an account of *kairos* capable of informing a system of ethics".

As mentioned in the abstract, the main aim of this article is twofold: to highlight and make explicit the connections between the notion of *kairos* and Mikhail Bakhtin's ethical and rhetorical vision, with a particular emphasis on his notion of carnival; secondly, to further support a Christian reading of Bakthin's work by making explicit the connections between this carnivalesque vision and a Christian reading of the ethical importance of *kairos* and its links with incarnation.

The next section of this article provides a brief historical overview of the use of the term *kairos*, firstly within the context of the classical world, but secondly with reference to its employment within a Christian milieu, beginning with its use in the Greek New Testament, but placing the most emphasis on the theologian who has more than any other incorporated this concept into modern thinking i.e., Paul Tillich. The section ends with an example of its use in modern liberation theology i.e., as part of the contextual theology of the South African liberation theologian, Albert Nolan.

The article then takes a brief look at Bakhtin's notion of carnival, as famously expounded in his doctoral dissertation, *Rabelais and his World*. Various, often diametrically opposed, interpretations of carnival, particularly from an ethical and political perspective, have arisen since Bakhtin's re-discovery, both within and without Russia, in the second half of the 20th-century. The position adopted here is that Bakhtin's (and thus carnival's) ethics are of an essentially (although implicitly and unorthodox) Christian nature. Given the incorporation of the notion of *kairos* into Christianity right from the beginning (i.e., the New Testament) this allows for, in this last section, a final bringing together of Bakhtin's notion of carnival and a Christian understanding of *kairos*.

2. A Brief History of *Kairos*

> Thus saith the Lord, In an acceptable time[2] have I heard thee, and in a day of salvation have I helped thee . . .

Isaiah 49: 8; Kings James Version. In Ancient Greece, *Kairos* was a god; and, as described by Sipiora (2002, p. 1) this god represented opportunity. As demonstrated by Tillich (1957, p. 33), *kairos* means ""the right time," the moment rich in content and significance". More broadly, the concept of *kairos* became "a seminal concept in ancient Greek culture that was strategic to classical rhetoric, literature, aesthetics and ethics" (Sipiora 2002, p. 1).[3]

One of the odd aspects of the early, classical use of the expression *kairos* is that its different meanings appear, on the surface, to be somewhat at odds. On the one hand, we have a sense of *kairos* as a force or power that breaks through the expected or the repetitive; it breaks, in particular, through *chronos* or mechanical time. It also explicitly assumes (or demands) human agency. In the words of White (1987, p. 13), it is "a passing instant when an opening appears which much be driven through with force if success is to be achieved". It is, moreover, something that is not predictable and that requires a special sensitivity to the contingencies of the immediate context; it is a force for dynamism and change. In the writings of ancient rhetoricians, such as Isocrates and Gorgias, *kairos* is associated with the use of language for particular times and particular purposes and deals directly with an ability to adapt and adjust, in terms of one's use of the spoken language in particular, to the context that one is in, to the topic at hand, as well as to the audience being spoken to. Of particular

---

2 καιρῷ in the Septuagint; a derivation of *kairos*.
3 It is tempting even at this point to make connections between *kairos* and the work of Bakhtin. This list of topics is almost a perfect catalogue of Bakhtin's interests which the Russian manages to bring together into a relatively stable but open theoretical oeuvre; Bakhtin received a thorough early training in the classics (Clark and Holquist 1984, pp. 30–34).

importance is that the ability to sense the right moment, to sense the *kairos*, cannot be taught on the basis of mechanically-applied, repeatable principles.

On the other hand, *kairos* is also identified with the right proportion and symmetry; concepts that tend to be associated with order, balance, and continuity:

> *Kairos* means also the "right measure" or proportion as expressed, in the saying of Hesiod, "Observe due measure, and proportion (*kairos*) is best in all things." The same idea is found in the maxims attributed to the Greek Sages, such as "Nothing in excess" (Smith 2002, p. 47).

The appropriateness of an action or utterance to a particular context is one way of thinking about this. As such, *kairos* calls for appropriate behavior in terms of both local and non-local contexts. The latter refer to broader, 'congealed', repeatable structures on an ethical, linguistic, and social level, while the former demand a suitable, potentially unique, response to the exigencies of an immediate context. Here we have a connection with the ethical implications of *kairos*. In Isocrates' system, for example, *kairos* was very closely related to *phronesis* (practical wisdom) as well as *paideia*, the latter referring to the education of the ideal member of the Greek polis. In *Panathenaicus* for example, Isocrates writes that educated people are those "who manage well the circumstances which they encounter day by day, and who possess a judgement which is accurate in meeting occasions as they arise and rarely misses the expedient course of action".[4] The ethical dimension of *kairos* and its link to *phronesis* in particular is, then, taken up by Plato (e.g., in the *Phaedrus*) and, perhaps most importantly, by Aristotle.

According to MacIntyre (2007, p. 154) in *After Virtue*, the virtue of *phronesis* in Aristotle's thinking "comes to mean . . . someone who knows how to exercise judgement in particular cases". This is later taken up by Aquinas as the Christian virtue of *prudentia* (prudence in English). Of interest here is that, within Aristotle's ethical system, particularly as provided in his *Nicomachean Ethics*, *phronesis* takes pride-of-place among the virtues: without the practical judgement that is subsumed under the notion of phronesis, the individual would not be able to appropriately cultivate the other virtues. Thus, drawing again on MacIntyre's (2007) analysis of Aristotle's ethical system, we note that "judgement has an indispensable role in the life of the virtuous man which it does not and could not have in, for example, the life of the merely law-abiding or rule-abiding man. A central virtue is therefore *phronesis*" (ibid., p. 154). Later on this author confirms that *phronesis* is "a virtue the possession of which is a prerequisite for the possession of other virtues" (ibid., p. 183). Here, we have an insistence on a level of independence from (although not a rejection of) abstract principles and rules.

The appropriation of *kairos* by the Christian tradition begins with its use in the New Testament. In Mark 15:1, we read, according to Sipiora (2002, p. 114), the first utterance of Christ: "The time [i.e., the *kairos*] has been fulfilled and the Kingdom of God has drawn near. Repent and believe in the Gospel". The word *kairos* is used extensively in the New Testament (86 times) and, in particular, is used by Jesus to refer to the Christian eschaton and, as in Ancient Greek rhetoric, is clearly distinct from *chronos* i.e., linear and chronological time. Here again, we have qualitative (and also divine) time and time that is filled with a sense of urgency and meaning. We again have the sense of a force (the eschaton in this case) breaking through the regular and the familiar.

One of the most important consequences of the appropriation of *kairos* into the Christian tradition (via the notion of the eschaton in particular), is its alignment with a particular conception of history, something that distinguishes it from the earlier Greek tradition, which had very little sense of history i.e., the notions of *kairos* and *phronesis* were conceptualized mostly in terms of the actions and education of the individual. We will see that this incorporation of *kairos* into a particular conception of history characterizes the appropriation of the term into modern theology, particularly by Paul Tillich and

---

[4] See Page et al. (1929, pp. 391–93).

modern liberation theologians. With this emphasis on history, we also find a link between the notion of *kairos* and that of prophetism, as commonly found in the Old Testament. As confirmed by Tillich (1957, p. 33), therefore, the Greek term *kairos* was also useful in terms of appropriating the "dynamic spirit of Judaism".

As mentioned, Paul Tillich appropriates the concept of *kairos* as part of a broader philosophy of history, which, as intrinsically Christian, "is more than a logic of the cultural sciences", and which he characterizes as "a summons to a consciousness of history in the sense of the *kairos*, a striving for an interpretation of the meaning of history on the basis of the conception of *kairos*" (ibid., p. 32). More specifically, for Tillich, "the kairoi are those crises in history ... which create an opportunity for, and indeed demand, an existential decision by the human subject—the coming of Christ being the prime example". This recognition of "an inescapable responsibility for the present moment in history" (ibid., p. 32) is something that is recognized and elaborated on by later liberation (and *Kairos*) theologians, as discussed briefly below.

Importantly for the purposes of drawing the connections between *kairos* and Bakhtin's work, Tillich (1936)[5] , makes a distinction between two 'lines' of spiritual history in his article entitled "*kairos* and Logos": the main one connected with Logos, the lesser one connected with *kairos*. With respect to the *Logos*-line he identifies "Kant's *Critiques* [as] its mightiest expression". On the other hand, he identifies the *Kairos*-line with "the mysticism and nature-philosophy of the late Middle Ages and the Renaissance", Schelling, Schopenhauer, and Nietzsche, and "finally as a philosophy of life at the turn of the nineteenth and twentieth centuries it raises a protest against the methodical formalism of the Kantians". We will see later that it is into this later *Kairos*-line that Bakhtin can be clearly and relatively unambiguously placed, not least because of his explicit critical stance towards Kantian ethics as well as his celebration of the Renaissance-spirit via his notion of carnival. The essentially anti-Enlightenment stance that Tillich (1957, p. 34) takes up, alongside Bakhtin, is against "the rational conception of reality as a machine with eternally constant laws of movement manifest in an infinitely recurring and predictable natural process. The mentality that has produced this conceptual framework ... has, in turn ... made itself into a part of this machine".

Of relevance too for the current discussion is Tillich's notion of balance between the necessity of change and becoming, on the one hand, and the preservation of form on the other hand:

> Therefore, it is impossible to speak of being without also speaking of becoming. Becoming is just as genuine in the structure of being as is that which remains unchanged in the process of becoming. And, vice versa, becoming would be impossible if nothing were preserved in it as the measure of change (Tillich 1951, p. 181).

This tension between two poles, one static and the other dynamic, is reflected in Tillich's description of the relationship between the Prophetic Spirit and the Law. This relationship is in turn directly linked to the notion of *kairos*, given that it is only at certain opportune moments (i.e., *kairoi*) that the Prophetic Spirit is able to break "through the barriers of the law" (ibid., p. 370). In his description of the interrelationship between the Prophetic Spirit and the Law, it is interesting to note that the two are clearly dependent on each other; without the Law, the Prophetic Spirit has nothing to break through and, in fact, Tillich insists that it is only as a result of a serious investment in (and commitment to) the Law that the need for something more (for a change) arises:

> For maturity is the result of education by the law, and in some who take the law with radical seriousness, maturity becomes despair of the law, with the ensuing quest for that which breaks through the law as "good news" (ibid., p. 370).

---

[5] I have unfortunately not been able to find a page-numbered version of this publication. Tillich also (exceptionally) does not italicize the word *kairos* and its derivations in his various publications.

From this perspective, *kairos* need not be considered as the equivalent of a radical form of antinomianism. It is only, in fact, when we resist the need for becoming (when we resist the *kairos*) that we experience a complete breakdown of form: "when the churches rejected this criticism or accepted it in a partial, compromising way, the prophetic Spirit was forced into sectarian movements of an originally revolutionary character" (ibid., p. 370). Important therefore, is that while *kairos* implies the irruption of the new, it does not necessarily imply the complete destruction of the old.

There are a number of further aspects that are central to Tillich's description of kairoi and which are relevant to the current discussion. Firstly, from an explicitly Christian perspective, Tillich is committed to distinguishing between what he refers to, on the one hand, as the great *Kairos* ("the moment of time in which God could send his Son, the moment which was selected to become the center of history" (ibid., pp. 369–70)) and, on the other hand, as the relative *kairoi*. Important here is that the great *Kairos* (i.e., Christ) stands as a criterion against which the relative *kairoi* can be judged. This is because it is clear for Tillich that kairoi can be both demonically distorted and erroneous. As an example of the first he refers to the rise of naziism in post-WWI Germany: "a demonically distorted experience of a *Kairos* [which] led inescapably to self-destruction" (ibid., p. 371).

With regard to each *kairos* moment being almost inevitably erroneous to some degree, there is a link here with the Greek notion of *phronesis* i.e., with a demand for a form of practical wisdom that cannot be encapsulated in a clear-cut rational or ethical vision: what Tillich calls the Prophetic Spirit, an ability to discern "the "signs of the times", as Jesus says when he accuses his enemies of not seeing them" (ibid., p. 370). There is also an emphasis on the need for (and the consequences of) practical involvement, which is necessary but, of course, involves risk and error: "it is not an object of analysis and calculation . . . it is not a matter of detached observation but of involved experience" (ibid., pp. 370–71). We will see later that a core aspect of Bakhtin's notion of carnival is that of involvement; and relatedly of incarnation. Important here too is that the practical wisdom demanded by the *kairos* moment does not exclude analysis and observation, but rather introduces them as an element into the *kairos* moment, as a source of clarification and enrichment. *Kairos* is not, therefore, anti-intellectual or anti-rational. It is meant to indicate a force (and a wisdom) that is, however, beyond (but nonetheless incorporative of) the intellectual and the rational.

The clearly political (as opposed to narrowly individual) implications of *kairos* within Tillich's system become clear as a result of his analysis of different forms of historical consciousness in the chapter entitled 'Kairos' in *The Protestant Era* (Tillich 1957). The prophetic spirit (i.e., the *kairoic* historical consciousness) is opposed to different forms of what Tillich (1957) refers to as absolute and relative forms of philosophies of history, all of which exhibit some degree of truth and falsity. The *kairoic* historical consciousness combines the true demands of these various forms into what, on the surface at least, appears to be a paradox:

> The tension characteristic of the absolute interpretation of history must be united with the universalism of the relative interpretations. But this demand contains a paradox. What happens in the *kairos* should be absolute, and yet not absolute, but under judgement of the absolute . . . this demand is fulfilled when the conditioned surrenders itself to become a vehicle for the unconditional . . . where there is an acceptance of the eternal manifesting itself in a special moment in history, in a *kairos*, there is openness to the unconditional (ibid., pp. 42–43).

Here, we clearly see a tension between the demands of the Kantian-like unconditional and the prophetic (*kairoic*) spirit that is sensitive to the demands of the particular time and place. While the unconditional certainly sits in judgement of the 'moment' (and is thus incorporated into our response to the 'moment'), at the same time,

> . . . there exists no direct way from the unconditional to any concrete solution. The unconditional is never a law or a promoter of a definite form of the spiritual or social life . . . the truth is a living truth, a creative truth, and not a law. What we are

confronted with is never and nowhere an abstract command; it is living history, with its abundance of new problems whose solution occupies and fulfills each epoch (ibid., p. 51).

Given Tillich's links to religious socialism, it is of course not surprising that Tillich is conceivable, with many provisos, as a forerunner of modern liberation theology (cf. Robbins 2015, pp. 163–65). Unsurprisingly, therefore, *kairos* has become a central term in modern liberation theology, and particularly in the South African 'brand'.[6] The *Kairos Document*, the central Christian anti-Apartheid manifesto of the 1980s, begins in the following way:

> The time has come. The moment of truth has arrived. South Africa has been plunged into a crisis that is shaking the foundations and there is every indication that the crisis has only just begun and that it will deepen and become even more threatening in the months to come. It is the **Kairos** or moment of truth not only for apartheid but also for the Church Kairos Theologians (Group) 1986 .

So-called *Kairos* Theology, as a form of liberation theology, has subsequently spread to other parts of the world, one prominent example being that of Palestine, which now has its own *Kairos Document*.

It also forms part of so-called contextual theology, also a sub-branch of liberation theology, and championed by the South African Dominican priest, Albert Nolan, who was also one of the main architects of the South African *Kairos Document*. Contextual theology, as the name suggests, is a form of theology that is responsive to the demands of the concrete time and place confronted by the Christian. Its clear links with ethics is reflected by its emphasis on orthopraxis as opposed to orthodoxy, something which it shares with many other strands of liberation theology. The links here with the Ancient Greek use of the term *kairos* in rhetoric and the related ethical concepts of *phronesis* and prudence should be obvious. In his book, *Hope in the Age of Despair*, Nolan (2009, pp. 77–79) provides a definition of *kairos* and a description of prophecy that have clear resonances with traditional Greek understandings of *kairos* and the related virtue of *phronesis* as well as with Tillich's notion of the Prophetic Spirit:

> "*Kairos* . . . refers to time as a quality. A particular *kairos* is the particular quality or mood of an event. This concept is clearly and succinctly expressed in the well-known passage from Ecclesiastes (3: 1–8):
>
> There is a time for everything;
>
> A time for giving birth
>
> A time for dying
>
> A time for planting
>
> A time for uprooting
>
> Etc.
>
> . . . For the Hebrew, to know the time was not a matter of knowing the hour or the date; it was a matter of knowing what kind of time it was.
>
> . . . This kind of time is not entirely foreign to us. It is particularly meaningful to those who inherit an African culture and even more meaningful when we are involved in an intensified struggle to change the times.
>
> . . . In the Bible the prophet was someone who could tell the time. He (or she) could see what kind of time it was and what kind of action would be appropriate now. The prophets could read the signs of the times, which means they could interpret the *kairos*."

---

6   For more on the incorporation of *kairos* into liberation theology see, for example, Boesak (2015).

In this section, we have briefly reviewed the use of the term *kairos* in both classical times and in terms of its incorporation into the Christian tradition. We now turn to Bakhtin's notion of carnival.

3. Bakhtin's *Carnival*

The Russian literary critic and philosopher Mikhail Bakhtin (1895–1975) received a classical training and was thoroughly familiar with Ancient Greek, Hellenistic and Roman culture, literature, and philosophy, as reflected, for example, in his work on the roots of the modern novel. His philosophy of language is, in addition, and in a manner clearly echoing the Ancient Greek and Hellenistic rhetoricians, clearly focused on the concrete utterance rather than on any abstract system underlying it. As with these early rhetoricians, his vision of the utterance includes a clear emphasis on appropriateness to context and audience.

The discovery and publication (and translation into English) of Mikhail Bakhtin's early work (as, for example, contained in the English-language volumes entitled *Towards a Philosophy of the Act* and *Art and Answerability*)[7] were of significance in that they were a corrective to the image of Bakhtin as a kind of proto-postmodernist (with distinctly Marxist leanings) that was prevalent in the West directly after his (re)discovery in the 1960s and 70s.

One side-effect of the publication of these early works, with their distinctly (although not exclusively) ethical slant, was a growing appreciation for Bakhtin's neo-Kantian as well as Christian (Russian Orthodox) roots.[8] Implicit in this Christian interpretation of Bakhtin's ethical vision, and one which connects his critique of Kant to his notion of carnival, is the emphasis on incarnation. We recall from the previous section that Tillich viewed Kant's critiques as the high-point of his so-called Logos-line (as opposed to the *Kairos*-line).

Bakhtin's whole oeuvre is moreover characterized by the motif of finding a (phronetic, prudential) balance between form and dynamics, as dealt with in the previous section with reference to Tillich. When it comes to his linguistics, Bakhtin attempts to find a middle-path between the extremes of individual subjectivism (the production of what is unique and non-repeatable in language) and abstract objectivism (the systemic and static in language). Furthermore, in the notion of genre, Bakhtin finds just such a balance, the genre being an example of "relative typological stability" (Bakhtin 1981, p. 85)[9] i.e., a relatively stable form that is nonetheless open to change. In his ethics, similarly, while rejecting the abstract, rigid framework of Kantian ethics, he does not fall into a nihilistic form of ethical relativism.

Bakhtin is without doubt most known for his notion of carnival as developed in his book *Rabelais and his World* (Bakhtin 1984). While the book itself is not explicitly a book on ethics—but is rather, on the surface at least, an example of literary criticism—many have drawn ethical, sociological, and political inspiration from it. The exact lessons to be learnt, however, differ from commentator to commentator, and, in this way, reflect different receptions of Bakhtin's work more generally.[10] On the one extreme, carnival can be viewed from within a Marxist perspective: basically as the eruption of radical forces which threaten the status-quo. On the other extreme it can be viewed as an integral function of a more conservative vision i.e., as the necessary mechanism for releasing the pent-up energies and frustrations created by the social order; and thus, part-and-parcel of the maintenance of this same social order.

Importantly, while on the surface, Bakhtin's description of carnival appears to be mainly a critique of the Christian (Catholic) church around the time of the transition from the middle-ages into the Renaissance (and has often been viewed as such), I would argue that it is in fact equally a critique of developments that took place after the Renaissance and, in particular, developments that began in the seventeenth century i.e., with the Enlightenment—a position supported in Charles

---

7   Bakhtin (1990, 1993).
8   See, for example, (Mihailovic 1997; Coates 1999; Pechey 2007; Bagshaw 2013).
9   See also (Bakhtin 1986).
10 See, for example, Emerson (1997, pp. 162–206) for a taste of some of the different 'takes' on Bakhtin's carnival.

Taylor's *A Secular Age*.[11] With the Enlightenment we find the beginning of "laughter's degradation" (Bakhtin 1984, p. 101). Bakhtin makes explicit reference to Descartes' "rationalist philosophy" and classicism in aesthetics as key examples of this development of a "new official culture [in which] there prevails a tendency toward the stability and completion of being" (ibid., p. 101). Here, we have a clear echo of Tillich's so-called Logos-line as described in the previous section.[12]

Again, as confirmed by Bakhtin (1984, p. 115), "in the seventeenth century an important process was started in all ideological spheres. Generalization, empirical abstraction, and typification acquired a leading role in the world picture". On an ethical sphere, this process, as described by Tillich, reached its apotheosis in the categorical imperative of Kant. In terms of theories of language it has as its height the abstract objectivism of a Ferdinand de Saussure or a Noam Chomsky. Carnival does not, however, imply the polar opposite of such abstraction and generalization. In the ethical sphere, it does not become a nihilist form of ethical relativism, and, on the linguistic level, it is not identifiable with the subjective individualism that Bakhtin contrasts with the abstract objectivism of a De Saussure.

The link between *kairos* and carnival is clear from the very outset. *Kairos* is, from one perspective, essentially a willingness to remain sensitive to the contingencies of time and place, to the peculiarities of context and to suspend abstract, mechanically-applied ethical solutions. It demands as such a willingness to incarnate.[13] The related concept of *phronesis/prudentia* demands exactly the same from the educated citizen i.e., involvement. Likewise, "these images [of carnival] are opposed to all that is finished and polished, to all pomposity, to every ready-made solution in the sphere of thought and world outlook" (ibid., p. 3). Moreover, references to time are replete in Bakhtin's description of carnival and the related concept of the grotesque. "Carnival was the true feast of time, the feast of becoming, change and renewal. It was hostile to all that was immortalized and completed" (ibid., p. 10); "the feast is always essentially related to time" (ibid., p. 9); "the relation to time is one determining trait of the grotesque image" (ibid., p. 24). In the following description of carnival time, if we abstract away from the references to feasts and "a festive perception of the world" we almost have a perfect description of the traditional conception of *kairos* itself:

> Moreover, through all the stages of historic development feasts were linked to moments of crisis, of breaking points in the cycle of nature or in the life of society and man. Moments of death and revival, of change and renewal always led to a festive perception of the world (ibid., p. 9).

Carnival time is also clearly historical time. Bakhtin refers to "a mighty awareness of history and of historic change" (ibid., p. 25). It is the exact opposite of what (Tillich (1957), p. 33) would consider to be a-*kairoic*, a-historical consciousness, one form of which "is rooted in the awareness of what is beyond time. This type of mentality knows no change and no history".

---

[11] Taylor (2007). This recognition should not detract from the fact that carnival is also a critique of (and an improvement on) the medieval world view: "Rabelais' task is to gather together on a new material base a world that, due to the dissolution of the medieval world view, is disintegrating. The medieval wholeness and roundedness of the world (as it was still alive in Dante's synthesizing work) has been destroyed ... There was destroyed as well the medieval conception of history ... in which real time is devalued and dissolved in extratemporal categories. In this world view, time is a force that only destroys and annihilates; it creates nothing new. It was necessary to find a new form of time" (Bakhtin 1981, pp. 205–6). The point is of course that the Enlightenment introduced its own set of extratemporal (a-historical) categories.

[12] It is also thus more than suggestive that given that Rabelais was a central figure of the Renaissance, that Tillich should describe the opposite spiritual *Kairos*-line as identifiable with "the mysticism and nature-philosophy of the late Middle Ages and the Renaissance" (Tillich 1936). Pechey (2007, p. 162) points out that "in telling the story of the later fortunes of the Gospel ethic Bakhtin distances himself from neo-Platonic elaborations and invokes against these the names of St Bernard of Clairvaux and St Francis of Assisi, those powerful figures of Western medieval spirituality to whom the Rhineland mystics owed so much".

[13] Bakhtin emphasizes the "obvious sensuous character [of] carnival images" (Bakhtin 1984, p. 7) and, in addition, that carnival always demands involvement and participation (i.e., incarnation and not spectatorship): "carnival does not know footlights, in the sense that it does not acknowledge any distinction between actors and spectators. Footlights would destroy a carnival ... Carnival is not a spectacle seen by the people; they live in it, and everybody participates because its very idea embraces all the people" (Bakhtin 1984, p. 7).

Turning to the grotesque as an essential component of carnival we note with Bakhtin, again in relation to time, that with grotesque images we find "both poles of transformation, the old and the new, the dying and the procreating, the beginning and the end of the metamorphosis" (Bakhtin 1984, p. 24). There is a clearly organic vision underlying the notions of carnival and the grotesque: Bakhtin (1981, p. 168) is at pains to point out that "everything that is good grows: it grows in all respects and in all directions, it cannot help growing because growth is inherent in its very nature. The bad, on the contrary, does not grow but rather degenerates, thins out and perishes . . . the category of growth is one of the most basic categories in the Rabelaisian world". Of course, the organic is a type (and metaphor) of the "relative typological stability" (i.e., continuity through change) mentioned already.

Of importance here too is Bakhtin's notion of grotesque realism and its intrinsic connection with the history of laughter. The important thing to understand about grotesque realism (as characteristic of the Renaissance period and as distinguishable from both the archaic grotesque as well as the modern grotesque) is that the critique that it delivers of the ready-made and the polished is not a solely negative one. It has a positive pole (i.e., as a mechanism for growth and transformation) and is in that sense linked to the modern Christian appropriation of the concept of *kairos*. Grotesque realism never devolves into pure (negative) satire of the modern kind. It is essentially a form of "gay relativity" (Bakhtin 1984, p. 11). This emphasis on gay relativity clearly sets the carnivalesque apart from modern-day concerns about the dangers of nihilism attendant upon ethical relativism (and as portrayed in the novels of Bakhtin's favorite author, Doestoevsky).[14] It would in fact, I believe, be completely incorrect to characterize carnival as a form of ethical relativity, in the same way that it would be an over-simplification to equate the rhetorical and sophistic theories of early Greeks, such as Gorgias and Isocrates, with modern-day ethical nihilism. That carnival is not opposed to ethical idealism is clear from Bakhtin's work: "the utopian ideal and the realistic merged in [the] carnival experience" (ibid., p. 10); Thus, in fact, a kind of idealism seems inherent to carnival:

> The feast had always an essential, meaningful philosophical content. No rest period or breathing spell can be rendered festive per se; something must be added from the spiritual and ideological dimension. They must be sanctioned not by the world of practical conditions but by the highest aims of human existence, that is, by the world of ideals (ibid., p. 9).

It is this ability to reconcile (and balance) the particular, the sensuous, and the changeable with the highest ideals that, I would argue, captures the essence of carnival, and is, I believe, the central motif of Bakhtin's complete work. In the same way, I would argue, does Bakhtin's notion of genre, his theory of language, and his ethical system capture the balance between form and dynamics. In the same way the ancient concept of *kairos* captures not a primitive form of ethical relativism, but rather the necessity of sensitivity to the concrete and the historical; to the exercise of the virtue of prudence that cannot be captured by mechanically-applied ethical formulae. The Christian irruption of the divine into human affairs (i.e., *kairos*) captures a similar balance. The relevant irruption does not come to destroy or overthrow the Law, but rather to fulfill it.

---

[14] Relatedly, Bakhtin emphasized the fact that the laughter and gaiety so characteristic of carnival is in no way incompatible with true seriousness (with tragedy to be more precise): "folk humour . . . was not opposed to all seriousness in general. It was opposed to the intolerant, dogmatic seriousness of the Middle Ages . . . tragic seriousness is universal . . . it is infused with the spirit of creative destruction. Tragic seriousness is absolutely free of dogmatism. A dogmatic tragedy is as impossible as dogmatic laughter . . . Both authentic tragedy and authentic ambivalent laughter are killed by dogmatism in all its forms and manifestations" (Bakhtin 1984, p. 121). There is nothing feckless therefore about carnival laughter. It is compatible with the highest idealism and is not to be equated with purely destructive ethical nihilism.

4. Conclusions

The above discussion has only provided the briefest of outlines of the historical development of the concept of *kairos*, and I believe that its importance for an understanding of Bakhtin's Christian ethos will require a book-length treatment of this development. Of particular importance here would be its connection with *phronesis* and the incorporation and development of the Aristotelian notion of prudence into Christian thought, particularly of the Thomist kind. Given the links explored above between *kairos*, prudence, and incarnation and Bakhtin's notion of carnival in particular, it would also be interesting to see what connections can be made between these concepts and what Richard Kearney refers to as *"the theological hermeneutics of incarnation* inspired by the phenomenological retrieval of Christian mysticism and exegetics"* (Kearney 2015, p. 121).[15] The history of the direct uptake of the notion of *kairos* into modern theology[16] also requires further investigation, with preliminary research in this regard, indicating a particularly important role that is played by Heidegger and the incorporation of his thinking about time into 20th-century theology (cf. Murchadha 2013; Schumacher 2015; Delahaye 2016). This all lies in the future, but it is my hope that this article has at least provided a reasonably convincing argument as to the clear similarities between certain key aspects of Bakhtin's thought and the understanding of *kairos* in its various stages of use and development.

Conflicts of Interest: The author declares no conflict of interest.

References

Bagshaw, Hilary B. P. 2013. *Religion in the Thought of Mikhail Bakhtin: Reason and Faith*. Farnham and Burlington: Ashgate.

Bakhtin, Mikhail M. 1981. *The Dialogic Imagination: Four Essays by M. M. Bakhtin*. Austin: University of Texas Press.

Bakhtin, Mikhail M. 1984. *Rabelais and His World*. Bloomington and Indianapolis: Indiana University Press.

Bakhtin, Mikhail M. 1986. *Speech Genres and Other Late Essays*. Austin: University of Texas Press.

Bakhtin, Mikhail M. 1990. *Art and Answerability: Early Philosophical Essays by M. M. Bakhtin*. Austin: University of Texas Press.

Bakhtin, Mikhail M. 1993. Toward a Philosophy of the Act. Austin: University of Texas Press.

Benedikt, Amélie Frost. 2002. On Doing the Right Thing at the Right Time: Toward an Ethics of *Kairos*. In *Rhetoric and Kairos: Essays in History, Theory, and Praxis*. Edited by Phillip Sipiora and James S. Baumlim. Albany: State University of New York Press, pp. 226–35.

Boesak, Allan A. 2015. *Kairos, Crisis, and Global Apartheid: The Challenge to Prophetic Resistance*. New York: Palgrave Macmillan.

Clark, Katerina, and Michael Holquist. 1984. *Mikhail Bakhtin*. Cambridge and London: Harvard University Press.

Coates, Ruth. 1999. *Christianity in Bakhtin: God and the Exiled Author*. Cambridge: Cambridge University Press.

Craigo-Snell, Shannon. 2011. Kairos in the *chronos*: A Rahnerian View. *Philosophy and Theology* 23: 301–15. [CrossRef]

Delahaye, Ezra. 2016. About Chronos and Kairos. On Agamben's Interpretation of Pauline Temporality through Heidegger. *International Journal of Philosophy and Theology* 77: 85–101. [CrossRef]

Emerson, Caryl. 1997. *The First Hundred Years of Mikhail Bakhtin*. Princeton: Princeton University Press.

Erdinast-Vulcan, Daphna. 2013. *Between Philosophy and Literature: Bakhtin and the Question of the Subject.*. Stanford: Stanford University Press.

Husserl, Edmund. 1992. *On the Phenomenology of the Consciousness of Internal Time*. Dordrecht: Springer.

---

[15] Of relevance here too are Bakhtin's Russian Orthodox roots. Thus Pechey (2006), paraphrasing Lock (2001), claims that "it is the long bimillenial continuity of Eastern Orthodox tradition—its innocence, too, of any Platonic or Aristotelian admixture—that gives Bakhtin the standing ground he needs to correct the Kantian tradition of the West, and that this also explains his kinship with those twentieth-century developments in Western philosophy which have reconnected with premodern thinking". Some of the twentieth-century developments with particular relevance to Bakhtin and incarnation (Bergson, Merleau-Ponty, Levinas) have been recently explored in Erdinast-Vulcan (2013). The theme of reconnecting with premodern thinking is, as is well known, a defining characteristic of Radical Orthodoxy and, in this regard, it is interesting to see how John Milbank has recently shown a growing interest in the Russian Orthodox tradition (Milbank 2009).

[16] Not only by Tillich and modern liberation theology, but also for example by Karl Rahner (cf. Craigo-Snell 2011).

Kairos Theologians (Group). 1986. *The Kairos Document: Challenge to the Church: A Theological Comment on the Political Crisis in South Africa*. Braamfontein: Skotaville Publishers.

Kearney, Richard. 2015. What is Carnal Hermeneutics? *New Literary History* 46: 99–124. [CrossRef]

Lock, Charles. 2001. Bakhtin and the Tropes of Orthodoxy. In *Bakhtin and Religion: A Feeling for Faith*. Edited by Susan M. Felch and Paul J. Contino. Evanston: Northwestern University Press, pp. 97–119.

MacIntyre, Alisdair. 2007. *After Virtue: A Study in Moral Theory*, 3rd ed. Notre Dame: University of Notre Dame Press.

Mihailovic, Alexandar. 1997. *Corporeal Words: Mikhail Bakhtin's Theology of Discourse*. Evanston: Northwestern University Press.

Milbank, John. 2009. Sophiology and Theurgy: The New Theological Horizon. In *Encounter between Eastern Orthodoxy and Radical Orthodoxy: Transfiguring the World through the World*. Edited by Adrian Pabst and Christoph Schneider. Farnham and Burlington: Ashgate, pp. 45–85.

Murchadha, Felix Ó. 2013. *The Time of Revolution: Kairos and Chronos in Heidegger*. London and New York: Bloomsbury Academic.

Nolan, Albert. 2009. *Hope in the Age of Despair*. Bandra: St Pauls.

Page, Thomas. E., Edward Capps, and William H. D. Rouse, eds. 1929. *Isocrates*. London: William Heinemann, vol. 2.

Pechey, Graham. 2006. Penultimate Words: The Life of the "Loophole" in Mikhail Bakhtin. *Literature and Theology* 20: 269–85. [CrossRef]

Pechey, Graham. 2007. *Mikhail Bakhtin: the Word in the World*. Abingdon: Routledge.

Robbins, Jeffrey W. 2015. Changing Ontotheology: Paul Tillich, Catherine Malabou, and the Plastic God. In *Retrieving the Radical Tillich: His Legacy and Contemporary Importance*. Edited by Russell Re Manning. New York: Palgrave Macmillan, pp. 159–77.

Schumacher, Eric. 2015. Heidegger on the Relationship between Sterēsis and Kairos: Heidegger's Interpretation of Aristotle's Sterēsis as the Basic Movement of Kairological Vision. *International Journal of Philosophy and Theology (IJPT)* 3: 78–84. [CrossRef]

Sipiora, Phillip. 2002. Introduction: The Ancient Concept of *Kairos*. In *Rhetoric and kairos: Essays in History, Theory, and Praxis*. Edited by Phillip Sipiora and James S. Baumlim. Albany: State University of New York Press, pp. 1–22.

Smith, John E. 2002. Time and Qualitative Time. In *Rhetoric and Kairos: Essays in History, Theory, and Praxis*. Edited by Phillip Sipiora and James S. Baumlim. Albany: State University of New York Press, pp. 46–57.

Taylor, Charles. 2007. *A Secular Age*. Cambridge: Harvard University Press.

Tillich, Paul. 1936. Kairos and Logos. In *The Interpretation of History*. Edited by Paul Tillich, Nicholas Alfred Rasetzki and Elsa L. Talmey. New York: C. Scribner's Sons, pp. 123–75.

Tillich, Paul. 1951. *Systematic Theology*. Chicago: University of Chicago Press, vol. 1.

Tillich, Paul. 1957. *The Protestant Era*. Chicago: University of Chicago Press.

Verhoef, Anné, and Willie van der Merwe. 2015. Paul Ricoeur se begrip van transendensie met betrekking tot tyd en narratief. *LitNet Akademies* 12: 196–210.

White, Eric C. 1987. Kaironomia: On the Will to Invent. Ithaca and London: Cornell University Press.

![religions](religions logo) **MDPI**

Article

Introducing Cardinal Cardijn's See–Judge–Act as an Interdisciplinary Method to Move Theory into Practice

Justin Sands

School of Philosophy, North-West University, Potchefstroom 2790, South Africa; Justin.Sands@nwu.ac.za

Received: 27 March 2018; Accepted: 12 April 2018; Published: 14 April 2018

Abstract: Interdisciplinary dialogues find researchers seeking better understandings of theories and concepts, such colonialism and capitalism, and the means through which these concepts impact both local and global cultures. The results of explorations such as these raise the question of how to translate the theories that are created by these dialogues into practice. Moreover, they ask where we can take these conversations, how can we focus them toward specific aims, and how can we effectively enact them as one collective group. This article introduces and proposes Joseph Cardinal Cardijn's See–Judge–Act method as a possible framework to better enable these discussions to move from theory to praxis. It proposes that such a theory may also allow the theoretical portions of these interdisciplinary dialogues to happen without any discipline ceding or 'shaving away' the core principles that respectively identify each discipline. The article begins by exploring Cardinal Cardijn's original articulation of the method. Then, it describes how the liberation theologians Leonardo Boff and Clodovis Boff employed the method in their development of a theological framework. Finally, this article explores how the See–Judge–Act method might be useful for other disciplines, such as African thought and philosophy, and critical theory.

Keywords: Joseph Cardinal Cardijn; liberation theology; African Philosophy; Critical Theory; methodology; Leonardo Boff; Clodovis Boff; Young Christian Workers

---

The issues of economic, social, and political inequality clearly span across writing genres and academic discourses. This is seen throughout this special issue, and especially in its subtitle: 'African Thought, Critical Theory, and Liberation Theology in Dialogue'. Indeed, each of these disciplines approach the concept of inequality from specific and important angles: African thought/philosophy employs a critical deconstruction that decolonizes prevailing socio-economic systems that persist in controlling how Africans should think and live. Critical theory's socio-economic analysis likewise attempts to uncover the presumed structures of society that promote and legitimize the hegemonies targeted by African thought's decolonizing efforts. Liberation theology, in turn, takes these critiques and analyses, and employs them through a praxis-based theology in pursuit of not just material liberation, but a spiritual one as well.

The scope of this special issue is to bring these disciplines together to create an encounter from which future discussions may arise. This encounter was premised by the notion that each discipline focuses upon oppression and possible liberation: oppression resulting from a myriad of events that become conceptualized through colonialism, capitalism, and social hegemony. Furthermore, it was also premised by the idea that we need to bring together these disciplines because these issues cannot be solved by a lone theory or discourse; we need to band together ideas and concepts from various discourses to address these mammoth problems.

Yet this banding together, as it were, raises a new problem: how should we proceed as an interdisciplinary group without talking past each other? Where can we take these conversations, how can we focus them toward specific aims, and how can we effectively enact them as one? There is a range between the academic and the activist within all three disciplines, which can sometimes become muddled when theory evolves into practice—in other words, when the description of the problem at hand transitions toward alleviating that problem. This is multiplied, I find, when various methods become entangled and possibly compete. In short, there needs to be a basic framework to structure these sorts of conversations, especially when theory transitions into practice.

What I propose in the following is a possible schema or method for structuring this conversation, and future interdisciplinary discussions, in order to produce effective dialogue and social change. What I will propose is Joseph Cardinal Cardijn's See–Judge–Act method of liberation theology. Although prominent in liberation theology circles, particularly in Latin America, the See–Judge–Act method is not as widely known in Southern Africa outside of having an instrumental influence in the development of the 1985 *Kairos Document*. It is beyond the scope of this article to explore the activist connections between Cardinal Cardijn's organization, the Young Christian Workers (or JOC), and South African politics, but it is important to note that the JOC did have an impact in South Africa as an activist movement, despite the lack of intellectual engagement with Cardinal Cardijn's method. Nelson Mandela, for example, gave a speech at the opening ceremony of the Young Christian Workers World Council in 1995, praising their efforts and activism during apartheid (Mandela 1995). In regard to Cardinal Cardijn's method, the only mention I could find within a South African context is tangential and relational; it was stemming from discussions around the 1985 *Kairos Document*, which is a joint theological proclamation against the struggle of apartheid in South Africa. In "Tracing the Karios Trajectory from South Africa to Palestine," Gerald West argued that "while the *European Kairos Document* follows *The* [Original, South African] *Kairos Document* in its basic See–Judge–Act process of production and documentary format, as do most of the 'kairos' documents, the 'Judge' moment is fairly thin theologically" (West 2012, p. 11). West later went on to detail Cardinal Cardijn's influence on the European document. In my research, I have not found substantial evidence that Cardinal Cardijn's thinking was influential from an intellectual perspective in South African theological circles—at least in comparison to its great influence in Latin and South America—yet West did show us that his thinking was closely aligned with certain aspects of African Christian theology.[1] Although a historical account of the JOC activities in South Africa is an endeavor well worth undertaking, my aim in this article is to present Cardinal Cardijn's method as a means to bring the interdisciplinary dialogue to fruition through praxis. Hence, I will leave the historical account aside to maintain clarity in my argument.

Cardinal Cardijn's method is a movement from engagement and solidarity, then to reflection and understanding, and finally to cooperative involvement and action. I think that it is a strong basis from which we can take ideas generated by discussions, such as the one we are having in this special issue, and employ them in an effective manner. Likewise, it gives us another possible methodological avenue through which academics and activists can explore issues of inequality in such a way that they do not become either too abstract or too personal to be persuasive or effective. I will begin with a brief summary of Cardinal Cardijn's See–Judge–Act method, and then will expand upon it by showing how it may be used to connect the various strands between our three dialoguing disciplines. I will conclude with an analysis of how I think that this method could be further developed to intellectually and actively address the issues of economic, social, and political inequality.

1. Cardinal Cardijn's See–Judge–Act as Practical Engagement

Born in Belgium in 1882, Joseph Cardijn was ordained as a priest in 1906, and actively worked in underground movements during World War I, which led to him being imprisoned for espionage in the latter stages of the war. After the Great War, he began unionizing local workers while appointed as a parish priest, beginning with the creation an organization called The Young Trade Unionists

---

[1] For more on liberation theology from a Catholic perspective, which hints at Cardijn's influence but does not directly cite/engage him, see the work of Albert Nolan, particularly: Nolan (1986, 1988).

(*Jeunesse Syndicaliste*).[2] In 1924, the Young Trade Unionists expanded and became an international network called the *Jeunes Ouvrières Chrétiennes*, or the Young Christian Workers (as mentioned above, often referred to as the JOC). This organization first attempted to mobilize the laborers for worker's rights, and later mobilized young persons according to a broad range of social justice causes.[3] It is during this early period of the JOC that he developed his See–Judge–Act method of addressing inequality, employing it with the JOC to engage communities in an effective and transparent manner. Coinciding with the success of the JOC and the growing admiration for his work, Pope Paul VI consecrated Joseph Cardijn as a bishop and a Cardinal of the Catholic Church in 1965. Cardinal Cardijn would die two years later, in 1967, with his legacy cemented as a pivotal figure in liberation theology, and with the JOC carrying on their mission to this day through various local Young Christian Workers groups and an international governing board, the International Coordination of Young Christian Workers (ICYCW).[4] Importantly, Cardinal Cardijn did not create his method just for social activism, nor did he create the JOC as just a worker's party movement. Rather, he saw both as means toward life formation. Although See–Judge–Act can be used as a teleological method, as I will show below, it is not merely a tool that is employed to achieve a particular end; Cardinal Cardijn originally thought of it as a way to fundamentally reorient one's life toward social justice and solidarity.[5]

What makes Cardinal Cardijn's method particularly fruitful is how it first seeks to understand the communities in which it is employed—particularly by those outside who enter into a particular community—to safeguard that what one does for social justice actively reflects the wills and wants of said community. In order to present the See–Judge–Act method, I will begin by first describing how Cardijn envisioned this for social activism so that we can gather its original uses. From there, I will show how liberation theologians such as Leonardo Boff and Clodovis Boff took this practical method of social justice and employed it as a theoretical framework for their theology. This latter part is crucial for our investigation, since it shows how See–Judge–Act is not just a practical operation, but also a groundwork for engagements of all kinds, especially the ones engendered by this special issue's ongoing discussions.

According to Cardinal Cardijn, the first movement of any engagement with another person or community should be to 'see': to observe and immerse oneself in the lives of that community. This goes doubly so when engaging those being oppressed, to be in solidarity with the poor or oppressed, to become more than just a bystander or outsider to injustice. By doing so, assuming that one is an outsider to the community,[6] one does not take one's own perspective as normative to the other, and thus can begin to attempt to see the world through the other's eyes—as close as one can do so. At the very least, one can develop a sympathy that moves toward understanding the situation(s) of the other, their community, and perhaps create a bridge between communities to further this solidarity. With regards to adequately 'seeing' the issue at hand, Cardinal Cardijn explicitly argues that one cannot "rely upon book knowledge or *a priori* ideas: They must, however, have accurate and current information available concerning living realities. [We] must learn to see through personal and collective investigations that are well-ordered and verified". Moreover, he continues to state that for one's investigation into a situation to be really "fruitful and instructive, it must be adapted with care to the mentality and to the ways of living and talking amongst the people in each locality. On this condition, we obtain through

---

2   I am indebted to the help of Stefan Gigacz, the editor of the new journal, *Cardijn Studies*, for his advice and expertise on Cardinal Cardijn's life and work.

3   For a broader overview of Cardinal Joseph Cardijn's work and thinking, see: Cardijn (1982); for an overview of his methodology, see pp. 72–106, especially pp. 72–76, 84–90.

4   For more, see the Young Christian Workers' website: www.ycwimpact.com, accessed on 9 February 2018; and the International Coordination of Young Christian Workers website: www.cijoc.org, accessed on 9 February 2018. For a list of YCW/JOC organizations in African nations, see: http://www.cijoc.org/region/africa, accessed on 9 February 2018.

5   Cardijn (1982), *La Pensée de Joseph Cardijn*, p. 72.

6   This is not necessarily always the case, obviously, and one can utilize this same methodology in one's own community as a practice of self-reflection, evaluation, and discernment. Also, some of those who use See–Judge–Act within liberation theology prefer the term, 'listen' over 'see' to emphasize how one should open oneself to the other and the other's community.

inquiry an accurate picture of [the other's state] and the exact knowledge of their religious, moral, intellectual, and/or economic situation".[7] What this seeks to prevent is the mentality held by many (usually) well-meaning activists that seem to know what is best for a community without actually understanding that community own its own terms. For example, there are several instances of aid given to African communities where those giving the aid have rarely set foot into the communities that they wish to help, nor do they actively engage them in solidarity.[8] Aid of this type is often given asymmetrically, where a chauvinistic imbalance between the giver and the receiver is maintained, and rarely does the giver truly instantiate a relationship with the receiver. Ultimately, the receiver loses agency in this exchange.

From an embedded understanding of the other, one can begin to adequately 'judge' the specific problems of the community that oppress the other, and in the process of that judging, look toward actual remedies to alleviate this suffering or otherwise move the other toward a sense of self-empowerment that helps the other take steps to alleviate it themselves. Here, 'judge' is a moment of discernment, and it is done in solidarity with those one seeks to help; it is therefore a community that works together toward this goal, rather than a particular person or group working on behalf of others. Once the proper judgments and/or discernments have been made, then and only then can one 'act' in solidarity with the community toward alleviating suffering—or, better still, act toward empowering the those who suffer to alleviate their own suffering.[9] As Cardinal Cardijn argues: "This judgment, finally, does not remain a dead letter, it leads to action: to solving problems, it turns to reality to change it and make use of it, to make daily life vast and beautiful".[10] Effectively, one acts to alleviate the suffering of others and this comes from a comprehensive and thorough discernment of their situation, thus preventing scenarios where aid appeals more to the concerns of the so-called 'liberator' than to those who need help. "*See, judge, act...*" Cardinal Cardijn summarizes, "this method of education is suited equally well to the masses as to the elites. It takes place in life and through life".[11] What Cardinal Cardijn envisioned was a movement rooted in community, where outsiders become a part of that community, and where this solidarity also informs and changes other global communities; a 'bottom–up' solidarity where local communities and the global world meet for social and spiritual liberation.

2. Leonardo Boff and Clodovis Boff: See–Judge–Act as a Theological Framework

For a more systematic formulation of this methodology, and to better fashion it for our task of exploring the how See–Judge–Act might work as a foundation for dialogue between academic discourses, we turn to the liberation theologians Leonardo Boff and Clodovis Boff, who expand these concepts to develop a liberation theology. While they do not exclusively receive their theological method from Cardinal Cardijn, it becomes abundantly clear that these three men approach the liberation of the oppressed from the same perspective, and one can immediately sense traces of

---

[7] My translation. See: Cardijn (1982), *La Pensée de Joseph Cardijn*, p. 85. The expanded French quotations are: "On ne peut, en effet, en ces matières, se baser sur des connaissances livresques ou sur des idées *a priori*: il faut, au contraire, disposer de renseignements exacts et actuels sur les réalités vivantes. Les jeunes travailleurs doivent apprendre à voir par des enquêtes personnelles ou collectives bien dirigées et bien contrôlées." ... "Mais pour que le travail des enquêtes soit fructueux et vraiment éducatif, il doit être adapté avec soin à la mentalité, à la manière d'être et de parler des jeunes gens de chaque localité. A cette condition, on obtiendra par l'enquête une image exacte de l'adolescence salariée de l'endroit et une connaissance exacte de sa situation religieuse, morale, intellectuelle, économique. À cette condition, on obtiendra par l'enquête une image exacte de l'adolescence salariée de l'endroit et une connaissance exacte de sa situation religieuse, morale, intellectuelle, économique".

[8] The work of journalists and academics, such as Nobel Prize-winning economist Angus Deaton, has moved from questioning the effectiveness of such aid to outwardly opposing it. For a brief overview and example, see: Swanson (2015).

[9] For a historical overview of how this methodology worked in Chile and Brazil, see: Mackin (2012), especially pp. 337–39.

[10] Cardijn (1982), *La Pensée de Joseph Cardijn*, p. 87. "Ce jugement, enfin, ne reste pas lettre morte ; il conduit à l'action: aux problèmes pour les résoudre, au réel pour le changer et s'en servir, à la vie quotidienne pour la faire grande et belle".

[11] Cardijn (1982), *La Pensée de Joseph Cardijn*, p. 88. "Voir, juger, agir ... Cette méthode d'éducation s'adapte aussi bien à la masse qu'a l'élite. Elle se réalise dans la vie et par la vie".

Cardinal Cardijn in the work of Leonardo Boff and Clodovis Boff.[12] From the outset, Leonardo Boff and Clodovis Boff echo the concerns of Cardinal Cardijn by explaining that "faced with the oppressed, the theologian's first question can only be: Why is there oppression and what are its causes"? From this seemingly simple question, a dialogue begins to form by 'looking at', or observing, the fundamental reasons for the oppression (Boff and Boff 1987, pp. 25–28). This effectively eschews two faulty explanations of oppression: the so-called 'empirical' explanation that the poor are poor because they are lazy, ignorant, or simply deserve their situation (that they are being punished or cursed by God, for example); and the 'functional' explanation according to which the impoverished/oppressed are simply backward-thinking people that need to be led to the right ways of living and doing (which often turn out to be Western or First-World ways of living and doing). Additionally, it alleviates the stereotype that the oppressed are always a minority culture or gender. Removing these assumptions, one sees the oppressed as *people first*, rather than lesser selves or 'poor little things' in need of help and pity. It allows them to be seen as people rather than as 'the oppressed', thus fashioning their relief from oppression as a dialogical, cooperative effort that is focused on community building instead of the lone actions of a person or group.

After performing this "mediation", as Leonardo Boff and Clodovis Boff describe it, a second, hermeneutical mediation must follow in which oppression and liberation are seen "in the light of faith", which is rooted in a theological reflection upon Scripture (Boff and Boff 1987, p. 32). In *Introducing Liberation Theology*, Leonardo Boff and Clodovis Boff explained that this hermeneutic follows a model of scriptural interpretation where the *use* of Scripture is given primacy:

> It is a hermeneutics that favors *application* rather than explanation. In this the theology of liberation takes up the kind of probing that has been the perennial pursuit of all true biblical reading, as can be seen, for example, in the church fathers—a pursuit that was neglected for a long time in favor of a rationalistic exegesis concerned with dragging out the meaning-in-itself. Liberative hermeneutics reads the Bible as a book of life, not as a book of strange stories. The textual meaning is indeed sought, but only as a function of the *practical* meaning: the important thing is not so much interpreting the text of the scriptures as interpreting life 'according to the scriptures'. Ultimately, this old/new reading aims to find contemporary actualization (practicality) for the textual meaning. (Boff and Boff 1987, p. 34)

Therefore, a theology of liberation, while it takes exegesis into account, heavily emphasizes the application of the biblical text in the lives of believers rather than a strict scriptural analysis.

Expanding upon this hermeneutical movement of faith in *Theology and Praxis*, Clodovis Boff emphasizes the nature of theological reflection and its relation to faith. After noting that we must be watchful that theology does not begin to fall into "speculative" or "empiricist" idealisms, he begins to highlight the "precise, operational sense" of faith, its need for works and acts, and how this can serve as an opening to theological reflection. Clodovis Boff explains: "we perceive that [faith] receives its semantic determination partly from the concept of salvation, and partly from the concept of theology [...] Faith, then, is a bridge. Or better, it stands at the intersection of theology and salvation" (Boff 1987, p. 118). Continuing, Clodovis Boff explains that faith embodies an experience of salvation (*fides qua*) and a deepening sense of understanding of theology (*fides quae*). From here, he summarizes that:

- *Salvation is the real apprehension of (the reality of) God in and through the practice of agape;*
- *Faith is the conscious apprehension of (the experience of) God in and through religion;*

---

[12] What is clear is that Leonardo Boff and Clodovis Boff were involved in the JOC (*(Juventude Operária Católica)* and the JUC *(Jeunesse universitaire chrétienne)*, both employed the See–Judge–Act method, and were a part of the *Ação Católica* (Catholic Action), an umbrella organization linked to the Young Catholic Worker's movement. It was within movements such as these that Leonardo Boff and Clodovis Boff first began their theological formation. See: Löwy (2007).

- *Theology is the theoretical apprehension of (the idea of) God in and through a conceptual system.*[13]

For our purposes, these sentiments are significant, because they show that this second mediation involves a theological reflection on the operative aspects of faith in and beyond Scripture. They are applicable to theology as a whole as it reflects the operational aspects of faith; faith, as the conscious apprehension of salvation, bridges theology to salvation. Therefore, any 'judging' aspect of a hermeneutics that involves itself in liberation theology must involve a critical, theological evaluation of the self's experiences, i.e., what one has seen (through the 'eyes of faith') in light of the tradition of the church and Scripture.

This leads us to a final consideration of this methodology that focuses on the issues of practicality and action after one completes, as best as one can, the hermeneutical inquiry of judging. Following Cardinal Cardijn, Leonardo Boff and Clodovis Boff wrote that at the end of the day, "liberation theology leads to action: action for justice, the work of love, conversion, renewal of the church, transformation of society" (Boff and Boff 1987, p. 39). In this mediation, liberation theology focuses on building a blueprint for action, based on the prior mediations, attempting to apply them to the sociological, economic, and historical situations of the oppressed. This process, by virtue of being decisive and active in the lives of others, is extremely complex and focuses more on experience than theory. "On this level", Leonardo Boff and Clodovis Boff explain (again, echoing the sentiments of Cardinal Cardijn's methodology), "wisdom and prudence are more useful than analytic reasoning. And in this, ordinary persons are often way ahead of the learned".[14] This is important to remember, since often "the learned" here are the 'liberators', and the "ordinary persons" fulfill the roles of 'the oppressed'. This form of doing theology is aware of the communal aspect of theological mediation and acting in accordance with the Gospel, and it is aware that the "ordinary person" is just as important and necessary to the process as the doctoral candidate, the professor, or the pastor.

Epistemic humility is foundational to this methodology, i.e., knowing the limitations of one's own perspective and attempting to see what best helps *the other*, not what seems like the best option for one's own self. Moreover, it also helps in evaluating a given situation or community, as it adds powerful moments of reflection in which the self acknowledges that its own role in the process of overcoming suffering should be secondary, or perhaps tertiary, to the overall task at hand. It removes the self from the center of the issue, shattering the illusion that the self is some sort of messiah or Superman, setting off to save the whole world (and remaking it in one's own image in the process). Rather, it embeds the self into the situation, where one recognizes their solidarity with the oppressed and realizes their situation as one's own, or as best as one can. Helping the other through solidarity with the other, then, brings the other closer to oneself, diminishing his or her 'otherness'. Thus, in solidarity, both work to eliminate oppression, not as a giver and receiver of aid, but through cooperation and in the spirit of community.

3. With and Beyond Theology: See–Judge–Act in Interdisciplinary Discourses

At first blush, one may be suspicious of whether See–Judge–Act, as a theological method rooted in the Christian tradition, could form the basis of a conversation between disciplines that do not adhere to the same foundations. This suspicion is valid, since one should not dissolve the differences between disciplines simply to enact dialogue between them. However, one could likewise be suspicious that the non-Christian-centric sentiments of African thought and the secular discipline of critical theory may bleed out the 'theology' within liberation theology, leaving only the 'liberation'. In other words, the dangers of interdisciplinary dialogue, broadly, is that either one or the other disciplines may need to concede or set aside certain founding principles for such a dialogue to work.

---

[13] Clodovis Boff (1987, p. 119). Emphasis is Clodovis Boff's and he separates them from the rest of the text, which I replicate here.

[14] Boff and Boff (1987, p. 41).

Surprisingly, this is why I think See–Judge–Act might function as a basis for such conversations. Although it is theological in origin, it is also a teleological method that is aimed at alleviating a particular concern or issue within the community and it does so by explicitly taking that community's socio-cultural context into account, and not just the context of the person entering into that community. In other words, while one brings one's context into the situation, one readily recognizes that the other's context is primary, and one's own is secondary. Therefore, if the community is Christian, it takes this into account when addressing that community's oppression. When that community is something other than Christian, it likewise takes this into account. As a teleological method that is aimed at alleviating oppression, its spiritual concerns are for those who are oppressed, not for its theological motives of alleviating that oppression on behalf of Christian doctrine or belief. Rather, the See–Judge–Act method begins with a particular community and its present issue and it ends by addressing those issues as best as it can. Although Leonardo Boff and Clodovis Boff see an intertwining between the issues of materialism and spiritual well-being (as well as salvation), their judgment and subsequent action do not privilege one over the other.[15] Ironically, following what was mentioned in the first section, although Gerald West finds the 'judge' portion of See–Judge–Act theologically thin, this is where this method shines brightest as an interdisciplinary method that is focused on a teleological goal. With this, See–Judge–Act can robustly function as a method of engagement outside (or better said, alongside) its spiritual and Christian concerns. Just because it stems from a theological orientation does not necessarily mean that it is wholly limited to theological matters.

When used outside of the Christian tradition and its praxis, this method thus begins with the notion that alleviating oppression is a form of salvation. Clodovis Boff's definition of salvation, as argued in the prior section, is a practical salvation. It takes into account that the apprehension of God comes through the experience of God through religion, and the theoretical reflections upon these experiences through theology. The importance of Clodovis Boff's argument for non-theological audiences is the connection between theory and praxis: how the former necessitates the latter, and how the latter may guide the former. In African thought, especially in decolonization, scholars often find themselves recovering beliefs, ideas, and practices that were long suppressed and covered over by Western, colonialist, and eventually capitalist encroachment. Therefore, they often rely upon personal and communal experiences of Western hegemony and work backward, archeologically pealing away Western thought to arrive at a nebula of memories and experiences to better understand African contributions to Western thought, pre-colonial African culture, and current expressions of African ideals and concepts.[16] Here, one sees clearly a link between praxis and theory, where the rediscovery of African praxis informs our notions of the 'thought' within African thought and philosophy. It also raises the question of who can 'practice' African thought and philosophy, and whether or not it can be performed by non-Africans (or at least those not directly related to the African diaspora): since praxis is fundamental to the rediscovery and contemporary re-articulation of these ideas and philosophies, can one rightly do so without experiencing this praxis themselves?

The See–Judge–Act model acknowledges this question through solidarity and 'seeing': solidarity only entails a communion or co-equal affiliation between the self and the other, rather than a dissolution between them. It maintains a difference through solidarity. Moreover, 'seeing' does not require one to become what one sees, but only that one sympathetically observes and finds understanding in league with the other. In this way, 'seeing' has much in common with Paul Ricoeur's concept of the sympathetic imagination. Ricoeur's hermeneutical phenomenology employs this concept in

---

[15] See, for example, Boff (2008). Here, Leonardo Boff examines various mythologies on care, showing how these myths reveal a cosmic and material sense of care where "the human being is both utopian and historical-temporal. . . . It is through care that the human being keeps these powers united and makes use of them to construct his or her existence in the world and history. It is because of this that care is essential care" (p. 41).

[16] From a methodological point of view, see: Smith (2008). For a specific example of this in operation, see the work of Mbembe (2001), particularly ch. 6: "God's Phallus" pp. 212–34.

the sense that the phenomenologist reimagines another's perspective, but not in a sense that one 'feels' the motivations and intentions of the other in a sense that they are one's own, "in their first naïveté" (Ricoeur 1972, p. 19). Rather, the phenomenologist "'re-feels' them in their neutralized mode, in the mode of 'as-if'. It is in this sense that phenomenology is a re-enactment in sympathetic imagination" (Ricoeur 1972, p. 19). Importantly, sympathy, as a second naïveté, acknowledges a separation between the self's imagination of the other's experience, and the actual experience of the other as he or she perceives it; it is a separation that the self cannot breach, the self cannot claim the other's experience as their own. They can only sympathetically appreciate it. Returning back to the question of African thought and praxis, it then becomes possible for those outside of these African communities and contextualities to have a solidarity with those within them without taking over, or 're-colonizing' to an effect, their experiences. By becoming in solidarity with the other, what is important is that both outsiders and insiders form a community that appreciates the difference of each person's experiences. All the while, by crafting this solidarity, they are also creating shared beliefs and appreciations. Solidarity, then, becomes a mutual, communal enactment toward a specific goal. In See–Judge–Act, that solidarity functions toward mutual understanding of the injustice in question, then deciding ('judging') how to best relieve this injustice, then moves toward action in pursuit of this relief.

Critical theory, as a Western discipline, would likewise need to employ such a practice of sympathetically 'seeing' the other. This is because critical theory's notions of mass culture need to be employed backwardly from colonization: in Africa, the proletariat had to be made first and before it could be exploited by the bourgeoisie. The conventional Marxist readings of mass culture and the expanse of capitalism thus need to be augmented with the African experience before, during, and after colonialism. This is something that African thought can provide to critical theory, and it can also become the reflection that comprises the 'judge' section of Cardijn's method. Leonardo Boff and Clodovis Boff's reference to the practical application of biblical sources functions in the same way that one may utilize Western philosophies such as critical theory within African dialogues. Taking Marx's thinking as an example and *Das Kapital* especially, there is indeed great value in the rigorous studies of this text in and of itself. This deliberate reading of *Das Kapital* in its own context resembles an exegesis. However, what makes this work important for such reading is its timeliness, meaning its applicability to present concerns and concepts. It has a practical value. This latter value, particularly in the context of African thought, lies in the theoretical reflection (theological reflection in Clodovis Boff's schema) of where African societies have been, where they are, and where they are going. The inclination that *Das Kapital* can help us better understand how capitalism and colonialism fundamentally changed African societies is an acknowledgement that one's reading of the text informs their judgment of the community as they see it.[17]

This may seem obvious to the critical theorist, and to other academics of various disciplines, but it comes with one important difference: action. Recall that See–Judge–Act is teleological in orientation. By focusing on a particular issue or form of oppression, this theory allows for a conversation that adequately traverses theory and praxis. It avoids the question of whether the discussion is purely theoretical (and therefore descriptive) or purely practical (and therefore prescriptive) by emphasizing the interrelation between the two. By resolving from the outset that all reflections should coalesce toward some action, this theory transcends the academic boundaries between scientific investigation and political engagement.

This is also why the theological aspects of the method cannot be cast away. Liberation theology, as described above through Leonardo Boff and Clodovis Boff, moves from theory and theological reflection to praxis. Its teleological aim is toward a goal that is shared by its dialogue partners, African thought and critical theory. Therefore, it can employ its theological foundations concerning the need to

---

[17] Indeed, one article in this special issue is doing just that, see: Lomola (2018).

satisfy both material and spiritual fulfillment for a sense of salvation, while also contributing insights to non-theological dialogue partners. It does not need to 'shave away', so to speak, its theological foundations to adequately help move theory toward praxis in this interdisciplinary dialogue; it merely needs to show how its theological foundations help inform the judgments and prescribed actions of its dialogue partners. This is especially seen in Leonardo Boff and Clodovis Boff's emphasis on giving primacy to application over exegesis when using biblical sources to better understand the injustice or oppression in question: the concern is not whether revelation within the Bible exists, but rather how this might inform us of a better path toward liberating action. Through its teleological orientation fashioned through See–Judge–Act, this form of liberation theology gains an ecumenical thrust that makes it a strong interdisciplinary dialogue partner concerning the injustices that are afflicted upon others.

4. Conclusions

As this special issue and the conference that instigated it has shown, all of the world's issues cannot be solved exclusively by one discipline or one method, and an interdisciplinary dialogue addressing specific concerns from local and global communities is not only necessary, but essential. What I have proposed above is just one method for such an engagement. However, I also recognize that this method will have limitations regarding its effectiveness, as do all methods that try to move theory into practice. Those limitations will be made clear if or when it is employed by such dialogues. I anticipate that its reliance on theological presuppositions may rattle some, or that its solidarity might overwhelm communities and strip away their cultural uniqueness through such exchanges and openings. Yet still, I think that this method could bear some fruit within these discussions, and it is my hope that it may become a means of open engagement between academics of various disciplines and activists of various causes; a means that is aware of the differences between these groups and tries to not strip away what makes their focus and expertise special.

This also presents this method as provisional, as something to be further explored and contemplated. Cardinal Cardijn envisioned the method to be more than a process of social activism; he thought of it as a means of faith formation and, subsequently, life formation. Just as both faith and living are ever-evolving, ever-developing tasks, this method too must adapt and change to meet the challenges that are posed to persons and their communities. This is the strength, I find, of the See–Judge–Act method: it knows that it is not static, and that social change changes both the self and the other. This change, when wrongly enacted, can be asymmetric and chauvinistic. Or, when thoughtfully considered, it can be dynamic and performed in solidarity. Embedded into See–Judge–Act's core is a thrust of liberation through community, of seeking understanding through solidarity and association, of knowing that one cannot force change, rather, one must change alongside others in communion. These are lessons that all interdisciplinary dialogues should learn before proceeding from theory to practice.

Conflicts of Interest: The author declares no conflict of interest.

References

Boff, Clodovis. 1987. *Theology and Praxis*. Translated by Robert Barr. Maryknoll: Orbis Books.

Boff, Leonardo. 2008. *Essential Care: An Ethics of Human Nature*. Translated by Alexandre Guilherme. Waco: Baylor University Press, pp. 31–41.

Boff, Leonardo, and Clodovis Boff. 1987. *Introducing Liberation Theology*. Translated by Paul Burns. Maryknoll: Orbis Books.

Cardijn, Joseph. 1982. *La Pensée de Joseph Cardijn, va Libérer mon Peuple!* Brussels: Vanbraekel Mouscron.

Lomola, Malesela John. 2018. Marx, the Praxis of Liberation Theology, and the Bane of Religious Epistemology. *Religions* 9: 74. [CrossRef]

Löwy, Michael. 2007. La théologie de la libération: Leonardo Boff et Frei Betto. *Autres Brésils: Un Déecryptage de la Société Breésilienne Pour un Public Francophone*, January 17. Available online: http://risal.collectifs.net/article.php3?id_article=2065 (accessed on 19 March 2018).

Mackin, Robert. 2012. Liberation Theology and the Radicalization of Social Catholic Movements. *Politics, Religion & Ideology* 13: 333–51.

Mandela, Nelson. 1995. Speech by President Nelson Mandela during the opening ceremony of the Young Christian Workers World Council. November 26, Oukasie, South Africa. Available online: http://testimonies.josephcardijn.com/nelson-mandela (accessed on 19 March 2018).

Mbembe, Achille. 2001. *On the Postcolony*. Berkeley: University of California Press.

Nolan, Albert. 1986. The Option for the Poor in South Africa. In *Cross Currents*. Hoboken: John Wiley & Sons, pp. 17–27.

Nolan, Albert. 1988. *God in South Africa: The Challenge of the Gospel*. Cape Town: David Phillip.

Ricoeur, Paul. 1972. *The Symbolism of Evil*. New York: Harper & Row.

Smith, Linda Tuhiwai. 2008. *Decolonizing Methodologies: Research and Indigenous Peoples*. London: University of Otago Press, pp. 80–85.

Swanson, Ana. 2015. Does Foreign Aid Always Help the Poor? *World Economic Forum*, October 23. Available online: https://www.weforum.org/agenda/2015/10/does-foreign-aid-always-help-the-poor (accessed on 13 March 2018).

West, Gerald. 2012. Tracing the 'Kairos' Trajectory from South Africa (1985) to Palestine (2009): Discerning Continuities and Differences. *Journal of Theology for Southern Africa* 143: 4–22.

![religions logo] *religions* MDPI

Article

Transforming the Conversation: What Is Liberation and from What Is It Liberating Us? A Critical Response to "Transforming Encounters and Critical Reflection: African Thought, Critical Theory, and Liberation Theology in Dialogue"

Justin Sands

School of Philosophy, North-West University Potchefstroom, Potchefstroom 2520, South Africa;
Justin.Sands@nwu.ac.za

Received: 5 June 2018; Accepted: 14 June 2018; Published: 19 June 2018

Abstract: The Religions special issue, "Transforming Encounters and Critical Reflection: African Thought, Critical Theory, and Liberation Theology in Dialogue," addresses the concern over the present postcolonial context in which African persons and societies find themselves. The issue attempts to gain a further understanding of this context through a dialogue between these three disciplines, but what emerges from this attempt? As a critical response to the issue as a whole, this article will reveal that each author presents different yet converging perspectives on the questions: 'what is liberation and from what are we being liberated?' This article begins by phrasing this question through Frantz Fanon's critique on the postcolony, where he sees that the same logic—what Schalk Gerber's article calls 'the logic of the colonizer'—is still employed in the postcolony. This article unpacks the entanglement created by this logic and how each author addresses it in different ways. Importantly, this is not a review of each article; rather, it seeks to reveal the narrative created by this interdisciplinary dialogue in order to further the conversation on oppression and liberation in an African context. In so doing, it reveals how each author addresses the concept of liberation or freedom and where they partially (or perhaps provisionally) agree that liberation entails embodied communal responsibility as being-with others, the importance of transparent dialogue, the need for new rationalities to enter the discussion of African self-determination, while also highlighting the dangers of appropriating these new rationalities when bringing them into an African context or when moving theory into praxis.

Keywords: decolonization; critical theory; liberation theology; African philosophy; African Theology; Postmodern philosophy; systematic theology; Postcolonialism; Joseph Cardinal Cardijn

1. Introduction

This article is an in-depth response to this *Religions* special issue since the conversations touched upon in this issue are themselves *in medias res*. "Transforming Encounters and Critical Reflection: African Thought, Critical Theory, and Liberation Theology in Dialogue" explores the founding principles of this conversation. What these articles reveal is a common thread running through the each respective discipline's questioning of what comes after the postcolony; what is next for African societies in particular but also for the global community at large. *This thread essentially is a questioning of what is liberation and from what is it liberating us?*

Franz Fanon's *Wretched of the Earth* crystalizes this question when he discusses the concept of "national consciousness" and its leaders (the "national bourgeoisie") in African nations after their liberation from colonialization:

Independence does not bring a change of direction. The same old groundnut harvest, cocoa harvest, and olive harvest. Likewise the traffic of commodities goes unchanged. No industry is established in the country. We [i.e., those in the postcolony] continue to ship raw materials, we continue to grow produce for Europe and pass for specialists of unfinished products. ... Yet the national bourgeoisie never stops calling for the nationalization of the economy and the commercial sector. ... *For the bourgeoisie, nationalization signifies very precisely the transfer into indigenous hands of privileges inherited from the colonial period.* ... For the dignity of the country and to safeguard its own interests, it considers it its duty to occupy all these positions. *Henceforth it demands that every major foreign company must operate through them, if it wants to remain in the country or establish trade. The national bourgeoisie discovers its historical mission as intermediary.*[1]

Fanon's aim here and throughout chapter three of *Wretched of the Earth* is to reveal how this so-called independence, or liberation, maintains the same power structure established by the colonialists. Moreover, this independence operates on the same logical foundations employed by the colonialists. The difference is that a group of the former colonized—the educated and well-connected 'national bourgeoisie'—replaces the European powers at the top. Yet still, as intermediaries to commerce and so-called development, they are still beholden to those European (or Western) powers. So the question arises again: is this liberation and from what are we being liberated?

In what follows, I will critically explore this questioning of liberation as it developed throughout the special issue. The special issue is divided into three parts, 'African Thought,' 'Critical Theory,' and 'Liberation Theology,' respectively, and what we will see is at once an expansion and tightening around the issue of liberation: The expansion, particularly in the Critical Theory section, will be toward the notion of freedom in a philosophical register, the questioning of liberation and from what opens itself to an inquiry on what it means to be free in the first place. The tightening results from the other two, book-ended sections which focus a notion of liberating freedom as at once a political and a spiritual concept within the African context. In what follows, I will show how interrelated each discipline's approach to the concept of liberation or freedom throughout the special issue.

The hope of "Transforming Encounters and Critical Reflection" was to re-examine the basis for these approaches in an attempt to find common ground for future discussions within academia and outside of it. It attempts to serve as a platform for future interdisciplinary dialogues in pursuit of better understandings of the world(s) in which we live and to push these theoretical understandings into more ethical and just praxes. Hence, before one can move to practically engage in liberation, we must have a more comprehensive concept of what is justice, what is freedom, and from what is this freedom liberating us.

2. An African Perspective on the Concept of Liberation through Dialogue and the Critique of Logic

Kelebogile T. Resane's article, "Transparent Theological Dialogue—*Moseka Phofu Ya Gaabo Ga a Tshabe Go Swa Lentswe'* (A Setswana Proverb)" explores a line of questioning liberation or freedom through an engagement with Christian dogma and the Christian struggle for liberation.[2] The proverb—roughly translated as "one must fight impatiently for what rightly belongs to him or her"—is used by Resane "as a special appeal to theology to speak vigorously, vivaciously, and vividly" concerning the role of dogmatic, theological convictions in relation to the type of logic Fanon highlights in the quote above and throughout his oeuvre. However, in Resane's case, this focus is on the *theo*-logical convictions at play in this so-called independence and liberation.[3] Although

---

[1] Fanon (2005, p. 100), emphasis Sands.
[2] Resane (2018).
[3] Resane (2018, p. 2).

Resane does not cite Fanon, he is aware that this appeal can fall into the same dangers of Fanon's national consciousness "since this proverb [also] carries the meaning of patriotism, it can be ascribed theologically as promoting Christian *apologia*."[4] As we shall see, Resane's concern against *apologia* links quite well with Schalk Gerber's description of the onto-theological constitution of metaphysics: for Resane, the suspicion against *apologia* resides in its defense of dogma and the faith, in Fanon's case it could be likened to a defense of national consciousness, and below Gerber reveals a similar concern through his dialogue between Achille Mbembe's and Jean-Luc Nancy's critiques of logical enclosures.[5] In all three cases, one can see a suspicion against institutions and persons defending and upholding a certain logic, and the more one entrenches oneself into that logic the harder it becomes to see without it, especially if one is a part of the privileged few in power. An *apologia* of certain dogmas and their metaphysical structures becomes a sort of enclosure or exclusion of other concepts, hence Resane's apprehension against certain kinds of patriotism and theological dogmatism, which he extrapolates throughout the article.

Against this apprehension, Resane reads this proverb as a provocation to re-contextualize what we mean by *dogma* or theological convictions by calling for a more transparent dialogue. Transparency, here, is seen as "clear, unhindered honesty" on part of all dialogue partners which also entails an unhindered license to listen and to allow those who have been silenced to speak.[6] For Resane, quoting Katrin Kusmierz, theology's role is to take up "the challenge of contributing to the shaping of common life" while knowing that this life "can only be meaningful and relevant if it takes into account its social, political, and economic context."[7] From here, one can see that Resane's appeal to theology is a contextual and political one, a position where Christian salvation—the impetus of several theological reflections—is placed upon questioning how one can experience that salvation in their own life. This entails liberation, but also cooperation through dialogue. As Resane argues, this type of theological reflection cannot exist on an island and must need "ecumenical cooperation."[8] Resane continues in his article to explore how this cooperation, through transparency and dialogue, might unfold. Skipping ahead somewhat in his argument, he then explores the dogmatic, or rational and *theo*-logical, implications of such a dialogue. His final argumentations give a rationale for type of liberation theology that is based upon praxis and dialogue without giving up its core convictions, a liberation theology that is "consonant with Christian *dogma* and *credo*."[9] Yet Resane has not forgotten the concerns against *apologia* and patriotism, rather, he finds that if theology emphasizes its dialogical, communitarian, and transparent roots, it can turn these concerns into at once warnings against past theological sins (a sort of hermeneutics of suspicion) while also being reminders of the purpose of the Christian Church and theology in general:

> Theology must be chiefly concerned with reasoning about relation between God and God's creation (including humans), together with their ethical behaviors (Pietersen 2015, p. 120). Furthermore, theology as a *moseka phofu* must become patriotic in such a way that its prophetic utterances can be heeded *by humanity in all spheres of life*.[10]

The patriotic thrust of *moseka phofu* becomes an inversion, and its apologetic thrust follows as well: theologians have often forgotten which side they should be on and their essential role in everyday life. They do not serve to 'protect *their* faith' and nor do they serve to 'uphold *their* society.' Their role is to better understand the relationship between God and *all* God's people, that the kingdom they serve is not on earth, that their patriotism should be focused on the Kingdom to come, one that involves all

---

[4] Resane (2018, p. 2).
[5] Gerber (2018).
[6] Resane (2018, pp. 2–3).
[7] Resane (2018, p. 2); Kusmierz (2016, p. 161).
[8] Resane (2018, p. 3).
[9] Resane (2018, p. 8).
[10] Resane (2018, p. 9); emphasis Sands'.

persons within all spheres and contexts. Therefore, transparency is needed for theologians to see these persons and spheres, to better understand their contexts and the logic(s) that suppresses others while also upholding the *status quo*.

Joel Mokhoathi's article, "From Contextual Theology to African Christianity: The Consideration of Adiaphora from a South African Perspective," seems to agree with the Resane's premise that contextual theological reflection in African communities must develop its own self-determination. Mokhoathi's first aim is to articulate that far too often this contextualization has been labelled as "syncretism" by theologians (mainly Western theologians), and therefore has been cast as an 'other' within the global Christian community: far too often Christianity in Africa is designated as "African Christianity," essentially a separation from the larger Christian community that falls in line with 'orthodox' dogmatic rationality.[11] This dogmatic rationality that Mokhoathi highlights closes off ecumenical and communitarian dialogue partners. Although unintended (I imagine), Mokhoathi appears to have taken up Resane's call for transparent theological dialogue—*moseka phofu*—and his article deepens its implications by looking at the "things in between" (*Adiaphora*), which could be revealed through such transparent dialogues.[12] His article explores the ways in which these dialogues were initially enclosed to uphold a theological Western rationality through mission work in Africa. He then continues to show how Christianity, in spite of this imposition from Western missionaries, grew within the contextualization and enculturation of Christian belief amongst and within African communities. This contextualization became the 'problematic' in African Christianity—the so-called syncretism—yet this happened *not* because Africans are uninterested in creeds or the essential teachings of Christianity, it happened because of the Western logic imposed by the missionaries cut off any dialogue with those whom they sought to teach the faith. In other words, instead of sharing their Christian beliefs to others and listening and learning from those others, they tried to impose *en masse* an unwavering metaphysics or logic that could not speak to the sensibilities of their African brethren and sistren. Mokhoathi argues thusly:

> The implications therefore, of African theology, are that imported theologies do not sufficiently touch the hearts of African believers because they are couched in a language that is foreign to them (Muzorewa 1985, pp. 96–97). And, that the building of communication between Christianity and the African cultural and religious heritage is best left for African theologians because they know how best to contextualize Christianity in a manner that can fully communicate with their African cultural and religious heritage (Muzorewa 1985). Thus, in this argument, Christianity needs to assume a local and Africanised temperament, where it can be communicated in a language that Africans can understand and appreciate; and be articulated in a manner that can touch the hearts of Africans. In its reproduction, it is exclusively the task of African theologians to contextualize Christianity so that it may fully communicate with the African cultural context. As to how this can be done, it is not clear. But what is apparent is that the contextualization of Christianity has resulted in the emergence of African Christianity.([13])

Mokhoathi's argument then goes on to map out the ways in which African culture and African Traditional Religions overlap with 'orthodox' (i.e., Western) Christianity and the ways in which so-called African Christianity develops its own theological rationale. Again, following Resane, Mokhoathi deepens our understanding of this transparent dialogue by unveiling what lies between 'African' and 'Western' Christianity. He locates where the convergences and divergences lay.

Relating back to our question concerning what is liberation and from what are we being liberated, his article enriches our understanding of the contextualities at play in liberation: Mokhoathi does not

---

[11] Mokhoathi (2018, p. 1).
[12] Mokhoathi (2018, p. 1).
[13] Mokhoathi (2018, p. 2).

want an African church liberated from the Western theological tradition, nor does he want to suppress any Western theological influence on the African church.[14] Rather, one of the aims in his paper is to show that the *theo*-logical rationale (and thus dogmatic or systematic formulation) of Christianity in Africa is more complex than mere syncretism or holding on to indigenous beliefs. It is interconnected with its pre- and post-missionary past, while also being connected to the global Christian community. Liberation, then, is not a freedom from something or a group, as in a separation from a particular Christian tradition. Liberation is again a contextual, ecumenical dialogue that opens Christian belief to all spheres of life. Both Resane and Mokhoathi find liberation to be communitarian. Liberation for them is dialogical, and through an emphasis on contextualities it seeks to address the Western rationality, a yoke, if you will, that is placed upon believers here-and-now, in this world, and their answer to liberation is to shed this yoke through solidarity, honest discussion, and an appreciation of others' traditions. They seek to reveal how this yoke and its rational justifications separates Christians, but it also separates all persons beyond Christianity, which becomes the focus of our next two authors.

Lawrence O. Ugwuanyi and Schalk Gerber's articles shift from this theological reflection toward African philosophical thought at large. In "Towards a Rational Kingdom in Africa: Knowledge, Critical Rationality and Development in a Twenty-First Century African Cultural Context," Ugwuanyi takes up the question of kingdoms and domains, but his attention is geared toward building an African self-understanding; one that is self-critical without being self-deprecating, one that is not fixed nor fixated on its past but is open for development.[15] It is a different kind of kingdom—neither a heavenly one nor a totalitarian monarchy of reason—and although Ugwuanyi does not share the theological motivations of Resane and Mokhoathi, he continues their engagement with the question of which logic has dominated African rationality and what logic might come after it. His article, in its own way and which does not cite Fanon, still follows Fanon's critique that the national bourgeoisie perpetuate the rationality of their colonial predecessors. However, where Ugwuanyi diverges is that he seeks to move beyond Fanon's critique. Likewise, his argument aligns well with Resane's emphasis on transparent, vigilant dialogue. Almost as if he is dovetailing both of these notions into his own logical system, Ugwuanyi emphasizes an emergent rationality that is essentially contextual and African in its own self-determination:

> My desired rational kingdom is one where different demands of reasoning will be realized in a complimentary manner [Sands: similar to Resane's and Mokhoathi's transparent dialogue] as against one where a strand or an aspect of reasoning will function to dominate and destroy others [Sands: similar to Fanon's critique]; where productive rational ethics will enable Africans to move beyond the current state of thinking which amounts to rational medievalism to one where critical but resourceful culture of modernity marked by innovative rationality define Africa's rational ethics.[16]

Ugwuanyi then gives a dialogical reading of the concept of reason—from its roots in Aristotle and Greek philosophy, to its contemporary, scientific formulations, to its recontextualization in contemporary Africa—all the while teasing out concepts and challenges to developing a rationality which would further African self-determination. Throughout, his aim is to present the conditions in which a *"creative and critical rationalism* [Sands: this includes being self-critical] is demanded by the African society" and possible avenues in which this demand can be satisfied.[17] However, like all rationalities, there is the question of limitations; or, if you will, who can be citizens in this rational kingdom and what ideas could be (or could not be) included in this kingdom's constitution. Ugwuanyi is not naïve about this, which is why his reading of what rationality is and what it may become in an

---

[14] See for example Mokhoathi (2018, pp. 5–7).
[15] Ugwuanyi (2018).
[16] Ugwuanyi (2018, p. 2).
[17] Ugwuanyi (2018, p. 7).

African context leads to two final sections that explore the developmental and cultural imperatives for building such a rational kingdom. Furthermore, one of his aims is to "problematize" the various traditions of rationality—both Western and African—in order to find a "desirable alternative."[18]

In a lot of ways, his article reminds me of Tsenay Serequeberhan's argument in *The Hermeneutics of African Philosophy*, where he argues that "the 'reconstructive challenge' of African philosophy is aimed at supplying a positive hermeneutic supplement to the concrete efforts under way on the continent. . . . Paraphrasing Ngugi wa Thiong'o, one could say that this is the process of 'decolonizing the mind' or, with Cabral . . . one can describe it as the struggle to 'return to the source.'"[19] Time and space precludes me from going into detail, but Serequeberhan likewise goes through an intellectual history of philosophical discourses in Africa, hermeneutically exploring and teasing out the ways in which rationality has become the domain of the powerful. His argument concludes that African philosophy is in a double bind; it is in a discourse stuck between beginning a-new and returning to the sources—something highlighted through the so-called ethnophilosophy and Professional Philosophy debates spurred on by the likes of Paulin Hountondji.[20] His response to this bind is similar to Ugwuanyi's in that he seeks a critical rationality (Serequeberhan's is rooted in hermeneutics) that explores the "lived circumstances" of the people in African communities and societies that is emancipatory at its heart; although Serequeberhan does not proclaim his emancipation through a metaphor of a kingdom, he does insist on a domain in which African thought and the cultures from which it springs can find self-determination.[21]

Returning to the question of what is liberation and from what are we being liberated, Ugwuanyi's article settles upon a liberation that allows African persons the freedom to express their own rationality, their own logic, through a critical reading of their traditions and the Western histories forced and forged upon those traditions. 'Liberation from whom' becomes the dominant rationality, the Western rationality, that in ways can be appropriated for African discourses but also must be resisted in some ways to allow space for African self-determination. Yet the question remains about whom and what is allowed in this kingdom, since kingdoms often require enclosures. Although Ugwuanyi follows Resane and Mokhoathi's call for dialogue, this question remains and it aligns well with Fanon's concern that those in power may still keep the same power structure of their former oppressors. Kingdoms still have kings, one could say, and who is the king of the African rational kingdom?

Schalk Gerber's article, "From Dis-Enclosure to Decolonization: In Dialogue with Nancy and Mbembe on Self-Determination and the Other," engages this foundational question through one of Fanon's contemporary interlocutors, Achille Mbembe, and the Continental philosopher Jean-Luc Nancy. What Gerber sees in arguments similar to the one Fanon makes above is what he calls "the logic of the coloniser."[22] Gerber explores this logic and what it means to decolonization through two overlapping explorations: In Nancy's work, Gerber finds a contemporary European thinker who seeks to deconstruct the dominant logical thinking from within his own European context. Nancy's exploration of the metaphysical assumptions undergirding this logic, Gerber argues, can give us an understanding of how the consequence of this metaphysics for "the subject or social body is a matter of exclusion. That is the exclusion of everything that does not fit the identity of the Subject or Social body, or in a reversal of terms, included as excluded."[23] He links this with Mbembe's social critique, particularly in his seminal work *On the Postcolony*. I will refer the reader to Gerber's article for the sake of time, but his questioning of the logic of the colonizer, and his placing European deconstruction in dialogue with African decolonization shows the covalent trends in both subfields of philosophy.

---

[18] Ugwuanyi (2018, p. 16).
[19] Serequeberhan (2012, p. 119).
[20] Serequeberhan (2012, pp. 1–12, 119–21).
[21] Serequeberhan (2012, p. 118).
[22] Gerber (2018, p. 2).
[23] Gerber (2018, p. 5).

It does so while revealing that questioning the logical structures—which makes Fanon's critique of the national consciousness and its bourgeoisie possible—is inherently necessary before we can begin to understand the political and intellectual implications of liberation.[24] This is especially so in a world dominated by Capitalism and an ever-interconnected (or, perhaps, entangled) world.[25]

Gerber's conclusion hinges upon the concept of a dis-enclosure as opposed to an enclosure or a logic (i.e., metaphysics) that necessarily excludes otherness to create order, or sense, of being-in-the-world. Dis-enclosure, aligned with Mbembe's decolonization, is an attempt to present a logic where:

> ... every other is seen as an origin, from where the world is co-created; the world occurs at each moment of the world, as each time of Being in the realm of being-with of each time with every other time (Nancy 2000a, p. 20). Consequently, there is no set example, origin, or identity, according to which to model others. What it means to exist is not given or enforced on someone by another in reference to an abstract principle or identity. Rather, each time of Being constitutes a singularly unique origin of the world, making up the plurality of origins. Furthermore, the with of being-with, which lies between the I (subject) and the other, belongs to neither. No one possesses the monopoly on the question of existence with others. The with, instead, exposes one to an-other.[26]

Gerber's argument is an attempt to realize the community and commonality (the being-with, or *Mitsein*) of being-in-the-world. In a decolonial measure, this involves a re-thinking of our identity outside of the "logic of the coloniser" and turning to an identity that recognizes both the responsibility and the facticity that our beingness is amongst others; it happens in a shared world.[27] Yet still, this responsibility requires recognition of the past and also for us to take "responsibility for ... the past, and also making sure that this kind of logic regarding race and the ontological status of the other does not continue in new forms in the future. It is then that the question of reparation can start to take place, of restoring the dignity of the other who co-exists in our shared world."[28] Gerber's emphasis on being-with others opens us to a shared world, but the fact that he (rightly) argues that this necessitates a responsibility for the past to ensure a future that does not replicate this past seemingly appears to recognize Fanon's charge: that independence which perpetuates the power structure—or, better said, the logic of the colonizer—is not a true independence at all. In this way, Gerber's reading of Nancy and Mbembe continues the call for dialogue and for self-determination, but its emphasis on responsibility raises another concern: what is the relationship between responsibility and freedom? If we are responsible for the past— to make reparations for it as well as to not replicate it—in what way are we liberated? And, furthermore, if liberation or freedom means to emerge a-new with a self-determined rationality, in all of its communitarian and dialogical praxis, how and where does this responsibility limit this freedom? From whom or what are Africans being liberated if not the past transgressions imparted by colonialism?

3. A Critical Theoretical Engagement with Freedom in an Economically Dependent World

This is where this special issue pivots toward an engagement with the concept of freedom and how one's (economic and political) engagement with others impacts one's freedom. Regarding this relationship, Abraham Olivier and Marcos Antonio Norris explore Jean-Paul Sartre's philosophy on different levels: Olivier questions what we mean by freedom or liberation concerning our historical situatedness; Norris, similar to Fanon and the authors discussed above, turns to the logic of the power structures; questioning what it means to have sovereignty in light of self-determination. Continuing the

---

[24] One can also see this sort of inquiry operating in Malesela John Lamola's contribution, as I detail below.
[25] Gerber (2018, pp. 4–7).
[26] Gerber (2018, pp. 8–9).
[27] Gerber (2018, p. 10).
[28] Gerber (2018, p. 11).

discussion, Mark Rathbone, similar to Gerber, returns to the concern over responsibility but situates it within an economic context by exploring how global Capitalism impacts our understanding of self-determination and accountability. Anné Verhoef then locates a particular lacuna in our concept of freedom or liberation, questioning whether our notions of these concepts might result in a deterministic outcome—which returns us back to Fanon's worry that independence in the postcolony only exchanges who yields the power yet does nothing but replicates the same logic of power used by the colonizer.

Olivier's article, "The Freedom of Facticity," initiates his analysis of Sartrean concept of freedom by asking of Sartre and his followers:

> How free are we from situations, particularly ones in which we are subject to collective identification? More exactly, how free are we from the situations—places, environments, histories, others—that we inevitably belong to, and which subject us to collective identities? How free are we from identification in terms of others? How free are we to transform such identification?[29]

To my mind, these questions align well with the contextual concerns and the implications of responsibility that I have highlighted already—particularly in the work of Mokhoathi, Ugwuanyi, and Gerber—but Olivier's questions give us a new perspective: freedom or liberation is not absolute; although Sartre claims that we are 'condemned be free' and that we maintain our freedom of choice regardless of circumstance, Olivier questions the ways in which our historico-cultural situation influences and sometimes limits this freedom.[30] For example, one is not free to just choose to ignore the facticity of their whiteness while living in South Africa because of the privileges that come with whiteness still influence one's position in that world and influence what one can and cannot do. This comes into sharper focus in an African context, particularly when one reads Ugwuanyi's concept of a rational kingdom as African self-determination alongside Olivier, and notices that Ugwuanyi's concept of rationality necessitates that African persons and communities cannot hold on to an abstract concept of reason; it needs to be lived and embedded in their lives and interpersonal engagements.[31]

Olivier gives an in-depth reading of Sartre's notion of the "facticity of freedom" in order to arrive at his own understanding of freedom, what he calls "the freedom of facticity."[32] This freedom of facticity is based upon the "intentional heteronomy of freedom," meaning "that choices are not in the first place the manifestation of the nihilating power of consciousness, but rather that they are originally based on and shaped by the options offered in particular situations."[33] Here, Gerber's employment of being-with others finds a dialogue partner, yet Olivier's intentions are to shift the focus from the self's awareness (or sense) of being-with others to otherness itself, or the object itself, and how this relation shapes the choices that one can and cannot make: "I [aim to] illustrate how choices between options are directed by objects in particular situations and their enabling conditions; second, more particularly, [I aim to illustrate] how choices between available options are learned in situations shared with others."[34] Olivier's argument, as we shall see below, touches upon Mark Rathbone's concerns about how global economic factors shape our lives.[35] Also similar to Rathbone, Olivier finalizes his argumentation through exploring Maurice Merleau-Ponty's concept of embodiment. For Olivier, Merleau-Ponty's concept of embodiment reveals how "we are 'born into' experiencing [the world] with its limits and options" and from this we are free to choose our own existential projects, such as joining a labor movement or political party: "freedom arises through such an existential project, through which,

---

[29] Olivier (2018, p. 1).
[30] Olivier (2018, p. 8).
[31] Ugwuanyi (2018, pp. 6–7).
[32] Olivier (2018, p. 2).
[33] Olivier (2018, p. 9).
[34] Olivier (2018, p. 9).
[35] It is also worth noting that both Olivier and Rathbone employ Maurice Merleau-Ponty's phenomenology and his concept of embodiment to illustrate these points.

together with others with whom I share a past and present, I give my life direction."[36] Where Olivier diverges from Merleau-Ponty is that he does not see one's situatedness and one's freedom as "two poles of tension," but rather that they have a more symbiotic relationship where the situation offers to oneself choices which thus may or may not change one's situation.[37] The final critical disagreement, and lynchpin to his argument, is that he finds "that freedom coincides with choice but [Olivier thinks] . . . that facticity gives rise to choice in the first place."[38]

One can immediately see how Olivier's article intersects with those discussed above in that: First, he shares with our other authors an awareness of our historico-cultural situatedness (one could go as far as saying that, to varying degrees, all of the authors covered thus far share a Gadamerian appreciation of ones *Wirkungsgeschichte Bewusstsein*); Second, freedom or liberation entails dealing with this situatedness and its historical implications; and Finally, that dealing with these issues is also dealing with others—whether it is via transparent dialogue, developing a critical and contextual rationality for self-determination, or re-orienting oneself toward being-with others as the initiate to responsibility.

Marcos Antonio Norris' article, "Existential Choice as Repressed Theism: Jean-Paul Sartre and Giorgio Agamben in Conversation," transitions these agreements and returns back to the pressing concern of who holds the power in the logic (i.e. metaphysics) of freedom and liberation.[39] Norris employs Agamben's notion of secularized theism over and against Sartre's concept of "sovereign decisionism," which he teases out of Sartre's struggle "to develop a political philosophy bereft of moral absolutes" and his concept of atheism which Marcos, referencing Kate Kirkpatrick, argues is "thoroughly Augustinian;" meaning that it was influenced by Augustinian notions of sin, being, and nothingness.[40] Norris goes so far to argue that "Sartre secularizes Augustine to fit his atheistic worldview, professing the death of God at the same time that he advances a traditional (though secularized) idea [of being in relation to willing to be]."[41] Marcos takes from this a concept of repressed theism in Sartre's phenomenology (and subsequently his concept of freedom and political philosophy) and in the next section he follows a line of reasoning similarly employed by Gerber by exploring and critiquing Sartre's understanding of metaphysics and its onto-theological foundation. Next, he places Sartre in dialogue with Giorgio Agamben to tease out the repressed theism he finds within Sartre's concept of existential authenticity (i.e., sovereign decisionism) to highlight how it maintains a sense of deification: "Sartre declares the end of morality while defending the metaphysical value of sovereign, self-originating choice."[42] Relating this back to the discussion of what is liberation and from what are we liberated, Norris has shown that the logic of power is still at play when one takes up a Sartrean position of freedom; even if one is absolutely free to make one's own decisions, there is still an issue regarding power and sovereignty. If we return to Olivier et al.'s arguments about historical contextualities and that one is always amongst others, the question of who holds the power—or who gets deified in this logic of power à la Norris—still remains and one's freedom may come at the expense of others. Fanon's critique still emerges and the cycle replicates itself in this notion of freedom.

This is not to say that Sartre has no place in the conversation, but within the context of liberation alongside other selves and in an increasingly interconnected world, what this special issues' authors have found is that one's freedom must but understood as freedom with others. This recognition between both selves becomes a focal point for liberation: liberation necessarily requires a comprehensive understanding of being-with others, how history or the past situates that being-with into a present, contextual event, and how this contextual event requires transparent

---

36 Olivier (2018, p. 11).
37 Olivier (2018, p. 11).
38 Olivier (2018, p. 11).
39 Norris (2018).
40 Norris (2018, p. 4).
41 Norris (2018, p. 4).
42 Norris (2018, p. 12).

dialogue in order to address oppression and express (i.e., enact) a more just independence, thereby moving one's community closer to freedom or liberation.

Mark Rathbone's article, "Adam Smith, The Impartial Spectator and Embodiment: Towards an Economics of Accountability and Dialogue," deepens these findings by exploring how a community's historical situatedness is enveloped in a global Capitalist economy and his work explores pathways to making this economy both more accountable to and more equal for all those involved, particularly those within an African context.[43] His exploration begins with Adam Smith whose master work, *An Inquiry into the Nature and Causes of the Wealth of Nations*, often overshadows his earlier work, *The Theory of Moral Sentiments*. Smith's *Wealth of Nations*, rightly or wrongly, is often seen as a founding text for Capitalism yet Rathbone argues that *Moral Sentiments* needs to be read alongside it to better understand how Smith envisioned his economic framework.[44] In *Moral Sentiments*, Rathbone argues that Smith's concept of the "impartial spectator . . . connects the individual to society. In this work, Smith's economics are far more complex than mere self-interest as the driver of commerce;" self-interest, here, is often misunderstood to be this driver to those who often cite *Wealth of Nations* as the essential text on Capitalism.[45]

Rathbone's tandem reading of both texts reveals that Smith envisioned a more communitarian economic system where the morality of commercial exchange held an equal importance to the economic gains resulting from such an exchange: for Smith, Rathbone argues, "self-interest functions within a socio-ethical framework that limits excess and narcissism."[46] Rathbone first reviews how "Smith's work has often been misused to justify selfishness" and rebuffs this misuse through a critical reading of Smith's understanding of moral behavior.[47] However, even though Smith envisioned a morality that "is directly linked to the socio-cultural system that condones behaviour, resulting in the joy of 'fellow-feeling' or mutual sympathy," Rathbone critiques this 'Smithian' position as being too deterministic. This determinism arises, for Rathbone, in Smith's "empiricist roots" that embeds moral development into an economy of exchange and a social system that approves of certain behaviors in support of maintaining said social system; one could say that the 'invisible hand' guides too much, approves too much, in order to maintain its primacy on regulating society.[48] As we shall see, Anné Verhoef's article locates a similar type of determinism within our global social system through his reading of Slajov Žižek.

Skipping ahead in his argument, Rathbone employs Merleau-Ponty's phenomenology and his concept of embodiment to tease out how "the body . . . is embedded in the interpretative process. . . . Therefore the situated subject, consciousness, and intentionality cannot be separated from the perceived environment or other people."[49] After employing this concept of embodiment over and against the empiricism and idealism of Smith's time, Rathbone then uses it to show how our historico-cultural situatedness entails a limitation on our freedom and also a responsibility. Rathbone's argument may well remind us of Resane's and Mokhoathi's argument for dialogue and contextuality, Gerber's call for responsibility in being-with others, as well as Olivier's and Norris' critique of Sartre. Consider thusly:

> The awareness of difference [amongst others and in our environments] highlights the possibility of other perceptions; because our perception of the world and others is inexhaustible and is not completely accessible to our consciousness and its intentionality, we remain free individuals. This freedom to act does not go beyond the existence of intersubjective relations between people; therefore, freedom goes hand in hand with

---

[43] Rathbone (2018).
[44] Rathbone (2018, p. 1–2).
[45] Rathbone (2018, p. 2).
[46] Rathbone (2018, p. 2).
[47] Rathbone (2018, p. 3).
[48] Rathbone (2018, p. 3–4).
[49] Rathbone (2018, p. 5).

accountability. The facticity of existence makes it impossible for empiricism to give way to idealism. We cannot be free in our minds with our self-determining consciousness if not also as bodily perceptive beings. For Merleau-Ponty, to escape self-determining consciousness, unlike Sartre's view that the consciousness is undetermined or "nothing", perceptions and freedom is always dependent on a particular situation. We are not determined to be an object in this world; however, there are limits to our freedom which require that we confront a situation and our assessment of it. We choose between various possibilities within a situation. There is no absolute freedom or absolute determinism, no idealistic norms for behaviour or behaviour that will gain approbation by others as envisioned by the impartial spectator. Rather, we are always embodied subjects within a particular situation and historical context provides the motivation for specific action. This is not a historicist reduction because the self remains different from others and the situation and can therefore act with freedom.[50]

Rathbone's final section, "Embodied Economics: Accountability and Dialogue," employs this reading of embodiment and its implications to freedom to suggest an economic framework that is based upon the fact that "the presence of others implies that the subject cannot simply act without recognition of others and *accountability*."[51] I refer the reader to the original article to see how Rathbone makes this argument. For our present purpose, his use of accountability functions in a similar way to the responsibility highlighted by Gerber, as well as Resane's argument that "theology as *moseka phofu* must become patriotic in such a way that its prophetic utterances can be heeded *by humanity in all spheres of life*."[52] As we have seen up until now, the question of liberation and from what we are being liberated becomes an issue of the synonymous concepts of responsibility or accountability, which always already necessitates being-with others.

Verhoef's article, "Encountering Transcendence: Žižek, Liberation Theology and African Thought in Dialogue," returns to the issues of the logical, metaphysical structures undergirding postcolonial independence, which is similar to Fanon's critique and to the critiques highlighted throughout my reading of this special issue: namely, that the logic of independence or liberation entails a metaphysical structure (highlighted in Gerber and Ugwuanyi), which requires us to explore how this logical apparatus, or any one that replaces it, orders concepts and understandings through a conceptual framework.[53] Verhoef employs the concepts of transcendence and immanence—as they are understood in African and Western thought[54]—in order to question whether these categories are "still needed and why? To what extent will the 'project of emancipation' (liberation) be furthered or hindered with the complete rejection of transcendence?"[55]

Verhoef first explores the meaning and implication of transcendence, highlighting how transcendence has often been co-opted for ideologies of oppression.[56] From here, Verhoef then explores Deleuze's concept of 'radical immanence' in order to see if a logical framework which proceeds without transcendence alleviates the ideological, oppressive tendencies that are often attributed to transcendence and/or in concepts of 'independence' like the one Fanon critiques is happening in the postcolony. His reading of Deleuze is informed by the work of Žižek, who eventually critiques Deleuzian radical immanence "for its inability to allow for human freedom. . . . this is ironic, because freedom is exactly what Deleuze intends to promote. . . . [Contrary to Deleuze and contrary to restoring

---

50 Rathbone (2018, p. 6).
51 Rathbone (2018, p. 7), I quote at length since it shows the convergence of ideas shared by many of the authors in this special issue.
52 Resane (2018, p. 9); emphasis Sands.
53 Verhoef (2017).
54 Verhoef (2017, pp. 2–3).
55 Verhoef (2017, p. 4).
56 Verhoef (2017, pp. 4–5).

a traditional transcendence-immanence framework, Žižek] emphasizes the need for epistemological and ontological transcendence, for a 'gap in the immanence' in *immanence*."[57]

From here, Verhoef goes on to articulate what Žižek intends with this gap in immanence. Skipping ahead for our present scope, the upshot of Verhoef's reading of Žižek is to show the ways in which Žižek's gap in immanence is "attuned" to liberation theology and African thought.[58] Because of time and space, here I will only explore Verhoef's main point concerning liberation theology.[59] For liberation theology, Verhoef sees the connection residing within liberation theology's "emphasis on social justice and on the emancipation of the poor and oppressed," where its concerns (contrary to, say, systematic or dogmatic theology) are more focused on "social action" than on "'the beliefs and truths of Christianity.'"[60] Verhoef finds that "in its quest for freedom, Liberation theology can find in Žižek's 'gap of immanence' a space for insisting on the 'more', the excess, the 'imperceptible something', the 'minimal difference' between Christ-man and man."[61] In other words, Verhoef thinks that Žižek's thinking may provide a way for liberation theology to keep its focus on 'liberation' without losing its 'theology'—as we shall see below, Malesela John Lamola's contribution to this special issue critiques liberation theology's use/appropriation of Marxist ideology critique, and here, in Verhoef's argument, we may find a way in which this Marxist emphasis on ideology and our emancipation from it does not overshadow or otherwise 'secularize' the theological foundation of liberation theology. Verhoef's aim in this article was not to completely reject transcendence but perhaps to reconcile it within a framework that is less inclined to become ideology; or, in the very least, to present Žižek as a dialogue partner for both liberation theology and African thought. Žižek's ideas—while critical of traditional logical and metaphysical frameworks—reveal new avenues to recontextualizing and reconsidering how we logically make sense of and construct our world.

Verhoef often employs the phrase "entry point" in the article and, returning to what I said about these conversations concerning liberation are *in medias res*, his suggestion of critiquing transcendent and immanent paradigms opens this conversation to new possibilities. The transparent dialogue expands, and the question of whom or what is included in the rational kingdom is re-examined. In this way, Verhoef's article connects with the ones previously discussed. Moreover, due to its exploration of ways in which each dialogue partner has something to learn from the other (Žižek, and, in general, liberation theologians and African philosophers), Verhoef also gives us means to transition to our third section, where the theoretical reflections gained thus far in this discussion are then weighed and measured for their practicality: we have partially settled on a communitarian, responsible, and dialogical understanding of liberation through self-determination alongside and along with other selves; furthermore, we have found that what suppresses liberation is often the logical, metaphysical framework which places the self's liberation over and against others. What this special issue turns to next is how this may become a possibility.

4. The Issue of Praxis and Warnings of Entanglement, What Can Be Gained from These Discussions?

Malesela John Lamola's article, "Marx, The Praxis of Liberation Theology, and the Bane of Epistemology," begins our exploration of turning our theoretical reflections into praxis by questioning the notion of praxis itself within liberation theology.[62] His concern for praxis focuses on the "epistemological break" within Marx's work and how it becomes a problematic for the practical

---

[57] Verhoef (2017, p. 6), emphasis Verhoef.
[58] Verhoef (2017, p. 11).
[59] Verhoef does a strong job exploring the *weltanschauung* of African Traditional Religions and of African thought writ large. To get into how he sees the connection between Žižek's gap in immanence and African Thought would require either an all too simplistic summary or an extensive section on its own.
[60] Verhoef (2017, p. 11).
[61] Verhoef (2017, p. 11).
[62] Lamola (2018).

and transcendent nature of liberation theology.[63] Referencing Louis Althusser, Lamola explores how Marx's epistemological break between his initial Feuerbachian theological position, the "'humanistic' early Marx," to his "'materialist-scientific'" later writings is an overlooked problematic for liberation theologians who often employ this break to overlay Marxian critique of ideology and society with a Christian spirituality.[64] "What are the ramifications of this praxis in theology," Lamola asks, "given that it arose out of Marx's epistemological break from speculative and contemplative thought typical of Hegel and Feuerbach during his discovery of dialectical-historical materialism?"[65] This question is also important for African philosophy and theology, given that several philosophers and thinkers in Africa—such as Paulin Hountondji, Ernest Wamba-Dia-Wamba, Kwame Nkrumah, Leopold Senghor, amongst others—employ a Marxist theory of praxis for postcolonial liberation.[66] For now, in order to keep our scope, we will continue only with Lamola's concerns about this epistemological break.

Lamola's primary aim in the article is to question "the content and value of the concept of praxis as the interpretive frame of reference that emerged from the post-Feuerbachian Marx, and the implications of this frame for theology as a discipline and mode of knowledge that is premised on Transcendence."[67] Essentially, his concern is whether a Marxian theory of praxis is compatible with theology as a whole—liberation theology is a sub-branch of Christian theological reflection, but does its emphasis on Marx sever it from the concept(s) of transcendence and therefore the larger theological doctrines that ultimately undergird Christianity? This was also a question for the Catholic Church in relation to Latin American liberation theology, even to the point of suppressing it.[68] Yet through Lamola we see new a concern arise considering whether liberation theology's reliance (over reliance?) on Marx for its emphasis on praxis "assumes the form of a pre-Feuerbachian Hegelian theosophy."[69]

Lamola unpacks this concern first through an in-depth reading of Althusser's analysis of Feuerbach's influence on early Marx and how Marx eventually transitioned into a materialist-scientific understanding of liberating the proletariat.[70] This transition is where the epistemological break in Marx appears and Lamola specifically locates where Marx's concern "about the theoretical integrity of the universe of ideas" eventually leads him toward a suspicion against ideology; where theoretical logic turns into a political force or power.[71] This again raises the concerns highlighted by Fanon and others in this issue, such as Ugwuanyi, Gerber, and Norris: what is the logic behind power, how does it replicate itself through ideology? But here, Lamola delves further into its epistemological implications and how it creates not just oppression, but a means to understanding and being-in-the-world. Lamola's next section goes on to explore how Marxian ideology critique became central to Latin American theology, which we will save for the reader. For our present scope, what emerges from Lamola's work is Latin American theology's concept of "orthopraxis," where, quoting Gutierrez, the aim was "to recognize the work and importance of concrete behavior, of deeds, of action, of praxis in Christian life."[72]

The concept of orthopraxis presented an epistemological understanding of the Christian faith through liberating works, which supplied the essential link between Marxian ideology critique and Christian theology.[73] One can see here a connection to the questions raised above about the logical

---

63 Lamola (2018, p. 2).
64 Lamola (2018, p. 2).
65 Lamola (2018, p. 2).
66 See: Wamba-Dia-Wamba (1991, pp. 129–33); Senghor (1971, pp. 6–7, 39, 61); Hountondji (1983, pp. 92–93, 139–41, 179–83). Also, Tsenay Serequeberhan critiques all of these authors and the concept of "Marxist-Leninism" throughout *The Hermeneutics of African Philosophy*; this book is where I found many of the citations in this footnote and Serequeberhan's book may make an interesting companion read alongside Lamola's article.
67 Lamola (2018, p. 3).
68 Lamola (2018, p. 9).
69 Lamola (2018, p. 3).
70 Lamola (2018, pp. 3–5).
71 Lamola (2018, p. 4).
72 Lamola (2018, p. 6), he is quoting from: Gutierrez (1973, p. 10).
73 Lamola (2018, pp. 9–10).

structures that undergird being-with others and also how it transforms into another ideology or metaphysics. Yet here, Lamola critiques it as a driving force for liberation in theology: does the *liberation* overtake the theology? This is Lamola's concern, and he goes on to give a few illustrative examples to show how this epistemology was enacted in liberation theology's history.[74] What he finds is similar, yet contrary and perhaps critical of, Mokhoathi's argument for how 'African Christianity' and 'orthodox/Western' Christianity can overlap, dialogue, and mutually develop. This statement highlights Lamola's critique: "Liberation theology reduces social processes and experience into theological dogmas; the result is that praxis, transforming reality, is then left conceived as a riddled system of dogmatic inconsistencies, which are perpetually in search of some form of an esoteric resolution or another. The most pertinent example of this resultant theoretic confusion we find in the application of the doctrine of sin as *theoria*, an interpretive principle in political analysis."[75]

Lamola's article is primarily a strong critique about the dangers of appropriation, which signals a warning bell to projects such as this special issue: when bringing into dialogue other theories, paradigms, disciplines, etc. what else are you unintentionally bringing into the conversation as well? When addressing the logic(s) of oppression through a multi-layered discussion, one must be vigilantly aware of all possible theoretical implications when moving toward praxis since it is undergirded by its own particular logic. Going back to Fanon, perhaps the national bourgeoisie did not realize that they were maintaining the same logic that brought them into colonialization. Through critical analyses such as Lamola's, we may become more aware of what we are unintentionally bringing with us in such dialogues, which, in Latin American theology of liberation, he says "develops mystical constructs out of historical contradictions;" one could easily connect the mystical here with Verhoef's concern for what happens to transcendence and/or immanence within these contradictions imparted by appropriating and adopting concepts/frameworks across disciplines or ideologies. As we shall see below through my contribution to the special issue, this may require us to find a provisional framework for such dialogues, so that certain concepts essential to each discipline/theoretical discourse involved are not forgotten, unintentionally assumed, or merely 'shaved away' to become retrofitted into a practical method of addressing oppression.

For now, in order to restore some optimism for us when exploring overlapping and intersecting dialogues on liberation and/or freedom, we turn to Ian Bekker's "Kairos and Carnival: Mikhail Bakhtin's Rhetorical and Ethical Christian Vision."[76] Our concern is still what is liberation and from what are we being liberated, and alongside Lamola's warning against contradictory appropriations when building a theory for praxis, Bekker returns us to the question of embodiment through an exploration of *Kairos* and the Russian theorist Mikhail Bakhtin's theory of carnival, which holds a notion of embodiment different than the one employed by others in this special issue. When in dialogue with Lamola's article, one perhaps can see that Bekker contributes a possible connection to the epistemological break highlighted by Lamola's reading of Marx and his Christian appropriation. However, due to space and time, we will mainly explore how Bekker's article contributes to the concern over praxis in this special issue through God's action (or interaction) in human history through human agency itself.[77]

Bekker first gives an appraisal of the term *kairos* from within Christian theology and tradition. Here, he aims to highlight how, "on the one hand, we have a sense of *kairos* as a force or power that breaks through the expected or the repetitive ... through *chronos* or mechanical time. ... On the other hand, *kairos* is also identified with the right proportion and symmetry; concepts that tend to be associated with order, balance, and continuity."[78] Through this tension of breaking into mechanical

---

[74] Lamola (2018), see Section 7, "Contemplative Epistemology Action".
[75] Lamola (2018, p. 11).
[76] Bekker (2018).
[77] Bekker (2018, p. 2).
[78] Bekker (2018, pp. 2–3).

(Greek/Western) temporality and the demand for balance and order, Bekker argues that we find "a connection with the ethical implications of *kairos*."[79] This was especially taken up, Bekker finds, in Greek philosophy, where this "ethical dimension" becomes tightly linked to "*phronesis*," or practical wisdom, in the work of Plato and eventually Aristotle.[80]

What is interesting to Bekker is how this Greek concept of *kairos* and its ethical imperative, crystalized through its linkage to *phronesis*, is appropriated within a Christian context. Here, he explores how the Gospels used the term *kairos* when speaking of Jesus Christ's divinity and how this breaking into mechanical time by the divine develops an eschatological vision. Bekker then articulates how this becomes incorporated in Christian doctrine, especially in Paul Tillich and the South African liberation theologian, Albert Nolan.[81]

After reading Lamola's warning, what I find interesting is that what Bekker shows here is how appropriation and incorporation may be possible. It may be fruitful, even. Particularly when considering how *kairos* was not only employed to understand the possibility of how Christ-as-divine can enter the world but also how it is used to further articulate the eschatological and ethical implications of this divine in-breaking.

Yet returning back to our understanding of liberation/freedom as communitarian, responsible, and dialogical—as well as self-critical of the logics which undergird these concepts—Bekker's next section attempts to place his theoretical insight into praxis through Backhtin's notion of embodiment. Bakhtin was a Russian literary theoretician, steeped in a Classical philology as well as Kantian philosophy.[82] What Bekker finds within his work is a connection, particularly to Tillich, between "finding a (phronetic, prudential) balance between form and dynamics . . . a middle path between the extremes of individual subjectivism . . . and abstract objectivism."[83] One can perhaps see a connection here with Olivier and Norris' critique of Sartre, as well as their critique of freedom in light of embodiment. Moving ahead, Bekker locates that Bakhtin's 'middle path' through a sociological, ethical vision within his concept of *carnival*, or incarnation, is a rejection of Enlightenment rationalism that he found to be too speculative, too abstract, and therefore it cannot adequately address the ethical importance of being a human body in the world amongst other bodies.[84] *Carnival*, Bekker warns us, can be interpreted in various extremes, which is worth a careful reading unto itself.[85] However, skipping ahead and concerning our present scope, what Bekker sees is that *carnival* as embodiment and *kairos*, with its double function as divine action within chronological time and its desire for order, is an ethical vision of balance:

> It is this ability to reconcile (and balance) the particular, the sensuous, and the changeable with the highest ideals that, I would argue, captures the essence of *carnival*, and is, I believe, the central motif of Bakhtin's complete work. . . . In the same way the ancient concept of *kairos* captures not a primitive form of ethical relativism, but rather the necessity of sensitivity to the concrete and the historical; to the exercise of the virtue of prudence that cannot be captured by mechanically-applied ethical formulae. The Christian irruption of the divine into human affairs (i.e., *kairos*) captures a similar balance. The relevant irruption does not come to destroy or overthrow the Law, but rather to fulfill it.([86])

Bekker's reading of *kairos* and *carnival*, then, holds a tension between being-with others, being-in-the-world, and our theoretical (here, Christian) understanding of these relationships. Through

---

[79] Bekker (2018, p. 3).
[80] Bekker (2018, p. 3).
[81] Bekker (2018, pp. 3–4, 5–6).
[82] Bekker (2018, p. 7).
[83] Bekker (2018, p. 7).
[84] Bekker (2018, pp. 7–8).
[85] Bekker (2018, p. 7).
[86] Bekker (2018, p. 9).

Bakhtin, Bekker seeks a practical method for implementing our partial answers to the questions what is liberation and from what are we being liberated; in a theological register, it is a method of understanding the need to balance our historical situatedness, its subsequent baggage (if you will), and our need for a theoretical vision of that world. One may reject or accept Bekker's proposal in the article, but one can see within his proposal a focused desire to see how the theory highlighted in the articles above and the impetus to employ them through praxis need a balance or tension.

Importantly, Bekker's article is not a rebuttal to Lamola. Rather, as I see it, both work alongside each other in a hermeneutical tension between the positive and negative implications of placing theory into practice and how this reflexively changes our theory. Concerning Ugwuanyi's desire for a rational kingdom, both Bekker's reading of *kairos* and Lamola's critique against the contradictions inherent in a Marxist-based theology have a place in this kingdom. Both can aid us in seeing what rationalities can or cannot be brought into such a kingdom, and how thorough we need to explore the presumed logic(s) within these rationalities. Returning to Fanon's critique of the national bourgeoisie, one can see that his critique likewise looms over Bekker and Lamola's contributions.

My article, "Introducing Cardinal Cardijn's See–Judge–Act as an Interdisciplinary Method to Move Theory Into Practice," attempts to facilitate and progress this special issue's conversation, with its implicit/explicit tensions, by positing a possible framework for future interdisciplinary discussions.[87] Lamola's critique of the contradictions that have arose within liberation theology's appropriation of Marxist critique impacted my decision to focus on what I find is the main problematic with interdisciplinary dialogues: How can we bring disciplines and theories into dialogue without entangling their various discourses and assumptions? How can we do so without creating a situation where each discipline has to abandon one of its essential or core concepts? Concerning liberation theology, how can it dialogue with critical theory, or a Marxist sociological analysis, without losing the 'theology' that orients its idea of liberation? Or, conversely and as addressed by Resane and Mokhoathi, how can African philosophy and theology dialogue with the Western Christian tradition or its ideological critiques of society without losing its African contextuality?

My proposal was to provisionally adopt a method crafted by Joseph Cardinal Cardijn, a Belgian priest whose work heavily influenced liberation theologians such as Leonardo and Clodovis Boff. Cardinal Cardijn's method, in short, employs three important meditations: first one must 'See' or embed themselves into the context they are engaging or the contexts of those whom one engages. The idea here, is not to overtake the other's perspective as one's one, in a sort of first naiveté, but in a second naiveté where one recognizes the distance between theirs and the other's context yet still tries to understand the situation from the other's perspective.[88] From Cardijn's and liberation theology's perspective, this prevents an asymmetrical relationship that one especially sees within the "mentality held by many (usually) well-meaning activists that seem to know what is best for a community without actually understanding that community own its own terms."[89] It is from this embedded reflection that one begins to understand the situation at hand in its own context, in how the other person sees it and how they wish to address it. From here, one builds with the community in which they are engaging, not on top of it or alongside it. From an interdisciplinary point of view, persons from each corresponding discipline begin to understand how the other discipline sees the issue at hand—in this case what is liberation and from what is it liberating us—and then begins to reflect upon how it differs from their own.

The next step, 'Judge,' is where one begins to formulate a plan of action or, in a dialogical attitude, a mutual understanding of how each person within the community can contribute to addressing the issue at hand. As I argue in my paper, the teleological impetus of this method (even before one gets to the 'Act' portion of the method) allows those in this community to focus their efforts on the given issue;

---

[87] Sands (2018).
[88] Sands (2018, pp. 3–4).
[89] Sands (2018, p. 4).

rather talking past each other they can see where their own expertise/ability/discipline can contribute to this particular problem.[90] I find that such a framework may alleviate concerns over, or at least make transparent (*pace* Resane), one's assumptions and/or presumptions when in dialogue. By focusing the energy on the *telos* of such a dialogue, one can begin to see the strengths and limits to their discipline when addressing said *telos*.[91]

From here, once some sort of consensus is made, then the community can adequately 'Act' toward the *telos*. This is where praxis takes a primary focus. Importantly, acting, here, does not need to be in unison; each discipline or actor may choose how they can best contribute to addressing the situation at hand. Acting can take up many forms as it follows the discourses of the previous stages or reflections, but these previous reflections allow each actor to engage in his or her own way. Using liberation theology as an example, I argue thusly:

> Liberation theology, as described above through Leonardo Boff and Clodovis Boff, moves from theory and theological reflection to praxis. Its teleological aim is toward a goal that is shared by its dialogue partners, African thought and critical theory. Therefore, it can employ its theological foundations concerning the need to satisfy both material and spiritual fulfillment for a sense of salvation, while also contributing insights to non-theological dialogue partners. It does not need to 'shave away', so to speak, its theological foundations to adequately help move theory toward praxis in this interdisciplinary dialogue; it merely needs to show how its theological foundations help inform the judgments and prescribed actions of its dialogue partners.[92]

Again and recalling the authors discussed above, one can see the call for transparent dialogue, a concern for each dialogue partner's historico-cultural situatedness (in academia, this also includes one's chosen discipline or method), and that such dialogues must maintain a tension between theories by focusing on how to move from dialogue to praxis. Importantly, I argued that my proposal for using such a method was provisional, that it may need to be further explored and adapted in order to function as a framework for dialogues such as the one in this special issue. Every method or framework has its limits, and as Lamola argues (as well as others in this issue) the limitations and contradictions of a given theory may become occluded when appropriated; creating a framework that is inherently contradictory. However, as I mentioned in the beginning of this critical response, the conversations in which we engaged in this special issue are *in medias res*, so perhaps after further reflection this method can help us engage in more fruitful conversations, to move out of talking past each other toward enabling us to act upon what we have learned.

5. By Way of Conclusion: Carrying the Conversation Forward

This special issue was named "Transforming Encounters and Critical Reflection" for the very important reason that it is through encounters with others and through a critical reflection of those encounters that we might find a better understanding of being-in-the-world. Within an African context, this entails a discussion on the postcolony, decolonization, and the liberation from oppression. In this critical response, I have highlighted the narrative thread which connects the articles published but also to show how they are products of encounters. They are products of engaging in interdisciplinary dialogue, of questioning their discipline's own assumptions while also contributing ideas to their correspondents.

This revealed that each discipline within this African context is essentially questioning what is liberation or freedom, and from what are we being liberated? I employed Fanon's critique because,

---

[90] Sands (2018, p. 7).
[91] Sands (2018, pp. 7–8).
[92] Sands (2018, pp. 9–10).

when reviewing all of the articles, it felt as if Fanon was hovering above the conversation. That his critique of the logic which upholds the (post)colony—initially published in 1961, even—is still with us and is still a concern for these three disciplines. Of course, this special issue did not 'solve' the problems and logic of oppression in the African context. Yet still, its questioning of the concept of freedom, logic, and the role of philosophy and theology in addressing this issue will be its main contribution to the ongoing conversations dealing with this oppression. Theory needs to become praxis, but how? Which theory? This issue highlighted how the concept of freedom is communal and historically situated, that it needs to address the past through communal responsibility, that it requires transparent dialogue, and that it needs to critically reflect upon the ways in which corresponding theories need to thoroughly explored before haphazardly being employed. The conversation over liberation and liberation from what continues, hopefully this special issue has aided in giving it a stronger direction.

Funding: This research was funded by the National Research Foundation of South Africa through a "Knowledge, Interchange, and Collaboration" grant.

Conflicts of Interest: The author declares no conflict of interest.

References

Bekker, Ian. 2018. Kairos and Carnival: Mikhail Bakhtin's Rhetorical and Ethical Christian Vision. *Religions* 9: 79. [CrossRef]

Fanon, Frantz. 2005. *The Wretched of the Earth*. Translated by Richard Philcox. New York: Grove Press.

Gerber, Schalk Hendrik. 2018. From Dis-Enclosure to Decolonization: In Dialogue with Nancy and Mbembe on Self-Determination and the Other. *Religions* 9: 128. [CrossRef]

Gutierrez, Gustavo. 1973. *A Theology of Liberation: History Salvation and Politics*. Translated by Inda Caridad, and John Eagleson. Maryknoll: Orbis Books.

Hountondji, Paulin J. 1983. *African Philosophy: Myth and Reality*. Bloomington: Indiana University Press.

Kusmierz, Katrin. 2016. *Theology in Transition: Public Theologies in Post-Apartheid South Africa*. Zuric: LIT Verlang GmbH & Co.

Lamola, Malesela John. 2018. Marx, the Praxis of Liberation Theology, and the Bane of Epistemology. *Religions* 9: 74. [CrossRef]

Mokhoathi, Joel. 2018. From contextual theology to African Christianity: The Consideration of Adiaphora from a South African Perspective. *Religions* 8: 266. [CrossRef]

Norris, Marcos Antonio. 2018. Existential Choice as Repressed Theism: Jean-Paul Sartre and Giorgio Agamben in Conversation. *Religions* 9: 106. [CrossRef]

Olivier, Abraham. 2018. The Freedom of Facticity. *Religions* 9: 110. [CrossRef]

Rathbone, Mark. 2018. Adam Smith, the Impartial Spectator and Embodiment: Towards an Economics of Accountability and Dialogue. *Religions* 9: 118. [CrossRef]

Resane, Kelebogile Thomas. 2018. Transparent Theological Dialogue—Moseka Phofu Ya Gaabo Ga a Tshabe Go Swa Lentswe' (A Setswana Proverb). *Religions* 9: 54. [CrossRef]

Sands, Justin. 2018. Introducing Cardinal Cardijn's See–Judge–Act as an Interdisciplinary Method to Move Theory into Practice. *Religions* 9: 129. [CrossRef]

Senghor, Leopold Sedar. 1971. *The Foundations of 'Africanté' or Negritude and Arabité*. Paris: Presence Africaine.

Serequeberhan, Tsenay. 2012. *The Hermeneutics of African Philosophy*. New York: Routledge.

Ugwuanyi, Lawrence Ogbo. 2018. Towards a Rational Kingdom in Africa: Knowledge, Critical Rationality and Development in a Twenty-First Century African Cultural Context. *Religions* 9: 96. [CrossRef]

Verhoef, Anné Hendrik. 2017. Encountering Transcendence: Žižek, Liberation Theology and African Thought in Dialogue. *Religions* 8: 271. [CrossRef]

Wamba-Dia-Wamba, Ernest. 1991. Philosophy in Africa: Challenges of the African Philosopher. In *African Philosophy: The Essential Rudings*. Edited by Tsenay Serequeberhan. New York: Paragon House.

MDPI

St. Alban-Anlage 66

4052 Basel

Switzerland

Tel. +41 61 683 77 34

Fax +41 61 302 89 18

www.mdpi.com

www.ingramcontent.com/pod-product-compliance
Lightning Source LLC
Chambersburg PA
CBHW051314020426
42333CB00028B/3340